T0318218

TOWARDS A COMPARATIVE POLITICAL ECONOMY OF UNFREE LABOUR

Case Studies and Debates

THE LIBRARY OF PEASANT STUDIES

TOWARDS
A COMPARATIVE
POLITICAL ECONOMY
OF UNFREE LABOUR

Case Studies and Debates

TOM BRASS

FRANK CASS
LONDON • PORTLAND, OR

First published in 1999 in Great Britain by
FRANK CASS PUBLISHERS
Newbury House, 900 Eastern Avenue
London, IG2 7HH, England

and in the United States of America by
FRANK CASS PUBLISHERS
c/o ISBS,
5804 N.E. Hassalo Street
Portland, Oregon, 97213–3644

Transferred to Digital Printing 2004

Website: www.frankcass.com

Copyright © 1999 Frank Cass & Co. Ltd

British Library Cataloguing in Publication Data

Brass, Tom
 Towards a comparative political economy of unfree labour:
 case studies and debates. – (The library of peasant studies)
 1. Forced labor – Developing countries   2. Agricultural
 laborers – Developing countries   3. Forced labor – Developing
 countries – Case studies   4. Agricultural laborers –
 Developing countries – Case studies
 I. Title
 331.1'173'091724

 ISBN 0 7146 4938 4 (cloth)
     0 7146 4498 6 (paper)
     ISSN 1462–219X

Library of Congress Cataloging in Publication Data

Brass, Tom, 1946–
 Towards a comparative political economy of unfree labour: case
 studies and debates / Tom Brass
     p. cm. – (Library of peasant studies, ISSN 1462–219X; no. 16)
 Includes bibliographical references and index.
 ISBN 0–7146–4938–4 (cloth). – ISBN 0–7146–4498–6 (paper)
 1. Peasantry–India. 2. Peasantry–Peru. 3. Agricultural
 laborers–India. 4. Agricultural laborers–Peru 5. Indentured
 servants–India. 6. Indentured servants–Peru. I. Title.
 II. Series.
 HD1537.I4B72   1999
 305.5'633–dc21   99–24213
                                                   CIP

Typeset by Regent Typesetting, London

For Amanda,
and for
Anna, Ned and Miles

'... the whole question of slavery is still before us. It has reappeared under the more pleasing names of "indentured labour", "contract labour" ... The whole thing will have to be faced anew, for the solutions of our great-grandfathers no longer satisfy. While slavery is lucrative ... it will be defended by those who identify greatness with wealth, and if their own wealth is involved, their arguments will gain considerably in vigour ... They will point to what they call the comfort and good treatment of the slaves. They will protect themselves behind legal terms. But they forget that legal terms make no difference to the truth of things. They forget that slavery is not a matter of discomfort or ill treatment, but of loss of liberty ... I know the contest is still before us. It is but part of the great contest with capitalism ...' – The concluding comments by Henry Nevinson [1906: 209–10] in his report on the working conditions of rural labour in the Portuguese colony of Angola during 1904–5.

'Whatever assigns to the people power they are unable to wield, in effect takes it away from them' – An observation by Agar [1944: 58].

Contents

Acknowledgements

In retrospect, my intellectual debts are few. At Cambridge the more fashionable theories and ideas circulating in the Social and Political Sciences Faculty where I worked throughout the 1990s seemed to me to be irrelevant to the concerns of development theory generally and to my own research interests in particular. In India the situation was different. There I participated in useful and occasionally heated discussions with a number of administrators, scholars and political activists, most notably K.B. Saxena, Pradhan Prashad, K. Gopal Iyer, Manjit Singh, Manjari Dingwaney and Sarma Marla. These were productive exchanges, since disagreement with their views frequently enabled me to clarify my own.

Most of the research presented here has been carried out with the fieldwork assistance of others. In Peru during the mid-1970s I received help from many peasants and labourers in the agrarian co-operative where I conducted research, in particular from my *compadre* Manuel Paredes and also from Teofilo Noblega. In India, Professor K. Gopal Iyer of Panjab University provided much valuable assistance during various fieldwork trips throughout the 1980s. Not only did he possess an unrivalled knowledge about conflicts and changes in the Indian countryside, but his laconic sense of humour frequently enlivened the routine of fieldwork. Dr M.C. Sarkar and Dr A.K. Jha, both of the A.N. Sinha Institute of Social Studies at Patna, assisted with fieldwork in Purnia District, Bihar, during 1990.

Assistance of another kind, no less crucial, was provided by Ramaswamy Sudarshan, then of the New Delhi Office of the Ford Foundation, and Professor John Dunn of the Social and Political Sciences Faculty at the University of Cambridge. Although neither of them share my views, both have extended valuable support when my politics came under attack in different contexts. Such principled action is nowadays rare, and does not deserve to remain unsung.

Thanks are due to Lydia Linford, of Frank Cass, who guided the book through production, and also to Dr Manjit Singh, who took the photograph reproduced on the front cover. It depicts the forcible capture of a migrant labourer in Punjab during the early 1980s.

Finally, the cliché about the support of one's family is not merely true but in my case applies rather more strongly than is usual. Without the multifaceted and unstinting support of Amanda, a scholar in her own right, this book would have remained unwritten. That it has been is due in a large measure to her, and also to Anna, Ned and Miles, who have learned tolerance and forbearance well beyond their years. This book is dedicated to them.

Since this book represents a synthesis of research conducted over a quarter of a century, earlier and substantially different versions of a few chapters have been published before. Chapter 2 combines materials which appeared in a number of different articles: 'Class Formation and Class Struggle in La Convención', *The Journal of Peasant Studies*, Vol.7, No.4 (1980); 'Agrarian Reform and the Struggle for Labour-Power', *The Journal of Development Studies*, Vol.19, No.3 (1983); and 'The Elementary Strictures of Kinship: Unfree Relations and the Production of Commodities', *Social Analysis*, No.20 (1986). Portions of Chapters 3 and 7 first appeared in 'Class Struggle and the Deproletarianization of Agricultural Labour in Haryana (India)', *The Journal of Peasant Studies*, Vol.18, No.1 (1990). Chapter 5 incorporates some materials from 'Slavery Now: Unfree Labour and Modern Capitalism', *Slavery and Abolition*, Vol.9, No.2 (1988), and also from 'Some Observations on Unfree Labour, Capitalist Restructuring, and Deproletarianization', *International Review of Social History*, Vol.39, No.2 (1994).

T.B.

December 1998
Richmond, Surrey

Introduction

Perhaps the best way of illustrating the complexities of the debate about the presence, meaning and economic role of unfree labour in India and Latin America is to consider four different ways in which the following episode might be interpreted. No longer owning a smallholding, a poor peasant turns to wage labour in order to earn a living. Used to working on a daily or seasonal basis for a number of cultivators in the vicinity, this agricultural labourer subsequently takes a loan from one of them and enters his employ on an exclusive and regular basis. The labourer in question ceases to offer himself for work as a daily wage labourer, and over time becomes the permanent worker of a single cultivator, either on a formal or informal basis. His kinsfolk are also drawn into this relationship, and themselves go to work in the fields of the employer, sometimes working in the latter's house as domestic labour. In a decreasing order of political optimism, this is how such a process can be interpreted by outside observers.

Some would point to the economic benefits this kind of working arrangement bestows, not just on the worker concerned but also on his kinsfolk. The worker, it is argued, now enjoys permanent and secure employment with one particular cultivator, from whom he might expect to receive additional economic perquisites and favours. These extend from the provision of personal items, such as clothing, to further employment opportunities for his kin, to occasional credit, and perhaps even to the provision of more substantial loans enabling the labourer to meet costly non-recurrent expenditures (such as marriage or death).

An economic arrangement like this, observers would insist, was and is a highly desirable and thus much sought-after working relationship made available only by the best employers. It is therefore evidence of the essentially free nature of the arrangement, into which a worker enters voluntarily. Moreover, if the agricultural labourer performs well, works hard and is particularly fortunate, his employer might at some future point offer to include the labourer's son or daughter in a similar kind of permanent economic arrangement.

Discounting the material benefits of such an arrangement, other observers would point to its non-economic advantages. These might extend from confirming the social identity of the worker concerned within a given locality – as a person of a particular status within his tribal, caste or village hierarchy – to proclaiming him a member of a specific national, ethnic or indigenous group in a wider context. Conceding that the economic aspects of the relation might not be beneficial or even correspond to free labour, these observers would nevertheless maintain that such considerations are for the worker involved of secondary importance, and thus of less significance than its non-economic dimension. Whether the arrangement is in a technical sense free or unfree is accordingly for them not the central issue.

Alternatively, another set of observers who interpret this economic arrangement more critically – as one whereby proprietors exploit their workers – point to the presence of grassroots (or 'from below') agency based on non-economic issues as an empowering countervailing element. Hence the view that resistance or assertiveness grounded in identity politics and ideology – about belonging to a tribal, ethnic, indigenous, village or national group – constitutes evidence for worker emancipation. Cultural identity, they maintain, not merely displaces economic identity but is a more effective method of organization and mobilization by agricultural labourers against any oppression on the part of their employers. By invoking their cultural identity, therefore, workers succeed in undermining a relation that is both exploitative and unfree.

Perhaps the least optimistic view is held by yet another set of observers who also categorize this working arrangement as unfree but deny that cultural assertiveness/resistance either negates this or is empowering. This is the view informing this book, which examines the character of unfree labour and also debates about its role in the development of capitalism. The focus is on bonded labour, an unfree relation frequently encountered in rural areas of the Third World. It is suggested here that the existence of such relations cannot be understood without regard to the process of class decomposition/recomposition (or restructuring) that accompanies struggles over the direction of agrarian change.

Much current writing about agrarian change in the Third World assumes that capitalist development in agriculture always transforms peasants into proletarians, that the expansion and operation of the industrial reserve army necessarily leads to and takes the form of free wage labour, and that where these exist unfree production relations such as debt bondage are archaic forms destined to be eliminated in the course of this process.

By contrast, it will be argued here that the incidence of unfree labour is much greater than generally supposed, may be incrasing in specific contexts, and that in certain situations rural employers actually prefer this kind of work-force. The central proposition of this argument is that the bonding of increasingly landless agricultural workers in Third World contexts amounts to a process of deproletarianization. It is therefore wrong to assume that economic development in agriculture always requires the emergence of a rural proletariat, and thus to categorize unfree production relations as anachronistic.

The threefold importance of political economy to the analysis which follows is simply put. First, it restores an approach linking macro-level economic processes to micro-level relational transformations, a combination which currently influential culturalist frameworks obsessed with the individual 'self' have (almost) managed to sunder. Second, it permits the debt bondage relation to be reclaimed from the many varieties of revisionism that have (almost) succeeded in banishing political considerations from theoretical debates about the existence and desirability of unfree labour in the Third World. The latter maintain that such relations are advantageous/beneficial for rural labour in one of two ways (or perhaps both): unfreedom is in their view empowering, either economically (as a form of patronage, subsistence guarantee or job security) or culturally (as a manifestation/celebration of 'otherness'). If this positive depiction of unfreedom is indeed accurate – a claim which this book disputes – then there is obviously no reason to abolish unfree labour, much rather the opposite. Herein lies the political basis of what is referred to here as a disempowering discourse: namely, presenting as good or desirable a working arrangement that the subjects of the relationship concerned themselves find bad/undesirable.

And third, political economy also reinstates an epistemologically crucial historical dimension missing from culturalist and other approaches. As presented here, the link between free and unfree labour is a dialectical one based on struggle (at local, national and international levels) between capital and labour, whereby free workers become unfree and vice versa. The objection to most texts about agrarian change in India, Latin America and elsewhere is that they subscribe to what is palpably an untenable concept of unilinear and irreversible *relational* (*not* systemic) transition.

After an initial consideration of the possible definitions of unfree labour and the elaboration of one in particular (Chapter 1), the first half of this book is devoted to the presentation of research data obtained in the course of fieldwork in Peru and India over the 1974–90 period (Chapters 2–4). The reasons for and the impact of the mis- or non-recognition of unfree labour on debates about the political economy of agrarian change are considered in the second part (Chapters 5–8).

Chapter 1 examines the socio-economic components of unfree labour, with particular reference to the debt bondage mechanism. The latter, it is argued, constitutes an unfree agrarian relation that involves the cancellation of cash/kind loans (or advances) with compulsory labour service. Since the meaning of unfree labour, and thus its historical and contemporary presence in Latin America, India and elsewhere, is not merely contested but also the subject of many and contradictory definitions, this chapter outlines the way in which unfreedom is conceptualized in this book, together with the reasons for this. The principal claim is that the bonding of landless workers amounts to deproletarianization, a process whereby labour-power is either decommodified or recommodified by someone other than its owner. Much of the epistemological confusion about unfreedom possesses methodological roots. Bonded labour is invariably seen as a relationship which does not occur in the kinship domain, does not affect migrant and non-permanent workers, and cannot exist without the legislative support of the state. The different and oblique forms of extra-economic coercion, together with their methodological accessibility and modes of economic appropriation, are rarely problematized. It is suggested in this chapter that one of the most effective ways of enforcing debt-servicing labour obligations is through the formal/informal control exercised through caste and/or kin networks, and further that such pressure can be sustained, even when workers migrate and where unfree labour is illegal.

Tracing the similarities and differences between the pre – and post-reform role of bonded labour in the eastern lowlands of Peru, Chapter 2 presents field-work data collected during the mid-1970s on an agrarian cooperative in the province of La Convención. These data suggest that rich and middle peasants who employed bonded labour at this conjuncture were replacing migrants with locals, the latter being composed for the most part of poor peasants whose smallholdings adjoined the larger properties belonging to their creditor-employers. This process of workforce recomposition allowed small capitalist producers to mobilize the labour-power of debt bonded poor peasants and their kinsfolk for harvesting coffee when the price of this cash crop was favourable. It also enabled them to use this kind of unfree worker in exchange labour groups, in individual exchanges of labour, or to redeploy it as substitute labour on to the cooperative sector. Political and ideological connections between creditor-employers and bonded labourers are also explored, particularly the important role in the reproduction of debt bondage played by actual/fictive kinship. The authority vested in the latter enabled rich peasants to enforce debt-servicing labour obligations indirectly, by invoking the idiom of kinship 'reciprocity' or 'duty' in the case of both local and migrant workers.

Turning to the Indian case study materials, Chapter 3 presents research findings from Green Revolution areas in the northwestern states of Punjab and Haryana, where fieldwork was carried out during 1983 and 1987. Evidence from Punjab, where unfree labour is supposed to have been eliminated by the development of a capitalist agriculture, indicates that in contrast to Peru, locals were being replaced by migrants. Debt bondage is considered in relation to class struggle in this labour scarce context, specifically with regard to its utilization by capitalist farmers to lower costs and maintain control over both local and migrant workers.

Empirical data from fieldwork in Punjab and Haryana also suggest that – as in the case of Peru – both permanent and casual labourers were bonded as a result of debt, the latter subjects being unfree only during the peak period of the agricultural cycle. Debt servicing labour obligations incurred by permanent or casual workers were enforced by fellow caste members, either informally or through the village *panchayat*. Loans taken by permanent or casual workers that remained unpaid due to illness, incapacity, old age or death, were also passed on to their domestic kinsfolk, who repaid such debts with personal labour in fields belonging to the creditor-employer.

Agricultural workers in Haryana and Punjab expressed a strong dislike of permanent attachment and a corresponding preference for free casual labour, citing as reasons the maltreatment of annual servants, their long working hours and low wages, and the inability of such workers to own livestock. This finding challenges directly the view that the subjects of bonded labour relations perceive such arrangements in a positive light, as a form of subsistence guarantee or employment insurance.

Chapter 4 presents research findings about bonded labour from fieldwork conducted during the latter part of the 1980s in two different locations in the northeastern state of Bihar: Nalanda District in central Bihar and Purnia District adjoining the border with Bangladesh and Nepal. The object is to compare the socio-economic characteristics of indebtedness, together with their effect on the agricultural labour market, in an unreformed area exhibiting a relatively low level of technological change with high growth areas where the implementation of the Green Revolution has generated capitalist development.

In common with their counterparts in Punjab and Haryana, therefore, agri-cultural workers in all the Bihar fieldwork villages disliked attachment and preferred casual employment as free labour. Many workers from Purnia District, where both permanent and seasonal labourers were bonded, now migrated to Punjab, Calcutta and Assam in search of better wages. Landholders in Purnia had as a result started to plant cash crops and to use tractors instead of plough bullocks. Instead of hiring free labour, however, employers began to withhold wages from casual workers in order to prevent them from migrating, thereby ensuring their (enforced) presence in Purnia District throughout the peak period of the agricultural cycle. The emancipation of male workers who managed to migrate was achieved at the expense of female workers who remained behind: in the process of meeting debt-servicing labour obligations incurred by male migrants, therefore, local female workers were themselves transformed into bonded labour.

In Nalanda District, a relatively more advanced area economically, only permanent labour was bonded. Unlike their counterparts in Purnia and also northwestern India, permanent workers in central Bihar owned livestock, leased in land, borrowed from different lenders, and the debt they incurred was not intergenerational. The comparatively privileged situation of permanent labour in Nalanda District stemmed from the capacity of such workers to repay loans with income generated by sharecropping, livestock sales, and off-farm employment by (non-bonded) domestic kinsfolk. The reduction in the amount of sharecropped land leased by creditor-employers to permanent workers in Nalanda District, however, posed a threat to the continued relative autonomy of these subjects and their kin.

Questions about the presence/absence of unfreedom, and its negative/ positive meanings, are addressed in the remaining chapters of the book. The epistemological differences between the way in which specific variants of Marxism and neoclassical economics interpret the connection between capitalism and unfree labour are examined in Chapter 5. Marxists who are exponents of the 'semi-feudal' thesis share with neoclassical economic histor-ians the view that unfree labour is a pre-capitalist relation which constitutes an obstacle to market formation and thus accumulation. Emphasizing the multiple role of unfree relations in segmenting an already existing labour market, and thus in cheapening/disciplining workers by undermining their bargaining power and/or growing class consciousness, other Marxists by contrast maintain that in particular situations bonded labour is not merely compatible with capitalism but actually its preferred form.

Only the latter variant of Marxism is able satisfactorily to explain both the persistence and the economic importance of particular kinds of unfree relation in the United States, the Caribbean and Australasia from the mid-nineteenth century onwards. Although neoclassical economic historiography claims that in all these contexts 'choice-making' free workers were exercising subjective preferences regarding employment, evidence suggests by contrast a process of workforce restructuring undertaken by agrarian capitalists. This entailed the deproletarianization of rural workers attempting personally to commodify or recommodify their own labour-power.

Chapter 6 examines the continuing debate about the historical existence and incidence of unfree labour in Latin America, with specific reference to the claims made in a number of influential texts by (among others) Bauer, Cotlear, Knight and Cross concerning the meaning and causes of debt peonage (the *enganche* relation) over the period 1870–1930. Instead of an exploitative insti-tution premissed on coercion, the *enganche* is presented in such texts as a benign, non-coercive and thus non-antagonistic form of patron-clientage. Having redefined debt peonage as a free relation, these analyses then identify economic security as the main reason why rural labour enters into and remains within such working arrangements. The chapter concludes by arguing that this idealized image of bonded labour, and the inability to recognize it as a form of unfreedom, has its roots in a corresponding failure to differentiate the peasantry in terms of class.

Chapter 7 looks at the analogous debate about the link between unfree labour and agrarian change in India, with particular reference to the way in which attached labour has been defined (and redefined) from the early nineteenth century onwards. This includes not just defenders of slavery and serfdom during the 1800s, but also the Wisers in the 1920s, the Agricultural Labour Enquiries of the 1950s, and more recently the work of Epstein, Rudra Bardhan, Breman, Harriss and Platteau.

Common to all these analyses is a positive conceptualization of attached labour in rural India, and consequently the elimination of its element of unfreedom. As in the case of the Latin American *enganche* system, the debt servicing labour obligations structuring attachment are depicted as materially reciprocal exchanges involving landholder and labourer. Widely regarded as a non-capitalist transaction, the debt bondage relation is presented as a desirable form of job security or subsistence guarantee unacceptable to and thus discarded by producers engaged in accumulation. Because unfreedom is perceived as incompatible with worker 'resistance'/'assertiveness', moreover, the latter is frequently mistaken as evidence for the demise of bondage, and thus as an indicator of proletarianization.

The final chapter draws together a number of political themes emerging from the debate about unfree labour in India, Latin America and elsewhere, and outlines the way which these are being applied currently in development theory. It begins by considering the historically enduring aspects of a discourse about the culturally advantageous nature of unfree relations, variants of which have been deployed in Europe, the Americas and India over the nineteenth and twentieth centuries. At the centre of this discourse, the object of which has been the defence of serfdom, slavery and bonded labour, is a politically non-specific concept of grassroots cultural empowerment associated with agrarian populism and nationalism. It is argued that such claims have been and remain politically disempowering, especially when deployed by national/international capital (or their representatives) in order to justify current workforce restructuring/recomposition.

Of particular significance is the way in which narratives about unfreedom-as-economic-empowerment are merging with those which proclaim unfreedom-as-cultural-empowerment. Hence the notion of uncoerced individual agency at the centre of neoclassical economic historiography fuses conceptually with a variety of contemporary analytical frameworks in which worker unfreedom is depicted as a culturally empowering form of ethnic/national 'otherness'. The latter view structures claims advanced by 'resistance' theory, 'moral economy', 'survival strategies', popular culture and postmodernism concerning the desirability and empowering aspects of a politically non-specific worker 'assertiveness'. This, it is argued, has in turn created an epistemological space for nationalist ideology.

Influenced by postmodernism, these analyses downgrade or deny struggle conducted 'from above', and thus underestimate the power of capitalist producers and consequently overestimate the efficacy of 'from below' resistance/assertiveness on the part of unfree labour. They also overlook the extent to which a discourse emphasizing the innateness (= 'naturalness') of cultural identity has been deployed historically by employers to undermine or roll back the growth of class consciousness and thus to divide workers.

Most significantly, postmodern arguments against metanarratives and universals that inform political economy are currently being invoked by employers, conservatives and neo-liberals in two politically disempowering ways. On the one hand, against the desirability of an empowering working class internationalism, whereby trade unions are condemned as culturally/ nationally inappropriate universals and/or Eurocentric impositions. And on the other, in support of the view that unfree labour is nothing more than a specific form of cultural 'otherness', and thus beyond the competence of political economy to change.

1

Towards a Definition of Bonded Labour

About the central historical role of free labour in the process of economic development, political economy generally has been unambiguous. In the course of its transformation into a commodity, labour-power becomes doubly free: free from access to land, and free from the control of a particular employer. It is the first of these two freedoms which is generally identified as the obstacle to the complete proletarianization of a workforce engaged in agricultural production. Hence the unwillingness of rural workers to be separated from their means of production, together with a corresponding inability of agrarian capital to effect this separation, is seen as the principal barrier to the formation of a market in free labour and the concentration of landownership, both the latter being regarded as the prerequisites to the development of an efficient and large-scale commercial agriculture.

This book will focus on the second of these two unfreedoms and its role in the accumulation process. It will be argued, by contrast, that resistance to proletarianization derives not from the 'innate conservatism' of a rural workforce that wishes to remain or become a peasantry, but rather from the specific conditions of capitalist accumulation. Against the view that characterizes it as a pre-capitalist relationship, unfree labour is regarded here as a crucial aspect of class struggle between capital and labour in specific agrarian contexts, and as such may be introduced (or reintroduced) by employers at *any* historical conjuncture: either to pre-empt the political consequences of proletarianization in situations where a proletariat is in the process of being formed, or to re-impose capitalist authority over the workplace in cases where a proletariat already exists.

A corollary of this view is that unfree labour is not only compatible with relatively advanced productive forces but also fulfils the same role as technology in the class struggle: capital uses both to cheapen, to discipline, or as substitutes for free wage labour. Accordingly, it is precisely when rural workers begin to exercise their freedom of movement or bargaining power to secure benefits such as higher wages, better working conditions, shorter working hours, etc., in the course either of the formation or the consolidation of a market in free labour that capital attempts to shift the balance of work-place power in its own direction once again by restricting labour mobility.

Employer response to worker mobility and/or militancy consists of either importing labour which is already unfree (chattel slaves, indentured or contract workers) or converting free workers into unfree labour. Compulsory work in India and Peru takes many forms (not all of which possess mutually exclusive characteristics), extending from customary labour, communal labour to varieties of labour-rent paid by tenants and sub-tenants. Here it is intended to focus on one form only: bonded labour, an unfree relation constituted by the debt bondage mechanism which involves cancelling cash or kind debts with compulsory work. The three main claims reiterated throughout this book are: first, that contemporary bonded labour is a modern form of unfreedom; second, that in the contexts under consideration this relation is an important method whereby capitalist farmers and rich peasants increase their control over and simultaneously reduce the cost of their workforce; and third, that this process corresponds to deproletarianization, the 'other' of proletarianization.

I

Any definition of what constitutes an unfree production relation has to begin by focussing on the labour-power of the subject as private property, and hence as an actual/potential commodity over which its owner has disposition. Unlike a free labourer, who is able to enter or withdraw from the labour market at will, due to the operation of politico-ideological constraints or extra-economic coercion an unfree worker is unable personally to sell his or her own labour-power (in other words, to commodify it), regardless of whether this applies to employment that is either of time-specific duration (for example, contract work, convict labour, indentured labour) or of an indefinite duration (chattel slavery).[1]

1.1 Debt Bondage, Decommodification and Unfreedom

A useful way of approaching the conceptualization of unfree labour is to begin by defining it negatively: in terms of its 'other', a free production relation. In order to be regarded as free, therefore, a worker of whatever kind must have unconditionally and on a continuing basis the capacity to re-commodify fully his or her own labour-power. Whether or not a worker actually exercises this capacity is irrelevant, since the categorization of labour as free depends on an act of commodification/recommodification which – if the workers so wishes – he/she must be able to put into effect. For the purposes of this definition, therefore, a worker is free in the sense that he/she possesses an ability personally to commodify or recommodify labour-power at any moment in agricultural cycle, an ability which the worker in question must retain throughout the whole agricultural cycle itself. Where such a capacity is constrained, either wholly or in part, because of debts owed to his/her employer, the worker in question cannot be considered to be free.

For many writers on the subject, the unfreedom inherent in chattel slavery derives from property rights exercised by one person over another. All forms of work relationship that do not entail ownership of persons are consequently regarded as free. Such a view, however, overlooks additional forms of unfreedom which occur in situations where labour-power is prevented from entering the labour market under any circumstances (in which case labour-power ceases to be a commodity), is prevented from entering the labour market in person (labour-power remaining a commodity in such circumstances, but is sold by someone other than its owner), and is permitted to enter the labour-market in person, but only with the consent and at the convenience of someone other than its owner. It is precisely these kinds of unfreedom which arise in the case of bonded labour.

In general terms, therefore, the debt bondage relation may be said to exist in circumstances where cash or kind loans advanced by a creditor (usually – but not necessarily only – a landlord, a merchant, a moneylender, a labour contractor, or a rich peasant) are repaid in the form of labour-service, by the debtor personally and/or by members of his domestic/affinal/fictive kin group (poor peasants or landless labourers plus spouses, sons, daughters, co-parents and godchildren). Where the creditor does not personally own land (merchant, moneylender, labour contractor), the labour-power of a debtor may be profitably leased to a third party that does. In contexts where the lender is only or also a proprietor who hires in workers (landlord, rich peasant, a landowning merchant/moneylender/labour contractor), the labour-power of debtors will be employed on those holdings under his control (land owned or leased).

Two apparently contrasting forms of initiating debt bondage may be identified. The first occurs when an individual voluntarily seeks a loan which he or she is unable to repay subsequently. Thus loans taken for non-recurrent items of expenditure, such as the purchase of medicines for illness, the finance of important life cycle ceremonies (such as marriage or death rites) may result in the labour-power of the debtor being acquired by the creditor. Because the advance is requested, this form lacks the coercive appearance of bonded labour: the worker becomes indebted and exits from the free labour market 'voluntarily'. Perhaps the best example of 'voluntary' recruitment coupled with an unfree production relation is famine slavery, a work arrangement which arose historically in times of great scarcity, when self-enslavement was the only alternative to starvation and death.[2]

In the second form a loan is neither sought nor is the necessity for doing so present initially. Indebtedness is involuntary, and furthermore appears as such.

It follows from a situation in which payment due a worker at the end of his contract is withheld by the creditor-employer precisely in order to retain his services, the resulting period of unpaid labour (engineered by the creditor-employer) necessitating recourse to subsistence loans on the part of the worker. Though different in appearance, both these forms are in substance the same, and initiate the cycle of debt-servicing labour obligations which constitutes bondage.[3]

Like chattel slavery, this relationship entails the loss on the part of a debtor and/or his kinsfolk of the right to sell their labour-power at prevailing free market rates during the period of bondage. Unlike chattel slavery, however, where the *person* of the slave is itself the subject of an economic transaction, in the case of a bonded labourer it is the latter's *labour-power* which is bought, sold, and controlled without the consent of its owner. Hence the frequent conflation of bonded labour with the free wage relation, notwithstanding the fact that while a free wage labourer may personally dispose of his or her own labour-power (by selling it to whomsoever s/he wishes, or withdrawing from the labour market altogether), neither a chattel slave nor a bonded labourer possesses this right. Both the latter may appear in the free labour market, therefore, but not as autonomous sellers of their own labour-power.

Although many local variants of bonded labour exist, each possessing historically specific oral or written contractual obligations (stipulating the form and level of remuneration, the duration and type of work, etc.), the core elements of the debt bondage mechanism as this occurs in India and Latin America consist of an advance payment (or loan) together with a prohibition on working for others without the consent of the creditor so long as the debt remains outstanding.[4] The object of this unfree relation is to ensure the availability to the creditor-employer of the worker thus indebted, the ideological decommodification of the wage, and ultimately to reduce the price of labour-power itself.

An important effect of the economic decommodification of labour-power is the ideological decommodification of the wage form itself, a process whereby labour-power is separated conceptually from the value it produces (analogous to the conceptualization of payment received by female workers as 'pin money'). In ideological terms, therefore, a bonded labourer works to pay off a debt rather than for a wage. When reinforced by kinship authority (see below), the process of ideological decommodification is particularly marked. The kinds of struggle generally pursued by unfree workers are also correspondingly distinct in terms of their political implications for an employer. Whereas resistance by bonded labour – when this occurs – usually takes the form of *individual* flight from the place of work, opposition by free wage labour not only entails a *collective* response in the form of trade union organization, but also remains within the labour process itself, and hence affects its reproduction.

Debt bondage has been – and continues to be – regarded as a form of unfreedom associated with serfdom, an involuntary agrestic servitude arising from the attachment of an individual to land through debt. Although this form is still important, as the examples of poor peasants in Peru and sharecroppers in Bihar confirm, it is argued here that contemporary debt bondage increasingly involves the bonding of *landless* labour, and on this criterion is more accurately viewed as a modern form of unfreedom amounting to deproletarianization.

1.2 Bonded Labour as Deproletarianization

Generally speaking, deproletarianization (or the economic and politico-ideological decommodification of labour-power) involves workforce restructuring by means of introducing or reintroducing unfree relations, a process of class composition/recomposition which accompanies the struggle between capital and labour.[5] In contexts/periods where/when further accumulation is blocked by overproduction, economic crisis may force capital to restructure its labour process either by replacing free workers with unfree equivalents or by converting the former into the latter.

The economic advantage of deproletarianization is that such restructuring enables rural employers first to lower the cost of local workers by importing unfree, more easily regulated, and thus cheaper outside labour, and then to lower the cost of the latter if/when the original external/local wage differential has been eroded. In this way it is possible either to maintain wages at existing (low) levels or even to decrease pay and conditions of both components of the workforce, thereby restoring/enhancing profitability and with it the accumulation project in (or linked to) the capitalist labour process.

In ideological terms, the object of the deproletarianization/decommodification of distinct forms of labour-power employed by capital is either to prevent the emergence of a specifically proletarian consciousness or to curtail the latter where it already exists. There are numerous instances of racist responses on the part of an existing agrarian workforce displaced by the nationally/ethnically/regionally specific labour-power of cheap/unfree migrants recruited by planters, landowners or rich peasants engaged in the restructuring of the labour process.

Where an initially progressive proletarian class struggle shows signs of being/becoming effective, the attempt by capital to demobilize it by means of workforce restructuring may convert what is an actually or potentially revolutionary situation into a politically reactionary combination of nationalism and racism. Accordingly, in such circumstances the form taken by class struggle waged from above in turn affects the form taken by class struggle waged from below. Although it may continue to reproduce itself in economic terms, therefore, and thus constitute a (segmented) class-in-itself, working class recomposition takes the all-important form of class-for-itself only where/when such politico-ideological division is transcended.

That the experience of the proletarian condition does not automatically generate an immediate, unambiguous or exclusive class consciousness on the part of workers, therefore, may in given circumstances be a consequence of the fact that the aim of deproletarianization is precisely to prevent, deflect or distort the development of just such a consciousness of class. For this reason, the experience of *becoming* a worker in the employ of capital, or the change from class-in-itself to class-for-itself, has crucial implications for the self-perception and the perception-of-others on the part of the labouring subject, as well as the forms taken by any resulting political action. Viewed thus, unfree relations of production are an integral part of both class struggle and capitalist accumulation in the context of much Third World agriculture.

II

It is important to make clear what such a definition of bonded labour excludes.[6] Apart from those analyses which recognize both the existence and the unfree component of debt bondage, approaches tend to adhere to one of three interpretations. The first denies that bonded labour exists any longer, a position which constitutes the most fundamental non-recognition of the relation. The second recognizes the presence of contemporary debt bondage, but disputes its classification as a form of unfreedom: the element of coercion is replaced by a concept of 'reciprocity', 'subsistence guarantee' or job security. The third recognizes neither the existence nor the unfreedom of bonded labour, and unproblematically elides it with free wage labour. For reasons which are examined in the second part of this book, bonded labour is regarded by exponents of the last two views as either economically or culturally empowering for the subject concerned.

1.3 What Bonded Labour Is Not

Among the more common causes of misrecognition are the following. Some texts dealing with bonded labour tend to confuse economic immobility with physical movement, concluding (wrongly) that evidence of the latter disproves claims about the presence of unfreedom. As not only the migration of slave and indentured labour but also the inter-employer transfer of debt (='changing masters') confirm, however, unfreedom is indeed compatible with the process of physical movement on the part of its subject, either on an individual or a collective basis.[7] Hence the occasional escape of an 'absconding' bonded labourer is not of itself a problem for the definition of debt bondage, any more than the occasional escape of a chattel slave has been a problem for the definition of slavery. Of equal significance in this regard is the fact that debt bondage is not incompatible with a technologically advanced labour process.

Neither is it the case that debt bondage automatically excludes the possibility of 'from below' agency on the part of an indebted worker, frequent claims to the contrary notwithstanding. Those who endorse the view that unfree agrarian relations are negated by worker 'assertiveness' usually do so because they also subscribe to an historically unsustainable contrast: since in their perception the unfree production relations which existed in the past generated workforce passivity, the fact that workers now challenge the legitimacy of such relations is regarded by them as evidence for the non-existence of bondage, and consequently as confirmation of the presence of free labour.

Nor is unfreedom simply an effect of employment duration, since debt bondage can apply equally to permanent/casual/seasonal workers, and does not require the intergenerational inheritance of debt.[8] Neither is it the case that, once unfree, labour remains bonded indefinitely. Workers who are bonded by debt do not necessarily remain unfree forever, and will – just like 'green' labour which is not unfree – begin to organize in furtherance of better pay and conditions if and when this becomes possible. Unlike free labour, however, unfree workers are faced with additional obstacles to successful political organization, not the least of which is the fact of their indebtedness to the targets of such mobilization. Although bonded labour is unlikely to remain passive, and does indeed make tentative attempts to improve its situation, therefore, these endeavours rarely end in success; if they do, there is always the likelihood that other unfree workers will be used to displace them.[9]

Of equal importance to the conceptualization of unfreedom adopted here is the fact that extra-economic coercion is not reducible to physical maltreatment; as is argued below, coercion frequently takes a nuanced form of socio-economic pressure that can be exercised directly or indirectly through actual/fictive kin and/or caste networks, and as such does not automatically entail the actualization of physical oppression. Nor is bonded labour necessarily synonymous with forced labour, notwithstanding their frequent conflation. Whereas forced labour encompasses the kind of infrastructural projects – for example, road building, clearing irrigation ditches, famine relief, etc., organized either by a local community or by the state – from which its subjects may benefit on a collective basis, debt bondage usually involves an arrangement between individuals occupying different positions in the class structure.

For analogous reasons, debt bondage is not the same as the forced commercialization of peasant produce, although here too there is a tendency to present the commodification of crops produced by peasant proprietors who owe debts or labour-rent to landlords, merchants or multinational corporations as evidence for the unfree character of these production relations.[10] When compared with bonded labour, however, such transactions involve the extraction of distinct forms of surplus by producers occupying similar class positions: whereas debt bondage entails the appropriation by capital from indebted workers of surplus-value, forced commercialization can involve the appropriation of surplus product by agribusiness from what are in fact other (small agrarian) capitalists. Moreover, as the Peruvian case study presented in Chapter 2 indicates, the forced commercialization of tenant produce by land-lords resulted in the unfreedom not of the tenants themselves, who were rich peasants, but rather of the poor peasant sub-tenants and/or agricultural labourers employed by these rich peasant tenants to meet their own labour-service obligations.

Neither is it a condition for the existence of bondage that debts be interest-bearing; equally, debt is itself not the same as credit, their apparent similarity notwithstanding. The difficulty in this instance stems from a tendency to confuse productive and unproductive loans, and consequently a failure to dif-ferentiate the reasons for and the outcome of borrowing in terms of class.[11] In part, this may explain the problems many texts about rural development have with the theorization of the negative consequences (such as unfreedom) arising from worker indebtedness. And just as 'high' wages may not indicate worker advantage or freedom, so low wages do not necessarily signal the presence of bonded labour.[12] Although low wages for all forms of labour may be both the effect and the intention behind the operation of the debt bondage mechanism, it is nevertheless the case that not all low-paid workers are them-selves unfree to sell their own labour-power to the highest bidder. A low wage is an effect of economic unfreedom, and hence not of itself constitutive of the debt bondage relation.

III

An important aspect of the continuing debate about the nature of unfree labour, and the difference between it and free labour, concerns methods. Hence the investigation of the structure and process of unfreedom, or the way in which coercion and its effectiveness is reproduced over time, is confronted with a central question: in what way does one measure and evaluate the relative importance of different kinds of control and enforcement. The latter extend from outright physical oppression (killings, floggings, violence) to more subtle ideological forms (actual/fictive kinship authority, patriarchy), and raise in turn another crucial issue: the role of gender in this process.

1.4 Methodological Considerations

As is clear from the differences between Marxist and neoclassical economic approaches to bonded labour (see Chapters 5, 6 and 7), methodological issues are central to the way in the agrarian workforce in Australia, the Caribbean and the United States during the nineteenth century and Peru and India in the twentieth has been characterized as either free or unfree. One result of the fetishization of oral history, quantification and fieldwork, however, has been that such methods come to be seen as being capable by themselves of providing satisfactory answers to complex theoretical questions about the free/unfree character of the workforce. The implication in such instances is that the adequacy of explanation is an effect simply of the latest methods which license access to unproblematically constituted 'facts', rather than theoretical rigour which asks what 'facts' are in the first place.

Such advocacy of fieldwork generally, and of measurement/testing and oral history in particular, overlooks two things. First, the fact that by its very nature methodological approaches to questions concerning free/unfree labour are part of the difficulty and not of themselves the solution. And second, it ignores the methodological impossibility of quantifying those concepts, such as power and coercion, which are central to the debate about the meaning/enforcement of unfree relations. Where bonded labour is concerned, not the least of the many difficulties with such a view are the following four interrelated problems.

The first is its innate empiricism, an approach in which the acceptability or otherwise of any explanation is dependent ultimately on the technique of research and not on the prefiguring theoretical framework. The second is that it fails to problematize both quantitative methods and oral history in terms of what such methods do and do not disclose about unfree labour. Third, it reproduces the traditional/modern dichotomy invoked by cliometricians, whereby novel methodologies displace existing theory simply because they are new. And fourth, it also reproduces a false polarity between a 'from-below' framework which emphasizes worker agency (= freedom) and a 'from-above' one in which, it is implied, workers are depicted as passive (= unfreedom).[13]

In this connection it is important to remember two things regarding the quality of the sources from which indirect/direct information about unfree labour is obtained. First, it is indeed ironic that many of those who claim that unfreedom is acceptable to its subject are in fact historians, given that in the majority of instances the written record on which the historian depends contain little or no evidence about what labourers actually thought of their work situation. And second, even the reliability of contemporary oral evidence gathered directly from workers themselves must be questioned, again for rather obvious methodological reasons: for example, in cases where unfree workers are interviewed in front of their employers, or where there is a fear on the part of bonded labourers that the fact and/or content of any such interview will be made known to an employer.[14]

In methodological terms, therefore, it is difficult to verify the existence of the debt bondage relationship for four reasons in particular. These concern questions of legality, the nature of the written and/or historical record, the manner in which coercion/enforcement is exercised (and by whom), and a failure to disaggregate what are claimed to be high wages. The first of these methodological problems applies only in cases where contemporary forms of unfree labour are being investigated, the second concerns the methodological limits faced by those investigating its past forms, while the third and fourth apply equally to historical and contemporary research methods.

1.5 Unfreedom, the Law and the State

There are three interrelated methodological issues here: first, where unfreedom is illegal, what effect does this have on attempts to investigate debt bondage; second, what is the nature of coercion, does it occur, and if so is it effective; and third, if it is effective, can unfree relations be enforced in post-abolition contexts where they no longer enjoy the support of the law and the repressive apparatus (police, judiciary) of the state.

Given that it involves questions of national/international legality, both governments and individual creditor-employers are generally unwilling to divulge information about the presence of bonded labour to outsiders.[15] For this reason, secondary data on the presence of unfreedom is either non-existent or unreliable.[16] At a global level, debt bondage contravenes not only the 1948 UN Universal Declaration of Human Rights but also the 1956 UN Supplementary Convention on the Abolition of Slavery, the Slave trade and Institutions and Practices similar to Slavery.[17] The governments of India and Peru are co-signatories of the 1956 UN Convention, and both endorse the 1948 UN Declaration.

In terms of domestic legislation, debt bondage is outlawed both in Part III of the Indian Constitution, and by Point 4 (which stated that 'bonded labour, wherever it exists, will be declared illegal') in the 20-Point Programme introduced during the Emergency of 1975–77. In addition to the extensive provisions contained in the Bonded Labour System (Abolition) Act passed by the Congress government in 1976, numerous legislative ordinances outlawing specific and localised variants of debt bondage have been enacted at various times during the twentieth century by individual state governments.[18] Unfree labour is similarly declared illegal under a variety of legislative ordinances passed by the Peruvian state.[19]

Unless an observer is informed of the situation by the bonded labourer in person (which in the view of the coercive nature of the relation is generally unlikely), is present at the transaction which results in debt, or has access to written records of these transactions (which, again by their very nature, are kept by the creditor-employer), therefore, the existence of debt bondage and its *modus operandi* tends to remain hidden.[20] The marked unwillingness on the part of governments and/or creditor-employers to collect or make available data/information about unfree agrarian relations is itself compounded methodologically by the lacunae in the historical record. In the case of the Latin American hacienda, for example, written agreements between employer and worker involving the cancellation of cash debts with labour-service are found (if at all) not in public archives but rather in the private accounts maintained by landlords, farmers, labour contractors, and peasant proprietors.[21] This underlines the fact that although certain sources may contain no reference to debt bondage, this does not constitute proof that it does not exist.[22]

The role of the state and the law in the reproduction of bonded labour relations immediately raises what is perhaps the most crucial, and certainly the most contentious, of all the methodological issues confronting the study of unfreedom: the nature of coercion, its presence/absence in given contexts, and the related question of its effectiveness. Of central importance, therefore, are the following methodological considerations: can debt bondage be enforced, even where/when it is permitted by law and supported by the power of the state; conversely, is it possible to enforce bonded labour in contexts where it is illegal and thus lacks the support of the state.[23] Hence the questionable proposition that once debt bondage has been abolished by the state, it cannot possibly be reproduced. A corollary of this view is that, where it is not – or no longer – sanctioned by law, bonded labour is *ipso facto* unenforceable. As evidence from eastern Peru and northwestern India confirms, however, the power of the state has not been a necessary condition for the enforcement of bonded labour relations in either of these two contexts.

For reasons which will be explored fully in the second half of this book, there are two opposing views concerning the existence/efficacy of coercion/enforcement in the reproduction of agrarian relations. Focussing on the continued presence of the class position/power of landlords/planters/contractors/rich peasants, Marxism argues that this is usually sufficient to enable any or all of the latter to exercise coercion in a variety of ways so as to enforce bondage, regardless of whether such a relation is supported by the state or the law. By contrast, variant forms of revisionism maintain that – even where these exist – penal statutes and other legislative ordinances enforcing debt-servicing labour obligations are insufficiently powerful to ensure the reproduction of unfreedom.

In most cases, methodological considerations are also informed by epistemological ones: neoclassical economic historiography, for example, denies the efficacy of unfreedom because employer collusion necessary to achieve this is lacking. The latter view emanates in turn from the assumption within a neoclassical economic framework that in a market economy rival capitalist producers by definition engage in competition for workers. The methodological implications of such an epistemology are equally predictable: because competition between landlords/planters/contractors/rich peasants enjoys the status of 'given', little or no attempt is made to investigate the presence of collusion between any/all of them in particular circumstances. An important determinant of unfreedom thus remains unexplored, notwithstanding evidence from many other sources that it exists and is effective.[24]

Any attempt to problematize the connection between unfreedom, the law and the state must begin by addressing the issue of class power: where powerful landholders remain unexpropriated, therefore, they also retain the capacity to frustrate/circumvent any attempt by progressive bureaucratic elements and/or NGOs to eliminate debt bondage. In such circumstances, legislative discourse proclaiming abolition is invariably contradicted/undermined by grassroots practice.[25] During the post-reform era in Latin America and India – when a landlord class had either been expropriated or could no longer rely on the automatic support of the state – capitalist farmers and/or rich peasants who were also creditor-employers have enforced debt-servicing labour obligations not directly on the individual concerned but rather indirectly, via the actual/fictive kin and/or caste network of an indebted worker.

1.6 Coercion and Enforcement

While most of the more important texts dealing with bonded labour in Latin America and India rightly identify the existence of debt linked to extra-economic coercion as a crucial aspect of unfreedom, they nevertheless fail to problematise the methodological accessibility of coercion, let alone the different forms this might take.[26] Thus the attempt to present the quantification of whippings as an indicator of compulsion in motivating slave labour in the antebellum American South has rightly been criticized.[27] Much the same point might be made concerning those instances where coercion appears to be absent from the process whereby rural workers repay debts in the form of labour-service. Here it is the (all-pervading) knowledge about and fear of the consequences following default that constitute coercion, rather than the (perhaps infrequent) operationalisation of the consequences themselves. It is easy, therefore, to interpret the absence of the latter as evidence for the non-existence of the former.

The fact that some forms of coercion are exercised in an indirect manner reinforces the problem of methodological accessibility. One of the most important (and ideologically most potent) methods of enforcing debt bondage obligations remains the formal and informal control exerted in the context of kin networks. Thus a creditor-employer may seek to enforce a debt obligation by compulsion effected against the close kin of debtor rather than against the debtor in person. This kind of socio-economic pressure may take many forms: for example, by threatening to appropriate or cut off access to land, crops, livestock, fodder, or water resources belonging to or enjoyed by the kinsfolk (or fellow caste members) of a debtor; by blocking the access of these kinsfolk to local sources of credit and/or employment; and, finally, by the threat of violence, caste disapproval, or sanctions from the caste or village *panchayat* against a debtor's kinsfolk.[28]

To end such pressure on themselves, these kin will in turn exercise variant forms of pressure on a debtor to fulfil his labour-service obligations to the creditor-employer. Similarly, the corporate ideology of kinship can be invoked to compel subordinate kin categories to become bonded labourers in order to meet debts incurred by senior kinsfolk, and in some instances debt bondage itself corresponds not only to an intergenerational relationship (sons/wives inheriting both debts and labour-service obligations of fathers/husbands) but also to an intra-kin group relationship (the cancellation of labour-service involving all the family members of a debtor's household).[29] As in the case of fear, such coercion exerted through kin or caste networks frequently remains hidden from outsiders, and for this additional reason poses severe methodological difficulties.

To the degree that it involves the labour-power of those beyond the individual actually in debt, research into unfreedom cannot but pose gender-specific questions concerning the fact of, the manner in which, and by whom social control is exercised over female workers.[30] Where the labour-power of women who are also actual/fictive kinsfolk of a bonded labourer is as a result also decommodified, in the double sense of non-payment and/or immobilization, it is important to understand both that and also how this is achieved. In short, the extent to which gender-specific unfreedom is itself a consequence of the capacity of a creditor-employer or debtor to invoke and sustain patriarchal and/or actual/fictive kinship authority with the object of compelling unwilling – and in an economic sense perhaps already free – female workers to undertake debt-servicing labour obligations incurred by men.

Even in cases where women are not compelled to enter bonded labour relations in order to discharge debts owed by males, affinal/consanguineal kinship authority can still be inscribed in (and structure the socio-economic reproduction of) gender-specific instances of unfreedom. Instead of making payment directly to female workers recruited, therefore, a labour contractor and/or creditor-employer may pass the wage on to the kinsfolk of the woman concerned, thereby reinforcing the element of control exercised by senior relatives over the disposition of female labour-power.[31] In some contexts this kind of transaction has involved the purchase/sale of a woman herself, either to redeem debts incurred by males in poor peasant households or to reimburse brideprice paid by her current husband to her previous spouse.[32]

1.7 Intergenerational Debt Transfers and Unfreedom

The methodological issues raised by the intergenerational transfer of debt are clearly important, since this process not only disproportionately affects the labour-power of women but is also often invoked as a (even the) defining aspect of bonded labour. In the case of India, for example, contemporary unfreedom is associated by some texts only with the presence of a long-term debt that is passed down through the generations; where this condition is not met, the production relation is regarded as free. The characterization of unfreedom simply in terms of the heritability of debt is itself problematic, since by definition this would appear to exclude first generation bonded labourers who enter attachment because of their own indebtedness.[33] In such cases, a worker does not inherit debt, nor indeed is it necessarily the case that existing indebtedness will be passed on to the subsequent generation. The unfreedom of the labourer in question, however, is palpable, notwithstanding the absence of an intergenerational transfer of debt.

Equally problematic are the kinds of sources/data on which assessments concerning the presence/absence of intergenerational debt inheritance depend. Few texts dealing with the *enganche* system in Latin America make any reference to a link between this relation and the intergenerational inheritance of debt, and no text has attempted to explore this connection in depth.[34] The extent to which inheritance of indebtedness continues to be an important feature of bonded labour relationships in the agrarian sector of India is similarly problematic. For the country as a whole, the 1978 NLI/GPF survey found that although intergenerational bondage was common in the states of Andhra Pradesh, Karnataka, Rajasthan and Tamil Nadu, this was not true of Gujarat,

Maharashtra and Orissa.[35] Neither Bhattacharya nor Bhalla make any reference to this dimension of agrarian relations in their studies of Haryana, although information presented below from village case studies in this state would suggest that intergenerational bondage is indeed an aspect of both attached and casual labour in Karnal and Rohtak Districts.[36] Despite the fact that the same is true of Purnia District in Bihar, the NLI/GPF survey calculates the existence in this northeastern state of only a twelve per cent incidence of intergenerational – as distinct from all forms of – bondage.[37]

These methodological problems notwithstanding, it is argued here that the presence/absence of unfree labour does not depend on whether or not debt is inherited on an intergenerational basis. Together with the limited job mobility entailed in the transfer of debts between masters (= 'changing masters'), the non-heritability of debts constitutes a precise relocation of unfreedom in terms of the rural labour process. This transformation corresponds to a shift in the immobilizing function of debt from a continuous and inter-generational basis to a more period- and context-specific basis. Its operationalisation is as a result confined to the months of peak demand in the agricultural cycle, when sellers of labour-power would otherwise command high prices for their commodity. Whereas the traditional form of bondage is unprofitable (requiring payment for time when labour-power is not engaged in productive activity), the modern form is not (and is akin to the kind of control exercised by a plantation over the seasonal labour-power of poor peasant households that reproduce their own subsistence during the off-peak period in villages on its periphery).

Accordingly, the fact that rural producers in some parts of India and Latin America dispense with the services of their bonded labourers, both for the duration of the slack agricultural season and/or on an intergenerational basis, is indicative not of a transformation from unfree to free rural labour but rather of an increasing cost-consciousness on the part of creditor-employers. The latter nonetheless continue to hold on to workers throughout the busy months and over succeeding agricultural cycles so long as it remains profitable to do so.[38]

1.8 Kinship, Migration and Unfreedom

Unlike economic compulsion or other forms of extra-economic coercion in cases where no kin or quasi-kin link is present, kinship ideology as a mechanism of social control is not limited by locational constraints. It is therefore possible to operationalise this form of compulsion not only on bonded labourers and poor peasants who inhabit the same locality as the creditor-employer but also on those who migrate from distant locations. Significantly, recruitment by means of advance payment is often effected on the basis of pre-existing kin ties, and economic relations between labour contractors or work gang leaders and bonded labourers are also structured and reinforced by the additional presence of kinship ties.[39]

Accordingly, when migrant labourers fail to return and meet their labour-service obligations to a creditor-employer, kin networks may be activated to secure compliance or else to recover the original loan. In cases where a bonded migrant labourer is a member of a work gang recruited in his own village, this form of pressure is particularly effective, since the gang leader (or labour contractor) is not only himself answerable directly to the creditor-employer but – since he shares a common point of origin with the absconding migrant – also possesses both the political power locally and extensive kin networks necessary to exert pressure in the migrant's home village or community.[40]

However, as with class relations and class struggle, so conflict and control linked to the operationalisation of the debt bondage mechanism is frequently excluded from the domain of actual/fictive kinship and gender. Symptomatically, the failure to recognize either the presence of unfree labour or its extractive economic role together with the enforcement of debt-servicing work obligations derives in many instances from the idealization or non-problematization of kinship. In these cases, the mystification of debt bondage arises in a situation where observers uncritically adopt the classificatory categories of informants which depict the unequal exchange of cash for labour-power as an equal exchange premissed on the material (as distinct from the ideology of) reciprocity based on caste, kinship, quasi-kinship, or patron-client relations.[41]

1.9 Work Intensity, Wage Levels and Unfreedom

A related methodological problem stems from the frequent misrecognition of the real level of the wage due to a corresponding failure to disaggregate remuneration made by a creditor-employer to indebted workers and their kins-folk. The same applies in the case of payments received by workers who owe debts to the estate store or to labour contractors. Without a contextualizing knowledge concerning the cause, extent and effect of appropriation therefrom, 'high' wages are by themselves proof neither of the advantage enjoyed by nor the economic freedom of the worker. Exponents of the latter view take no account of the debt component of the wage, or the extent to which a 'high wage' is actually nothing more than largescale borrowing.

In cases where a substantial proportion of the wage is composed of debt (loans, advances, etc.) owed to an employer or contractor, therefore, the dis-posable element will be much lower, not only necessitating further borrowing for consumption purposes but also reproducing thereby the very conditions which give rise to unfreedom. Accordingly, the emphasis placed on the compilation of wage data, to the extent of recommending this as the way forward for research into bonded labour, ignores the fact that quantification without an adequate theorization of what precisely is being measured proves nothing other than the veracity of the computer programmer's adage 'gigo' (garbage in, garbage out).[42]

To know whether or not workers did (and do) well out of a particular arrangement, therefore, and why high wage levels or wage increases may not actually benefit labour, it is necessary to operate theoretically with a concept of exploitation that goes beyond the surface appearance of (invariably 'official') wage data. This approach would include not just elements such as working conditions, duration of working day, but also issues like surplus appropriation (by employers, contractors, and kinsfolk, or any combination thereof) from existing wages, and the levels at which wages ought to be. Thus a consequence of the reification of non-disaggregated wage levels is a corresponding failure to identify what the worker actually gets for the sale of his/her labour-power, who manages to appropriate the difference, together with the why and how of this.[43] In so far as they do not (and in methodological terms cannot) identify the following specific forms of appropriation, therefore, wage levels *per se* cannot serve as an indicator of worker advantage and worker freedom.

The first concerns the higher rate of exploitation which results from an increase in the workload and/or the length of the working day. That such appropriation is determined by worker unfreedom is evident from the case of Indian state of Haryana, where during the late 1980s indebted casual labour either worked for the same wages but longer hours than its non-indebted equivalent, or for the same hours but at lower wages than the latter.[44] Without this kind of knowledge about variations in the duration of the working day, therefore, it would be possible to argue that similar payments received by indebted/non-indebted casual labour precluded a differential rate of surplus-value (or surplus labour) extraction, and thus to conclude that no difference existed between the two forms as regards exploitation and ultimately relational substance.[45]

The reification of the undisaggregated wage also overlooks the second form of appropriation, or the dual forms of surplus extraction that occur within the domain (and are licensed by the ideology) of kinship: that is, appropriation from and by kinsfolk. With regard to the first variant, involving appropriation from a whole kin group, in cases where debt repayment involves family members having to work alongside the indebted wage earner, multiple units of labour-power receive no more than the payment of a single unit. Accordingly, non-disaggregated wage levels hide the fact that they are not for individuals so much as for family groups, and it is therefore necessary to know how many workers the concept 'wage' covers. Rather than benefitting the agricultural labouring family, therefore, debt bondage may actually permit a landholder to obtain and retain the labour-power of its separate members at a far cheaper rate than he would otherwise have to pay them individually as free wage labourers.

The second variant takes the form of intra-kin surplus extraction, where wage appropriation is effected not by non-kinsfolk from a kin group but rather within the latter context itself. In the Dagua region of southwestern Colombia, for example, private ownership by the male household head of the means of production on peasant farms enables such rich peasant patriarchs to accumulate on the basis of control exercised over the labour-power of female and younger male members of the peasant family (who are themselves either poor peasants or propertyless), a form of intra-familial surplus extraction premissed on unfree kin labour which belies the claim that Colombia is yet another location where 'wages were ... a function of market forces'.[46]

The third form consists of the appropriation from wages effected through the estate store, by labour contractors and by creditor-employers. Despite its important connection with the presence of unfree labour, many texts fail to mention the central role of the estate store in generating worker indebtedness, and thus its contribution to the economic reproduction of bondage.[47] This is a serious ommission, given that the real purchasing power of wages, the capacity on the part of workers to buy subsistence items without incurring debt, the ability of the estate to recover (and thus nullify) any wage increases obtained by the workforce, together with the positive/negative nature of worker reactions to the estate store in times of crisis, are all important indicators of whether or not it is possible to conceptualize debt bondage as a form of worker advantage.[48]

The same is true of the relationship between a labour contractor and migrant workers, which is frequently depicted as unproblematically benign, a tension-free arrangement whereby the former not only represents the best interests of the latter but also automatically passes on to them any wage increase obtained on their behalf.[49] Here the methodological difficulty stems from an inability to conceptualize this as a relation in which contractors appropriate wage increases and withhold existing wages, thereby necessitating further debt that either initiates or reproduces bondage which in turn leads to or intensifies the decommodification of migrant labour-power.[50] Appropriations by the estate store and/or labour agents, both at the point of workers' consumption and at the subsequent point of sale of workers' labour-power, suggest that a significant proportion of what employers identify as 'high labour costs' go to storeowners, contractors – or even to employers themselves – in the form of profits and not to workers in the form of wages.[51]

Finally, just as a labour contractor does not always pass on to the workers under his control the full amount he receives from an employer to whom such labour-power is provided, so a creditor-employer can also ensure that bonded labour does not actually receive the stipulated/declared wage or the total payment due.[52] This kind of appropriation by a creditor-employer extends from non-payment, through 'withholding wages', to the capacity to insist on repayment by the worker of a portion of the wage actually received.[53] In such circumstances, therefore, a discrepancy arises between the declared payment (or the 'official' wage), which may register the existence of a 'high' wage, and the amount retained by a worker from the sum received from the creditor-employer.

Since he is the one who sets the amount of labour service to be performed by a debtor cancelling a loan, the creditor-employer and/or labour contractor also possesses the power to fix the 'wage' rate at which the debt is paid off below the free market rate.[54] The fact that in some contexts the remuneration of free wage labour is barely above that of bonded labour is proof not of the economic indistinctiveness of debt bondage but rather of its effectiveness, since the object of introducing unfree components into the labour market is precisely to lower the price of *all* forms of labour-power.[55] A more fruitful comparison is therefore not between free and unfree labour in terms of differential remuneration but rather between the lowest level of remuneration after the introduction of unfree labour and the level at which an average wage would be if no unfree labour existed.

1.10 Conclusion

The central proposition advanced in this chapter is that the current decommodification of landless labour by means of the debt bondage mechanism corresponds to a process of deproletarianization. Many texts dealing with the issue of agrarian change, however, omit any reference to the presence of debt bondage. Those which do recognize its existence not only utilize different and contradictory definitions but also fail to consider important aspects of the relation. Bonded labour is seen as a relation which does not occur in the kinship domain, does not apply to migrants or non-permanent categories of worker, and cannot exist without the overarching support of the state. The distinct and oblique forms of extra-economic coercion, together with their methodological accessibility and modes of economic appropriation, are rarely problematized. One of the most effective ways of enforcing debt-servicing labour obligations, it is argued, is through the formal/informal control exercised through caste and/or kin networks. Such pressure, moreover, can be exercised on those who migrate, and also in contexts where the law forbids unfree labour.

About the defining characteristics of unfree labour, together with the reasons for its reproduction, political economy is unambiguous. Hence the categorization of any production relation as free or unfree depends only on whether or not its subject currently enjoys the ability personally to commodify his or her own labour-power. For this reason , unfreedom can exist even when employment is not permanent, and despite the presence either of physical movement (migration, 'changing masters') on the part of the labourer or of worker agency/'assertiveness'. Unfreedom also occurs regardless of whether entry into the relation is voluntary or involuntary. In a similar vein, the enforcement of unfreedom does not depend on the support of the state, nor does it require that a worker remain in the same locality as the debtor-employer, or the exercise by the latter of continuous and unremitting physical maltreatment. Not only is it possible for labour contractors to enforce bondage over long distances, therefore, but where compliance with debt servicing labour obligations is concerned, sanctions mobilized from within actual/fictive kinship authority are just as effective as legislation promulgated by the state.

In contrast to received wisdom about unfree labour in India, Latin America and elsewhere, which regards bonded labour as a pre-capitalist relation, here unfreedom is viewed as a way in which capitalist farmers and rich peasants cheapen, discipline and control rural workers by means of deproletarian-ization. This economic and politico-ideological decommodification of labour-power constitutes a process of restructuring, or workforce recomposition whereby capital replaces more costly free labour with less costly unfree variants. The advantages for creditor-employers engaged in capital accumula-tion of using the debt bondage relation instead of free labour are obvious. Debt bondage undermines, distorts or deflects the growth of a specifically proletarian consciousness in a number of ways. Not only does ideological decommodification conceptually devalorize the wage form, therefore, but it also individualizes struggle (flight, absconding). This in turn 'naturalizes' and thus facilitates the exercise by creditor-employers of certain kinds of authority, which it does by transferring conflict into the domain of 'innate'/'immutable' and historically longstanding identities (actual/fictive kinship, caste) sup-ported by religious concepts of the 'sacred'. One effect is the segmentation of the labour market through the reproduction of 'natural' divisions within the workforce (ethnicity, gender).

The non/mis-recognition of unfreedom stems from two distinct method-ological causes: on the one hand obstacles placed by those (employers, the state) with an interest in preventing information about bonded labour from being collected, and on the other the inadequate questioning of historical sources and/or contemporary accounts by those conducting research. Although the first cause – in which landholders, labour contractors and/or state representatives deny or downplay the incidence of contemporary unfreedom –is not the fault of an outside observer, this is not true of the second. In the latter case many of the difficulties can be traced to a failure to raise issues such as the methodological accessibility of coercion, and consequently the researcher is him/herself to blame for the conceptual non-problematization of unfreedom. Accordingly, the inability to recognize the presence of unfree labour and thus its reproduction by capital is due to a number of theoretical and methodological shortcomings. Hence a failure to search for evidence of coercion is itself frequently the result of a benign interpretation of the debt bondage relation, whereby compulsion is epistemologically decoupled from the act of lending, which in turn licenses a positive interpretation of debt as being to the benefit of the worker who borrows. A consequence of the inability to comprehend the nature, range and effectiveness of coercion is that the latter is deemed to be absent.

The mis/non-recognition of unfree labour usually derives from the non-problematization of class, coercion and kinship. The result of not different-iating debt incurred by rich peasants and landless labourers, therefore, is the conflation of productive and non-productive borrowing. Similarly, the under-estimation of the coercive authority vested in kinship/gender ideology (for example, patriarchy) is a failure to recognize the indirect enforcement of bondage, and hence the assumption that debt-servicing labour obligations are unenforceable. Where compulsion has no physical manifestation, therefore, it is assumed either to be ineffective or non-existent. An analogous difficulty arises in the case of physical mobility and the intergenerational inheritance of debt: the presence of the former and the absence of the latter are frequently taken as evidence for relational freedom. Such interpretations, however, not only conflate physical and economic mobility, but also overlook the fact that – even when temporary in duration – unfreedom covers those parts of the agricultural cycle when earning capacity is at its maximum. In such a situation, moreover, freedom is confined to periods when employment is either unavailable or else poorly remunerated.

Another methodological problem concerns supposedly hard data on wage levels and work intensity/duration where no attempt is made to differentiate such categories in terms of free and unfree workers. A consequence of not dis-aggregating wages received by a bonded labourer include a failure on the one hand to register the fact that remuneration generally covers not individuals but kin groups (the per capita wage being as a result much lower), and on the other to identify appropriations effected from such payments by creditor-employers, labour contractors, senior kinsfolk and/or the estate store. Bonded labour also finds it more difficult than its free counterpart to negotiate with employers over working practices, and thus to resist the prolongation of the working day, the intensification of the work rate, or the imposition of additional and/or more onerous tasks.

NOTES

1. For useful general accounts of unfree labour, see Miles [1987] and Cohen [1987]; for a critical evaluation of their arguments, see Brass [1988]. Neither of these texts utilises the same theoretical approach to unfree labour adopted here, nor do they examine its occurrence in the areas covered here. Miles's analysis focuses on unfree labour in the Caribbean and Australia over the seventeenth, eighteenth, and nineteenth centuries, South Africa until the early twentieth century, and post-war Western Europe. On the basis of a dualistic modes of production framework, he concludes that, due to a combination of uneven capitalist expansion and the persistence of peasant smallholding, labour shortages prevented the universal commodification of labour-power and thus the emergence of free wage labour on which the capitalist mode of production depends. By contrast, Cohen examines current forms of unfree labour in the Caribbean, South Africa, and Western Europe. He rejects the dualistic notion of coexistence between an autonomous non-capitalist mode of production and capitalism, in which the former withholds labour-power from the latter and thereby generates the shortages which necessitate the introduction or perpetuation of unfreedom. Unlike Miles, however, Cohen defines unfree labour largely in political terms; it is therefore loosely equated with the absence of rights to citizenship, settlement, and global mobility.

2. The link between unfree labour, starvation and famine has been reported in many different contexts. Thus instances of self-sale during times of famine have been recorded in Russia, Africa and Latin America (Hellie [1982: 329–30], Arnold [1988: 90–91], Langer [1989:151]), while specific historical categories of famine slave – such as *anákála bhritta*, or a person 'maintained in a famine' – exist in the case of India (Banaji [1933: 45–52, 209, 211–2], Chanana [1960: 67], Dingwaney [1985: 284]). Significantly, the incidence of outmigration by Indian indentured labour also rose during the famines or poor harvest years of the late nineteenth century [Tinker 1974: 118–9].

3. This conceptualization of labour as unfree, regardless of whether entry into the relation is voluntary or involuntary, is the subject of debate. According to Rao [1999], for example, unfree agrarian relations are characterized by the involuntary entry of a worker into and his/her retention within an employment relationship. This is different from the definition adopted here, where only an inability to exit from a relationship defines it as unfree.

4. On this, see, *inter alia*, Banaji [1933: 69–73], McBride [1934], Kloosterboer [1960], Thorner [1962: 21–38], Katz [1974], Nagesh [1981], Marla [1981], Ennew [1981], Shankaran [1983], and Patnaik and Dingwaney [1985].

5. A common form of historical and contemporary restructuring is the decentralization of the labour process itself, a transformation which entails the displacement of existing factory production by a smallscale outwork/putting-out system based on unfree sweated labour. In a study of the clothing trade in nineteenth century London, Schmiechen [1984] has argued that the introduction of the sweatshop system was a result of industrial growth rather than stagnation, and suggests that

the switch to production with low-paid workers in unregulated/non-unionized premises during the second half of the century was a direct response by employers to the consolidation in the first half of a well-organized, militant and highly unionized workforce protected by factory legislation. For accounts of a similar restructuring process in the contemporary period, see Levidow [1981], Mattera [1985], and Mitter [1986]. The way in which unfree relations are enforced within these smallscale units is outlined by Hoel [1982].

6. All the problematic definitional issues raised here will be considered in greater detail in the second part of the book.

7. References to its existence in the United States (see Chapter 5), Latin America (see Chapter 6) and India (see Chapters 3 and 7) all confirm that the transfer of a worker's debt – and thus the worker concerned – between creditor-employers is a ubiquitous form of unfreedom.

8. The contention that unfreedom encompasses workers who are not employed on a permanent basis finds much support in the literature on agrarian relations and rural change. Evidence from China during the 1930s [*Tawney* 1938: 71–2], for example, suggests that seasonal workers there were not just at the beck-and-call of creditor-employers but bonded for reasons and in ways that are basically no different from their unfree counterparts in Latin America and India nearly half a century later:

> [In China] rich peasants need a great deal of seasonal labour for planting and harvesting, but are always in fear that they will not be able to secure an adequate number of people. Thus when the poor peasants, many of them tenants, borrow grain from the rich during the spring, the debtor contracts for seasonal labour in payment. The peasant then works in his creditor's field during the busy season, just as an ordinary hired labourer, except that the value of the grain borrowed is deducted from the wage that he is supposed to receive. There is no interest charged on the grain loan, because the value of the grain borrowed is always fixed by the creditor at a supposed maximum market price, in the spring – a price which in fact gives the creditor more than ample interest. The balance between the grain price and the wage must always be made good, either by additional labour or sometimes by extra payment in cash. The contract demands, however, that this sort of seasonal labourer must abandon his own work whenever his creditor is in need of him.

9. For examples of unsuccessful political action carried out by bonded labourers in northern Peru just before the first World War, see Blanchard [1979: 70]; for a similar instance of unsuccessful strike action undertaken by attached labour in Haryana, see Chapter 3.

10. Claims about enforced commercialization are most frequently made with regard to smallholders contracted by agribusiness enterprises to cultivate specific crops for the international market [*Watts*, 1992]; in this framework peasants tend to be depicted as an homogeneous socio-economic category uniformly exploited by capital, rather than having within their ranks some rich peasants who themselves exploit the labour-power of others. Such an approach fails to distinguish between two very different kinds of contracting arrangement. That is, between on the one hand arrangements whereby agro-industrial capital subcontracts production to large capitalist farmers who not only own substantial holdings of fertile, irrigated land, provide their own seed, credit, and technology, but also hire in and supervise agricultural labour. And on the other arrangements whereby agribusiness trans-

national corporations subcontract production to small, so-called 'independent' growers who are no more than workers on land which they may own (or lease from elsewhere). In other words, it is necessary to distinguish what is essentially a production or marketing arrangement between large and small capitalist enterprises from what is a relation of production between capital and labour.

11. The problems arising from a failure to differentiate borrowers in terms of class are examined in more detail in Chapter 6. Here it is sufficient to note that the focus of much development literature is on credit provision to farmers, mainly for the purpose of agricultural production, and not on the effect on the labour market of debt relations as such. This nuanced epistemological distinction is significant, in that credit has a generally positive connotation linked to the process of acquiring and/or setting in motion the means of production, whereas debt conveys an altogether less favourable image linked more usually to a process of separation from the means of production and/or loss of control over the personal commodification of labour-power. Attributing the absence of economic growth to a corresponding lack of agricultural credit, such analyses recommend access to low-/no-interest loans as the best solution to the problem of rural poverty. Unsurprisingly, one effect of such credit provision to farmers is that better-off cultivators then utilize newly acquired funds to bond the labour-power of poor peasants and workers.

12. Hence the problematic claim made by the Bonded Liberation Front (*Bandhua Mukti Morcha*) of India, which defines debt bondage in terms of the low wage recieved by its subject, the inference being that all workers who sell their labour-power at less than the legal minimum wage are thereby characterized as unfree. For this claim, see the *Statement by the Indian Government Observer in the UN Working Group on Slavery and Slave-like Practices*, Geneva, 10 Aug. 1983.

13. As will be argued in the second part of this book, such a view ignores the fact that for Marxists it is precisely because workers engage in active class struggle as free wage labour that employers on farms and/or plantations resort in turn to immobilizing mechanisms/legislation.

14. In many ways still the most interesting and fruitful analysis of the methodological problems associated with the investigation of contemporary forms of unfree labour is that by Shankaran [1983].

15. Various sources from different contexts testify to the methodological difficulties deriving from the illegality of debt bondage relations, and thus obstacles posed by employers of unfree labourers to research aimed at uncovering their existence. For example, Stetson Kennedy, who gathered much information on debt peonage in the turpentine camps of Florida at the beginning of the 1950s, and provided evidence on the subject to the joint United Nations and International Labour Organization Committee on Forced Labour [*UN/ILO*, 1953], comments [1959: 136]: 'Getting into the camps was not easy; it was necessary to tell the bosses that the purpose of the expedition was to record folksongs'. It is perhaps significant that the two most successful investigations of unfree labour in Latin America, by Turner in the tropical sisal and tobacco plantations of Yucatan and Oaxaca in Mexico during 1908, and by Casement in the rubber producing Putumayo area of Peru during 1910, were allowed to proceed because the plantation owners and government officials in both cases were under the impression that the investigators were potential investors with large amounts of capital [*Turner*, 1911: 7; *Singleton-Gates and Girodias*, 1959: 231]. Similar methodological difficulties have been experienced during research conducted in the Indian state of Gujarat by Breman

[1985b], and the political sensitivity on the part of the landlord class concerning the existence of bonded labour in Andhra Pradesh is noted by the Rural Wing of the National Labour Institute [1977: 541–2]. My own research experience in Peru and India (see following chapters) confirms the accuracy of the kinds of difficulties highlighted by these accounts.

16. Estimates for the number of bonded labourers in India during the 1980s vary from the Union government's own figure of 120,000 and the National Sample Survey Organization 1979 figure of 345,000 to the 2.6 million calculated by the National Labour Institute and Gandhi Peace Foundation joint survey carried out in 1978, and the figure of five million mentioned by the Bonded Liberation Front in 1983. The Union government figure is based on information submitted by individual states; for the NSSO figure, see 'States Slow on Identification of Bonded Labour', *Hindustan Times*, 9 Sept. 1983; for the NLI/GPF survey, see Marla [1981: 154]; for the Bonded Liberation Front estimate, see Bandhua Mukti Morcha [1983].

17. For the texts of the relevant international conventions on slavery, forced labour, and servitude, see Sieghart [1983: 235–66].

18. For example, the Bihar and Orissa Kamiauti Agreements Act (1920), the Bombay Moneylenders Act (1946), the Orissa Debt Bondage Abolition Regulation (1948), the Rajasthan Sagri System Abolition Act (1961), the Orissa Dadan Labour (Regulation and Control) Bill (1975), the Uttar Pradesh Landless Agricultural Labourers Debt Relief Act (1975), and the Maharashtra Debt Relief Act (1976). For an account of the legislation on bonded labour in India, see Kulkarni [1982].

19. Variant forms of unfree labour are outlawed in Peru by, *inter alia*, Acts No. 605 and 479 of 6 October 1920 and 2 August 1921 prohibiting unpaid labour, the Peruvian Penal Code of 1924, Article 55 of the 1933 Constitution, and the 1979 Constitution. Replying to allegations made during the early 1950s concerning the existence of unfree labour within its national territory, the Peruvian government claimed that such relationships had successfully been eradicated and therefore no longer existed [*UN/ILO*, 1953: 299]. For a detailed account of Peruvian domestic legislation extant at the end of the 1950s against the employment of unfree labour, see the International Labour Conference [1962: 261] and Núñez del Prado [1973: 155–9].

20. Katz [1974: 13] and Loveman [1979: 485] make this point with regard to the methodological inaccessibility of debt bondage in Latin America. Writing about the continued existence of debt peonage in the American South, Daniel [1972: 191] comments: 'For peonage has been like the dark side of the moon; it existed, but only exceptional circumstances enabled one to see it.'

21. This is a methodological consideration that is rarely given the importance it deserves. The difficulties generated by the partial nature of the historical evidence, and consequently what it is possible or not possible to say about the presence/absence of debt bondage at a particular historical conjuncture, can be illustrated with reference to claims regarding the free/unfree character of the coffee workforce in late nineteenth century Puerto Rico. In a number of texts published during the 1980s, Bergad [1983a; 1983b; 1984] insisted that the coffee boom years of 1885–97 coincided with a transformation in rural Puerto Rico from unfree to free production relations. As Bergad makes clear, however, his analysis is dependent on and structured by the limited and uneven nature of the documentary sources: only those debts entered in notarial records are revealed by his kind of archival research. Not only was Bergad unable to examine the account

books for any nineteenth century coffee farm, therefore, but after the abundant material generated by the 1849 *jornalero* law he [1983b: 121] accepts that 'documentation on the rural labor force declines in quantity and quality'. Perhaps the most significant admission made by him [1983b: 193, note 109] in this connection is that:

> documentation on the labor force for this period [1883–97] is weak. The Lares municipal archive contains very little material on labor systems since there were no governmental dispositions regulating labor, as had been the case in the 1850s on the *jornaleros*, or in the 1870s after emancipation. The Yauco municipal archives contain practically nothing on labor for this period.

Given these lacunae, Bergad's [1984: 155] confident assertion that 'the rural working class [experienced a change] from conditions of "unfree labour" to the mobility and availability of labour so characteristic of the coffee boom years of 1885–97' is misplaced, particularly since much of the non-archival data and evidence suggest otherwise (see Brass [1984; 1986c]).

22. Although Brading [1978: 36] and Bauer [1979a: 44] both deny the existence in Latin America of debt bondage on the basis that the relevant estate records for the historical period contain no reference to the presence of this relation, neither indicate precisely what sort of archival or written evidence they would expect to find that would for them confirm its existence.

23. Hence the view of one neoclassical economic historian [*Shlomowitz* 1991b: 222] that 'reverse bondage' could not be unfree 'because workers who owed money ... were not legally compelled to return to [their] employer'. In a similar vein, elsewhere [*Shlomowitz*, 1986: 108] it is noted that '[t]he starting point for an analysis of the labour trade in the Western Pacific is the recognition that the structure of this trade was defined by a legislative framework [structured by] the notion of the sanctity of legal contracts voluntarily entered into by both parties, who were then obliged to faithfully fulfil the terms of these contracts'. Another text on unfree labour informed by the same theoretical framework is that by Steinfeld and Engerman [1997], which, because it operates with an analogous concept of a socio-economically disembodied law, also tends to fetishize legality.

24. Writing from a neoclassical economic view, Shlomowitz [1991a; 1991b; 1997] incorrectly interprets what he takes to be a lack of evidence about employer collusion as being synonymous with the absence of collusion itself. There is, however, plenty of evidence to the contrary: not merely of collusion between employers of bonded labour, both to prevent competition between them for such workers and to keep wages low, but also of its effectiveness. Hence full-time servants in 1930s rural South Africa [*Lacey*, 1981:163] who were unfree 'had limited options even within their own districts. Not only would a farmer be reluctant to poach his neighbour's servants, but the farmers together tacitly agreed about keeping wages down at the same low level.' Instances of employer collusion in India extend from Bihar [*Das*, 1979: 22], where a 'manager of a local quarry had been persuaded to deny employment to the freed bonded labourers who went to him when they got no work in the fields', to Maharashtra [*Deshpande*, 1982: 109], where unfreedom 'is recognized and enforced by the sanction of society, but not by ... law ... [a] bonded labourer is thus not given any work by others in the surrounding area'.

25. Even where institutions such as co-operatives are introduced with the object of undermining/circumventing the moneylending capacity of landlords and/or rich peasants, as long as the class power of the latter remains intact so does their

ability to subvert or take over the institution concerned. This happened not only in eastern Peru during the mid-1970s (see Chapter 2) but also in the Indian state of Bihar [*Roth*, 1983: 26, 29], where:

> The fact that a small landowning rural upper class controls the key positions of village administration, money market and village co-operatives quickly leads to the inference that a personal union exists between the officeholders in the village cooperative and the moneylenders. Thus, the grotesque situation arises that one and the same group of people guard over interests which pursue opposite objectives, since the co-operatives were primarily organized in order to curb the power of the moneylender. It is a paradoxical situation in which those people administer the institution which was created to eliminate them.

26. See, for example, Bauer [1979a: 36]. An exception to this criticism is the All-India Rural Credit Survey [*Reserve Bank of India*, 1954: 172], which observes that:

> Usually, the compulsion which [the moneylender] depends upon is one which he has reason to hope will operate more or less automatically. If need be, of course, he is prepared to exert himself and set in motion the forces of compulsion. Those forces are social or economic or both. They are different for different debtors, but are in each case related to how the debtor is circumstanced in the village. The social compulsion is connected with considerations such as loss of "face" or local prestige, caste disapproval, possible pressure through the caste panchayat, and a variety of other social sanctions which, because they happen to be intangible, are not on that account any the less powerful.

There are also paradoxical instances of texts that make extensive reference to both the presence and the operation of socio-economic networks coercing and imposing sanctions on defaulting debtors, yet which then go on to deny the existence of bonded labour relations. Thus, having indicated that 'a larger social group [within the community] may enter the picture by standing as a guarantor ... [and] will exercise pressure on debtors to give back the money owed to an embarrassed creditor. The pressure is likely to be effective. Social compulsion can be readily used in such circumstances: considerations such as "loss of face" in the eyes of the entire community, social marginalization ... and physical harassment are strong weapons which individuals cannot easily counter', that 'debtors cannot easily run away from the village community ... with the result that any default or violation of the implicit social code entails heavy social and economic costs', and that 'social sanction [against debt defaulters] can be very effective ... the community performs an important function of social control ... through a built in mechanism of social ostracization', Platteau and Abraham [1987: 468–9, 474–5, 478] nevertheless conclude: 'So long as "bondage" is taken to imply a recourse to extra-economic coercion to force the labourer into a relationship with a given "patron" ... we have not met any convincing evidence that this phenomenon [exists in the fishing villages of south Kerala].'

27. On this point, see Sutch [1975: 342], who notes: 'The frequency with which a punishment is administered is a poor measure of its effectiveness ... it is the *fear* of eventual punishment which motivates behaviour ... A slave need never have felt the lash to know the consequences of disobedience' (original emphasis). An analogous sentiment was expressed by Kofi Annan, the UN Secretary General, when in 1998 he observed in connection with the possibility of military action against Iraq that 'the best way to use force is to show it in order not to have to use it'.

28. The important policing role of actual and fictive kinship in the reproduction of

contemporary bonded labour relations in India and Peru is examined in Chapters 2, 3 and 4. Both the affective and coercive aspects of actual/fictive kinship were crucial regulatory mechanisms in the case of the unfree workforce employed on the plantations in the antebellum southern states of the USA, where 'family ties prevented slaves from running away or kept them close to home when they did run ... few slaves would leave permanently if they had to leave their mothers behind to face the master's wrath' [*Genovese*, 1975: 650; see also *Gutman*, 1976: 201–29, 324–5]. The unfreedom of black farm labour in South Africa during the 1940s was similarly enforced by the threat of sanctions applied to kinsfolk: thus, under the 1932 Native Service Contract Act, 'the whole family is liable to eviction if one member fails to render the [labour] service required ... if a young son who is liable to work on a farm goes off to work elsewhere, the livelihood of the whole family is jeopardized' [*van de Horst*, 1942: 285]. The historical importance of caste and kinship networks as methods of enforcing social compliance – of which debt is one element – has been noted by many commentators on rural India (see, for example, Risley [1908: 275], Beidelman [1959], and Mayer [1960: 251ff.]). As will be seen in Chapters 3 and 4, two indirect forms of coercion were particularly crucial in the villages of Haryana and Bihar where fieldwork took place in 1985 and 1987. This involved, firstly, the denial by landholders of access to fodder resources needed by livestock-owning agricultural labourers; the latter subjects in turn exercised pressure on workers from the same caste who did not own livestock to comply with debt-servicing labour obligations. And secondly, the invocation of authority for the same ends by *panchayat* members who belonged to the same caste as bonded labourers.

29. Examples abound illustrating the extent to which bonded labour in Asia, Latin America and Africa is not only enforced but also initiated from within the sphere of kinship. Nevinson [1906: 51,100–101] records that in Angola at the beginning of the twentieth century children were sold into slavery by their mother's brother; the latter had rights of possession over nephews, who could be pawned to cancel debts. For a more recent case of a similar intra-kin group relationship in Northern Ghana, see Goody [1959: 78–80]. Gough [1981: Chs. 16 and 17] indicates the way in which village level sanctions (including debt enforcement) were operationalised in South India during the early 1950s. Debt-enforcing coercion aimed at the kinsfolk of a debtor have also been recorded in the Jharia coalfields of Bihar during the early 1960s [*Srivastava*, 1970: 400]. Marla [1977: 424–7] reports a case in Medak district of Andhra Pradesh where the younger of two siblings worked as a bonded labourer in order to meet debts incurred by the elder sibling, and Kamble [1982: 81] of how in Karnataka children entered bondage as a consequence of debts incurred by parents. In Northern Peru, and also in the Thana and Nasik districts of Maharashtra when he cannot pay brideprice, the bridegroom works for his father-in-law as a bonded labourer [*Miller*, 1967; *Kulkarni*, 1979: 563]. Writing about the Philippines during the 1920s, Sturtevant [1976: 68] notes:

> If debt bondage had been terminated by death, eventual escape might seem feasible. Indebtedness, however, was normally transferred to the decesed debtor's children. Wayward youths who attempted to repudiate parental obligations felt the ire of entire villages and often experienced ostracism from friends and neighbours.

30. Claims to the contrary [e.g., *Kapadia*, 1995b; *Olsen*, 1997] notwithstanding, a large and longstanding literature on the gender-specific elements of unfreedom

already exists. Among the texts published in the earlier part of the twentieth century which have attempted to address the question of a link between unfreedom on the one hand and gender and/or kinship/family relations on the other are those by Nieboer [1910: 9–25], Tawney [1938: 82–5], Lasker [1950: 16, 22, 43, 66, 90, 92, 132 247, 292ff.], and Douglas [1964], as well as the Report of the Royal Commission on Labour in India [1931]. More recent examples of analyses which attempt to problematize gender and patriarchy in relation to unfree labour in the Americas, Africa, Asia and Europe include the Indian School of Social Sciences [1976: 12–13, 85ff.], Guy [1981], Phongpaichit [1982], Robertson and Klein [1983], Rubbo and Taussig [1983], Gupta [1985], Stoler [1985], Honig [1986], Griffiths [1987], Jaschok [1988], Beall [1990], Zegeye and Ishemo [1989], Beckles [1989], Tsurumi [1984; 1990], and Anderson [1993]. The texts by Kapadia [1995a] and da Corta and Venkateshwarlu [1999] are the latest contributions to this literature.

31. The payment of wages earned by unfree migrant women not to them directly but rather indirectly to their kinsfolk is reported for Meiji Japan [*Tsurumi*, 1990: 60–61] and 1970s Thailand [*Phongpaichit*, 1982], where remuneration took the form of a cash advance made by a labour contractor to the family of a female worker recruited from a rural area.

32. Transactions which mimic that of 'changing masters', the transfer of women to repay male debts, are reported for 1930s China and 1970s India and Peru. In the case of China [*Tawney*, 1938: 84], therefore,

> Among poorer families ... the young daughter-in-law once she has stepped into her husband's home has sealed her fate. By custom she has to obey her parents-in-law and her husband who have the right to command her labour and even to sell her should they deem it necessary. It is a fact that many a daughter-in-law has thus changed her husband and home against her own desire. There are many peasant women ... who have been sold and re-sold as many as four times ... Another form of acquiring labour power in the peasant family is through concubinage. Instead of hiring wage earning agricultural labourers by the year, many rich peasant families take in concubines who are considered from the point of view of field work to be much less expensive.

Women in polynyandrous households in sub-Himalayan Uttar Pradesh were the object of a similar kind of transaction [*Saksena*, 1962; *Indian School of Social Science*, 1976; *Hasnain*, 1982; *Gupta*, 1985]. For a married woman the only alternative to remaining within an oppressive household is divorce (*choot*); the latter, however, is conditional on the reimbursement of the original brideprice. In order to obtain this sum, a woman is either sold to another husband willing to make this payment, or else borrows from a moneylender. Cancellation of the loan requires her becoming and remaining a prostitute in Delhi until the debt is cleared. This practice of indebted males sending female relatives into prostitution in order to pay off debts dates from 1915, but became widespread after 1940 when 'the object was to earn freedom for the men of the family from the local moneylender ... men got into debt while buying their wives, and later these very brides were sent into prostitution to earn their husbands' release' [*Indian School of Social Science*, 1976: 62–3]. A similar arrangement involving the intra-kin group deployment/ control of peasant women workers is also encountered in Peru during the early 1970s. In this particular case, a member of the rural bourgeoisie in the province of Canas, the department of Cuzco, provided his urban counterpart – who was his kinsman, and from whom he wanted a favour – with a 'gift': the labour-power of a female from a peasant household in his area to work in his town house as an unpaid domestic servant [*Orlove*, 1980: 124].

33. In his analysis of bonded labour, Rao [1999] characterizes unfreedom in terms of the heritability of debt.

34. The sole exception in the case of Peru is Blanchard [1979: 73], who reports that in the northern Peruvian sierra at the beginning of the twentieth century, 'unredeemed debts were being passed on to the widows and children of dead *enganchados*'.

35. For the NLI/GPF survey findings concerning the incidence of intergenerational bondage, see Marla [1981: 24].

36. The views of Bhattacharya and Bhalla are considered in more detail in Chapter 3.

37. See Marla [1981: 55]. It should be noted, however, that this figure may constitute an underestimation, since only those cases where a preceding kinsman had actually taken the loan (and then passed on the unpaid debt) are considered as evidence of intergenerational bondage, whereas the much higher number of persons who had themselves taken a loan is excluded from the category, notwithstanding that even these debts may also be inherited by their families and/or kinsfolk at some future date. Tiwary [1985: 203] gives a much higher figure for Santal Parganas, where intergenerational debt inheritance occurs in over eighty per cent of all bonded labour relationships in this socio-economically backward district of Bihar. By contrast, 85 per cent of indebted attached labourers interviewed in a survey of Begusari District reported that their fathers had not worked for the same master [*R.A.P.Singh* 1985: 81], which suggests extensive regional variation as regards intergenerational bondage in Bihar.

38. This growing cost-consciousness on the part of creditor-employers is further attested by the fact that attitudes toward the issue of bonded labour emancipation vary according to the age – and hence the utility – of the worker concerned.

39. Because he regards actual/fictive kinship relations between labour contractors and agricultural workers in the Peruvian Andes in an unproblematically positive light, Cotlear [1979: 34, 48, 51] dismisses the possibility that such intermediaries were able to exercise an effective extra-economic control over labourers recruited by means of the *enganche* system. Rather than as an enforcer of debt obligations owed by peasants to landlords, therefore, the contractor is depicted as a trusted guarantor against maltreatment, under- or non-payment, a benign protector of migrants who was – and is – able to 'coax' them onto the free labour market through the offer of cash advances (for an analogous theorization, see Figueroa [1984: 56, 72]).

40. In the case of India, Cholia [1941: 59, 67, 70–71] outlines how in the 1930s Bombay region labour contractors recruited/controlled gangs of unfree migrants from their own villages on the basis of caste/kinship, while Breman [1985a: 249–50] cites the case of a labour contractor operating in the state of Gujarat who in his own village 'had a permanent stock of labourers who were bound to him by advance loans, and although he did not require all of them each time [his work gang migrated], they could not easily refuse if he called upon them'. The same is true for Peru. For a similar account of how kinship and village networks in the Yanamarca valley were used at the beginning of this century by local merchants and wealthy peasant sub-contractors (*sub-enganchadores*) to enforce labour-service obligations owed by indebted migrants to mining companies in the central highlands, see Mallon [1983a; 1983b: 188–9, 203]. The function of kinship networks in inaugurating and enforcing long-distance migration in other contexts is

well documented. For its role in the recruitment of both Melanesian labour for the Queensland sugar industry in Australia and Indian *kangani* labour for the Ceylon coffee and tea plantations towards the end of the nineteenth century, see Graves [1984: 117, 129ff.] and Sandhu [1969: 90–91].

41. Significantly, one consequence of this positive theorization of kinship is ultimately the redefinition of chattel slavery itself as a form of kinship [*Miers and Kopytoff*, 1977], a process which entails purging the slave relation of its coercive and unfree content in order to present it as a variant or extension of the kin relation. To some degree this position is prefigured in the work of Leach [1967: 13, 23–4], where the same criterion (unfreedom/coercion ≠ kinship) is applied to the debt bondage relation:

> At the opposite extreme [to chattel slavery] we meet with various institutions which are sometimes labelled debt-slavery or bond-slavery. In this system an individual mortgages his person as guarantee for a debt. The bond-slave remains a human being in the fullest sense and it is by no means clear to me why institutions of this kind should be considered objectionable; indeed they only become objectionable when Europeans for reasons of their own label them as 'slavery'. It is very significant that ... the status of the 'bond-slave' in respect of his master is very close indeed to that of a 'son-in-law' ... there is a very radical difference between the status of the chattel slave as he appeared in Greece and Rome and the latter-day Americas, and such categories as ... bond-slave which were found ... everywhere in modern Asia. The chattel slave had no kin and was not really fully a human being; the bond-slave was a person with kin and in an entirely different economic relationship with his master.

This is the mirror image of the position adopted here, that in specific conditions kinship incorporates the characteristics of slavery and bonded labour.

42. Examples from Africa and Asia underline the dangers inherent in failing to disaggregate contractually-stipulated wages. Thus one text [North-Coombes 1990: 73] on the South African sugar industry notes that:

> A report of the Native Economic Commission of 1930–32 drew attention to the practice of securing the services of migrant workers through the payment of cash advances. By this method employers were able to effectively dispense with any wage payments to the migrant workers during the duration of the contract, as they were entitled to recover the loans and transport costs from the labourers' wages. The report estimated that a [a migrant working] on an eight month contract would need to hand over 38 per cent of his potential earnings from task work to repay his rail fares and 42 per cent to redeem the usual £5 cash advance. Out of a potential maximum wage of £12 for the entire period of his contract ... he would effectively receive at best £2.10 at the end of his term of service. However, there was no guarantee that such a cash wage would in fact be paid ... Thus wages in the sugar industry until the eve of World War II bore little relation to actual earnings.

More generally, Tinker [1974: 184ff.] has warned against accepting at face value 'official' wage levels paid on Asian plantations, since these were usually peak and not average rates.

43. That labour contractors not only withhold wages but do not pass on the full payment made by employers for labour-power hired in this manner is clear from the case of China [*Honig*, 1986: 117], where a contractor supplying unfree labour to the employers in the Shanghai docks paid his workers only 20–40 per cent of the

wage rate he himself received from the company for their labour-power. Information on wage levels says nothing about the frequency of actual payment, and thus whether or not wages remain unpaid, for how long, and with what effect. In the case of unfree migrant labour employed on sugar plantations in nineteenth century Queensland [*Parnaby*, 1964: 141], for example, 'the 1868 act provided for payment at the rate of £6 per annum in coin of the realm, but the act contained nothing about when wages should be paid. Consequently, the employers did not pay [Pacific island workers] until the end of the [contract] ... [w]hile there was no provision for ... regular payment, the labourer had little security for his wages'. The connection between the withholding of payment and economic unfreedom in the same context is also noted by Graves [1983: 114], who observes:

> Though in theory workers were able to draw upon their bank accounts at will, it was extremely difficult for them to do so ... But whatever form of their account, workers were permitted [by employers] to withdraw their savings only at the termination of their contracts. The wages of most workers were thus locked up for the entire period of their contract ... .

44. For details about Haryana, see Chapter 3. In the case of coffee-producing estates in nineteenth century Puerto Rico, indebted labour employed in harvesting not only worked from sun-up to sun-down but also a night-shift tending machinery used for drying coffee beans [*Díaz Hernández* 1981: 51–53, 86]. For a working day of similar duration in the case of workers employed on sugar plantations, see Ramos Mattei [1985: 171].

45. Thus a lack of information in a text by Shlomowitz [1981: 86, 89–90, 91] regarding the length of the working day and the intensity of labour by unfree Melanesian workers employed in the Queensland sugar industry over the latter half of the nineteenth century does not prevent him from asserting that no exploitation took place in this context. For a very different view regarding the long hours and arduous working conditions experienced by unfree Melanesian labour employed in the Queensland sugar industry, see Saunders [1982: 73–4].

46. For the reference to wage determination by 'market forces' in the Dagua region of Colombia, see Shlomowitz [1991a: 218]. For the control of peasant family labour-power in the same national context, see Brass [1990a]. For the repayment with the labour-power of children of debts owed by parents in a coffee-growing area of Puerto Rico during the mid-nineteenth century, see Picó [1979: 66]. That labour recruitment for the Queensland sugar plantations involved intra-kin appropriation/coercion is clear from the work of Graves [1984: 117, 129–31], who shows how village headmen in Melanesia received trade goods from contractors (or 'passage masters') in exchange for providing them with the labour-power of junior kin, and also how this enabled senior kin to accumulate/consolidate political and economic power within the clan hierarchy.

47. In the case of the plantation system in Queensland, it is clear that employers who sold subsistence items to their Pacific island workers occasionally 'gave [the latter] no choice except to buy at exorbitant prices or not at all' [*Parnaby* 1964: 141]. A similar point is made by Graves [1983: 114–16].

48. The way in which debts incurred at the company store were used as a form of control in Canadian mining enterprises at the beginning of the twentieth century is outlined by Mellor [1983: 13–15]. Companies in Nova Scotia operated a policy of charging indebted workers much higher prices for subsistence goods, thereby intensifying the element of dependence; miners were unable to change jobs so long

as money was owed to the company store. That an important role of the company/
plantation store was to claw back any wage increases secured by the workforce is
also clear from the following example from the United States [*Corbin*, 1981: 32,
185]:

> The greatest drain on the miner's wages was the company store. Coercion, the
> scrip system, and physical distance combined to force the miners to deal at the
> company store, and through the monopolistic control of food and clothing and
> tools and powder, the coal companies were able to render wage rates and wage
> increases meaningless to the miners ... Wage advances were always absorbed,
> 'in whole or in part,' by price increases at the company store. This was a
> common complaint among the southern West Virginia miners – wage increases
> were valueless as long as the company store existed ... .a miner complained to
> a US Senate investigating committee: 'When a wage increase is given the
> miners, the store management increases prices to offset it.' He explained that
> the miners in his mine 'won a wage increase at one o'clock, Sunday morning.
> By Tuesday morning, prices were advanced exactly enough to absorb the wage
> increases.' [...] The miners at Sharon, Cabin Creek, wrote to the governor that
> 'the prices in their company stores have advanced so much since that [wage]
> agreement was made that we as the laborers of said place ... have resolved that
> instead of receiving an advance in wages, we deem it under the prices now in
> the company store of said place, a reduction'.

Unsurprisingly, workers in West Virginia attacked and burned the company/plan-
tation store during strike action and demanded its abolition [*Corbin*, 1981: 33, 203,
222].

49. The mistake in assuming a correspondence between wages paid to contractors and
those ultimately received by migrants is pointed out in a study of the way in which
workers were recruited by contractors for the cotton mills in Bombay during the
first decades of this century. It notes [*Newman*, 1979: 281–2]:

> Most studies of recruitment ... have emphasized the connection between labour
> supply and the level of wages, but this connection may need to be modified to
> take account of the jobber's powers ... One of the most serious difficulties in
> relating wages to labour is the unreliability of the data. The shortcomings of the
> available statistics have been freely admitted by previous writers but it is per-
> haps worth asking whether any statistical series based on wage books of the
> companies could reflect the involvement of the jobber in the cash relationship
> between employer and worker. The monthly wage was subject to fines and
> *dasturi* and possibly to other deductions connected with the jobber's services
> outside the mill. The wages which the millhands carried out of the compound
> were not necessarily the wages which the pay clerks had handed over the
> counter.

The same is true of textile mills in China during the early 1930s, where some 60
per cent of earnings by female workers recruited from rural areas by labour contractors was retained by the latter [*Chuan-Hua*, 1934: 20].

50. Generally speaking, the origins, role and profitability of labour contracting remain
an under-researched aspect of the literature about unfree labour. A recent and interesting exception is the monograph by Tadman [1989: 204ff.] on the chattel slave
trade within the American south during the first half of the nineteenth century,
which suggests that the business of labour contracting yielded a high annual rate
of profit (ranging from 60–80 per cent in 1817–19 to 15–30 per cent in the

1840s/1850s) and generated substantial wealth for individual traders. Of equal interest are the findings that store owners in Queensland and Sumatra during the late nineteenth century not only became wealthy labour contractors but this process was linked to worker indebtedness [*Graves*, 1993; *Breman*, 1989b: 110]. For the background, role, and power of labour contractors in Colonial Asia, and the profitability of labour contracting in the case of mining and the textile mills in China during the early twentieth century, see Chuan-Hua [1934: 20–22], Honig [1986: 111–12] and Breman [1990: 20ff.].

51. That wage maximization is not of itself incompatible with appropriation is made clear by Newman [1979: 293], who notes that although labour contractors in Bombay did indeed go from mill to mill in search of higher wages for their workers, the resulting increases went not to the latter but the former. As instances from Fiji and the United States confirm [*Gillion*, 1962: 48–9; *Daniel*, 1981: 178], workers in general and the labour movement in particular have expressed an unambiguous view about such practices, not least by their demand for the abolition of contracting and in the form of physical attacks on recruiters.

52. That the purpose of 'withholding wages' on the part of an employer has been and is to immobilize the worker, in order to prevent him or her from personally commodifying their own labour-power, is evident from, for example, its object in the case of female workers employed in Japanese textile mills during the Meiji period (1868–1912). In the latter context, therefore, 'amounts from an individuals' pay were regularly held back to be confiscated in case she ran away before her term of employment was complete ... ' [*Tsurumi*, 1984: 6]. Much the same point is made by Breen [1983: 92] with regard to the immobilization of farm servants in Ireland during the twentieth century: 'Servants might be paid monthly, or receive a monthly allowance and a lump sum at the end of their term. Should they leave prematurely, they forfeited this money.' Its pervasive occurrence at different historical conjunctures not only in the United States (see Chapter 5) but also in Latin America (see Chapters 2 and 6) and India (see Chapters 3, 4 and 7) suggests that 'withholding wages' is a near universal form of unfreedom.

53. One consequence is that the actual income of unfree labour is not just low but also delayed/deferred/denied, a situation which in turn necessitates further borrowing and thus reproduces/reinforces bondage. Instances of employers demanding repayment of a portion of wages received by their workers include not only late nineteenth century Queensland and late twentieth century Mexico [*Graves*, 1983: 114; *Baird and McCaughan*, 1979: 160] but also Punjab during the early 1980s, where bonded labourers were compelled to repay the difference between the legal minimum wage and the (lower) pay rate fixed by the landholder to whom they owed debts and for whom they worked (see Chapter 3).

54. See Cholia [1941: 59] for an example of the capacity of labour contractors to fix the wages of their workers.

55. Thus one observer [*Olmsted*, 1953: 90] noted of the slave states in the American South during the 1850s that: 'It is even said – and, as I have shown, it is practically true, at least wherever slavery has not in great measure withdrawn from the field – that white labour cannot live in competition with slave labour. In other words, the holder of slave labour controls the local market for labour.' Employers in many different historical contexts themselves place an emphasis on lowering wage costs as the reason for using unfree labour. In the case of Peru, for example, north coast sugar planters defended the need for a cheap workforce composed of *enganchados*

during the 1880s and 1890s because of the damage to sugar producing estates wrought by the invading Chilean forces during the War of the Pacific (1879–83) combined with the simultaneous decline in world sugar prices [*Blanchard*, 1979: 68–69]. Much the same kind of defence was made in 1901 by Guatemalan coffee planters [*Cambranes*, 1985: 325–6].

PART I
Case Studies

2

Bonded Labour in Eastern Peru

This chapter examines the contribution of unfree labour to capitalist re-structuring in the agrarian sector of eastern lowland Peru, a process whereby bonded labour replaces free wage labour. Debt bondage is analysed in relation to class struggle in a labour scarce context, the province of La Convención, specifically with regard to its utilization by capitalist producers to lower the cost and simultaneously maintain control over both the migrant and local components of their workforce.[1] The economic and extra-economic modes of compulsion required to enforce labour-service obligations incurred as a result of indebtedness are also considered, in particular the role of actual/fictive kinship. Since this kind of agrestic servitude involves the attachment through debt of workers not so much to land but to an individual employer, contemporary bonded labour is theorized as a modern form of unfreedom that is compatible with capitalist production.

The first section examines the way in which the debt bondage relation structured labour-rent paid by tenants to landlords in La Convención during the pre-reform era. The second outlines the post-reform role of actual/fictive kinship in the reproduction and enforcement of unfree labour, with reference to local and migrant workers employed by capitalist peasants in the province. The final section considers the part played by unfree labour in the process of agrarian restructuring which occurred during the post-reform period, when better-off peasants replacing migrants with local workers deployed the unfree labour-power of the latter in three distinct contexts: on their own small-holdings, in exchanges with other peasant proprietors, and on the agrarian cooperative.

I

Forming the northernmost and largest province in the Department of Cusco, La Convención is situated on the semi-tropical eastern slope of the Peruvian Andes, and constitutes an ideal location for the cultivation of cash-crops such as sugar, cocoa, coca and coffee. Although its inaccessible geographical location prevented extensive colonization and settlement of this frontier region until the early twentieth century, the area has since the mid-sixteenth century formed part of the rural estate (or *hacienda*) system imposed at the Spanish Conquest. From its inception, latifundist agricultural production in this area of Peru has been based not just on various forms of unfree labour but also a migrant workforce drawn from the Andean highlands. Over the seventeenth and eighteenth centuries, therefore, bonded labour was employed on the highly commercialized sugar estates in La Convención; these were owned and operated by the Jesuits, specifically with purpose of manufacturing cane alcohol (*aguardiente*) for local consumption.[2] By the mid-nineteenth century migrants from the highlands were already coming on a seasonal or permanent basis to work on estates producing cash-crops in La Convención and elsewhere in the eastern lowlands.[3]

During the early part of the twentieth century, owners of these *latifundia* leased uncultivated plots (on the non-demesne sector of the estate) to peasant migrants from the southern highlands, who thereby became tenants (*arrendires*) contributing a contractually stipulated number of days labourservice on the landlord enterprise (or demesne sector of the estate) as rental. Labour service contributions by tenants in La Convención took a number of different forms.[4] Of these the most important was *condición*, which consisted of the requirement on the part of a tenant to provide the landlord with a given number of working days per month, varying between 10 and 25 days according to the size and fertility of the holding and the duration of the lease.

Also important was *palla*, or the obligation on the part of a tenant to provide the landlord with 10–15 days of labour four times annually, in order to gather the coca harvest, this work being undertaken by the female kin of the tenant. *Maquipura* was the requirement to supply between two and six working days per year for sowing the landlord's crops. *Wata-faena* encompassed the annual work necessary for clearing irrigation canals and repairing roads on the estate, and *pongueaje* or *semanero* consisted of domestic service undertaken by female kin of the tenant either in the estate house itself or in the town house of the landlord. Although aditional forms of labour-rent existed, the most common and most onerous were *condición, palla* and *pongueaje/ semanero*.

2.1 Debt Bondage in Pre-Reform La Convención

In La Convención, as elsewhere in rural Peru, labour rent has long been regarded as a form of agrestic servitude, an unfree relation by means of which landlords extracted surplus labour from tenants. Since debt and coercion were also part of this relation, labour rent has for many commentators been indistinguishable from debt bondage (*enganche*), which has been and remains an unfree relation that involves cancelling debts with compulsory labour service.[5]

Many historically and contextually specific accounts suggest that the *enganche* involved not only involuntary recruitment but also bad working and living conditions, non-compliance with minimum wage legislation, absence of welfare benefits and physical violence, all of which were common features of the relation.

Although data concerning the historically-specific operational modalities of the debt bondage system in La Convención during this century are patchy, the information that does exist on the *enganche* system prior to the 1960s (mostly in the form of brief references by early travellers to the region) stress three important features: its connection with labour shortages, its coercive inception, and the role of the state in the reproduction of such relations. In all the texts which refer to its presence, the *enganche* is linked to the scarcity of labour in this tropical eastern lowland region.[6] Thus Kaerger, who was instructed by the German Emperor William II to investigate potential investment opportunities in Peru (and thus to identify any obstacles to the development of commercial agricultural production) reports that in 1899 the main economic problem faced by landlords in La Convención was a shortage of labour.[7] Most of the large landowners in the valley employed labour contractors (*enganchadores*) who obtained workers on their behalf from villages and peasant communities in the Andean highlands.[8]

Since peasants from the highland regions were unwilling to work in the eastern lowlands, Kaerger noted, landlords in the latter context adopted one of three methods to obtain labour: recruitment by means of the *enganche* system, thereby compelling highland peasants who owed money advanced by labour contractors to work off these debts on lowland estates; subletting to highland peasants smallholdings on the lowland estates themselves; or the purchase of another estate in the highlands, the tenants of which were then required to pay labour rent with work on lowland estates already belonging to the new owner.[9] A variant of this last method was for landlords who were faced with a seasonally-specific labour shortage either to lease in tenants from another estate in the Andean highlands or to purchase the debts (and thereby acquire the labour-power) of workers who owed money to another landlord.[10]

The coercive way in the *enganche* system operated at this period is illustrated by the manner in which the Yale Peruvian Expedition forcibly recruited porters from among peasants with the assistance of local officials in the Vilcabamba area of La Convención during 1911.[11] Labourers obtained by such means received the cash equivalent of three to four days wages for arduous work that lasted considerably longer than four days.[12] Even in the late 1950s local officials in the highlands were still involved in organizing and enforcing the *enganche* system in order to provide lowland estates with labour-power: one anthropologist carrying out fieldwork in the Pisaq area himself attempted to 'break the chain of authority from prefect to governor' whereby the latter recruited workers for the lowland estate owned by the former.[13]

Describing the *enganche* in La Convención during the early 1940s, Cuadros claimed that it possessed both beneficial and negative effects.[14] In his view the positive aspect consisted of the accompanying economic and ideological change; casting off indigenous woven fabrics for more modern factory products, an illiterate and economically backward Indian peasant from the Peruvian highlands was transformed thereby into to a forward-looking embourgeoisified and Spanish-speaking tenant, now able to read, write and undertake commercial transactions. Apart from its period-specific racist overtones, Cuadros misplaces the element of causality: any economic improvement wrought in such instances was determined not so much by the relation governing the process of migration structured by the *enganche* as by the access to land in La Convención that resulted.

Of greater interest are the negative aspects of the *enganche* relation which Cuadros highlights. These include aspects such as deception practiced by the labour contractor regarding the benefits to be enjoyed, and the consequent situation whereby a tenant ended up by working hard in an inhospitable climate for a low wage that was insufficient even to cover his minimum subsistence requirements. Unable as a result to repay the full amount of the original cash advance, the tenant had to borrow more money and was compelled thereby to work for the landlord on an indefinite basis. Given the interconnection in La Convención between labour shortages, the *enganche* system and the resulting centrality to the landlord/tenant relation of labour rent, changes in the amount of latter that occurred after 1940s led to increasingly acute class struggle, the outcome of which was the elimination of the landlord class and the abolition of labour-rent.

2.2 Debt Bondage, Labour Rent and Class Struggle

Before the 1940s labour-rent payments by tenants to landlords were low. Following the rise during the next two decades in the global demand for primary commodities grown in the province, however, landlords increased the amount of labour-rent payable by tenants. The latter in turn recruited one or more sub-tenants (*allegados*), to whom they leased a portion of the holding, and who henceforth discharged the labour-service contributions owed by the tenant to the landlord. Significantly, the Spanish word for 'sub-tenant' – *allegado* – also means kinsman, and in La Convención sub-tenants were frequently related to tenants by blood, by marriage, or by ties of fictive kinship (see below). In such circumstances, actual/fictive kinship within and beyond a given peasant household also corresponded to production relations determining issues such as surplus appropriation and the division of labour, and thus constituted evidence for the presence in the pre-reform era of distinct class positions transecting what otherwise appeared to be homogeneous smallholding units. The existence of class relations within the peasant household gave rise in turn to class conflict involving landlord, tenant, sub-tenant and landless labourer, albeit projected by means of a discourse about actual/fictive kinship. [15]

With the rise in coffee prices, a small but economically powerful stratum of rich peasants began to accumulate capital by growing this cash crop for the export market.[16] Tenant obligations to the landlord now became an economic obstacle to further accumulation, as a decline in the real level of the remuneration paid by the landlord to substitute workers fulfilling labour-service requirements coincided with a rise in the amount of labour-rent per leased hectare.[17] Accordingly, these capitalist tenants increasingly came into conflict with the landlord class in the province over the control of labour-power and means of production on the estate system. The result was that during the period 1958–62 La Convención became the site of one of the most important peasant movements in Latin America. In a period during which the price of coffee (the main tenant crop) was high, and faced with increased levels of labour-rent together with the threat of eviction from land on which to cultivate this commodity in the event of an inability to meet these rental demands, rich peasants in La Convención who were estate tenants joined the most radical political group, the Trotskyist FIR (Revolutionary Left Front) led by Hugo Blanco.[18] It was these same rich peasants who, as tenants, spearheaded the anti-landlord mobilization.

The resulting peasant movement not only advocated the expropriation of landlord class and the redistribution of property among tenants, but also undertook direct action (land invasions, non-payment of labour-rent) in furtherance of these objectives, culminating in a general strike throughout La Convención in 1961. The outcome was that tenants ceased to provide the landlord with labour-service, thereby undermining the economic and political power of the landlord class in the province. Among the many existing relational forms not challenged by this peasant movement, however, was the *enganche* system as this applied to migrant labour.[19]

When in 1962 the ending of labour-rent deprived the demesne of its main source of labour-power, the landlord was compelled to transform the labour process on this sector. In the case of one particular estate, Pintobamba Grande, labour-intensive crops such as cocoa and coca (the cultivation of which depended on tenant-derived labour-power) were replaced by capital-intensive crops such as tomatoes, maize and dairy produce.[20] The result was a mixed arable and stock farming system on the demesne sector, which required not only increased levels of investment in specialised plant but also a reduced workforce. During the decade after 1962, therefore, the landlord demesne functioned as an independent unit within estate production. Following its expropriation, ownership of the demesne sector in La Convención generally passed from the landlord to co-operatives composed of peasant proprietors owning holdings on the non-demense sector.

The legal abolition of labour rent did not result in the demise of the *enganche* system, much rather the contrary. Its continued economic importance for an emerging class of rich peasants is overlooked, however, since many of the more recent secondary sources which confirm the presence in La Convención of the *enganche* relation confine references about the exploitative/surplus-extracting nature of debt bondage in the pre-reform era solely to its use by the landlord class in an attempt to secure unpaid or below-cost labour from tenants.[21] With a few exceptions, therefore, no mention is made of the resort by tenants to the *enganche* in order to obtain workers during the pre-reform era.[22] Tenants who became rich peasants, and themselves required labour-power, similarly recruited/controlled agricultural workers by means of the debt bondage mechanism. As in the case of landlords, such tenants obtained their workforce from the Andean highlands, and in the pre-reform period either settled them within their holdings as sub-tenants or employed them as seasonal migrants.[23]

2.3 Debt Bondage, Feudalism and Nationalism

The absence of references to bonded labour employed by tenants in La Convención is due in part to the pervasive influence of the prefigurative discourse about the role of unfree labour: namely, the fact that historically critics of the *enganche* system saw it (wrongly) as an obstacle to capitalist development in Peruvian agriculture. This is evident from the way in which this relation was theorized in authoritative texts from an earlier period, such as those by Mariategui and Castro Pozo, where forced labour was equated with the exploitation/oppression of tribal and/or highland indian populations in Peru by a 'foreign' landlord class.[24] Hence the locus and meaning of the debt bondage relation was trapped ideologically and politically in a powerful relay in statement, whereby external domination = landlordism = unfreedom = feudal/semi-feudal relation = absence of capitalist development = national economic backwardness.

In the debates of the 1920s and 1930s, indigenous unfree labour employed by landlords on the estate system of Peru was accordingly linked discursively and politically to the reproduction of national economic backwardness, stemming in turn from external (= European and/or North American) domination, the principal effect of which was the semi-colonial and thus the unproductive (= feudal/semi-feudal) character of the agrarian sector. Peasant struggle with the landlord class was perceived largely in terms of a wider *national* struggle against imperialism, and not as part of the intra-national *class* struggle by workers against capitalism of whatever ethnic/national origin. Within this discourse, therefore, not only did agrestic servitude become associated mainly and unsurprisingly with the landlord/tenant relation, but the latter (and thus the former) was also depicted principally in terms of ethnic/cultural/national rather than class identity.

Many of these same concerns inform the way in which debt bondage was interpreted with regard to its role in the pre-reform agrarian structure of La Convención. In the latter case, therefore, the elimination of the power exercised by the landlord class over an emerging class of capitalist peasants, composed of rich tenants, is interpreted by many texts as signalling the demise both of feudalism and thus of pre-capitalist relations of production, of which the *enganche* was the most notorious example. Because debt bondage is categorized as a semi-feudal relation, the end of one is interpreted as evidence for a decline of the other: accordingly, unfree labour is necessarily regarded as being incompatible with capitalism.[25] Fieldwork evidence from La Convención in the post-reform era suggests that such a view is wrong.

II

It has been argued by Deere that, following the 1969 Peruvian agrarian reform, the expropriation of the landlord class was accompanied by a corresponding demise of patriachal control over peasant family labour.[26] Since the latter was determined by the amount of land to which the household head had access, and this in turn was dependent on the goodwill of the landlord, kinship authority among the estate peasantry was ultimately structured by the presence of a landlord as its guarantor. Such a view, however, overlooks both the fact that authority emanating from actual/fictive kin relations is supported as much by sanctions operationalized from within the peasantry, and also the consolidation of peasants' material base after the expropriation of the landlord class, which gave them access to new and improved means of production – as individual proprietors and as co-owners of co-operatives.

2.4 Debt Bondage in Post-Reform La Convención

Deere overlooks the extent to which fictive kinship complemented and reinforced patriarchal relations among the peasantry during the post-reform era, through the reproduction of an analogous structure and idiom that stressed intra-kin group hierarchy and obligation. In short, the power and authority vested in and mediated by this fictive kin link constituted the politico-ideological framework necessary for the enforcement by peasant proprietors of debt bondage relations on which the reimposition of pre-reform control over the labour-power of increasingly landless kinsfolk depended. And it was this latter process that enabled sections of the rich and middle peasantry in La Convención to become or remain small capitalist producers.

The topography of the subtropical regions in the eastern lowlands of Peru where coffee is grown prevents mechanization and, apart from the use of pesticides and fertilizers, precludes substantial investment in labour-saving techniques. Furthermore, a consequence of coffee price fluctuation on the international market has been that better-off peasants with investments in costly technical inputs are most vulnerable when prices fall or export quotas are reduced.[27] The fact that this labour-intensive cash crop is a highly seasonal one increases the importance of access to and control over an adequate supply of cheap labour-power. Thus higher output and profitability necessarily involves increasing both the availability and the intensity of labour while simultaneously reducing wage levels.

To ensure the success of the accumulation process on peasant holdings in La Convención during the post-reform era meant that labour-power for coffee production had to be available in sufficient quantities, at the right price, and when required. Although the expropriation of the landlord class signalled a victory, it nevertheless possessed contradictory aspects from the viewpoint of capitalist peasants. Far from solving the problem of scarcity of labour in the province, the agrarian reforms of the late 1960s created further difficulties for such producers as regards access to and control over labour-power. At the same time as new land was becoming available in La Convención as a result of landlord expropriation, therefore, the implementation of the same reform process in other areas of Southern and Central Peru deprived proprietors of the labour-power necessary for cultivating this land.[28] These reasons help explain why in the province during the post-reform era the standard method of recruiting, maintaining control over, and cheapening labour-power continued to be the debt bondage mechanism.[29]

In the ex-estate of Pintobamba Grande in La Convención during the mid-1970s, debt bondage was used to secure the labour-power of local poor peasants and landless migrants contracted from outside the province to work on both the peasant sector and the co-operative sector.[30] In the case of bonded migrant labour, indebtedness was incurred subsequent to recruitment. The migrant entered employment with his account in balance, and occasionally left it at the end of the contract period in credit, receiving his total cash wage in a lump sum. Generally, however, the employing rich or middle peasant deducted the cost of subsistence items consumed by the migrant from his wage, with the result that on the termination of his contract the labourer owed money to his employer. The latter then advanced a further lump sum, thereby committing this migrant to a further period of work in order to pay off the debt. In this manner, capitalist peasants in La Convención secured the labour-power of migrant workers for those periods of the agricultural cycle when the demand for labour in the province was at its highest, and the competition for this labour from other capitalist peasants correspondingly acute.

In the case of the local bonded workforce, recruitment occurred subsequent to indebtedness; this was possible because of poor peasants' inability to cover the cost of large non-recurring expenditures, on illness, funerals and marriage.[31] Here indebtedness was a consequence of increasing commoditization, poor peasants being squeezed between the rising cost of living and the declining level of real income. The effect was to raise the level of poor peasant indebtedness to rich and middle peasant creditor-employers while simultaneously depressing the wage rate at which debt was cancelled in the form of labour-service. In many instances, the extent of indebtedness required a poor peasant to commit not only his own labour-power to its cancellation but also that of domestic kin resident in his household, thereby extending the concept of unfreedom from individuals to whole peasant families.

2.5 Patterns/Results of Worker Indebtedness

A comparison of the structure of indebtedness as this affected both migrant labourers and permanent locals in Pintobamba Grande revealed significant differences in terms of the amount borrowed, the frequency of and the reasons for borrowing. The pattern of debt incurred by seasonal migrants over the years 1973–5 indicates that generally only small sums were borrowed at regular intervals during the period of employment. More than three quarters of all cash advances made to these subjects involved amounts of less than S/.50, and just three per cent of loans were of sums in excess of 1,000 Soles.[32]

The average interval between cash advances made to migrants was once every six days, and the day-to-day list of subsistence purchases effected with this money specified items such as bread, sweets, trousers, sandals, a nylon shirt, a haircut and a bar of soap. Apart from recording the economic structure of migrants' consumption patterns, this detailed and intimate list of subsistence purchases is also an indicator of the ideological power exercised by a rich peasant creditor-employer over these workers. Although no reason existed for providing information beyond the amount of money lent, therefore, in many cases the record nevertheless identifies the expenditure for which cash was required, a form of itemization that not only suggests a lack of privacy on the part of the borrower but also conveys a sense of the latter having to justify the purchases made.[33]

In contrast to seasonal migrants, poor peasants and labourers who constituted the local workforce borrowed larger sums less frequently. The detailed accounts kept by the same rich peasant reveal that 80 per cent of all cash advances made to these subjects were for sums of over S/.50, 16 per cent were for amounts of over S/.500 and that five per cent involved single payments in excess of one thousand Soles. Locals also borrowed less frequently, at an average interval of 16 days. In the case of locals, the principal reason for borrowing was to cover the cost of large non-recurring items of expenditure such as house construction, burial or medical expenses. Information on cash advances made by a rich peasant indicate that two poor peasants borrowed large sums (S.2,280 and S/.5,400) in order to purchase corrugated iron sheets for roofing, while another borrowed S/.200 for expenditure on a burial. However, smaller sums were also lent for the purchase of items such as milk.

Other cases of poor peasant and labourer indebtedness indicate how non-recurring items of expenditure led to bondage. One example concerned a labourer who in 1975 got food poisoning, as a result of which it was necessary for him to borrow S/.750 from a rich peasant member on the co-operative in order to meet the costs of medicines and hospital treatment. Another involved combined expenditures occasioned by illness and death. When one particular sub-tenant (a poor peasant with usufruct rights to 0.66 of a hectare) in Pintobamba Grande died in 1962, therefore, his burial expenses were met by his tenant (a middle peasant with a holding of 7.93 hectares). The resulting debt was passed on to his son, who in the following year obtained ownership rights to his dead father's sub-tenancy. In 1966 this poor peasant himself became seriously ill, and the heavy medical expenses were once again met by the same middle peasant (*lo he llevado al médico, he gastado un montón de plata*). If the accumulated debt was not met, the middle peasant threatened, he would absorb the poor peasant's holding within his own land which surrounded it (*tu chacra esta dentro de mi parcela, y ahora: ¿que dices?*).[34]

Since that date, in order to pay off these two debts amounting to some S/.3000 (or 150 working days at the time of fieldwork) the poor peasant concerned worked for this middle peasant as domestic or agricultural labour in the dwelling and on the land owned by his creditor-employer, as well as on behalf of the latter on the co-operative land itself, on land privatised by members of the cooperative, and on holdings owned by other peasants.[35] Informants on the cooperative pointed out that even this poor peasant's participation in an extensive network of exchange labour groups (*ayni*), composed of poor peasants in the vicinity, was under threat since debt-servicing work for his middle peasant creditor-employer prevented him from returning labour contributions to those who belonged to the same network (that is, his reciprocal labour obligations).

2.6 Actual/Fictive Kinship and the Discourse of 'Reciprocity'

One of the principal and ideologically most potent methods of enforcing debt bondage in La Convención was through the formal and informal control and authority (not consensus) exerted in the context of actual/fictive kin networks. Of particular importance to the accumulation process in La Convención, there-fore, was the fact that although actual/fictive kinship is capable of projecting an ensemble of positive meanings that may serve to deflect class antagonism, it also enables an employer to exercise a unique and powerful form of social control (based on patriarchal authority) over the labour-power of kinsfolk, co-parents, and/or god-children.[36] Since they not only originated from the same highland communities as bonded migrants, but were frequently actual/fictive kinsfolk of the latter, labour contractors who recruited them and organized the migration process also utilized this kind of authority to enforce compliance with labour-service obligations incurred as a result of debt.[37]

As elsewhere in the Andean region, ritual or fictive kinship (*compadrazgo*) is established as a result of baptismal, marital, or confirmational sponsorship of a child (*ajihado*) by godparents (*padrinos*) who also become co-parents (*compadres*) of its parents. The resulting triadic relationship not only entails specific forms of behaviour and mutual obligation but also creates a formally recognized structure of superiority and subordination. The mutual obligations imposed on both parties to the relationship involve strong behavioural norms. Godparents are required (altruistically) to sacrifice their self-interest in favour of their godchild, a process whereby gifts are made to the latter or to his/her (co-) parents, which in turn generates a cycle of reciprocal changes. Accordingly, regular prestations by generous sponsors both reproduce the relationship and require co-parents and/or a godchild to undertake counter-prestations.

Like actual kinship, fictive kinship is premissed on 'sharing without reckoning'.[38] Paradoxically, therefore, although it serves both to initiate and reproduce material exchanges between co-parents, the ideology of fictive kinship nevertheless supresses any attempt to calculate the economic content of these transactions.[39] Such a framework of politico-ideologically non-calculable reciprocity between fictive kin was particularly suited to the godparental/co-parental exchanges occurring in the post-reform class structure of La Convención.[40] Baptismal or marital sponsorship of labourers and poor peasants was not only the occasion for initiating debt by advancing cash sums subsequently repaid (or reciprocated) in the form of labour-service but also for reproducing and augmenting debt (and labour-service) through the periodic 'gift' from a 'generous' rich or middle peasant godparent to a poor peasant or landless labourer co-parent.[41]

2.7 Actual/Fictive Kinship, Debt Enforcement and Local Workers

Despite the fact that fictive kin links are asymmetrical, and involve god-parents and co-parents from different positions in the class structure, many texts about *compadrazgo* in the Andes fail to distinguish between the discourse of equal exchange that permeates this relation and its economic content.[42] The institution of ritual co-parenthood is accordingly presented as operating to the benefit of both landholders and landless, in particular the latter for whom it serves as a 'security network' or 'social insurance' in a context of scarcity or uncertain subsistence.[43] A variant of this position is contained in studies of Andean peasant economy which, although accepting that egalitarian idioms projected through the discourse of fictive kinship mask unequal exchanges between godparents and co-parents, nevertheless regard such transactions as non-capitalist.[44]

However, even texts which address the politico-ideological advantage that external capital/capitalism derives from actual/fictive kinship usually emphasize hegemonic elements, such as legitimation, rather than more directly coercive aspects of this relation.[45] Accordingly, proponents of the view that it is the privileged access to low-paid or unpaid kin labour-power which permits petty commodity production either to survive in conditions where capitalist enterprises go bankrupt or to produce cheaper commodities than capital fail to problematize the central issue: exactly how peasant smallholders maintain control over and secure the availability of this form of cheap labour-power.[46] Such a view omits a consideration of the extent to which owning/non-owning, manual labouring kinsfolk within a single household or an extended kin unit may at particular conjunctures possess not just different but opposed economic interests.[47] Where kin labour-power that constitutes the peasant work-force cannot enter the labour market, therefore, it is necessary to identify mechanisms which prevent this from happening: the coercive element inherent in actual/fictive kinship.

The fact that debt bondage relations structured actual/fictive kinship, and that the result was a form of coercion used by better-off peasants in La Convención to discipline and maintain control over the labour-power of poor peasant co-parents and/or godchildren, was evident not merely to the outside observer but also to the subjects of these relations. Hence the utterances made in the course of a particularly antagonistic exchange between on the one hand a poor peasant and on the other a middle and rich peasant, in which the former accused both the latter of having secured the services of their father-in-law, brother-in-law, and co-parent – all of whom were bonded labourers – as 'slaves' (*esclavos*). This incident took place in the context of a beer drinking group convened by a number of peasant *socios* privately occupying and cultivating portions of the cooperative land; the confrontation itself was the outcome of the very public joking and teasing of the rich and middle peasant concerned by the poor peasant, a situation which rapidly escalated into the trading of insults.[48] The existence yet ineffectiveness of these utterances equating the employment of indebted relatives with unfreedom (actual/fictive kinsfolk = bonded labourers = 'slaves') bears testimony to the effectiveness of the discourse naturalizing kinship obligation/ authority which informs such relations.

Thus the authoritarian structure of fictive kinship is an explicit aspect of this relation. The ascribed inequality of actual kinship is also projected on to the fictive kinship hierarchy, as manifest in the joint exercise of parental/ godparental power over a godchild, itself a form of politico-ideological domination installed and strongly sustained by Catholic religion.[49] Significantly, however, fictive kinship in La Convención is not limited just to a restricted triad of godchild, parents and godparents but extends laterally and vertically to include all the brothers and sisters of the godchild's parents as well as its grandparents, the latter becoming senior co-parents (*compadres mayores*) and the former classificatory co-parents to the sponsors of the child. Similarly, the godparents' own siblings and grandparents become in turn classificatory fictive kin to any co-parents of the child's mother and father.[50] Thus the ties of ritual co-parenthood not only spread beyond (and in some cases overlap with) consanguineal and affinal links but also – and unlike the latter – encompass different class subjects.

Accordingly, the authority of fictive kinship may be invoked by a rich peasant in order to mobilize local opinion directly against an indebted poor peasant co-parent (or a member of the latter's family) who fails to fulfil labour-service obligations. It may also be invoked indirectly, in order to prevail on rich or middle (classificatory) co-parents (or members of their family) not to give employment to any poor peasant or landless labourer who owes him money.[51] Given the extensive range and heterogeneous social composition of fictive kinship in La Convención, sanctions threatened or actualised through its network are correspondingly powerful. Idioms of patriachal authority, duty, obligation and reciprocity can be utilized to control a workforce of debt bonded labour composed of godchildren, co-parents and classificatory co-parents while at the same time disguising the class basis of this control.

2.8 Actual/Fictive Kinship, Debt Enforcement and Migration

Much the same was true of the migrant workforce, where fictive kinship reinforced economic sanctions contained in the penal clauses of labour contracts.[52] The latter specified not only the duration of employment, the rate of pay, and the amount of the cash advance paid by the peasant proprietor to a seasonal migrant, but contained also a separate clause imposing a fine in the event of conditions not being met. In Pintobamba Grande during the 1966–73 period, the fine for non-completion amounted to no more than 17 per cent of the final cash wage, and although not inherently large it nevertheless contributed to a situation in which some 65 per cent of the wage was structured by potential debt (the cash advance accounting for remaining 48 per cent). Notwithstanding the fact that the fine applied to both parties to the contract, in reality it was a sanction available only to the employer, who could invoke non-completion of contractual obligations as a reason for withholding a portion of the migrant's wage.

As the following example illustrates, pressure exercised through kinship and fictive kinship networks was also an effective method of enforcing debt servicing labour obligations on on young migrants.[53] Two of the seasonal migrants from the Province of Canchis employed by a rich peasant in Pintobamba Grande were themselves linked by kinship. The elder of the two was father-in-law to the younger and, since the latter was below eighteen years of age, also his legal proxy in contractual negotiations with employers. Although the younger labourer had received two loans of S/.1,850 and S/.110 from the rich peasant with which to repay outstanding debts owed to others, he nevertheless failed to turn up for work on the agreed date.

Accordingly, the rich peasant sent him a letter – significantly via his guarantor and father-in-law – instructing him to report for work at once since the coca crop was ready for harvesting, and reminding him that he had already received a cash advance so as to repay another debt he owed.[54] The original labour contract, drawn up in July 1973, stipulated that the elder of the two labourers 'undertake in my capacity as guarantor to ensure that my son-in-law [name] complies with these conditions' (*Yo ... acepto los terminos precedentes en todas sus partes comprometiendome en mi condición de garante, hacer cumplir la obligación adquirida por mi hijo político ...*). Pressure was exercised through him as guarantor and kinsman of the absent, potentially absconding, and indebted son-in-law to ensure that the latter turn up as arranged. The younger of the two labourers did in fact commence work for the rich peasant shortly thereafter.

III

Although the post-reform pattern of capitalist development in the coastal and highland regions of Peru may have reduced or eliminated the need for bonded labour in these areas, the opposite remains true of the accumulation process in the semi-tropical eastern lowlands.[55] Instead of hastening the disappearance of debt bondage on the large estates (now expropriated and divided between peasant holdings and co-operative production) in the province of La Convención, the 1969 agrarian reform contributed to the resurgence of this unfree relation through the provision of additional land for co-operative cultivation. It is important, therefore, to understand why better-off peasant proprietors who – as members of the cooperative were the beneficiaries of the agrarian reform – acquired control over the labour-power of poor peasants and landless labourers, and also how such unfree relations enabled them to accumulate.

2.9 Bonded Labour and Agrarian Capitalist Restructuring

Fieldwork evidence from Pintobamba Grande suggests that over the 1973–5 period rich and middle peasants who employed bonded labour were replacing migrants with local labour, the latter composed for the most part of indebted poor peasants whose smallholdings adjoined the larger landholdings belonging to their creditor-employers.[56] Higher profitability and more effective control were the principal objectives of this shift employment patterns.[57] The change eliminated expenditures, both on the commission payable to the labour contractor and also on the transportation of migrants to and from their home communities. Similarly, residence within the social domain of the creditor-employer enabled the latter to enforce labour-service obligations more effectively. And finally, whereas the external workforce was absent for much of the agricultural cycle (now extended in duration as a result of production on the co-operative sector), a creditor-employer had continuous access to the labour-power of a local debt bonded poor peasant household.

This process of restructuring, whereby cheaper and more easily regulated components of unfree labour replaced more costly variants, allowed rich and middle capitalist peasants to employ agricultural workers in a number of different ways: not only to mobilize immediately the labour-power of debt bonded poor peasants and their kin for harvesting coca and coffee when the market price was favourable, but also to use them in exchange labour groups (*mink'a*) and reciprocal exchanges of labour (*ayni*) with other rich and middle peasants, or to redeploy their workers on to the co-operative sector which possessed more advanced productive forces (irrigation, mechanized power) and a dissimilar pattern of production (tomatoes, maize, livestock).[58] The presence of bonded labour in exchange labour groups and reciprocal exchanges of labour on peasant holdings, together with the redeployment of unfree workers from the latter context on to the co-operative sector, all constitute instances of the way in which unfree labour in La Convención was inserted into what appeared to be a free market.[59]

The developments licensing this workforce restructuring are not difficult to discern. In the post-reform era, the difference between the low 'wage' rate paid to bonded labour employed on peasant holdings and the relatively high wage received by any form of labour employed on the co-operative sector encouraged rich and middle peasants to redeploy their workforce composed of unfree poor peasants on to the co-operative land during the slack season on their privately-owned land.[60] As a co-owning member of the co-operative, a rich or middle peasant received the higher wage rate for each unit of (bonded) labour redeployed in this manner, but the latter subjects received only their usual low 'wage'; the wage differential between the two sectors of production was accordingly appropriated by the creditor-employer. Central to this process of appropriation, however, was the incapacity on the part of unfree workers to personally commodify their own labour-power.

Both the fact of and the increase in bonded labour redeployed in this manner coincided with two specific developments in the structure of the cooperative workforce. The first of these was a decline in the number of poor peasant members, many of whom were expelled from the cooperative. This in turn was due to an inability on their part to fulfill the statutory labour requirement necessary for continued member status, as a result of which poor peasants were deprived of co-ownership rights to cooperative means of production together with material benefits this conferred (interest-free loans, subsidized fertilizer, below market price meat and milk provisions, etc.).

The second was a corresponding decrease in the number of free wage labourers directly employed by the co-operative as its permanent workforce. Components of the latter were relatively speaking the most privileged category of the rural labour in La Convención, and received not only the high wage payable to workers employed on the co-operative sector but also the full range of entitlements that composed the social wage (insurance and medical cover, paid holidays, paid Sunday rest-day, living quarters, meals, maize beer, coca rations during rest-periods of the working day, etc.). These permanent workers preferred to be employed on the cooperative sector as free labour rather than on peasant holdings as unfree labour, giving as reasons the lower wages and harder working conditions imposed by proprietors in that context. While bonded labour redeployed on to the co-operative sector assumed many of the functions and characteristics of the displaced permanent free wage labour, the former nevertheless did not receive any of the social wage entitlements received by the latter.

Significantly, both the expelled members of the cooperative and the free workforce employed on this sector were composed of poor peasants and local landless labourers who were also in debt to and related by actual/fictive kinship ties to rich and middle peasant members of the same agrarian unit. The latter had acquired control over the labour-power of these subordinate actual/fictive kinsfolk through the debt bondage mechanism, and the disappearance of poor peasants and free landless workers from the co-operative sector was a result of a corresponding inability to personally commodify their own labour-power. Hence the expulsion of poor peasants from co-operative was the direct result of the debt bondage mechanism, which prevented them from carrying out their statutory labour contribution necessary for membership. These same poor peasants and workers subsequently reappeared on the co-operative, but now as unfree labour deployed by rich and middle peasant members.

As in the case of the privately-owned peasant holdings, therefore, this shift in the employment pattern corresponds to the capitalist restructuring of the cooperative labour process, whereby more costly forms of (free) labour-power were replaced by less costly (unfree) variants receiving (at the end of the total accounting procedure) lower payment and no rights to the social wage.[61] Co-operative members in general, and rich and middle peasant capitalists in particular, were as a result able to extract a higher rate of profit from the transformed workforce in both sectors of production on the ex-estate system in La Convención during the post-reform era.

2.10 Conclusion

Class struggle is central to an understanding of the dynamics structuring the reproduction of the debt bondage relation in the province of La Convención in eastern Peru during the pre- and post-reform era. Initially, this conflict involved landlord and tenants over the issue of labour rent on the estate system. When additional land became available as a result of the expropriation of the landlord class, it became a struggle between different peasant strata for access to and control over labour-power on the agrarian co-operatives. In La Convención debt bondage was used to secure the labour-power of both locally-hired workers and those contracted from outside the province to work on a seasonal basis. The local workforce was recruited from poor peasants resident on the non-demesne sector.

Whereas in the pre-reform era debt bondage was used to obtain the labour-power of those who then settled in the province as tenants or sub-tenants, and for whom ufruct rights to land offered the possibility of landownership, in the post-reform period by contrast the workforce has been composed of land-poor or landless bonded labour. Over the twentieth century, therefore, while the rural workforce employed in La Convención has become increasingly one with only the single commodity labour-power to sell, unfreedom has nevertheless remained a pervasive aspect of production relations in the province. As such, it has entailed the decommodification of both local and migrant labour-power employed by capitalist peasants, first on the estate system and subsequently on the co-operatives. For epistemological reasons, however, the presence/incidence of debt bondage, together with its crucial role in the accumulation process, has not always been recognized.

Hence a failure by much of the literature about pre-reform La Convención to extend the concept of unfreedom to production relations involving tenants, sub-tenants and workers stems from three interrelated assumptions: that debt bondage is restricted to the landlord/tenant relationship on the estate system, that it is a pre-capitalist relation and thus incompatible with (or an obstacle to) accumulation, and that it could not be enforced once the landlord class had been expropriated and unfreedom was no longer supported by the law and the state. A consequence of this epistemology (debt bondage = pre-capitalist relation) is that unfreedom is similarly absent from much of the literature about the nature of the production relations in post-reform La Convención, particularly in cases where capitalist producers redeploy poor peasants and agricultural workers onto the newly-formed co-operatives in the province.

In part, a failure to recognize the presence of bonded labour in post-reform La Convención is due to a corresponding failure on the part of texts analysing agrarian change in the province to differentiate the peasantry in terms of class, a lacuna the theoretical effects of which in are examined in Chapter 6. Thus the abolition of labour rent did not signal the end of debt bondage, since tenants who were or became rich peasants relied on it to accumulate, and themselves utilized this mechanism to recruit/cheapen/discipline/control migrant and/or local workers. Nor did the fact that – following the agrarian reforms of the 1960s – the debt bondage relation could no longer rely on political and/or economic backing from the landlord class, the law and the state hinder its reproduction, since after this conjuncture its enforcement was effected by means of actual/fictive kinship authority mobilized from within (and ideologically sustained by) the peasantry itself.

In an attempt to account for both the fact of and the manner in which peasant proprietors retain privileged access to cheap labour in a situation of intense competition for scarce agricultural workers, therefore, it has been argued that in post-reform La Convención this involved the reimposition of pre-reform control over the labour-power of kin and quasi-kin. This control took the form of politico-ideological authority exercised by rich and middle peasants in the context of extensive and hierarchical networks, with the object of enforcing debt servicing labour obligations incurred by subordinate actual/ fictive kinsfolk. Converted from free to unfree labour through the operational-ization of the debt bondage mechanism, poor peasants and landless workers who constituted these actual/fictive kin were as a result prevented from seeking higher wages and better working conditions.

Not only was the workforce employed by rich and middle peasants either on the co-operative or on their privately owned holdings not composed of other equivalent and autonomous smallholders, therefore, but each sector of the agrarian labour process on the ex-estate system of La Convención was similarly differentiated in terms of class: between on the one hand owning and co-owning subjects who exercised supervisory functions on both the co-operative and the peasant holdings, and on the other the non-owning subjects who carried out manual labouring tasks in these same two contexts. The rich and middle peasants who owned private and co-operative means of production advanced money to secure, cheapen and retain the labour-power of actual/fictive kin. This enabled them to cultivate cash-crops for the national and international market, to reinvest in trading activities, to purchase agricultural inputs, and to buy land elsewhere in the province. In short, the employment of bonded labour enabled such proprietors either to become or to remain small agrarian capitalists.

NOTES

1. Fieldwork on which this chapter is based was carried out in Peru between January 1974 and April 1975, and funded by the Social Science Research Council (SSRC). All prices are expressed in terms of 1975 Peruvian *Soles* (S/.), and at the time of fieldwork the exchange rate was approximately S/.100 = £1.

2. For the employment of unfree labour on seventeenth and eighteenth century Jesuit estates, in Cuzco as well as in the rest of Peru, see Macera [1966; 1968]. As Mörner [1975: 366] points out with regard to the workforce employed on Jesuit estates in the Cuzco region during the eighteenth century, 'without debts there were no workers' (*sin deuda no había trabajador*). Following the expulsion of the Jesuits in 1767, a number of their estates in La Convención passed under the con-trol of the Franciscans, who at the start of the nineteenth century were similarly reported to be enaged in the successful commercial production of coca, coffee and cacao as well as sugar [*Marcoy*,1872: 402ff.].

3. Around the middle of the nineteenth century, Marcoy [1872: 351] describes in the following manner an encounter with migrant labour from the Andean highlands travelling to work in eastern lowlands of Peru:
   a company of poor Indians of both sexes ... were crossing the Cordillera to the Valley of Occobamba [where they] were going to gather, for the benefit and satisfaction of others, sweet-potatoes, coca, manioc, and cacao, undergoing

misery, hunger, and sickness, and perhaps, after all, leaving their bones in the Valley ... .

4. Different combinations of labour-rent depended on the type of crop produced by the landlord on the demesne, and consequently on the variations in and timing of the labour input to the latter [*Villanueva*, 1967: 39ff.; *Hobsbawm*, 1969: 39–40; *Fioravanti*, 1974: 74–8]. For an account of labour-rent obligations payable on the estates in the neighbouring province of Paucartambo, see Palacio Pimentel [1962]. The two most useful texts on the development and contextually/historically specific variants of labour rent on the Andean *hacienda* system are those by Reyeros [1949] and Zavala [1978; 1979; 1980].

5. The Spanish term *enganche* (literally 'the hook') is synonymous with the Quechua word *jurk'a* (the ritual act of recruiting an unwilling person for forced labour), and both refer to the coercive inception and surplus-extracting function as well as the compulsory and arduous nature of the work itself. In pre-reform La Convención the term *jurk'a* applied to a whole range of similarly exploitative agrarian relations: that between landlord and tenant, and also the obligatory and costly sponsorship by a tenant of religious office in the fiesta system [*Brass*, 1986b].

6. See, for example, Bowman [1920: 74], Cuadros [1949: 105], and Craig [1967: 10ff.], all of whom attribute the reproduction of the debt bondage relation to a scarcity of labour in the eastern lowlands of Peru. Macera [1968: lxxxv] reports that during the second half of the eighteenth century landowners in the La Convención area employed guards on their estates specifically in order to prevent workers from leaving.

7. See Kaerger [1979: 17].

8. See Bowman [1920: 64]. Even in the 1760s, landlords in the La Convención region employed labour contractors (*guatacos, buscadores*), not just to obtain workers for their estates but also to pursue those who attempted to leave employment without first clearing their debts [*Macera*, 1968: lxxxv]. Contractors continued to recruit male, female, and child labour in the Andean highland on behalf of landlords in La Convención up until the agrarian reforms of the 1960s. When challenged by an anthropologist opposed to the exploitation of the *enganche* as to the legality of this relation [*Núñez del Prado*, 1973: 19–20, 51], one contractor is reported to have replied: 'The Indian is the best business, and you are spoiling it'. Large commercial enterprises in the province, such as the tea producing estate Huyro, relied particularly heavily on contractors for their seasonal labour requirements. Workers were recruited in the neighbouring provinces of Apurímac, Grau, Acomayo, Calca, Urubamba and Cotabamba by means of the *enganche* system, and contractors received a commission for each labourer delivered. As the following Table shows, in real terms payment made by Huyro estate to contractors for each unit of labour-power increased tenfold over the first half of this century.

Year	Index
1906	100
1952	625
1969	945

Source: Calculated from data contained in Seminario de Investigación sobre Movimientos Campesinos [1974: 22].

9. The practice of diverting tenant labour-service obligations from estates in the Andean highlands onto those owned by the same landlord in the eastern tropical lowlands was still in operation during the mid-1950s. Examples include tenants on estates in Q'ero, who were sent to work on other estates owned by the same landowner (a journey of 92 kilometres), and tenants from Kuyo Chico, who were also required to meet labour-rent payments owed to local *hacendados* on estates owned by the latter in La Convención [*Núñez del Prado*, 1973: 3, 26]. For a similar example from the northern Peruvian *Sierra*, where the owner of a coastal sugar planation purchased an estate in the highlands in order to have access to the labour-power of its tenants, see Miller [1967: 169–70]. Exactly the same kind of objective lay behind the purchase in northern Argentina during the 1930s and early 1940s of highland estates by owners of lowland sugar plantations [*Rutledge*, 1975; 1977]. One of the largest and most powerful landlords in La Convención, Alfredo Romainville, reversed this procedure, and sent workers from his estates in the province to work in his textile mills situated in the highlands.

10. The way in which *haciendas* in the Cusco region acquired labour-service linked to debts during the eighteenth century is outlined by Macera [1968: cxx–cxxi]. For example, a merchant who provided goods or services on credit to a particular worker then sold this debt to a landlord in exchange for goods produced on the latter's estate; the worker's debt was thus transferred to the estate, in which context he was now required to cancel it with labour. A similar system of inter-estate transfers of labour was still operating in the Urubamba valley during the mid-1950s, where landlords of one *hacienda* rented out their tenants to other estates in the same locality; payment for work done was made not to the tenants themselves but to their landlord [*Núñez del Prado*, 1973: 3]. As is indicated below, a similar form of surplus appropriation linked to labour redeployment was operated by peasants who were co-owning members of an agrarian co-operative in La Convención during the mid-1970s.

11. According to Bingham [1951: 124–6], porters for the expedition were recruited in an unambiguously coercive manner:

> When they [the officials] were so fortunate as to find the man of the house at home or working in the usual Indian manner, a [Peruvian] silver dollar was slipped into the palm of his right hand and he was informed that he had accepted pay for services which he must now render. It seemed very hard but this was the only way in which it was possible to secure carriers ... When an unfortunate Pampaconas Indian found he had a dollar in his hand he bemoaned his fate but realized that service was inevitable. In vain did he plead that he was 'busy', that his 'crops needed attention', that his 'family could not spare him', that 'he lacked food for a journey'.

12. Bingham [1951: 128] comments without irony that porters 'were good for fifty pounds [weight] apiece ... suffered from the heat [and] found it more and more difficult to carry their loads'.

13. For this particular incident, see Núñez del Prado [1973: 48–9, 51, 155–9].

14. See Cuadros [1949: 105–6].

15. On these points, see Cuadros [1949], Tupayachi [1959], CIDA [1966: 206ff.], Craig [1967; 1969], Villanueva [1967: 33ff.], and Hobsbawm [1969]. One of the few exceptions to a general failure to recognize the connection between kinship and class is the case study by Miller [1967] of a commercial hacienda in northern Peru during the late 1950s, which confirms that sub-tenants who were related by

marriage to tenant households were required not only to pay off labour-rent owed by the latter to the landlord but also to work on the tenant's own holding, and how this led to acrimonious conflict between tenant/sub-tenant kin. On this point, Miller [1967:188] observes:

> The son-in-law was obliged to work not only his own plot, but, with the help of his wife's brother, the land of his father-in-law. He brooded constantly about being ordered about like a peon and receiving only an inadequate parcel [of land] for his own use. In addition he, along with another sub-tenant, had to pay the whole labor [rent] to the hacienda ... Life as a sub-tenant to one's father-in-law is in many ways more difficult than if one is a sub-tenant to a complete stranger, for along with the duties of a sub-tenant, a son-in-law is obliged to render bride service ... A man who gives his daughter [in marriage] is motivated more by the desire to incorporate another worker in the family than to become related to the groom's family.

16. Coffee was ecologically more adaptable to cultivation on tenant holdings than on the landlord demesne. During the period 1945–54 the price index for this crop increased from 100 to 1221 [*Craig*, 1969: 283], and over the years 1940–50 the index for coffee output in the province increased from 100 to 187 [*Fioravanti*, 1974: 94, Table 18]. Tenants and sub-tenants are categorised as belonging to the rich, middle or poor peasant stratum on the basis of the quantity of non-demesne land possessed. The latter was a significant element in differentiating the peasantry because of its crucial role in the production of coffee, the most profitable cash-crop grown in the province. Increases in coffee output were obtained by expanding the area under cultivation (and hiring in more workers). Accordingly, the area of non-demesne holdings available for current and future coffee production became an important factor in the non-demesne accumulation process and levels of profitability on the peasant enterprise. Rich peasants operated in excess of ten non-demesne hectares, and constituted the economically dominant element among the tenants; they not only possessed the most extensive holdings but also disposed of the largest quantity of uncultivated land on which to expand coffee production. Middle peasants held between five and ten hectares of non-demesne land, and although possessing less extensive holdings than rich peasants they were nevertheless capable of sustained and substantial accumulation in good harvest years. Poor peasants had less than five hectares of land, and virtually no reserves for future expansion.

17. The rapid rise in labour-rent during this period is illustrated by one example from the estate of Pintobamba Grande (see below) of an ex-tenant rich peasant proprietor, who in the mid-1970s owned a holding of 14.85 hectares. When his father, the original tenant, was leased land on this estate in 1900, the holding covered a total area of 29.54 hectares, and labour-service amounted to two working days per month. The rental increased to 20 working days per month in 1955, 28 in 1957 and 30 in 1960, increases which necessitated the introduction of seven sub-tenancies to meet the labour-rent contributions to the landlord demesne, a process requiring the sub-letting of 14.69 hectares and decreasing by half the initial area of this holding.

18. In the discourse of Hugo Blanco, the seemingly radical institutional framework of 'dual power' to be established following the expropriation of the landlord class turned out to be a return to the traditional peasant 'community' and unconnected with the concept as theorized by Trotsky [*Brass*, 1989a]. The resulting idealization

of both the struggle and its objective was not merely compatible with but supportive of accumulation project of rich peasants. The latter were able as a result to depict the struggle as that of an homogeneous peasant mass ranged against oppressive landlords, and its objective as the recuperation of a pre-existing and egalitarian rural 'community'.

19. Blanco [1972: 33] justifies this failure to address the issue of the *enganche* system in the following manner: 'The agricultural labourers, because they were migratory labourers who came only intermittently to [La Convención], took very little interest in the [peasant] union. When they did show some interest in it, it was with regard to the problems of their own regions.' A more likely explanation for this failure is an unwillingness on his part to risk antagonizing those rich peasants who not only discharged an important role in the movement but themselves employed bonded migrant labour, and who would most certainly have withdrawn their support in the event of any attempt to question the *enganche* relation. Regarded by Blanco as the most progressive component of the peasant movement, rich peasants were the most active elements in the struggle against the landlord [*Alfaro and Ore*, n.d.: 17–18]; indeed, Blanco [1972: 73] points out with approval that 'a number of such farmers were members of the guerrilla band'.

20. Much of what follows is based on detailed fieldwork conducted during the mid-1970s on this particular ex-estate (on which see Brass [1980; 1982; 1983; 1986b; 1986c; 1989a; 1989b]). Although it is important to stress all the usual caveats about the specificity of this example, it is nevertheless the case that in terms of size and tenure pattern Pintobamba Grande was in fact typical of many other ex-estates in La Convención at this conjuncture; accordingly, the developments outlined with regard to this context may possess a wider relevance for the province as a whole. Situated a short distance outside the provincial capital Quillabamba, Pintobamba Grande covered an area of just under one thousand hectares divided between two different but structurally interrelated sectors of production. One was the landlord enterprise (or demesne), which consisted of some 50 hectares of irrigated best flat land on the valley floor, and contained not only the most fertile crop and pasture land but also extensive infrastructural development. Until 1972 this sector remained the property of a single landlord, and after this date it became the property of the combined membership of a Production Committee (*Comité de Producción*). Prior to its expropriation, therefore, this area of the estate corresponded to the landlord demesne and was the site of the landlord enterprise, whereas after this point it formed the cooperative sector. The remaining area within Pintobamba Grande corresponded to the peasant enterprise (or non-demesne), which consisted of some seven hundred hectares of hilly and less fertile land lacking the irrigation and transportation facilitites available to the demesne. Before the agrarian reforms of the 1960s, individual plots of land on this sector were leased by the landlord to numerous tenants and sub-tenants, who were required in turn to supply the demesne with variant forms of labour-service. After the agrarian reforms, tenants and sub-tenants became the owners and operators of land which they had rented hitherto. During the mid-1970s, the average rich peasant landholding in Pintobamba Grande amounted to 15 hectares, that for middle peasants to seven hectares, and that of poor peasants to just over two hectares. There were no sub-tenants among the ranks of the rich peasants, while the middle peasantry consisted of sixty per cent tenants and 17 per cent sub-tenants. By contrast, only a quarter of poor peasants were tenants, and

nearly seventy per cent of them sub-tenants; the economically inadequate nature of their landholdings was recognized in the official designation of those ex-sub-tenants with access to insufficient means of production as *deficitarios*.

21. See, for example, the references to the *enganche* by Cuadros [1949: 105–6], Vásquez [1961: 25], CIDA [1966: 211], Craig [1967: 11,30], Neira [1968: 86–7, 91], Hobsbawm [1969: 38] and Fioravanti [1974: 68]. The same is true of Chevalier [1982: 198, 205, 212, 240–42], who maintains that coerced labour has ceased to exist in eastern Peru after 1945, despite references in his own text to the continued presence there of debt bondage relations.

22. Among the exceptions are Pumaruna [1968: 9 note 9], Huxley and Capa [1965: 149], who note the existence of child labour on the estates of La Convención during 1961, and CIDA [1966: 211]. The latter text, however, categorizes migrants who worked in La Convención on a seasonal basis as 'an authentic rural proletariat', a doubly incorrect designation given that such labourers were recruited by means of the *enganche* relation and in some instances continued to own smallholdings in their home communities.

23. Sub-tenants were required not only to discharge the labour-rent obligations owed by rich tenants to the estate landlord but also to work on the non-demesne holdings of these subjects. In the course of an interview during 1974, an agricultural labourer who was himself the son of an ex-tenant characterized pre-reform tenants as small landlords who leased tiny plots of land to sub-tenants in order to secure labour-power, both for their own non-demesne holdings and also to carry out their labour-service obligations to the owner of the estate (*cuando tu eres arrendire, asi es que vas a partir el arriendo a fin de que te ayude en tú chacra y en la hacienda al mismo tiempo. Así es que ya eres como segundo hacendado, es como mini hacendado, asi es que al allegado tú lo obligas*). This view was confirmed by a poor peasant ex-tenant who, describing the tenant as a landlord in his own right, explained that in the pre-reform era it was necessary to work six days per month on his tenant's land, and then to undertake a further six day's work on the latter's behalf in order to meet the labour-rent payable on the demesne (*al arrendire lo hacía condiciones de seis días al mes, y a la hacienda otro seis días por cuenta de eso otro también. Gamonal era, pues, el arrendire*). The use of the term *gamonal* in this manner is significant, in that a perjorative word generally applied by peasants only to landlords in order to signify the parasitic socio-economic role of the latter is here extended to include the tenant, who is thereby identified by the sub-tenant as the same kind of exploiter/oppressor.

24. For their views on the *enganche* system in Peru, see Mariátegui [1968: 72–8] and Castro Pozo [1947: 9]. Described as 'the most important Latin American Marxist theoretician in the 1920s' (Caballero [1986: 160]; for the influence of his ideas see Choy *et al.* [1970] and Melis *et al.* [1971]), José Carlos Mariátegui (1894–1930) designated such relational forms as feudal, and lamented the displacement of 'traditional subsistence cultivation' on the part of smallholders by an externally financed/owned export agriculture on the Pacific coast, a process cited by him as evidence for the colonial nature of the agrarian sector in Peru [1968: 76–7, 78–9]. Much the same is true of Hildebrando Castro Pozo (1891–1945), a founder member of the Peruvian Socialist Party who became a member of the Constituent Assembly in 1931 and a Senator in 1945. He pioneered the study of peasant and tribal populations in Peru, and was instrumental in the attempt to set up a Ministry of Native Affairs. Writing mainly about the sugar, rice and cotton producing

estates on the Pacific coast of Peru, Castro Pozo – like Mariátegui – objected to the *enganche* system because it led to the separation of smallholders from their means of production, and thus undermined the indigenous Andean peasant community.

25. As will be see in subsequent chapters, the equation of unfree labour in India with 'semi-feudalism' resulted in a similar misrecognition of the link between bonded labour and agrarian capitalism. Among those who regard the peasant struggle in La Convención as signalling the end of feudalism are Villanueva [1967: 19ff.] and Bejar [1970:35]. In making much the same point, Fioravanti [1974: 215] observes that '[p]re-capitalist forms of production had disappeared from the region for ever, the conditions for an unfettered development of a capitalist agriculture being present'. Notwithstanding the inference that debt bondage had ceased to exist, elsewhere in the same text he concedes [1974: 134] that sub-tenants who owed debts to tenants both worked for and were 'dependent' on them.

26. See Deere [1978: 424ff.]. Making a similar case with regard to industrial capitalism, Folbre [1982: 326] notes that an outcome of the extension of generalised commodity production is the inability of small businesses dependent on family labour to withstand competition for their workforce from large firms. It is precisely because of this inability to compete economically that concepts of intra-kin group obligation assume such central importance in the struggle by such enterprises to hold on to family labour-power.

27. During the period 1958–72 the price of Peruvian coffee on the international market averaged US$778 per metric tonne; partly because of the Brazilian frosts in 1969, 1972 and 1975, the price of this same commodity increased to US$2,083 in the years 1973–77 [*Araya et al.*, n.d.: 76–77, 89].

28. By providing peasants in La Convención with additional land, the reform exacerbated the demand for labour; at the same time, by distributing land to erstwhile migrants in their communities of origin, the reform reduced the supply of labour from outside the province. Scarcities in other parts of Peru compounded this difficulty. Matos Mar and Mejía [1982: 104] estimate that in the post-reform era the casual manpower requirements in the cotton-growing co-operatives on the Coast rose by 15 per cent, this increase being met by migrants from the Central Highlands. The redistribution of land in the highland communities of Cuzco was the reason most frequently invoked by proprietors in Pintobamba Grande who complained about lack of workers from that region. That capitalist peasants operating in areas of low population density explicitly blamed the scarcity of labour on the redistributive effects of the reform programme is confirmed by a study of Satipo [*Shoemaker*, 1981: 177, 180, 189], a lowland tropical forest area in eastern Peru similar in many respects to La Convención.

29. Evidence for the continued existence of debt bondage in the eastern lowland region of Peru is contained in Chiriftirado *et al.* [1975], Alfaro and Ore [n.d.], Seiler-Baldinger [1980: 246], Shoemaker [1981: 95–6], Chevalier [1982: 198–9, 205, 240–42], and Collins [1988]. For example, during the mid-1960s Piro Indian children could still be purchased as domestic servants or maids in the Gran Pajonal area in the Department of Junín, and in the adjoining Department of Loreto during the mid-1970s Yagua Indians enmeshed in the *enganche* were compelled by logging contractors to fell trees and float them down the headwaters of the Upper Yaguas river [*Huxley and Capa*, 1965: 149; *Seiler-Baldinger* [1980: 246].

30. Data concerning the operation of the debt bondage mechanism in Pintobamba Grande were contained in and obtained from notebooks belonging to a rich

peasant, in which were entered extensive details concerning sums of money advanced by him throughout the period 1973–5, both to poor peasants inhabiting the same locality and to seasonal migrant labourers contracted from outside the province for periods of between ninety and 120 days over the rainy season (November to February). Also recorded was the extent of indebtedness at different dates, the days on which each of the individuals who owed him money worked for him, and the number of the domestic kinsfolk of the debtor who accompanied the latter to work in the fields of this particular creditor-employer. For example: *Ajuste Julián Huallpataipe el 16 mayo 1973 quedando el saldo deudor de S/.190; me vino 3 de marzo 1 dia plantación de cafe ... ajuste el 9 octubre de 1973 me debe S/.1000 como adelanto para el trabajo le di a Pancho Lopa, vino el 21 noviembre trabajar Pancho Lopa, su mujer 1 dia y su chiquita,* etc. (the two individuals mentioned here were both poor peasants resident on the same agrarian cooperative, and each owned less than two hectares of land) The way in which these data were obtained underlines the fortuitous nature of collecting written information on bonded labour. After having provided numerous personal documents about land purchases, etc., from an old trunk in his dwelling, the informant concerned left this writer alone in the room to copy these papers. In his absence, further investigation into the contents of this trunk uncovered a number of notebooks in which were recorded details of loans, debt, and labour-service. These data were rapidly copied out into a separate notebook, and the originals were then replaced where they had been found. Although an excellent informant, the rich peasant concerned never volunteered information about these relationships, nor was he made aware that – let alone how – it had been obtained. Instead, questions put subsequently to other informants confirmed both existence and manner in which he operated the debt bondage mechanism.

31. The following two Tables demonstrate the extent to which cumulative indebtedness on the part of poor peasants is linked to an increase in labour-service contributions. The data refer to poor peasants owning between 0.25 and two hectares, all indebted to and employed by a rich peasant owning 36.65 hectares in Pintobamba Grande during 1973–75.

	1973[b]		*1974*		*1975*	
Area[a]	*Debt*	*Work*[c]	*Debt*	*Work*	*Debt*	*Work*
2.00	271[d]	8	140	4½	115	4½
1.00	1207	34	6915	227	5210	208
0.63	993	28	793	26	530	21
0.25	1146	32	3801	124fi	2717	108½
	3617	102	11649	382	8527	342

Notes: *a* Refers to size of non-demesne holdings; *b* Debt/work balance for the last day of 1973 and 1974, and for the last day of February 1975; *c* The amount of debt and number of work days owed is calculated by dividing the total debt by the adult non-demesne wage; *d* At 1975 prices. *Source*: Compiled from data contained in work records and account books maintained by an informant.

The table below shows the actual average monthly labour input supplied to this same rich peasant by these bonded poor peasants:

Average Monthly Labour Input[a]			
Area	1973	1974	1975
2.00	0.0	0.2	0.0
1.00	2.0	4.6	13.5
0.63	0.1	1.9	3.0
0.25	9.2	6.6	8.0
	11.3	13.3	24.5

Note: a Refers to the number of working days per month of personal and kin labour contributed by each of these poor peasants. *Source*: See previous table.

32. The capacity to lend money in this manner derived in part from the fact that control over cooperative resources enabled rich and middle peasants not only to deny poor peasants access to institutional credit from this source but also themselves to borrow interest-free from it, money which was then lent on to the same poor peasants in order to establish or maintain debt bondage relationships [*Brass*, 1982: 272ff.].

33. This lack of privacy, together with the suspicion that migrants might not voluntarily indicate on what they wished to spend money, is conveyed by one entry recording that a particular subject borrowed S/.50 in order to buy 'knickers for his wife' (*calzon para su mujer*).

34. This kind of economic pressure against property was effected by creditor-employers not just with regard to private land owned by those who owed them money but also with regard to cooperative landholding rights of those who attempted to poach their bonded labourers. Thus one rich peasant member (*socio*) threatened to initiate the expulsion procedure against another *socio* because the latter had attempted to employ as substitute workers in the Production Committee two poor peasants who owed debts to and worked for the former. Significantly, the rich peasant member expressed his anger regarding this attempt to poach his own bonded labourers in terms of the concern he felt as a co-parent responsible for their welfare. In addition to being the creditor-employer of these debt bonded poor peasants, he was also baptismal godparent to their children.

35. When asked about his relationship to his middle peasant creditor-employer, the poor peasant replied that 'he is my tenant, nothing more' (*es mi arrendire, no mas*). This utterance is doubly significant: not only does it indicate that the link between creditor-employer and a debt bonded poor peasant was in the mid-1970s still referred to in terms of the pre-reform tenure but it also confirms that the debt relation was an integral part of such relations.

36. The enforcement of debt servicing labour obligations by means of actual/fictive kinship networks/ideology has a long history in this area, and helps to explain the preponderance of unfree child labour. On the commercialised estates owned by the Jesuits in the Cusco region during the eighteenth century, for example, the whole family was held accountable for debts incurred by its individual members [*Macera*, 1968: cxiii, cxxi]. Not only were the debts incurred by parents met with

the labour-power of children, but any payment due for the work performed by the latter was made not to them but to their parents. The same was true of Brazilian Amazonia during the early 1950s, where children of parents who owed debts to godparents worked as servants in the household of the latter [*Wolf and Hansen*, 1972: 134].

37. Instead of using labour contractors, during the mid-1970s some peasant proprietors in La Convención recruited and collected migrants in person. Not only was this cheaper, but it also established a personal link between employer and the migrant's social milieu, and in particular with the kinsfolk of the latter, which could then be used to enforce compliance with debt obligations. For a similar development in the case of Punjab during the 1980s, see Chapter 3.

38. See Fortes [1970: 238]. The ideological potency of 'reciprocal' exchange is twofold. Thus the initial component, equal exchange (= 'sharing without reckoning'), has as its sub-text the additional premiss that those who undertake such exchange are themselves equal; it is the latter aspect which attempts to supress references to class distinctions. This double meaning is made clear by Leach [1982: 150], who observes that 'reciprocity is *like-for-like* [exchange] and the message that is encoded in the action is roughly: "we are friends and we are of equal status" (original emphasis).

39. The most obvious case of misrecognizing bonded labour due to the non-problematization of actual/fictive kinship is the study by Figueroa [1984], whose conceptualization of an internally homogeneous peasant family in Peru during the post-reform era precludes not only the existence of a division of labour, ownership and authority pattern within this unit but also the epistemological effects of disregarding all the latter. Having constructed a 'typical' peasant family, undifferentiated in terms of its household composition, Figueroa's neoclassical economic approach is then able to focus on the way in which such a (mythical) unit *chooses* to follow a path of risk-avoiding economic strategies (self-employment, migration, local employment, etc.).

40. For instances of an overlap between fictive kinship and debt bondage relations in the province during the post-reform era, see Alfaro and Ore [n.d.: 19–21] and Seminario de Investigación Sobre Movimientos Campesinos [1974: 37–38].

41. This pattern of indebtedness generated at the inception of fictive kinship and reproduced within its politico-ideological framework was common in Pintobamba Grande during the early 1970s. Thus a rich peasant would sponsor not only the marriage of poor peasants and landless labourers who composed his permanent workforce but also the baptism of their children. Both marriage and baptism were occasions for the receipt of cash advances from sponsoring godparents, who thereafter lent them small sums from time to time in exchange for which landless labourers, poor peasants and their kinsfolk would (in the words of one rich peasant) 'pay with labour' (*ellos pagan con trabajo*). Cash advanced on the same religious occasion was also a method of inaugurating a debt bondage relationship in the Scottish mines during the seventeenth and eighteenth centuries: this system, known as 'arling', took the form of the receipt by a collier on the baptism of his child of a 'present' of money from a coal-master, which committed the family of the former to work permanently in the mine owned by the latter (see Anon [1899: 121ff.], Page Arnot [1955: 5–6, 9–10]).

42. Thus, for example, Long [1984: 16] observes that: '[non-wage relationships] cannot be assigned a monetary value [and] can only be understood in terms of

benefits perceived and derived by the participants themselves. Many non-wage relationships are in fact based on sentiments of kinship ... '. Skar [1984: 93–4] draws an analogous contrast between wage and non-wage relations on the basis that the latter contain a 'strong emotive quality based on reciprocity'. For similar theorizations, see Nuñez del Prado [1973], Béjar [1970], and the contributions in Alberti and Mayer [1974]. In the case of La Convención, Huizer [1983: 33] holds the same kind of idealized view when outlining the preferential treatment licensed by actual/fictive kinship relations. '[T]he owner of a plot', he observes,

distributes the work in such a way that his relatives or *compadres* (those workers with whom he has a relationship of patronage or acts as godfather) get more densely cultivated parts which are easier to pick and can thus earn a larger piecework remuneration than those who are less familiar, who then feel themselves to be victims of discrimination.

43. For examples of this view, see Mintz and Wolf [1968] and Wolf and Hansen [1972: 131–5]. Another example is the study by Chevalier [1982] of the Pachitea Valley in eastern Peru, where ritual co-parenthood is presented in terms of equal exchanges (the presence of capitalism notwithstanding), thereby attributing a concrete existence to the idiom of reciprocity. Actual kinship, Chevalier [1982: 325–6] argues, permits only intra-class transfers of wealth, whereas fictive kinship by contrast licenses inter-class resource transfers from rich godparents to poorer co-parents. By choosing rich peasants as baptismal or marital sponsors for their children (or, in the latter instance, for themselves), poor peasants turn the institution of fictive kinship to their own advantage. Rich godparents are forced into expenditures on a godchild, and in this manner contribute to his/her material well-being and that of the whole co-parental poor peasant family.

44. See, for example, Orlove [1977], Sánchez [1982], Fioravanti-Molinié [1982], Mallon [1983a] and Smith [1985]. In so far as the dominant godparents are not petty capitalists, therefore, appropriation licensed by fictive kinship is regarded as either unconnected with capitalist accumulation (surplus-*labour* is extracted in the course of non-reciprocal exchanges; trading profits accrue to merchants *outside* the production process) or else only indirectly connected with capitalist expansion (accumulation *elsewhere* entails the reproduction of this non-capitalist relation). Thus Sánchez argues that the fictive kin relation is used by rich peasants to obtain cheap labour-power from poor peasant households which receive goods and/or services in return, scarcities occasioned by capitalist development compelling the latter subjects to become clients of the former. By contrast, Fioravanti-Molinié presents non-reciprocal transactions involving fictive kin as part of a wider system of 'vertical' exchanges that structures Andean peasant economy. Such transactions, albeit unequal in content, are still perceived by Sánchez and Fioravanti-Molinié as non-capitalist: that is, involving peasant producers who – although subordinated to the circuit of capital – do not themselves accumulate.

45. Although Smith [1985] rightly argues that the 'moral economy component' inherent in Andean community institutions such as reciprocal labour, intra-kin group unpaid labour, and exchanges between fictive kin enable smallholders to extract absolute surplus-value from a local non-commodified workforce, he nevertheless fails to pursue the basic contradiction between the positive ideological sentiments and the coercive aspects of these economic relations. His suggestion, that this method of retaining cheap labour is both non-antagonistic and specific to peasant economy, is problematic.

46. Thus, for example, Long and Richardson [1978: 205] argue that 'the extensive utilization of available family labour – children, wives, old people – allows informal enterprises to adjust labour inputs as circumstances change', without asking how exactly this is achieved. Similarly, Chevalier [[1982: 157] notes that '[i]t is on the basis of ... market determined calculations that a smallholding unit may decide not to sell its own labour power or to sell only a part of it in order to maximize its limited revenue and secure the reproduction of its means of production'.

47. Rather than contributing to the reproduction of a peasant smallholding composed of non-partible land, a household member or kinsman of the household head may derive more benefit from selling his or her own labour-power on the open market. This may be the case, for example, where agriculture is seasonal, and consequently the demand for labour (and thus its remuneration) is higher during certain months of the production cycle; or in conditions where a general upturn in the production cycle favours increased output not only by peasant smallholders but also by their capitalist competitors. Both these situations generate a demand for additional labour-power, and thus offer the workforce on which peasant producers rely the opportunity of obtaining alternative and better-paid employment elsewhere.

48. On the importance of beer drinking groups as contexts in which class antagonism is expressed, see Brass [1989b]. When the same poor peasant resigned from his post on one of the Cooperative Committees shortly after this incident, he referred to this episode in bitter terms, indicating that 'the work we are carrying out in the allotments ... and as I have pointed out before I have no labourers nor do I wish to exploit (... *del trabajo que tenemos en parcelas ... i como los digo que no tengo peones ni quiero explotar*). This letter of resignation was addressed by the poor peasant to the rich peasant, in the latter's capacity as President of the Cooperative Committee involved; although an attempt had been made by its author to erase the final part of the text (' ... nor do I wish to exploit'), it remained legible, as did its inference about the nature of relationship between on the one hand the rich and middle peasant and on the other their actual/fictive kinsfolk who were bonded labourers.

49. Significantly, the act of baptism symbolizes a twofold bonding process: it inaugurates dependence on and obedience to a spiritual master in heaven and simultaneously to a secular master on earth. Equally significant is the way in which 'natural' religious authority embodied in fictive kinship is supportive of debt bondage in Latin America is replicated in the case of unfree labour in India, where during the 1920s the Wisers' interpretation of the *jajmani* relation was similarly informed by notions of 'natural' authority vested in Christian hierarchy (see Chapter 8).

50. Godchild, parents and classificatory co-parents in Pintobamba Grande were expected to accord a baptismal or marital sponsor 'respect' (*honradez*), to address him as *señor compadre* and to treat him as 'an important person' (*como grande*), whereas a rich or middle peasant godfather regards a poor peasant co-parent as a 'subordinate' (*como pequeño*). One rich peasant, godfather to the child of his bonded labourer, described the latter – an adult worker – as being 'like a son' (*es como mi hijo*). The same bonded labourer had to work for his godparent whenever required to do so, it being impossible to refuse a 'request' from the latter even though he himself might be engaged in some important task elsewhere.

51. In this respect, fictive kinship fulfils much the same role as caste in rural India (see Chapters 3 and 4).

52. For the existence of an overlap between debt relations and fictive kin linking con-

tractors and migrants employed on sugar plantations in northern Argentina at this conjuncture, see Whiteford [1981: 45, 60].

53. The historical function of actual/fictive kinship networks in inaugurating and enforcing the long-distance migration in Peru of unfree labour is well documented. For an example of how this sort of compulsion was exercised by a creditor-employer on a debtor's kinfolk who acted as sureties, see Long and Roberts [1984: 115–16]. On this point Laite [1981: 101] makes the following observation regarding the central highlands during the first two decades of this century:

> The *enganchador* would use the debt relation to coerce poor peasants to work in the mines. If a migrant did not complete the necessary working days owing to illness or death, the debt was passed on to his family, and the children often spent years working off their father's debts. One way of cancelling the debt was to sell the family lands to the *enganchador* ... The seizures of land by *enganchadores* led to the bitterest family disputes.

For similar accounts in the context of the Yanamarca Valley at the same period, see Mallon [1983a; 1983b: 187ff., 194–5].

54. The Spanish text of the letter was as follows:

> *cuando vas entrar [.] no me agas esa farsa ... as dicho que vayas regresar pronto y tey [te he] dado adelanto para que pagues a Ilares. asique te debes darte cuenta no hay que ser asi te espero tu viaje pronto [.] la cosecha de coca me vense todo esta de pallar [.] me ases el gran servicio de venir pronto.*

The letter was entrusted to the father-in-law and guarantor of the indebted migrant labourer in question, who delivered it in person to the latter.

55. For accounts (using analytical frameworks different from that adopted here) of the operation of the debt bondage mechanism on the sugar and/or cotton plantations of the west coast and the pastoral estates and mining enterprises in the central highlands of Peru during the late nineteenth century and the first half of the twentieth, see among others Rodríguez Pastor [1969], Macera [1974], Huertas Vallejos [1974], C. Scott [1976], Martinez-Alier [1977: 73ff.], Gonzales [1980; 1985], Laite [1981], Mallon [1983a; 1983b], Albert [1984], and Deere [1990: 44ff.]. Although claims advanced by many of the latter concerning the elimination of unfreedom in Latin America are examined in more detail in Chapter 6, the kinds of difficulties faced by arguments about the emergence of a rural proletariat are immediately evident from contradiction encountered in a text by Miller [1967: 143]: namely, the juxtaposition of the assertion that even in the late 1950s the plantation workforce in northern Peru was composed of free labour, and the admission that it was bonded by planters on a temporary basis for the duration of peak seasonal demand in the agricultural cycle.

56. It should be noted that in some cases this process involved not a shift from migrant to local labour but rather the settling of migrants within the locality, in effect converting it into a local workforce. As will be seen in Chapter 3, this kind of transformation was also taking place during the 1980s in the Indian states of Punjab and Haryana.

57. The politico-ideological domination exercised by creditor-employers over their bonded labourers took a number of forms. One example is the requirement for a bonded labourer to consume his meals in the kitchen, alongside the female members of his creditor-employer's family, and making him carry shopping purchases a respectful two paces behind the creditor-employer, acts whereby a male bonded labourer is symbolically reconstituted as a classificatory female, a subordinate

socio-economic category. Another consists of rousing a bonded labourer from bed at midnight, in order to get him to corroborate a story his irate creditor-employer was recounting to this writer.

58. In eastern Peru *ayni* corresponds to a dyadic relationship involving just two small-holders who agree to work on each other's land over a given period, while *mink'a* refers to a large work party called for a particular day during which many small-holders discharge a day's labour owed to the peasant on whose land the *mink'a* takes place. Both these forms of institutionalized exchange labour are also accompanied by festive drinking and eating, and are therefore frequently theorized as non-monetary but materially reciprocal transactions which characterize the tradi-tional (non-capitalist) Andean peasant economy (see, for example, Alberti and Mayer [1974], Guillet [1980] and Skar [1982]). In La Convención, however, such exchanges were called by capitalist peasants producing cash-crops for the nation-al and international market, and were structured not only by the employment of substitute workers for whom monetary payments were made but also by the social division of labour. For example, middle or poor peasants exchanged their own per-sonal labour-power on such occasions, whereas two rich peasants linked by an *ayni* relation exchanged not their own personal labour-power but that of their workers. Similarly, middle or poor peasants contributed their personal labour to a working group, thereby repaying days of labour owed to its organizer. By contrast, repay-ment of working days owed by a rich peasant took the double form of personal labour together with that of his worker. Bonded labourers who participated in such exchanges, and accompanied and/or discharged the work obligations of their employer, not only received payment from the latter for this participation but also undertook the more difficult agricultural tasks allocated by the peasant organizing the *mink'a*. For a useful account of how these 'traditional' socio-economic forms are used by rich peasants in the Peruvian highlands, see Sánchez [1977; 1982].

59. The availability within the ex-estate system of these different employment oppor-tunities, with correspondingly distinct work conditions, hours of work, levels of remuneration, etc., on the one hand, and on the other the inability of poor peasants and labourers to choose between them, challenges the view expressed by Cotlear [1979: 2, 34ff., 42] that peasants and workers recruited by means of the *enganche* willingly enter such relations due to the lack of alternative employment. Other examples from Peru which similarly undermine this positive theorization by Cotlear include the descriptions of the *enganche* system on the coastal sugar plan-tations at the turn of the century [Gonzales 1980: 298], in the Vilcapampa region of La Convención in 1911 (see above), and in the Mantaro Valley during the 1940s (see Chapter 6).

60. The change in the real value of the daily cash payment received for each unit of labour-power employed on the demesne/cooperative and non-demesne/peasant sector of Pintobamba Grande during the pre-and post-reform periods is indicated by the following table:

Year	Daily Payment	
	Demesne/ Co-operative sector	Non-demesne/peasant sector
	-S/.	S/.
Pre-reform		
1942	13.3[b]	50.0
1962	3.8-5.8[b]	57.7
Post-reform		
1971	61.7	26.6
1975	60.0	25.0

Notes: *a* In 1975 Peruvian Soles; all rates cited refer to the sum received by an adult male worker only, the rates paid to female and child labour being in many cases considerably less. *b* refers to payment for *condición*, the most common variant of labour rent in La Convención. *Source*: Based on data in Brass [1982: 214, Table 3–1].

61. Over the 1973–5 period, the average cost to the co-operative of directly employing a free wage labourer was 91 Soles per day, compared with the equivalent cost of only 50 Soles for each working day of labour-power employed indirectly, or supplied by members who redeployed such workers to the co-operative from their own private holdings [*Brass*, 1982: 678, Table C–8].

3

Bonded Labour in Northwestern India

The focus of this chapter is on the desirability – or otherwise – of unfree relations as seen from the viewpoint of the labouring subjects themselves. Fieldwork data from Punjab in 1983 and Haryana in 1987 not only confirm the central role of debt in conflicts between landholders and their workforce, but suggests further that – as in the case of La Convención in eastern Peru – both permanent and casual labourers are bonded as a result of indebtedness. Debt-servicing labour obligations in northwestern India are enforced by fellow caste members, either informally or through the village *panchayat*, and loans taken by attached or casual workers that remained unpaid due to illness, old age, or death, are also passed on to their domestic kinsfolk who repay such debts with personal labour in fields belonging to the creditor-employer. Agricultural workers expressed a strong dislike of attachment and a corresponding prefer-ence for non-bonded casual employment, citing as reasons the maltreatment of annual servants, their long working hours and low wages.

I

Because the state of Haryana did not have a separate existence from the rest of Punjab until 1966, information concerning both the particular form taken by and the numbers of the workforce employed in agriculture is difficult to dis-aggregate before this date. A comparison of two important texts, by Bhattacharya and by Bhalla, dealing with the social composition of the work-force in the Punjab/Haryana region, demonstrates significant continuities and discontinuities between pre-and post-Independence agrarian labour.

3.1 Pre-Green Revolution Labour Attachment

Over the period 1870–1940, landholders in this area utilized four kinds of labour: that of *sepidars*, peasant smallholders, *siris*, and casual workers.[1] A distinctiveness in terms of their relationships to the means of production notwithstanding, at specific historical points all the latter categories were char-acterized by an element of economic unfreedom, in so far as this entailed the inability of the labouring subject personally to dispose of his labour-power on the open market. The *sepidari* system consisted of caste-specific specialised craftsmen who also undertook agricultural work, and were paid with a share of the crop they harvested. By the 1880s, the *sepidari* system had declined in importance, and was replaced by seasonal labour drawn largely from the kinsfolk of indebted tenants and family farmers. Possessing insufficient land to meet their subsistence needs, these subjects depended increasingly on cash advances received from rich peasants or landlords in order to reproduce their material base. In these circumstances, the control exercised over the subsistence resources (land, loans) of smallholding peasants and their kinsfolk was also a potent form of controlling their labour-power.[2]

The most important form of permanent worker employed in agriculture during the early twentieth century, however, was the *siri*.[3] Its subjects were full-time labourers who worked for rich peasants, and were also recruited through the mechanism of cash advances. Receiving as payment one fifth of the crop harvested, *siris* were required to accept contractually-stipulated terms and conditions of work agreed before a witness who 'symbolized power and authority and could evoke feelings of submission and obedience'. Such labourers were not permitted to leave a creditor-employer without first repaying the whole cash advance together with 50 per cent interest.[4] The growth of a rich peasantry together with the cultivation of labour-intensive crops meant that throughout this period there was a corresponding increase in the demand for seasonal labour. In response to the latter development, casual workers followed the harvest and migrated from the arid southern region of Punjab to the wheat and cotton producing irrigated areas in the centre and north.[5] This kind of seasonal occupation in agriculture was supplemented with earnings from urban employment during the off-peak period in the winter months.

On the question of post-Independence labour attachment in Punjab and Haryana, both the First and Second Agricultural Labour Enquiries (together with other texts) support the contention that at this period it corresponded to an unfree production relation. In the area of Punjab, attached workers were known by the regionally-specific terms of *Siri, Sanjhi, Saipi, Athri, Nokar* or *Kamin, Hissadar* and *Koli*, and allocated by peasant producers to all kinds of agricultural tasks, in particular night-time crop irrigation. They were employed on a contract basis for periods of between one month and a year, and could not leave a creditor-employer without first repaying in full the cash advanced they had received.[6] The Second Enquiry is clear about the reason for rising levels of worker indebtedness: deductions by employers from the wages of attached labourers occasioned shortfalls in basic income, which in turn generated a need for further borrowing from the same source.[7]

3.2 Post-Green Revolution Labour Attachment

More recently, long-term labour attachment as a result of debt has risen to prominence once again in Haryana, where it emerged following the introduction of the new technology associated with the Green Revolution in the early 1970s. A comparison by Bhalla of the three regions in the state indicated that 57 per cent of the total agricultural workforce in the economically most advanced areas centring on Karnal District was composed of annual servants (*salana naukar*), whereas this same category of labour accounted for only 30 and nine per cent respectively of the workforce in the two less irrigated areas consisting of Rohtak and Hissar Districts on the one hand and the arid region bordering Rajasthan on the other.[8] Labour contracts of annual servants employed in Karnal District at this period were not only of longer overall duration (three to five years) than those of sharecroppers (*sanjhis*) but also incorporated both a formalised witness system and an interest-free cash advance. Those called upon to guarantee (and, significantly, enforce) such contracts included rich peasants, shopkeepers, and what Bhalla refers to as 'modern institutional leaders': the village *sarpanch* and the *pradhan* of the Cooperative.[9]

Of particular interest from the view of free/unfree nature of these labour relations was the accompanying (and inbuilt character of) indebtedness, and on the one hand the way this constructed and regulated the economic activity of its subjects in the workplace, and on the other the constraints it imposed on their entry into and operation within the labour market. Accordingly, an important consequence of payment based on cash advances was the reproduction and consolidation of worker indebtedness. Since the cash advance made to an attached labourer in June amounted to only four to five month's wages, it was necessary for him to borrow interest-bearing consumption loans from his creditor-employer in order to cover the remaining one-and-a-half to two-and-a-half month-period before he received the next payment (in mid-January on *Lohri* day). This diminished the wage component and increased the loan element contained in the next cash advance, thereby inaugurating a cycle of accumulating debt-servicing labour obligations over the succeeding years. The only way any outstanding loan might be repaid in such circumstances was by means of a cash advance taken from another landholder, to whom the labourer became attached as a result.[10]

3.3 Attached Labour and Agricultural Commercialization

What emerges clearly from the texts of both Bhattacharya and Bhalla is the historical link in the Punjab/Haryana region between on the one hand the increased commercialization of or capitalist development in agriculture, absolute and relative shortages of labour, and the enhanced bargaining power of rural workers, and on the other the extension and intensification of permanent forms of unfree labour subordinated/controlled by the debt bondage system. In short, the centrality of the latter mechanism (together with its socio-economic apparatus of enforcement) to the process of class struggle between labour and capital.

Bhattacharya shows how in the earlier period the employment of the two principal modes of attached labour was a result of the expansion in labour-intensive cash-cropping by an emerging rich peasantry. From the late 1870s until the capitalist crisis of the 1920s, relations between landholders and both *sepidars* and *siris* were characterized by the utilization of debt as a means of controlling the mobility and bargaining capacity of labour, work boycotts, strikes, together with demands for higher payments in cash and kind, the form and level taken by the latter being determined in this process of struggle.[11]

Bhalla notes a similar increase in the incidence of unfree permanent labour in the Green Revolution areas of Haryana during the early 1970s, where it was a response by capitalist farmers to the rising demand for workers on the one hand, and thus to the improved bargaining position of rural labour on the other.[12] Both these historically-specific instances suggest that the periodic upturns in the accumulation cycle were in this particular context also accompanied by a rising incidence of bonded labour, together with an acute process of struggle over the work conditions and remuneration levels received by (or imposed on) its subjects.

II

The development of a capitalist agriculture in the northwestern Indian state of Punjab following the implementation of the Green Revolution (in the form of access to HYVs, irrigation, marketing and transportation facilities, state-sponsored credit schemes, etc.) is well documented.[13] During the early 1980s, 83 per cent of Punjab was cultivated, compared with the All-India figure of 47 per cent.[14] Similarly, 85 per cent of the sown area in Punjab at this period was irrigated, as against only 27 per cent in All-India; and while the All-India cropping intensity amounted to 119 per cent, the equivalent figure for Punjab was 156 per cent.[15] The total farm labour requirement had increased correspondingly, by some 79 per cent between the mid-1960s and the early 1970s.[16]

3.4 Capitalism, Unfree Labor and Migration in Punjab

A consequence of this transformation in the structure of agricultural production, together with the changes in the division of labour which accompanied economic growth in Punjab from the mid-1970s onwards, was that the labour shortage of the first phase of the Green revolution became even more acute in the second phase.[17] Thus a relative decline in capital-intensive wheat production and a corresponding increase in the output of profitable but highly labour intensive paddy was only one aspect of a general shift to more intensive cropping patterns which entailed a decrease in the amount of slack period in the agricultural cycle. Since irrigation (unlike mechanization) increases labour requirements in agriculture, the profitability of capital investment by Punjabi farmers was determined at this conjuncture by their capacity both to recruit sufficient labour and to maintain control over this resource.[18] A shift to non-farming occupations had simultaneously deprived the agrarian sector of its local workforce as, on the one hand, jat Sikh family members withdrew from on-farm manual labour and, on the other, scheduled caste workers emigrated to better-paid occupations in the Gulf States.[19]

Factors such as scheduled caste outmigration, the shift to non-farming occupations, the extension of paddy cultivation and higher urban wages, all of which combined to intensify labour shortages in Punjab, also strengthened the bargaining power of local farm workers who remained. Hence the rise in the real level of farm wages, together with the fact that between the late 1950s and the late 1970s there was a fourfold increase in the average annual membership of the Punjab Agricultural Workers Union (*Punjab Khet Mazdur Sabha*).[20] The response of peasant farmers in Punjab was to replace this relatively costly and increasingly politicized local workforce with cheap migrants from Bihar and Uttar Pradesh.[21] The intensity of the competition between peasant farmers for labour may be gauged from a phenomenon known as 'forcible capture', a twofold form of coerced indebtedness (and subsequent bondage) which during the early 1980s was initiated in Ludhiana railway station in Punjab throughout the first two weeks of April, when between 1,000 and 2,000 migrant labourers arrived by train each night from eastern India.[22]

In the first (or direct) form, labour contractors recruited tribals from villages in north Bihar and transported them in groups of 20–100 by train to Punjab, where they were sold to Jat Sikh farmers waiting in the station at rates of Rs 300–400 each.[23] This sum was regarded by the employer as a debt contracted by the tribal, and the latter was accordingly compelled to work for two to three months without pay. After the expiry of this initial period of unpaid labour, a monthly wage rate of Rs 60–80 was fixed by the farmer, but actual payment was frequently withheld.[24] The delay in payment of wages not only amounted in the long term to non-payment but also ensured that a labourer thus deprived became increasingly dependent on the employer for his subsistence, in the process losing his freedom to re-enter the market both as a consumer and a worker. This in turn enabled the employer to make further deductions from the notional 'wage', thereby denying the labourer a capacity to save sufficient money to break out from the employer's economic control.

The second (or indirect) form arose in situations where ticket collectors and railway police deprived migrants arriving at Ludhiana station of their tickets before they reached the exit gates, and then detained them for not possessing a ticket.[25] If migrants had money, they were able to purchase their freedom at this point; if, as was more usually the case, they did not, one of the many farmers waiting at the station entrance offered to pay the required sum on behalf of the arrested migrant, and thus secured the labour-power of the individual concerned. As in the first form of induced debt, the migrant labourer was compelled to cancel the loan (or advance) with unpaid labour.[26]

3.5 Bonded labour and Capitalist Restructuring in Punjab

Fieldwork in Punjab during 1983 suggests that at this conjuncture the debt bondage mechanism played a significant and multifaceted role in the attempt by large capitalist farmers (operating between 20 and 500 acres of irrigated land) to solve the problems of labour availability and cost, and the corresponding absence of control over their own labour process.[27] It suggests further that bonded labour was to be found not only among local workers but also among migrants at all the different points in the migratory process: that is, unfreedom arose as a result of being indebted variously to employers in Punjab, to labour contractors from Punjab and Bihar, and to moneylenders in Bihar. As in the case of La Convención considered in the previous chapter, therefore, an increased demand for labour had in this particular instance been met not by free wage labour but rather by recourse to an unfree workforce.

The process of workforce recomposition on large capitalist farms was evident from the fact that migrants (*bhaiya*, literally 'brother', but possessing a derogatory connotation of 'labourer' when used by Jat Sikh farmers) from Bihar and Uttar Pradesh were replacing scheduled caste locals as permanent or attached workers (*siri*) who traditionally worked on an annual basis for a single employer.[28] The workload for this component had increased, while payments in cash (and kind) had begun to decrease in real terms. There had been a similar decline in the employment of locals as seasonal or casual farm labour (*dehadi*, literally 'daily wage') for harvesting and paddy transplantation, these subjects being compelled to accept lower wages, or else displacement, by cheaper migrant workers. Within the local component itself, females were replacing males as agricultural labour.

In the context of competition for workers, debt bondage was increasingly the principal method whereby large capitalist farmers in Punjab held both permanent and seasonal labour on-farm cheaply; that is, in a situation where free market wage levels would otherwise have tended to rise. In the case of migrants who settled in the state on a permanent basis, this bonding process took three forms.

The first was made possible because although the migrant workers themselves settled permanently in Punjab, their kinsfolk remained in the village of origin as sureties/'hostages' for debts incurred there.[29] In order to cancel the latter, migrants who settled on a permanent basis took cash advances from their employers in Punjab, thereby transferring the locus (and the institutional apparatus) of debt bondage from Bihar or Uttar Pradesh to Punjab.[30]

The second form derived from the fact that permanently settled migrants who worked for a single employer for nine to ten months of the year were nevertheless faced with two or three months of slack season annually, when no wages were paid. This necessitated recourse to the employer for loans that were then cancelled with unpaid work at a lower 'wage' rate during the following peak season.[31] A consequence of this procedure was that migrants who remained permanently in Punjab were then required to take further advances subsequently, thus initiating and reproducing a cycle of debt servicing labour.[32]

The third form consisted of partial access to the labour market in Punjab, but always under the control of the employer and always at his convenience.[33] This occurred when, for example, crop prices fell, a situation in which the creditor-employer might permit a bonded labourer to seek alternative employment. Such limited access to the labour market was nevertheless strictly conditional on the repayment by the worker concerned of any outstanding debt owed to the original creditor-employer, a condition which required the worker to obtain a large cash advance from (and thus become indebted to) his next employer, in effect transferring the debt bondage relation from one peasant farmer to another. It is important to note that this transaction (= 'changing masters') corresponds not to the purchase of labour-power by a capitalist producer from the worker in person but much rather to the purchase of the labourer's debt by one proprietor from another.

Migrants and locals who worked as seasonal or casual farm labour, from the period of wheat harvesting until paddy transplantation, were similarly enmeshed by the debt bondage system.[34] Although receiving smaller loans than migrants settled permanently in Punjab, seasonal migrants who returned to Bihar or Uttar Pradesh each year after the harvest also received cash advances from employers (or labour contractors) to cover the cost of travelling, illness, etc. Such loans committed a recipient to return and work for the same employer again the following year in order to cancel the debt. Before the harvest period began, local female labourers who continued to work in agriculture on a seasonal or casual basis also took cash advances from their employers. The latter made it clear that the intention behind the offer of this advance, and a condition governing its receipt, was that these female workers were as a result not free either to seek alternative employment with or accept offers of better-paid work from other peasant farmers during the harvest period.[35]

As with the majority of permanent locals and permanently settled migrants, there were instances of employers themselves recruiting and dealing directly with the non-permanent components of their workforce. In such cases, control was exercised directly by the employer, who personally enforced the debt obligations incurred by his workers.[36] More commonly, seasonal locals and seasonal migrants worked in groups organized and supervised by a gang leader or labour contractor who had borrowed money from a farmer in Punjab and recruited on his behalf. Loans for travelling, subsistence, etc., were advanced to seasonal workers who became indebted to the labour contractor or gang leader, and through the latter to a particular employer in Punjab. As in the case of La Convención, Peru, recruitment of both local and seasonal migrants for work in Punjab was effected on the basis of family links with a labour contractor or gang leader, and labour service obligations incurred as a result of debt were enforced indirectly, through affinal and/or consanguineal kin networks. In these ways permanent and seasonal migrants, many of whom entered the labour market as free workers, were transformed into unfree labour.

III

During 1987 fieldwork was carried out in five village locations in Haryana state: two in Karnal District and three in Rohtak District.[37] In terms of population increase and social composition over the period 1971/81, the fieldwork villages broadly reflect the patterns of their respective districts.

3.6 Village A, Karnal District, Haryana

Shortages of labour, both absolute and relative, were identified by the land-holders of this village as one of the foremost problems they faced. Farmers generally complained that it was difficult to hire local workers at sufficiently cheap wage rates during the period of peak activity in the production cycle. Attached labour was particularly difficult to obtain, because workers preferred urban employment on construction sites at the nearby power station, at the local petrol refinery, and in the town itself. All these enterprises, farmers argued, competed for workers that would otherwise be available to them as attached labour.

There were more than two hundred and fifty attached labourers employed in this village, the only form being the landless annual servant (*salana naukar*).[38] The yearly contract between labourer and farmer was signed in the presence of a reputable person from the village at the beginning of each June, when the whole yearly payment of Rs 4000 was also received in the form of a cash advance.[39] During the course of the year, the attached labourer borrowed further sums from his creditor-employer, up to a total of Rs 1,000; this amount was then deducted from the cash advance he received in the following June. As long as this cash advance, or any other form of loan, remained unpaid, an attached labourer was not permitted to sell his own labour-power to other landholders; even the local labour court, it was pointed out, would sometimes find against him in such circumstances.[40] The only way in which an annual servant could change employment was to repay his present creditor-employer by obtaining a cash advance on future wages from another landholder.

In the majority of cases, farmers declared, there were no disputes with attached labourers.[41] Those disagreements which occurred arose as a consequence of attempts by indebted workers to leave the employ of a landholder without first repaying loans they owed him. Such conflict was resolved by, in the words of one farmer, 'bringing in important people' from the village: the *panchayat* was convened, the issue was discussed, and a binding judgement made.[42] The potency of this kind of social pressure, landholders observed, derived from the presence on the *panchayat* of scheduled caste members; it was necessary to rely on the *panchayat* to enforce labour attachment rather than have recourse to the labour court, farmers added, because the latter institution occasionally decided in favour of the worker.[43]

The dependence of labour attachment on this system of enforcement suggests the existence of a fundamental antipathy on the part of the village workforce to such relationships, and indeed *all* the casual labourers interviewed expressed a strong dislike for employment as attached labour. Reasons given for this view stressed the much harder work intensity and schedule imposed on annual servants, together with the consequent inability of the latter to tend (and hence to own) livestock.[44] Significantly, casual workers compared labour attachment as a form of incorporation into the family of the creditor-employer; that such a prospect was perceived negatively was evident from the opinion uttered by one labourer that 'it is better to ask for alms [i.e. to beg] than to be an attached labourer'.[45] Only through the compulsion of debt, it was repeatedly emphasized, would a casual worker become a permanent attached labourer.

With regard to the process of labour recruitment, locals were approached by landholders on the day before they were actually needed, and then engaged for a whole month's work. This transaction generally involved the receipt at this stage of a non-formalized cash advance (as distinct from the formalized payment made to an attached labourer) from the monthly wage of Rs 600, the balance of which was usually paid when the period of employment had finished. Those who took cash advances in this manner were required to work not only for this particular creditor-employer (and no other) throughout the peak agricultural season but also at a lower daily wage rate (Rs 15 instead of Rs 20).[46] Local casual workers complained that contract labour for village landholders frequently entailed spending time travelling long distances to and from the work location, covering more than the contractually-stipulated acre of land, and completing unpaid overtime.

During the off-peak season, when no employment was available in agriculture, local casual labourers either tended their own livestock, worked in the town or at the nearby power station, or took loans from village landholders and shopkeepers.[47] Unlike borrowing specifically for consumption purposes, the more substantial loans taken by casual workers for marriage, illness, or emergencies, were not only formalised but carried an annual interest rate of twelve per cent.[48] In cases where repayment of the principal was not possible within the stipulated time limit, an indebted casual labourer either borrowed money from another landholder in the village so as to pay back the first creditor or else became the attached worker of the farmer who made the loan. If the amount owed remained unpaid due to the death or illness of the debtor, his wife and/or children were required to cancel the outstanding sum by working in the fields belonging to the creditor-employer.

For the past five years, landholders in this village had been engaged in acute conflict with agricultural labour over levels of payment and conditions of work. In the course of this struggle, casual labourers had not only agitated for higher wages (their principal demand) but also mobilized collectively in order to prevent any of their number accepting lower wages. All five of the agricultural labouring castes (Ziwars, Chamars, Balmiki, Kumhar and Badi) had combined to elect two representatives each, and the latter had then selected a *pradhan* to formulate policy and decide on tactics in their confrontation with the village landholders.

The response by peasant farmers to this show of worker militancy had been fourfold.[49] First, individual landholders approached individual labourers and offered to pay them higher wages so long as no other cultivator in the village was informed of this fact. Second and third, farmers threatened both to deny livestock-owning workers access to fodder for their animals and to recall any outstanding loans or cash advances made to labourers generally. And fourth, the big landholders of the village began recruiting migrants with the object of undermining the wage bargaining position established by local casual workers.[50] The latter subjects attempted to warn off migrants from coming to this village in search of work, and emphasized that to proceed with this would amount to strike-breaking; however, the blockade was broken by the land-holders themselves, who travelled to regional urban centres in order to recruit migrants directly, and then escorted them back to the village workplace. Had these migrants not come, local casual workers observed, wages would now be much higher.

3.7 Village B, Karnal District, Haryana

Around 100 landless attached labourers were employed by the landholders of this village on a permanent basis as annual servants, and their number had been gradually increasing during the recent past. For seasonal labour require-ments, large landholders utilised local workers, and a few also employed migrants. All landholders complained of labour shortages, particularly at peak seasonal periods in the agricultural cycle; with the arrival of the rains, one farmer noted, every landholder began to sow paddy simultaneously, and consequently labour was at a premium.

In this village an annual servant was still called a *hali*, literally 'a plough-man', despite the fact that such workers now drove tractors. Attached labourers also participated in wheat sowing, and operated the combine during the wheat and paddy harvests. In addition to the Rs 4,000–5,000 per annum, paid in a lump sum on 1 June, these workers also took loans of Rs 2,000; when the annual contract was renewed, any accumulated debt (that is, whatever had been borrowed from the employer during the preceding 12 months) was deducted from the cash advance received at this stage. Over succeeding agricultural cycles, therefore, the actual wage component of the money received from an employer was displaced by formal loans; it was impossible to change masters without first clearing this debt, a situation which required an annual servant to borrow from another landholder in order to repay the present creditor-employer.[51]

Landless labourers in this village preferred casual employment for a number of reasons, the most important being the higher wage obtained during the peak demand period in agriculture by those able to bargain with employers over the price of their labour-power. Incessant verbal (and sometimes physical) abuse was another reason cited by labourers for rejecting attached labour relationships.[52] Yet another was the length of the working day; one of the worst aspects of being an attached labourer, they pointed out, was having to be available for all kinds of work throughout the whole 24-hour period.[53] Although the wages paid to annual servants had increased, workers still refused to enter attached labour relationships voluntarily; in all instances, the sole cause of attachment was debt.

Casual labourers found employment in agriculture for six months of the year. During the remaining period of unemployment, propertyless workers borrowed cash or kind from the landowning *khatri* caste.[54] Though these periodic consumption loans involved petty amounts, usually in the range of Rs 25–100, over time such debt tended to accumulate, and repayment progressed along a specific trajectory. Initially, therefore, it entailed the common practice of borrowing from one landholder in order to pay back another, a system of circulating debt which remained feasible only as long as the level of debt stayed low.

When it rose beyond levels that permitted reborrowing (Rs 1,500–2,000), an indebted casual labourer was required to work for the last creditor on a beck-and-call basis; this restricted the freedom of the subject concerned to sell labour-power during the peak season in the agricultural cycle, but – unlike attachment – it did not include continuous work in the domestic context of a creditor-employer. The indebted casual labourer's wage was adjusted against the sum owed, and he received the same daily wage as a non-indebted hired labourer; whereas the latter worked for the the normal eight-hour day, however, the former was required to complete a much longer working day in the fields.[55]

The final stage in the trajectory of debt repayment was reached when the amount of money owed compelled a casual labourer to enter full-time attachment, thereby not only undertaking domestic as well as agricultural work on behalf of his creditor-employer but also diminishing the possibility of debt repayment. When either an annual servant or a casual labourer died or became incapacitated without first having cleared his debts, these were transferred to his son, even if the latter had formed an economically independent household unit within the village.

3.8 Village C, Rohtak District, Haryana

Landholders complained of high labour costs in general, and in particular of labour shortages during the period of peak seasonal demand (April to May and from October to November), attributing this specifically to alternative and better-paid employment opportunities available in the locally-situated brick kilns and the nearby town.[56] No migrants came to work in this village, compounding the already acute seasonal labour scarcity. An annual servant, the permanent form of landless agricultural labour in this village, was paid yearly the sum of Rs 4,800 plus meals.[57] Half his total annual wage was taken as a cash advance at the end of June, when contracts were renewed.

Local casual labourers obtained four to five months employment annually in agriculture, and were paid at the rate of Rs 20 a day. For the remaining seven to eight months those who did not own income-generating milch buffaloes worked either in the local brick kilns or on urban construction sites, or else took consumption loans.[58] The most common determinant of worker indebtedness in this village, however, was expenditure necessitated by marriage and other ceremonial activities.[59] Casual landless labourers who owned livestock repaid such debts with money obtained from the sale of milk, whereas propertyless workers attempted to save from their off-farm earnings. The annual rate of interest on these loans amounted to 24 per cent, and repayment of the whole sum was required within a seven to eight month period. Propertyless labourers unable to meet this schedule borrowed from other landholders at a higher rate of interest, and then repaid the first creditor; becoming an attached labourer was regarded as the final resort, when this form of circulating debt increased to the extent where a landholder imposed attachment as a condition of lending money.

During the peak agricultural season all casual labourers who owed debts to a landholder, but were nevertheless not yet attached to him on a permanent basis, were not permitted to seek alternative employment, either in agriculture, in the brick kilns, or in town. Servicing debts in this manner entailed both a longer working day in the fields of the creditor-employer and lower wages.[60] When a casual labourer died, any outstanding loans were automatically passed on to his son; asked what was to prevent the latter subject from disowning such debt, particularly in cases where a separate household (and therefore work patterns and socio-economic obligations) had already been established, agricultural labourers responded that by virtue of being a resident in the same village a son would have no alternative but to meet debts incurred by his father, even if this involved him personally having to work in the fields of the creditor. Where necessary, they added, pressure would be applied by the village *panchayat* in order to enforce the repayment of such loans.

The ownership by landless agricultural labourers of income-generating milch buffaloes, together with alternative non-agricultural employment, enabled agricultural labourers both to bargain with peasant farmers over wage levels and to avoid total dependence on consumption loans in order to survive the long period of seasonal unemployment. Notwithstanding the claim by the village *sarpanch* that no bondage was to be found in this village, it is clear from the information provided by workers that it did indeed exist. Those who identified themselves as free agricultural labourers (*mazdoori*) took loans for ceremonial or consumption purposes became unfree during the period of peak seasonal demand, thereby having to work longer hours at lower wages for a particular creditor-employer. If such loans taken by free workers remained unpaid, they became intergenerational, sons being pressured by the *panchayat* to honour debts incurred by their father even when economically independent of the latter. Bondage based on the phenomenon of 'changing masters' also occurred, since one way to postpone debt repayment for propertyless labourers was to borrow at a higher interest rate from one peasant farmer so as to repay another, earlier creditor; as in the case of village *B* in Karnal District, at some stage this cycle of borrowing-repayment became economically impossible, the amount owed being too high, and the debtor was as a result compelled to become an attached labourer.

3.9 Village D, Rohtak District, Haryana

In this village attached labour took two forms: landless annual servants and sharecropping tenants. The former variant was the more common relationship, there being some one hundred annual servants for the village as a whole. Locals employed permanently as sharecropping tenants were paid Rs 4,000 plus 3.6 quintals of wheat annually. All casual labourers interviewed preferred daily wage work to permanent employment; reasons given for not liking attachment included the low payment received by this type of labourer, having to do odd jobs and all types of work, being continuously abused by the employer, and having to remain constantly on call in the house of the latter for the full 24 hours.[61] If a *sahji* or a *naukar* fell ill and consequently became unavailable for work, a member of his household or kin group was required to act as a replacement.[62]

Employers complained about rising wage costs, and since 1977 – when production increased following the installation of irrigation facilities – large landholders had been recruiting migrants from Uttar Pradesh for work during the peak agricultural season. Local labourers expressed anger at this development, and pointed out that their own wages would now be higher if the migrants had not come. Although work boycotts had been attempted, these failed because on the one hand landholders united and collectively labourered in their own fields and on the other they prevented livestock-owning workers who were on strike from collecting fodder for their animals.

Landless casual labourers resident in the village worked for three months annually in agriculture and five months in the nearby town (on construction sites or as rickshaw pullers). During the remaining three to four months months of the year, they either tended their employers' cattle, sold milk produced by their own livestock, or took consumption loans in kind from an employer. Indebtedness was widespread among the landless population of the village, and derived mainly from loans of Rs 2,000–5,000 taken for marriage and ceremonial purposes; the annual interest on these debts amounted to 36 per cent. The principal was repaid in cash and the interest in labour, the latter in two forms: working in the creditor's fields and looking after his cattle in the debtor's own house. As long as such loans remained unpaid, it was necessary for indebted casual labourers to obtain permission from their creditor-employer before seeking alternative employment, particularly during the peak season. Similarly, when a casual labourer died, any outstanding debt was passed on to his wife and children, who had to cancel it by working personally in the fields of the creditor-employer. Wages were fixed by the landholder, there being no difference between the payment received by an indebted and a debt-free worker.

Keenly aware of the economic disadvantages of becoming indebted to a landholder, casual labourers observed that attempts to reduce the cost of marriage and other ceremonial expenditure were negated by rising price levels. They also pointed out that large farmers had appropriated *panchayat* lands, thereby depriving them of the only area on which to graze their livestock. This in turn cut down their ability to generate earnings from the sale of milk during the period of agricultural unemployment, a crucial source of income which enabled them to avoid indebtedness and therefore bondage.

3.10 *Village E, Rohtak District, Haryana*

Since this village consisted principally of small peasants who utilised family labour, few of the landless were employed as attached workers, no migrants were recruited, and the most common form of production relation was casual day labour. Subjects of the latter obtained work in agriculture for three to four months a year; in spite of dissatisfaction with the existing low wage rate, casual labourers had not agitated for higher payment because of the fear that peasant proprietors would deny them access to fodder with which to feed the livestock they owned.

For the remaining eight to nine months of the year, when no agricultural work was available, landless casual workers took loans from peasants, repayable at an annual interest rate of 24 per cent. As long as such debts remained unpaid, casual labourers were free to seek other agricultural work during the peak season or alternative local employment only if not required to work in the fields of their creditor-employer. Although receiving the same daily payment as non-indebted labourers hired by the latter, they nevertheless had to work for an extra two hours a day. In the event of sickness or death, any outstanding debt owed by a casual labourer was automatically passed on to his son.

When questioned about the desirability of long-term attachment to a single creditor-employer, casual labourers in this village (as in all the others) indicated a strong preference for daily wage work, and emphatically rejected attached labour because of the low wages paid to the subjects of these relations. The annual income of Rs 1,080–1,440 earned by a casual worker from just three to four months' employment in agriculture exceeded by some one hundred per cent the low annual payment of Rs 600–720 made to the few attached labourers in the village. Even if offered usufruct rights to land as part of the arrangement, casual workers stressed they would not voluntarily enter attached labour relationships.

3.11 Conclusion

It is clear that, historically and contemporaneously, there is a link between various forms of unfree relation and the commercialization of agricultural production in northwestern India. Over the 1970s and 1980s, unfreedom has been a central component in the struggle between landholders and agricultural workers in Punjab and Haryana. In a context where alternative and better-paid employment is available, and labourers are as a result capable of sustaining their unwillingness to enter attachment at any price, landholders have not only to make labour-power available but also to make it available cheaply. Both these objectives are realized through the operation of the debt bondage mechanism, which constricts or eliminates the free movement of labour in the market. It therefore deprives the subjects of these relations of the ability to sell their own labour-power to the highest-paying purchaser, thereby preventing them from acting as a proletariat, and simultaneously making them even more dependent on landholders for subsistence provision in the form of loans or cash advances.

Rather than encouraging the development of free wage labour, therefore, competition between agrarian capitalists in Punjab during the early 1980s led to the consolidation of unfree production relations. This took place in a wider context of workforce recomposition, a process whereby migrant workers not only replaced locals but were themselves transformed into bonded labour. Rural migrants who settled permanently in Punjab became unfree as a result of having to borrow from their employers during the off-peak season, while those who managed to re-enter the labour market did so not by selling their labour-power but by borrowing from – and thus transferring their indebtedness to – another creditor-employer. In the case of non-permanent migrant and local workers, borrowing also resulted in unfreedom, albeit confined to the peak period of the agricultural cycle. Debt-servicing labour obligations incurred by migrants and locals in Punjab were enforced by employers and/or contractors by means of pressure exercised through kin networks.

Much the same was true of agrarian relations in Haryana during the late 1980s. On a number of fundamental socio-economic indicators, differences existed not only between fieldwork villages in Karnal and Rohtak Districts, but also within each of the latter. Hence the developed agriculture of the Karnal villages provided labourers with more than six months employment annually, compared with less than five months in the Rohtak villages. By contrast, with regard to such aspects as the presence/absence of sharecropping relations, together with wage rates paid to and hours worked by indebted casual workers, divergencies occurred on an inter-village basis. Thus share tenancy was found in villages of both Karnal and Rohtak districts. Similarly, indebted casual labourers worked for lower wages but the same hours as their non-indebted counterparts in one of the Karnal villages but not the other, and also in two out of the three Rohtak villages; the pattern was reversed in one Karnal village and two Rohtak villages, where indebted casual labourers received the same pay as non-indebted subjects but worked for longer hours.

All the Haryana villages, however, exhibited a marked uniformity with regard to the socio-economic characteristics signalling the presence, enforcement, and dislike of unfree labour relationships. Accordingly, not only were interest-bearing loans incurred by both permanent attached and casual workers for subsistence and/or ceremonial purposes, but these were repaid to a creditor-employer in the form of debt-servicing labour contributions, the subjects of which forwent the right to sell their own labour-power so long as cash or kind loans remained unpaid. Any undischarged debts left when an attached or casual labourer died, or was unable to continue working due to illness or old age, were automatically inherited by his domestic kinsfolk, a liability which committed the latter to clearing such loans with personal labour in the fields of the creditor-employer (the existence of already-established prior socio-economic obligations notwithstanding). The methods of enforcing these debt-servicing labour-obligations were in all cases the same: pre-emptive socio-economic pressure was exerted on an actual (or potential) defaulter, either by fellow caste members generally, or by two or three of the latter in their formal capacity as *panchayat* officers. This system of compulsion was itself necessitated by the strong dislike of attachment on the part of both the subjects of this relation and casual workers.

Notwithstanding the clear difference between the villages in Karnal and Rohtak as regards the percentage of landless agricultural workers in the population, landholders in each district nevertheless complained about shortages of both kinds of labour. Initially, this points to the existence in these contexts of on the one hand a scarcity of labour throughout the whole year (and hence the unmet need for attached workers), and on the other a period-specific labour shortage confined to particular moments in the annual cycle (and thus the demand also for casual workers). However, it was clear from the nature of the utterances by both landholders and labourers on this point that the fundamental issue was not so much the absolute shortage (or non-existence) of agricultural workers as such, but much rather the unavailability of existing labour-power.

The frequent complaints about rising labour costs and the difficulty of obtaining local workers cheaply for either long-term attachment or casual/seasonal employment identified the reasons for this shortage as perceived by landholders themselves: not the absence of labour *per se*, but the fact that (actual or potential) subjects of these relations chose to work either for other landholders, who paid higher wages, or in towns and brick-kilns. Significantly, landholders in Haryana expressed their preference for migrants over locals not only in terms of harder work for lower wages but because the former were regarded as more 'reliable' and 'loyal' since they did not 'move to other farmers'. In this politico-ideological discourse, therefore, the application by landholders of the concept 'unreliable' to local workers means nothing other than a willingness on the part of the latter 'to go wherever payment is highest': that is, in a context where a demand for (and competition over) labour-power exists, its subjects sell this commodity to the highest bidder.

By contrast, the politico-ideological view of agricultural labourers themselves concerning employer/employee relations constituted a mirror image of – yet simultaneously confirmed and complemented – that projected by landholders. What the latter regarded as evidence of workforce insubordination, therefore, local workers experienced (and articulated) as resistance to the imposition of unacceptable current pay rates and/or conditions of employment. Against the views attributed to them in texts by – among others – Rudra, Bardhan, and Breman (see Chapter 7), attached labour in Haryana was regarded by its subjects as neither a desirable and much sought-after form of 'subsistence guarantee' or 'employment insurance' nor as a mutually beneficial solution to problems of 'risk' and 'uncertainty'. In none of the fieldwork villages, therefore, did agricultural workers choose either to enter or to remain in these long-term unfree relationships.

To begin with, the fact that only through debt would a free labourer become an annual servant underlines the coercive inception of attachment. Furthermore, in all the fieldwork villages in Haryana casual workers expressed a strong antipathy towards attached labour relationships, both on politico-ideological grounds (the combination of agricultural and domestic labour, continuous verbal – and sometimes physical – abuse from the creditor-employer) and for economic reasons (the low overall wage, the intensity of the workload involved, the prolonged duration of daily labour, the beck-and-call nature of the relation, and the consequent inability to tend their own cattle). The strength of this feeling on the part of landless workers was amply demonstrated by their emphatic rejection of labour attachment, even were it to be accompanied by usufruct rights to land.

In addition to contestation on the terrain of meaning, class struggle between landholders and agricultural labourers in the Haryana fieldwork villages also involved specific and countervailing forms of political action. Accordingly, local casual labourers not only resisted work conditions and payment levels imposed by landholders, sought out the best-remunerated agricultural and non-agricultural employment, and attempted to establish a minimal level of economic autonomy through income generated from live-stock ownership, but also engaged in worker organization and mobilization that culminated in the withdrawal of labour (boycotts, strikes, picketing the village workplace against migrants). In short, they both exhibited the characteristics of and operated as a rural proletariat. The response by land-holders to this worker resistance and miltancy took the multiple form of recruiting migrant labour, the threat to recall outstanding loans or cash advances, and the prevention of access to fodder for cattle.

This conflict also highlighted the dual yet contradictory role of livestock ownership by agricultural workers: on the one hand it enabled them either to avoid or else to repay debts (thus preventing bondage), while on the other it required those who owned cattle either to enforce the debt-servicing labour obligations of propertyless attached and casual workers or to break their political solidarity so as to retain access to fodder resources. Since in relative terms they constituted the most powerful economic and political elements among the landless rural workforce, livestock-owning labourers were not only vulnerable to threats from landholders regarding fodder resources on which their own animals depended, but were also in a position to exert effective sanctions against propertyless workers of the same caste concerning the fulfilment of debt-servicing labour obligations owed to village landholders.

The village *panchayat* in Haryana continued to discharge a crucial role in this struggle between landholders and agricultural labourers, specifically with regard to the enforcement of bondage, although a fundamental shift appears to have occurred in the identity of the class subject exercising pressure from within its context. As the study by Bhalla indicates, during the early 1970s debt-servicing labour obligations incurred by permanent components of the agrarian workforce in Haryana were enforced directly by the creditors them-selves (landholders, shopkeepers, moneylenders, etc.). During 1987, however, this kind of social pressure was exercised both indirectly and by a different class subject: through landless (but, significantly, livestock-owning) workers belonging to the same caste as the labourer concerned. In so far as it mystified (and therefore to some extent defused the antagonisms arising from) the socio-economic origins, interests and object of debt enforcement, this downward shift in the class position of the enforcing subject(s) permitted a landholder to exercise more effective control over labour-power in the workplace itself. This corresponds to a process whereby conflict between capital and labour was relocated in structural terms, and – in politico-ideological terms – became instead a conflict within the domain of (and thus between) kinsfolk and/or caste members. In short, it entails a politico-ideological transformation, both in the kind and hence the idiom of authority exercised over labour-power, thereby contributing to the overall effectiveness of the economic class struggle waged by agrarian capitalists.

NOTES

1. See Bhattacharya [1985: 105ff.].
2. Rather than being regarded as peasant proprietors (in so far as this involves a certain element of control over the means of production), such small family farmers are more accurately theorized as a workforce trapped in the debt cycle premissed on the forward buying of their standing crops by rich peasants or merchants to whom they owe money. Although not formally separated from their means of labour, the land cultivated by these smallholders is in fact controlled by the creditor. Bhattacharya [1985:121] rightly makes the distinction between capital advanced for the purpose of obtaining money interest, which does not require its possessor to control the labour process owned and worked by nominally independent peasant proprietors, and capital advanced by a rich peasant for the purpose of generating surplus-value extracted from unfree workers (peasant family members, *siris*, etc.) employed in his own labour process.
3. For details of the *siri* relation, which in some areas of Punjab was known as *sajji* (or *sanjhi*), see Bhattacharya [1985: 124–27]. In the course of post-Independence capitalist development in the Punjab/Haryana region, the pre-existing historical link between sharecropping and unfree labour has undergone a radical transformation. Whereas in the pre-Independence era the subjects of cropsharing relations, such as *siri* or *sanjhi*, were not allowed to work for anyone else without first obtaining the permission of a creditor-employed to whom they owed debts, a consequence of the decline in sharecropping following the Green Revolution has been that 'much of pure tenancy has been driven underground ... and re-emerged in the form which does not qualify as tenancy at all. This metamorphosis has been much more common in [Karnal District], the Prime Green Revolution area, than elsewhere' [*Bhalla, 1977:* A-11]. Accordingly, an outcome in Haryana of on the one hand fears concerning tenancy legislation, and on the other the increased profitability of direct cultivation was that sharecroppers either became the object of tenancy switching or were deprived of usufruct rights altogether, as both large and small landholders resumed direct cultivation of their property in response to the new inputs provided by the Green Revolution. Where leasing-out has continued, moreover, it has been not so much on a product share basis to poor peasants or landless workers but much rather on a cash-rent basis to rich peasants and capitalist farmers seeking to expand their operations and/or fully utilize their machinery. An exception to this process is noted by Bhalla [1983: 835–6]. '[T]he big landowners who lease out land', she writes,
   generally do not give land on rent for straightforward economic reasons. Most

are quite capable of cultivating it efficiently on their own. They are said to lease out ... as one informant put it, 'to bring a few smallholders within their political orbit.' ... Although it is not specified in the tenancy agreement, the landlord may expect the tenant to work for some days in the busy season on the landlord's farm. The tenant may also be asked to do occasional odd jobs for the landowning household. In short, the remnants of the old 'begar' system [of forced labour] do survive in Haryana – though to a very limited extent.

Thus, in the course of this change in tenure patterns, the element of unfreedom as a mechanism of control exercised by landholders over subordinates has shifted from sharecroppers (who enjoyed a modicum of usufruct rights) to landless labourers.

4. Job mobility took the familiar form of transferring debts between masters. This shifting of debt from one master to another by *sajji* labour employed in Karnal during the 1860s was described by one Settlement Officer in the following terms:

His [the worker's] account is seldom cleared off, and till it is cleared off he does household work also; so that he becomes attached to his master as a sort of serf, and if a second employer takes him, he is bound to first settle his account with the old employer. The debt is looked upon by the people as a body debt (*sarir ka qarzah*) and they hold that they are entitled to compel the man to work till he has cleared it off, and grumble much at our law refusing to endorse this view. In all cases the [*sajji*] is expected to do much of the hardest part of the labour (cited in Bhattacharya [1985: 126]).

The nature of the sanctions invoked against labourers who refused to comply with this precondition is equally clear: 'Often a *siri* or *sanjhi* attempted to break out of the relationship to take up an alternative job. Force could be used to compel him to stay' [*Bhattacharya*, 1985: 126]. The similarities between these characteristics and those of contemporary attachment in the Haryana village case studies outlined below should be noted.

5. See Bhattacharya [1985: 127–9]. The latter text has nothing to say about either the way in which migration was organized or the production relations governing this process. The impression conveyed is that migrants during this period consisted of free wage labourers. The fact that such emigration from the unirrigated south-eastern areas of Punjab (present-day Haryana) was determined in part by the droughts and famines which took place in the years 1896–97, 1899–1900 and 1906–7 [cf. *Bhattacharya*, 1985: 147, 157, footnotes 104 and 106] suggests the presence of conditions which give rise to debt bondage and the movement of what is unfree migrant labour.

6. See Government of India [1952: 151; 1960: 80–81].

7. The Second Enquiry [*Government of India*, 1960: 81] notes that:

in some cases when an attached labourer absented himself from duty and failed to supply a *badli*, the employer deducted wages for the period of absence at the local wage rates for which casual labourers were employed. This deduction hit the agricultural labourer to such an extent that at the end of the season there was a considerable reduction in the amount of wages.

8. See Bhalla [1976: A-25, Table 1].

9. Of these latter subjects, Bhalla [1976: A-26] observes: 'Their position as witnesses and – by well-understood implication – as enforcers of labour contracts, brings home the ... character of power relations in a progressive Haryana village.'

10. A consequence of this system of payment, Bhalla [1976: A-26] points out, is that

'the worker commonly ends the year owing in the neighbourhood of Rs 600 to his employer of the year just ending. This is 'cleared' in the cases where the labourer is hired by a different cultivator, by the repayment of the debt to the former employer by the new one. Otherwise it is cleared by an advance from the new year's first installment of wages. In either case, for current consumption purposes, the labourer must take a loan from somewhere'. The same text also reports the occurrence of 'managed borrowing'; rather than providing the loan himself, the landholder in such instances acts as a guarantor with respect to the repayment by his attached labourer of money borrowed from another person (a shopkeeper or a different landholder).

11. See Bhattacharya [1985: 116, 118, 126, 141–2, 155 note 59]. Significantly, Bhattacharya [1985: 118] observes that 'in the south-east, around Gurgaon or Rohtak, the situation was perhaps different ... [h]ere the protests of *kamins* were perhaps less effective and they were forced into submission more easily'. He also notes the withholding by landholders of customary rights to produce as a way of controlling *sepidars* [1985: 119]; this method of subordination still occurs, as the Haryana village case studies presented below demonstrate, but with two crucial differences. First, it is fodder for livestock – not a portion of the crop – that is withheld; and second, this kind of compulsion is exerted indirectly, on workers actually owning livestock, who in turn exercise pressure on propertyless attached labourers to comply with debt-servicing work obligations.

12. A long quotation from Bhalla [1976: A-28] serves to emphasize this point. She writes:

[T]he main force making possible the emergence and consolidation of an agricultural labourers' class consciousness (as opposed to 'Jat/non-Jat' or scheduled caste/non-scheduled caste consciousness), is hightened by the demand for labour. Although this has not led to collective bargaining, it has given them individually 'a place to stand', and the beginnings of an active collective self-consciousness. Individually, the casual agricultural labourer can, and does, say on occasion to one of the cultivators who hires him: 'I will not work today'. And the cultivators complain that their permanent labourers 'report sick', or go off for their sisters' marriages, more than they used to do ... Collectively, in action – far removed from collective wage bargaining – labourers in a village may arrive at some sort of consensus that for the coming harvest each should stick to a demand for Rs 'y' per day instead of the lesser sum of Rs 'x', which was paid last year. But this is a consensus which is implemented by individuals. The counterbalancing force is the whole process of personalised indebtedness relations being built into permanent labour contracts, very formally, on an individual labourer basis. This can best be interpreted as the landowners' response to a worrisome improvement in the bargaining position of labourers ... Thus the embryo expressions of solidarity among labourers has been nipped in the bud, and counterbalanced by the reinforcement of traditional individual relations of awe, subservience and dependency. So far, this counter-attack has been entirely successful in Haryana.

Bhalla concludes by pointing out that

the factor which ties the labourer more closely to his employer is not the level of interest rates ... nor is it the amount of debt ... the factor which has offset the rise in inherent bargaining strength is the direct link which has been forged in the prosperous regions [Karnal, Rohtak] between employment and new forms of indebtedness. In the poor region [bordering Rajasthan] ... the labourer is still constrained by the scarcity of jobs, but in high employment regions, he is now kept more or less in line by a complex set of new relations of production.

13. An early but still useful account of this process is that by Frankel [1971].
14. See Government of Punjab [1982].
15. Government of Punjab [1982].
16. Singh and Sidhu [1976].
17. Between 1955/56 and 1968/69 the annual demand for labour in Punjab increased from 235 to 348 million working days.
18. A study of Punjab by Oberai and Singh [1983: 115ff., 403] suggests that even in the case of mechanization the labour displacing effects tend to be overexaggerated.
19. Sidhu and Grewal [1981]. Oberai and Singh [1983: 399] observe that '[t]he rate of outmigration from the rural areas [in Ludhiana District, Punjab] is higher than the combined rate of inmigration and return migration, suggesting that some of the shortage of labour reported from the region may be due to migration, and not to new methods of agriculture.'
20. Daily wages for harvesting increased in real terms from Rs 12.33 to Rs 16.34 at 1982 prices [*Government of Punjab*, 1982: Tables 15.13 and 17.10]. For increases in union membership, see Singh [1980: 19–31].
21. In 1979 the total number of migrants from Bihar and Uttar Pradesh amounted to 219,000, or eight per cent of the total agricultural workforce in Punjab [*Grewal and Sidhu*, 1981: 172–3]. During the early 1980s even newly arrived migrants were beginning to to move to the towns in search of higher wages, a process which accentuated the problem of control exercised by capitalist farmers over their workers. This labour mobility is noted by Oberai and Singh [1983: 195, 196, 212 note 2], who show how outstate migrants from Uttar Pradesh and Rajasthan constituted an increasingly important component of the total migratory flow to Ludhiana city (rising from 30 per cent in 1962/63–1966/67 to 44 per cent in 1972/73–1976/77) where they were rapidly absorbed into the urban labour market. Complaints of labour shortage and mobility were frequent among farmers interviewed during fieldwork in 1983. One Sikh, who operated 67 acres, grumbled that other farmers in the vicinity enticed 'his' migrants away with offers of higher wages, and lamented that once migrants became aware of local wage differentials 'they get new wings', and wished to work in other rural or urban enterprises where pay and conditions were better.
22. See Singh and Iyer [1981: 4–5], and Arora and Kumar [1980: 8–9]. Employers spent many days waiting at stations in order to obtain labour, and the extent of the competition among them when migrants arrived manifested itself in scenes such as the following:

   The moment Mr Dina Nath, a 35-year-old farm labourer from Darbhanga in Bihar got down from the Howrah Express at Ludhiana, he was *gheraoed* by a group of farmers. About 15 minutes later the deal was struck with a farmer from Jagraon. Along with seven persons belonging to the same group, Dina Nath jumped into a waiting tractor-trolley and was virtually whisked away ('Scramble for Migrant Farm Labour in Punjab', *Indian Express*, 21 April 1983).

23. During the 1970s, contractors were themselves prominent local farmers (owning between 15 and 70 acres each) who had become involved in the recruitment process because of labour shortages on their own farms. They were replaced sub-

sequently by contractors who lacked the same extensive landholding base, but who were well-connected with local political and bureaucratic networks and operated through agents in Bihar who recruited at village level [*Singh*, 1981: 79–81].

24. Singh and Iyer [1981]. The latter provide many examples of the ill-treatment of bonded labourers in Punjab.

25. Between 50 and 60 migrant labourers had their tickets forcibly extracted from them in this manner each night [*Singh and Iyer*, 1981: 5].

26. Forcible capture as a form of induced indebtedness also structured peonage in the American South during the first half of the twentieth century [*Kennedy*, 1959: 131–46]. This system entailed the arrest for 'vagrancy' of blacks who subsequently worked off debts on the land of farmers who paid their fines (see also Chapter 5).

27. Fieldwork was conducted in the Districts of Amritsar, Jullundur and Kapurthula, with assistance from Professor (then Dr) K Gopal Iyer of the Sociology Department, Panjab University, Chandigarh, and from Dr Amanda Bevan, then at Clare College, Cambridge University.

28. For the *siri* relation in Punjab during the early twentieth century, see above.

29. Details about the existence/enforcement of this form of debt bondage in Bihar itself are examined in Chapter 4.

30. All permanent migrants in the fieldwork survey owed cash debts to their employers in Punjab, and one third also owed debts to moneylenders in Bihar and Uttar Pradesh (the latter being cancelled by means of remittances sent to the home village).

31. Despite the claim that, because employers in south Gujarat have ceased making loans to finance marriage, debt is no longer an aspect of relations between farmers and their permanent servants, Breman [1985a: 268] concedes that '[c]ertainly, most permanent labourers still now and then receive consumption loans [of about Rs 100] called *khavati* – literally "in order to eat"; they try to wheedle this in small amounts from their bosses when there is no work for them.' Although loans made specifically for the purpose of marriage may have ended, therefore, permanent labourers in south Gujarat are – as in the case of Punjab – nevertheless still indebted to their employers for consumption loans. This, Breman continues, enables

> farmers [to] ensure a low price for the services of their subordinates in the future. *Actually, it is a form of advance wage payment, with the added advantage that there is no need to pay out more the moment there is a labour shortage. The pressure on labourers in permanent service to supplement the continuous deficit in their means of subsistence thus robs them of the profit they would otherwise gain from peak periods* (emphasis added).

32. This mode of bonding is still possible even when permanent migrants are in receipt of wages throughout the year. In the course of a fieldwork interview, one large capitalist farmer boasted proudly how he managed to circumvent minimum wage legislation. For the purpose of registering compliance with the law, the full amount would be paid into the bank accounts of his permanent workers; the latter, however, were then required to repay the difference between the minimum daily wage of Rs 14 and the actual daily wage of Rs 10. These same workers were also heavily in debt to this employer. If widespread, this maneouvre would undermine the reliability of official statistics regarding payment of minimum wages, and suggests not only that aggregate wage levels throughout rural Punjab might have been

much lower than indicated but also that what was classified as 'free wage labour' may in many instances have hidden what were in fact debt bondage relationships.

33. The common occurrence of this particular form of bonded labour is indicated by the existence of similar examples of restricted and conditional access to the labour market, not only elsewhere in India (see Chapter 7) but also in Latin America (Chapter 6) and the United States (Chapter 5).

34. Eighty per cent of seasonal local workers were bonded, either through cash or kind debts owed to employers, or through wages withheld by the latter. In the case of seasonal migrants, 55 per cent were indebted to their employer in Punjab and 64 per cent also owed debts to moneylenders in Bihar. These figures accord with findings from three other studies (Grewal and Sidhu [1981: 171], Singh and Iyer [1981: 7], and Arora and Kumar [1980: 12–13]) which reveal that 71, 66 and 42 per cent of migrants – whether permanently settled or seasonal remains unclear – were indebted to village moneylenders in Bihar, and that a third of all those who migrate did so in order to pay off debts incurred in Bihar.

35. A similar restriction on the freedom and mobility of permanent and seasonal or casual migrant labour working on Punjab farms is reported by Arora and Kumar [1980: 17].

36. The method used in Punjab to enforce debt obligations incurred by local workers is indicated by reference to the kind of power exercised by large farmers, one of whom divulged in the course of an interview that he personally administered beatings to male workers who consorted with female workers (he forbade males working alongside females since this reduced efficiency) or else handed them over to the local police who administered the beating on his behalf. A graphic illustration of this explicitly coercive kind of enforcement is provided by Breman [1985a: 268; see also 411–12]:

> One farmer who ... helped his farm servant with wedding money told me that he had brought in the police to give the man a thrashing in order to 'persuade' him not to leave his service ... it became clear that the man's refusal to work resulted from the lowering of his daily wage from Rs 3 to 2, by way of enforcing the discharge of his debt.

37. Two important contextual factors should be noted. First, the proximity of the field-work villages to urban centres (and therefore alternative sources of income and employment). And second, the Assembly election in Haryana during May 1987, in which Congress (I) was heavily defeated by Lok Dal (a political situation which clearly influenced worker militancy expressed in the course of fieldwork interviews).

38. Fifty of the village landholders employed two or more annual servants, 100 landholders employed a single male adult attached labourer, and 50 landholders employed only a single male child attached worker.

39. Workers pointed out that the *siri* relationship, whereby a permanent labourer was paid one fifth of the crop grown on property leased from the creditor-employer, had been discontinued by the village landowners who now farmed such holdings themselves. Some attached labourers were paid only Rs 3,600, and were forced as a result to take consumption loans from their creditor-employer in order to supplement the shortfalls occasioned by this low income. One annual servant indicated that if he was absent from work for as much as a day because of illness, he received no payment; when this happened, he borrowed money from the landholder to make good the deficit.

40. When describing the dynamics of these relations, landholders were quick to claim that no bondage was involved (itself an interesting – and unprompted – intervention on their part); an attached labourer sometimes remained with the same employer for a decade or more, landholders affirmed, the implication being that workers undertook this voluntarily because they liked this kind of long-term relation. This may be compared with the findings from another study of three villages in Karnal District during 1988, where 86 per cent of farmers who engaged in moneylending openly admitted that its object was not to obtain interest but to tie labour-power on a seasonal or permanent basis [*Jodhka*, 1990: 258–9, Table 5.11].

41. This view was contradicted by one large landholder, who observed that disputes between farmers and their attached workforce were becoming more common. He recounted how three days before this particular interview, one such confrontation had led to the arrest of the labourer concerned; the latter had attempted to leave his employer without first repaying the cash advance, and the the landholder had called in the police.

42. The *panchayat* had the legal right to impose fines of up to Rs 250 on any labourer for non-attendance at work.

43. Significantly, this kind of social pressure from fellow caste members was also exercised both at an earlier stage against attached labourers and against indebted casual workers. Thus, witnesses to a formalised loan invariably included one person from the same caste as the borrower; this witness, usually a landless worker who owned livestock, was required to act as a guarantor and repay the loan – or himself become a substitute worker – in the event of a debtor absconding. Scheduled caste witnesses to loan transactions, it was emphasized, were always called upon to operate as replacement labour themselves. In order to avoid this possibility, pre-emptive sanctions were mobilised from within the same caste community as a potential defaulter. Accordingly, when an attached (or casual) labourer failed or refused to meet his debt-servicing work obligations to a village landholder, the scheduled caste involved assembled eight or nine persons who would go and 'talk' with the subject concerned, and persuade him either to return and personally cancel his debt to the creditor-employer in the form of labour (that is, to continue working as before), or else to repay the outstanding loan in full with cash, together with interest for the whole year. Unsurprisingly, when confronted with these options, indebted (attached or casual) labourers 'chose' to work – albeit unwillingly – to clear the debt. One large landholder noted that if a dispute reached the *panchayat*, conflict over debt enforcement was invariably settled through this kind of intervention, particularly from the two or three members belonging to the labourer's own caste, and especially in cases where the subject concerned reneged on his debt-servicing labour obligations. The same informant added that such social pressure was sufficiently effective to ensure compliance.

44. Attached labourers in this village received no holidays, and were not only required to undertake domestic labour in the house of the creditor-employer on a beck-and-call basis, but also worked long hours (from 5 a.m. until 9 p.m.) during the peak agricultural season in the fields of the landholder, after which they had to stay behind in order to operate the irrigation system throughout the night. This schedule was regarded by casual workers as hard for three reasons: because of the intrinsically onerous nature of the tasks involved, because of the continuous duration of work, and because it prevented them from looking after the livestock they themselves owned.

45. The strength of feeling about labour attachment may be gauged from the negative response by a casual labourer when asked whether becoming an annual servant would be more acceptable if a plot of land was part of the arrangement. The same informant had earlier expressed a desire to possess land. In his 1988 study, Jodhka [1990: 263, 264] found that 80 per cent of all agricultural workers preferred casual employment to attached labour, and 29 per cent equated attachment with debt bondage; one respondent is reported as saying that 'an attached labourer is like being the wife of a farmer [over] whose body the farmer has complete control'.

46. Casual labourers who took these wage advances, or who borrowed for consumption purposes during the off-peak season, were particularly vulnerable to coercion exercised by village landholders when it came to debt repayment in the form of work at a lower rate of remuneration during the subsequent peak season. As one labourer observed,

> there is compulsion from the farmer; he comes [to our homes] in the evenings and demands that we work, because we owe him money – or else that we repay the debt. We have to work, we have to follow his direction – there is no choice. We have always given in to this kind of pressure from the farmer: there is no conflict [over it].

Given the politico-ideological potency of the debt issue, and in particular the threat to recall outstanding loans if the demands of the creditor-employer were not met, it is unsurprising that worker indebtedness played such a major role in this village during the struggle by farmers to prevent or defuse attempts on the part of casual labourers to organize collectively in pursuit of higher wages (see below).

47. One casual labourer from the Balmiki caste explained that, as he raised pigs during the off-peak period of the agricultural cycle, he did not hire out his labour-power during these six months of the year. Although he borrowed large sums (up to Rs 2,000, mainly for investment in pig breeding) from a landholder, he experienced no difficulty repaying this amount in installments of Rs 100–400, the latter corresponding to money obtained through the sale of pigs. Significantly, whereas village shopkeepers who did not own land required that loans made to casual labourers be repaid in the form cash from wages earned during the next peak agricultural season, landholders (and landowning shopkeepers) required that repayment take the form of work in their fields at a below-market wage rate. Even those casual labourers who managed to obtain loans from institutional sources risked bondage through this form of borrowing; it was neccessary to rely on village landholders as witnesses to the transaction in order to have access to this kind of credit, and – in the words of one agricultural worker – 'when [we] take the farmer along [to the bank in the town] as a witness, [we] have to leave a family member to work for him as an unpaid labourer'. Since landholders controlled access to outside institutional credit, they were able to impose the condition that casual workers send domestic kinsfolk into attachment as a price of this access, an arrangement which accounted in part for the large number of child attached labourers in the village.

48. Around 80 per cent of the Ziwar community (the principal agricultural labouring caste in the village) owed amounts varying between Rs 200 and Rs 1000, debts incurred as a result of marriage and consumption loans. Repayment of such debts entailed working for the creditor-employer concerned for a lower wage on a beck-and-call basis (particularly during periods of peak agricultural demand), and being allowed to seek alternative employment only with his permission. A casual

labourer described the relationship thus: 'When we take a loan, we are bound to the farmer, we have to accept lower wages because he comes in a position of power'. Similarly, casual workers belonging to the Chamar and Balmiki castes observed that 'we also have to take loans for marriage, emergencies, and the like, from a landowner who can as a result compel us to work for him'. According to another text, 45 per cent of debt incurred by agricultural workers in Karnal District during 1988 was for marriage costs, 21 per cent for house construction, 17 per cent for subsistence, and 12 per cent for medical expenses [*Jodhka*, 1990: 239, Table 5.5].

49. With regard to this fourfold response, a casual worker from the village observed: 'We [labourers] want to unite, but it is difficult for us to organize unions in support of our wage bargaining, because farmers always bring these pressures against us to break our people'.

50. In the words of one capitalist farmer, who owned 60 acres of land and was the brother of the village *sarpanch*, 'the landholders here brought in migrants from outside to break the power of local workers bargaining for higher wages'. To an important extent, this restructuring of the workforce was determined by the need on the part of large farmers in the village to establish (or re-establish) better control over labour-power in the face of strong competition for this commodity, both from others farmers and from non-agricultural employers in the vicinity. This involved, in short, reimposing worker discipline and regulation in the capitalist labour process. Noting the general lack of a significant cost differential between local and migrant labour, the village *sarpanch*, a capitalist farmer owning sixty acres of land and who himself employed 30–40 migrant workers from Panipat specifically for paddy transplantation and harvesting, stated that he preferred migrants because 'they work harder and are more committed to the farmer; local workers don't show the same loyalty, and move to other farmers'. In a similar vein, another capitalist farmer operating 23 acres responded to an open question inviting him to identify the main problem area in agriculture by pointing out that labour was very costly, and that although there was little difference in this respect between locals and migrants, the latter were more 'dependable'. He regarded local workers as unreliable, since they went to whichever employer offered them the highest payment. What emerges clearly, both from the nature of the response to worker militancy and from the views expressed by the landholders themselves about this, is the interrelatedness of on the one hand the process of capitalist restructuring and regulation, together with the use of the debt mechanism to impose labour control, and on the other labour mobility as a crucial form of bargaining power exercised in this context by agricultural workers. It should be noted that the argument concerning restructuring is shared neither by Ahlawat [1988: 88], who holds that migrants coming to Haryana complement rather than replace local workers, nor by Jodhka [1990], who makes scant reference to migrant agricultural labour.

51. Landholders describing this system of 'changing masters' by transferring debts between creditor-employers emphasized that it involved no coercion on their part to make an annual servant remain in their employment. However, workers themselves gave a different account of the same practice, indicating that employers to whom debts were owed did in fact exercise considerable pressure on annual servants to continue working for them. The ability of attached workers to change masters is cited by Jodhka [1990: 272, 275] as evidence for the non-existence of debt bondage, despite the fact that 'for a majority of the attached labourers it was

not very easy to opt out of the relationship if they so desired', and that the element of unfreedom is recognized by both creditor-employer and labourer.

52. Employers taunted their indebted permanent servants with the constant refrain that 'You have taken my money, why aren't you working?'; from the worker's view-point, a major shortcoming of the extended work relationship was that many of his tasks were carried out in the home of his creditor-employer, and thus under the continuous supervision of the latter. This situation also possessed implications for fieldwork, since it proved difficult to interview attached labourers generally, and impossible to interview them without their master also being present. Information concerning these kind of workers was obtained from casual labourers whose kins-men worked as annual servants, or (more commonly) themselves acquired such information from these subjects directly when working alongside them in the fields. With regard to the methodologically problematic issue of obtaining data on coercion, one casual labourer confirmed that in the presence of outsiders an employer will 'behave correctly' towards his annual servant; when no one is around, however, verbal abuse and (less frequently) physical assault takes place. The same informant reported that recently in this village an attached labourer who was also a tractor driver was beaten so badly by his creditor-employer that his hand was broken. No compensation for the cost of medical treatment was received from the landholder in question, who then cut the attached labourer's wages for time taken off work due to injury!

53. Labourers stressed this point, stating that 'you have to work as long as the creditor says, at whatever task he indicates – in the house or in the field'.

54. For the role of the *khatri* caste as village moneylender, shopkeeper and grain-dealer in pre-Independence Punjab, see Darling [1925].

55. The casual labourer providing this information indicated that the extension of the working day in the case of indebted workers frequently entailed the application of 'some force' on the part of employers when it came to preventing those who owed money from leaving the fields at the same time as those who did not.

56. Six brick kilns had been operating on village land since 1972, when landholders leased usufruct rights to kiln-owners who supplied bricks to urban construction sites. Other landholders resented this, as it not only deprived them of labour-power for crucial seasonal agricultural tasks but also enabled workers to maintain wages at existing levels. One large landholder, who required 500–1,000 working days of labour for production during the peak season, protested that the landless workforce had been the principal beneficiaries of brick kiln operations.

57. The number of annual servants employed in this village during 1987 was around 50.

58. A landless casual worker who owned two buffaloes estimated that his earnings from the sale of milk in the local town amounted to Rs 2,400–3,000 per annum, a sum equivalent to the whole of his annual income from work as an agricultural labourer.

59. In this village expenditure on marriage amounted to Rs 7,000.

60. Casual labourers who owed debts to their employers were required to work a ten hour day in return for Rs 15 (and Rs 10 if the landholder was 'tough', an informant noted), instead of an eight hour day for Rs 20.

61. A sharecropping tenant employed full-time by a village landholder earned only 63–72 per cent of the annual wage received by a casual labourer who worked for three months in agriculture and five months in an unskilled urban occupation, even

without taking into account any income generated by the latter through livestock ownership.

62. Because of conflict with landholders over the conditions in and payment for agricultural work in the village, casual labourers expressed the wish to work in town full-time, even if this entailed lower overall wages.

4

Bonded Labour in Northeastern India

The northeastern state of Bihar has long been considered a redoubt of latifundist agriculture, and thus also as the epitome within rural India of the characteristics associated with this: landlordism, economic backwardness and agrestic servitude. In this regard, the agrarian structure of Bihar is invariably depicted as the mirror image of its counterpart in the Punjab/Haryana area.

For these reasons, the focus here will be on a number of crucial issues linked to the historical and continuing presence in this state of unfree agrarian relations: namely, the socio-economic conditions conducive to the reproduction of bonded labour, and conversely its connection with the reproduction of sharecropping relations, migration patterns and questions of kinship/gender. Also presented in this chapter are the findings of fieldwork conducted in two Districts of Bihar at different conjunctures: Nalanda District in 1985, and Purnia District in 1989/90.

I

The economic backwardness of Bihar in relation to Haryana is evident from the relative position of both in the same set of agro-economic indicators cited in the previous chapter: during 1978/79 only 35 per cent of the sown area in Bihar was irrigated, compared with 53 per cent in Haryana.[1] In terms of crop output, the per acre yield of paddy and wheat in Bihar during 1980/81 was respectively 10 and 16 quintals; the latter quantities are less than the equivalent crop figures not only for Haryana (26 and 27 quintals) but also for All-India (13 and 17 quintals).[2]

4.1 Feudalism, Capitalism and Debt Bondage in Bihar

As in the case of Peru, the reasons for the historical existence and reproduction of unfree labour in northeastern India are the subject of dispute. In rural Bihar debt bondage has been an integral part of labour organization as well as the outcome of the expropriation and pauperization of sharecropping tenants.[3] This twofold historical origin of unfree agricultural labour has been outlined by Tiwary in the case of Santal Parganas District in Bihar.[4] Forms such as *kamiauti, harwahi* and *kandh* constituted the traditional pre-colonial production relation, and involved bonding landless workers to particular masters in exchange for cash or kind loans, whereas forms such as *kishani, palhaiti* and *bhaoli* were the property relations that developed following the Permanent Settlement, and corresponded to rent-in-kind or labour-rent payments for land.

By contrast, Mundle argues that in the case of Palamau district the *kamiauti* system emerged only towards the end of the nineteenth century as a result of capitalist penetration.[5] Here moneylending constituted a preferred method adopted by capital for controlling, cheapening, or disciplining labour-power in a context where, due to worker outmigration coupled with a low incidence of landlessness, rural wage levels would otherwise have increased. For Mundle, the existence of the debt bondage relation in this district of Bihar permits a creditor-employer to extract absolute surplus-value from unfree workers employed in a technically backward agrarian labour process formally subsumed under capital.

This interpretation is disputed by Chopra and Tiwary, both of whom regard the debt bondage mechanism as an archaic survival unconnected with capital accumulation, through which unproductive landlords extract pre-capitalist forms of rent from smallholding tenants or sharecroppers.[6] Yet another interpretation is offered by Vijayendra, who argues that debt bondage persists in contexts where agriculture is backward and in situations where capitalist production is undertaken by ex-landlords on the basis of pre-existing class relationships.[7]

As with post-Independence labour attachment in Punjab and Haryana, the section in the First Agricultural Labour Enquiry dealing with Bihar during the 1950s similarly points to its unfree character at this period. Known as *harwahas* or *charwahas* in Saran and Muzaffarpur Districts, as *kamias* and *bagals* in Manbhum and Singbhum Districts, as *baniharas* in Palamau District and as *munish* in Santal Parganas, the Enquiry reported that attached workers were 'employed under contract with their employers, who advanced loans to them and kept them in perpetual bondage'.[8]

During the early 1950s an attached labourer in Bihar was not permitted to seek employment on another farm unless the creditor-employer to whom he owed cash or kind debts had no work for him. The First Enquiry concluded that attached labourers were ill-treated, paid in inferior grain, required to work longer hours yet at lower levels of remuneration than casual labourers, undertook domestic labouring tasks, and were forbidden to change employers during the busy seasons.[9]

Unsurprisingly, Indian government officials in Bihar espouse a different view. In October 1977 District Magistrates on whom depended the implementation of the 1976 Bonded Labour System (Abolition) Act were instructed by the Bihar government not to regard attached labour as a form of bondage, and therefore to take no legal action against creditor-employers over this issue.[10] Accepting the widespread existence of attached labour in the rural sector, officials nevertheless deny this is bonded on the ground that such workers enjoy better conditions than free wage labour with regard to assured subsistence, security of employment, perquisites in the form of clothing, cultivable and homestead land, and interest-free loans.[11] It is clear that the official interpretation of rural labour attachment has much in common with the way debt bondage is theorized by revisionist texts (see Chapters 5, 6 and 7).

Regardless of whether it is employed in a capitalist or a non-capitalist agrarian labour process, the presence of contemporary bonded labour in regions such as Bihar can in general be linked to a particular combination of socio-economic conditions.[12] Where a highly unequal land tenure system co-exists with an underdeveloped economic structure and surplus population, therefore, large sections of the poor peasantry owning insufficient (or unproductive) holdings and landless agricultural labourers are dependent for the major portion of their income on the proceeds from the sale of their labour-power. In these circumstances the unreformed tenure structure, the low level of development of the productive forces, and demographic growth all combine to reduce the bargaining power of the rural workforce in the context of the labour market.[13]

As in the case of the Punjab/Haryana region in the pre-Independence era, the resulting low wage levels together with their landless or landpoor situation, requires agricultural worker and poor peasant households to take loans from creditor-employers in order to supplement subsistence or income deficits. Since their wage rates and asset base are usually insufficient to enable the the repayment of such loans, rural workers in Bihar are as a consequence trapped in a vortex of rising debt. The latter in turn entails ever-diminishing returns from the sale of their only commodity, labour-power, and thus an even greater dependence on consumption loans from creditor-employers.

4.2 Bonded Labour and Migration in Bihar

One of the main problems concerning the existence of debt bondage in Bihar is the extent to which this relation structures the process of seasonal and/or permanent labour migration from the state to other work locations. Historically, debt bondage has been an important method of recruiting and controlling migrant labour, both within India itself and in cases where indentured workers from India were supplied to British colonial plantations in Africa, the Caribbean and the Far East.[14] As Omvedt makes clear, much of the workforce that migrated from Bihar to the Assam tea gardens and the Calcutta jute mills during the half century from 1880 to 1930 was composed for the most part of unfree labour, bonded by loans to landlords at the point of origin or by cash advances to labour contractors.[15] However, agreement concerning the historical importance of bonded migrant labour notwithstanding, many studies of contemporary rural–rural migration patterns within India fail to raise the issue of its unfree component.[16]

The problematic nature of the connection between labour migration and the debt bondage relation may be illustrated by reference to the following example. Where little or no employment is available in an economically backward area, a village moneylender might require a debtor to migrate so as to obtain sufficient money for repaying the loan. Accordingly, the debtor migrates to an economically developed region where wage levels are better, sells his labour-power to the highest bidder, and on returning allocates a portion of his enhanced income to cancelling the outstanding loan.[17]

Since in this instance the debtor is compelled neither to work in the labour process belonging to a creditor-employer, nor as a consequence has to accept a below-market payment for the sale of his labour-power, two important defining characteristics of the debt bondage relation are absent. However, in so far as the same debtor is working to pay off a loan, may be under local social pressure to migrate in order to do this, and is by virtue of his indebtedness permitted neither to chose his place of work nor to withdraw from the labour market, significant elements of the debt bondage relation also remain.

Of additional importance is a consideration of how the relations governing the process of migration change over time. Thus seasonal or permanent migrants from Bihar, who enter the labour market as free workers, may eventually become debt bonded to new creditor-employers outside the state; conversely, unfree migrants who are required to work for a particular labour contractor so long as cash advances received from him remain outstanding might subsequently become free wage labourers. A study by Singh and Iyer of annual labour migration between Bihar and Punjab suggests that only the 10,000 tribals who travel from south Bihar to work as permanent agricultural workers in Punjab (specifically, the districts of Hoshiarpur, Jullunder and Amritsar) are bonded, either to labour contractors or to creditor-employers in Punjab itself.[18]

The major portion of this annual migration is composed of backward castes from north Bihar, who work in the agrarian sector of Punjab on a seasonal basis; because these are not recruited by labour contractors, it is argued, such migrants are free workers. Although the same study indicates that even tribals cease to be bonded once they have become accustomed to the process of migration, it nevertheless remains problematic the extent to which – and just how – both tribal and non-tribal migrants manage to break out of the debt cycle.[19]

Given these problems of definition, together with the existence of contradictory and/or area-specific estimates, it is difficult to calculate both the current extent of debt bondage and the changes in its incidence for Bihar as a whole. For example, while Mitra and Vijayendra imply that bonded labour is increasing in the Kosi region of Purnia District, Singh indicates that in the Begusari region the same relationship is on the decrease.[20] The survey of debt bondage throughout India carried out by the National Labour Institute and the Gandhi Peace Foundation in 1978 estimated that only 111,000 bonded labourers were to be found in Bihar, or less than two per cent of the rural work-force in the state.[21] By contrast, surveys carried out at approximately the same time by the A.N. Sinha Institute of Patna indicate that 57 per cent of all rural households and 72 per cent of agricultural labour households in Monghyr District took consumption loans, a prime cause of bondage.[22]

Similarly, a sample survey during 1971 of 11 villages in the Kosi area of Purnia District shows that over half the landholders owning 10–20 acres and over three quarters of landholders owning more than 20 acres employed attached labour.[23] As both consumption loans and labour attachment are usually accompanied by debt bondage relations, the incidence of unfree labour in Bihar is likely to be much higher than the figure suggested by the NLI/GPF survey.[24] Another reason for the under-reporting of the incidence of bonded labour in Bihar is its frequent underestimation in the case of female workers, a point illustrated below with regard to fieldwork findings from Purnia district.

4.3 Debt Bondage and Sharecropping in Bihar

Most commentators on rural Bihar agree on the current widespread existence and historical importance in this context of the sharecropping system (*batai*), frequently contrasting this situation with the absence or diminished incidence of such relations in the economically more advanced agriculture of Punjab and Haryana.[25] The usual pattern nowadays of such a crop leasing arrangement is that the owner of the land provides means of production (land, finance, technical inputs, seeds, etc.) and supervises the labour process, while the sharecropper contributes his labour-power and sometimes that of his kinsfolk.

The crop itself is usually apportioned between owner and share tenant on a 50–50 basis, although this varies according to the context and the power of the respective parties. A survey carried out in Bihar during the late 1960s reports that 25 per cent of all peasant households in the state sharecropped non-owned land in addition to cultivating their own land, and that a further seven per cent worked only non-owned land on a share-tenancy basis.[26]

The continued preponderance of sharecropping relations in Bihar derives from three interrelated causes: the unequal structure of landownership, demographic growth, and the agrarian reform legislation of the early 1960s. During 1901–81, the population of Bihar increased from 27 million to 70 million people; the decennial growth rate itself has risen from ten per cent in 1951/61 to 24 per cent in 1971/81.[27] The pattern of land tenure in Bihar is characterized by a marked polarization: 72 per cent of cultivating households possess holdings of less than five acres, while only 11 per cent of households possess in excess of ten acres.[28] And since large landholders have been required to undertake direct cultivation in order to retain ownership rights under the provisions of the land ceiling legislation in the 1961 Bihar Land Reforms Act, tenants have been evicted and subsequently re-engaged as non-occupancy sharecroppers.[29]

It is important to recognize the contrasting roles of indebtedness with regard to the existence of sharecropping. On the one hand, a poor peasant proprietor may increase his level of debt during a sustained period of economic crisis, with the result that his land is acquired by a creditor in lieu of unpaid loans and the smallholder is transformed into a sharecropper. On the other hand, a landless labourer or poor peasant owning insufficient land may sharecrop property belonging to a rich peasant or landlord, and subsequently become indebted to the latter as a consequence of cash or kind loans received in order to cultivate sharecropped land.

From the viewpoint of a creditor-employer, these transactions possess distinct objectives: whereas the purpose of the first is to acquire land, the second involves control over labour-power, and therefore raises the issue of debt bondage. Accordingly, in rural Bihar sharecropping can be a means of either cancelling debt (and remaining free from bondage) or, conversely and more usually, inducing indebtedness (and entering an unfree relationship with the owner of the leased land).[30]

These different trajectories have contributed to the existence of opposing views about the connection between debt bondage and sharecropping. The 1978 survey by the National Labour Institute and the Gandhi Peace Foundation concluded that three quarters of all bonded labourers in Bihar did not receive any land from their creditor-employers, and that only a third of all unfree labourers in the state were bonded for land.[31] This points to a weak correlation between debt bondage and access to land through sharecropping arrangements.[32] By contrast, Mitra and Vijayendra suggest a strong connection between sharecropping and debt bondage in the district of Purnia, where historically this form of tenancy has been a method of securing not the product but the labour-power of the worker.[33]

In general terms, the persistence of sharecropping may be theorised in three distinct ways. The first concerns ideological causes that stem from the social division of labour. Thus Beteille argues that sharecropping derives its impetus from the wish of high caste landlords to avoid not only ritually polluting and physically onerous manual labour associated with wet paddy cultivation but also personally having to supervise this work.[34] These conditions, however, could just as easily be met by the employment of wage labour and by fixed cash or kind rents.

The second and third viewpoints locate the sharecropping relation within the context of class struggles, but in diametrically opposed ways: one regards sharecropping as evidence of a successful outcome for landlords and rich peasants in their conflicts with poor peasants and/or wage labourers, whereas another views the same relation as reflecting the objectives not of the former but rather of the latter. Where a latifundist tenure structure is combined with the absence of non-agricultural employment opportunities, and thus with a strong demand for land from rural workers or peasants with insufficient holdings, the high produce rent paid by these subordinate socio-economic categories may be regarded as an indication of the power exercised by landlords or rich peasants.[35]

By contrast, sharecropping arrangements may also be the result of successful struggles carried out by landless workers and poor peasants.[36] For example, Martínez-Alier reports that a return to pre-Civil-War sharecropping contracts in rural Spain during the 1960s was a response by landowners to the scarcity of cheap labour which resulted from collective action by agricultural workers to secure minimum wage levels.[37] Similarly, Bardhan notes that increases in the incidence of sharecropping in India correlate both with high agricultural wages for harvesting and with advanced agricultural production based on technical inputs.[38]

The fact that in rural India sharecropping and credit relations usually overlap, however, suggests that rich peasants and/or landlords are able to turn even initially unfavourable tenancy arrangements to their own advantage by combining sharecropping leases with the debt mechanism. Although landlord/rich-peasant control over a poor peasant or agricultural labourer may be absent at the inception of a sharecropping arrangement, therefore, in the process of class struggle it *becomes* part of the relationship. Unless located within this framework of conflict, the changing nature of the linkage between debt bondage and sharecropping in Bihar remains problematic.

II

The main findings of the 1985 research in Nalanda District and the 1989/90 research in Purnia District provide further details about the structure, the reasons for the existence and the socio-economic impact of bonded labour in Bihar.[39]

4.4 Bonded Labour in Nalanda District, Bihar

During 1985 fieldwork was carried out in three villages of Nalanda District, an area of intensive cultivation located on the South Bihar Plain of the Middle Ganga Valley. Until 1972, this region was part of Patna District, and Nalanda became a separate administrative and census unit only after this date; for this reason, a comparison with the rest of Bihar as regards demographic growth and social composition remains problematic.[40] Thus the high pre-1972 population density stems from the presence in the same district of the state capital: in 1971, the number of inhabitants per square kilometre for Patna District (643) was double that for the state of Bihar (324).

Similarly, the proportion of urban population (23 per cent) for Patna District was twice that for the state as a whole (ten per cent); however, as Kumar shows, the urban population level in the Nalanda area has increased only marginally throughout this century, from four per cent in 1901 to five per cent in 1941 and fourteen per cent in 1981.[41] The social composition of the district broadly reflects that of the state: in 1971, therefore, cultivators amounted to some 43 per cent of the rural working population in Bihar, while labourers constituted 39 per cent; in 1981, the figure for cultivators in Nalanda District was 40 per cent, and that for agricultural labourers 42 per cent.[42]

Over half the cropped area in Nalanda District is irrigated, and – as with Haryana – rainfall constitutes the main supply of water used for agricultural production. In 1981/82 tubewells were the most important source of non-rainfed irrigation (50 per cent), followed by tanks (40 per cent) and canals (eight per cent).[43] During 1982/83 more than three quarters of the land in the district was sown, compared with only half throughout the state of Bihar; this, together with a cropping ratio of 130 per cent, derives from the soil fertility in the area.[44] Another consequence of the latter is the high per acre crop yield; accordingly, the yearly output of paddy and wheat in Nalanda District over 1979/80 amounted to 12 and 14 quintals respectively, production figures which exceeded the annual average yields for the state as a whole.[45]

During the late 1970s and throughout the 1980s Nalanda District has been a site of acute struggles between landholders and agricultural labourers. This conflict took multiple forms, and included work boycotts and strike action on the part of rural labour; as in Haryana, landholders responded to worker militancy by prohibiting these subjects from either grazing livestock on or collecting fodder from fields they owned. The CPI(ML) has been active in the district from 1979 onwards, specifically in the organization of crop seizures.[46] Over this time strikes were organized in the northwestern region of the district (Hilsa block) around issues such as higher wages, access to village land and water resources; as a result of this mobilization, foodgrain wage payments in the area were increased to two and a half times their former levels in ten of the fifteen villages affected.[47]

4.5 Village A, Nalanda District

Peasant proprietors in this village belonged to the Bhumihar caste, the majority of whom were smallholders cultivating around five acres of land with the labour of male family members.[48] Intra-caste leasing of land on a share-cropping basis was also practised.[49] Although such producers owned pumpsets, this important source of non-rainfed irrigation had remained inoperative for the past two years (1983–85) due to unrepaired fallen power lines.[50] The yearly average per acre yield for the village as a whole amounted to ten and eight quintals respectively in the case of paddy and wheat.

The nine *Mochi* and 150 *Musahar* households in the labourers' colony provided the agricultural labour-power utilised by landholders in the village. Informants estimated that of these households, some 20–25 could be characterized formally as containing bonded labour (*bandhua mazdoor*); that is, the subjects concerned both identified themselves and were recognized as such. The casual labour households numbered around 100–125. In this village an attached labourer worked for his creditor-employer throughout nine months of each year, principally on agricultural tasks such as ploughing and bunding.

Together with the family labour-power at his disposal, this subject under-took the transplantation/harvesting/threshing of paddy and the harvesting/threshing of wheat. For these tasks, the daily payment-in-kind varied between 2.2 and 2.6 kilos per working family member.[51] An attached worker in this village had usufruct rights to between quarter and half an acre of land on which to cultivate paddy and wheat, usually sharecropped on a 50/50 basis with the landholder.[52]

During the off-peak season, when no agricultural employment was available, attached labourers in this village worked as casual labour in the local town, either transporting goods for merchants, in brick kilns, or on con-struction sites, at daily wage levels which varied between Rs 6–10. No ob-jection existed to their working elsewhere in this manner, one annual servant commented, only so long as there was no work for the master: whenever the latter had a task which required completion, it was necessary to work for him.

Bonded labourers incurred cash/kind debts mainly for three reasons: sub-sistence provision, to pay for the cost of medical treatment, and to finance the ceremonial expenditure associated with marriage, death rites, and religious observance. Although total expenditure on marriage varied between Rs 2,000 and Rs 5,000, less than half this amount (Rs 1,000–1,300) was actually bor-rowed from a current creditor-employer. The same was true of debts incurred as a result of medical treatment.[53] By contrast, cash/kind loans necessitated by subsistence shortfalls, religious ceremonial, or death rites, were usually taken only from the creditor-employer.[54]

In all cases where debts were owed by the attached labourer to his current creditor-employer, it was impossible to change masters without first undertaking full repayment. When asked what would happen in circumstances where a bonded labourer did in fact attempt to withdraw from the existing relationship without repaying outstanding debts, an informant replied that the creditor-employer concerned would beat him and then force him to work. Another annual servant pointed out that bonded labour had to work much harder than casual labour for less wages: casual workers, the same informant observed, did not undertake ploughing, which was the hardest of all agricultural tasks. It was also necessary for bonded labourers to wade through the mud over long distances carrying the heavy wooden plough, in order to cover all the scattered plots of land owned or operated by the creditor-employer.

Two individual case studies of worker indebtedness in this village reveal not only the frequent necessity for and the multi-sourced nature of borrowing but also the important role played by disposition over family labour in loan repayment. The first case study concerns a bonded labourer who was the household head in a family composed of five working adults. In 1979 he spent Rs 3,000 on the marriage of his eldest son; two thirds of this sum was financed by the sale of pigs the subject himself had reared, while the remaining one third was borrowed from his employer.[55] This debt was still outstanding six years later, and the informant reported that he was not free to leave the employment of his master until the full amount had been repaid.

Further large-scale expenditure was incurred by this same subject as a result of two illnesses in the family: thus, his own medical treatment necessitated borrowing Rs 700 in cash from three local landholders at an annual interest rate of 48 per cent, and that for his spouse required taking additional loans from both his creditor-employer and another landholder. The interest on the first of these two debts was met from the non-agricultural earnings of his son, while repayment of the second took the form of deductions made from his portion of the harvest on land (0.44 of an acre) sharecropped with his creditor-employer.[56] Because illness prevented him from working full-time, this same bonded labourer also had to take a supplementary loan in kind (0.4 of a quintal of rice) at 50 per cent interest from his creditor-employer in order to offset the resulting shortfall in his annual wage.

The second case-study concerns an attached labourer whose household consisted of seven working members. His two eldest sons were both married during the same ceremony in 1974 at a cost of Rs 2,600: half this sum came from the sale of a cow owned by the informant, while the remaining amount was financed by sharecropping revenue (31 per cent) and a loan from his creditor-employer (19 per cent).[57] This latter debt was also subsequently cleared with revenue generated from sharecropping. In order to pay for the double marriage ceremony of his youngest son and daughter in 1984, it was necessary to obtain Rs 5,000: a further sale of livestock together with family income from eight to ten months' work in a local brick-kiln provided 60 per cent of the required amount, the rest taking the form of cash borrowed from his wife's brother and a brick-kiln owner.[58]

The debt owed by this particular attached labourer to his present creditor-employer in the village amounted to only Rs 150; the latter amount was taken for subsistence purposes, and would have to be repaid before he personally could seek alternative work. He had also taken two further loans: one of Rs 600 at 36 per cent annual interest from a landholder in a neighbouring village, and another of Rs 5,000 from the government for the purchase of a horse-cart.[59]

4.6 Village B, Nalanda District

Much of the land in this village previously belonged to a single landlord.[60] In 1985 the village was composed of 145 households, of which 50 owned land. *Bhumihars* and *Lalaji* constituted the two main landowning castes: 35 *Bhumihar* households (24 per cent of all village households) and 15 *Lalaji* households (ten per cent) owned respectively 71 and 20 per cent of the total village land. Only 14 per cent of *Bhumihars* owned more than twelve acres of land, while the remaining 86 per cent owned less than this amount. Although important village proprietors, members of the *Lalaji* caste had urban occupations; accordingly, all their holdings were leased out to lower castes. There were fourteen privately owned pumpsets but no tractors in the village; the yearly average per acre output amounted to 12.8 quintals of paddy and 9.6 quintals of wheat.

The workforce was composed of subjects from the 60 landless *Musahar* households.[61] Known as *harwaha* (literally, 'a plough', or 'the person behind the plough'), the 60 attached labourers in this village generally worked for a single employer for between ten and 20 years on the basis of a recurrent yearly contract.[62] These annual servants were employed in agricultural production throughout eight to ten months each year; during the off-peak season of May and June, such labourers were either permitted by their masters to seek alternative work in local brick kilns and construction sites, or else took subsistence loans at 50 per cent interest from village moneylenders and landholders.[63] These debts were repaid from the harvest wage and/or in the form of produce from land leased to the permanent worker.

Each attached labourer rented a plot of land from his master; the area of such holdings varied in size between 0.13 and 0.22 of an acre. The lower figure was the most usual, and indeed attached workers complained that the average size of these plots had declined in the recent past, from a quarter to around one tenth of an acre. For every working day spent in the uprooting and transplantation of paddy, annual servants received one-and-a-half kilos of rice plus a kilo of parched grain (*salthu*) as payment-in-kind; at harvest-time, these subjects retained one tenth of the paddy and wheat crop they collected.[64] In this village, male and female casual labour (*chut mazdoor*) was employed by landholders only for the agricultural tasks of uprooting and transplanting paddy, and received the same daily payment as attached workers.

Landholders accepted that the older attached labourers in the village were bonded, principally because of loans taken for marriage, yet denied this was true of younger permanent workers on the grounds that now such debt was both repayable and no longer intergenerational.[65] However, they also agreed that in general permanently attached workers preferred employment as casual labour, although 'economic compulsion' – the absence of casual work combined with access to land being conditional on attachment – prevented this.

Prolonged strike action undertaken by attached workers for higher wages constitutes additional evidence against the view that subjects of this relation perceive it in a positive manner. As a result of a four-month strike by attached labourers in 1984, village landholders were compelled to increase daily payment made to these workers for uprooting and transplanting paddy from a kilo of rice plus 700 grammes of parched grain to one-and-a-half kilos of rice and one kilo of parched grain (increases amounting to 50 and 43 per cent respectively). Throughout the strike, all the manual labouring agricultural tasks were carried out by the landholders themselves: *Bhumihars* ploughed their own land for the first time, and all the members of this caste mobilized their personal labour collectively in order to plough and transplant each other's holdings.[66]

Because the strike was timed to coincide with the period of peak seasonal demand in the agricultural cycle, when there was a requirement for labour-power in neighbouring villages, attached labourers were able to sustain their political action without having to compromise on its economic objectives.[67] Accordingly, during these four months striking labourers worked as casual labour in nearby villages. However, as a result of social pressure exerted by their erstwhile employers on fellow *Bhumihar* caste members in these villages, workers on strike were forced to enter once again previous attached labour relationships in this village.[68]

4.7 Village C, Nalanda District

In this village there were 40–45 landholding households, nearly half of which were composed of *Bhumihars*, the principal cultivating caste.[69] Although means of production took the usual form of animal power and a rainfed water supply, there were nonetheless two tractors and twelve pumpsets privately owned by individual landholders.[70] Non-rainfed crop irrigation was inadequate, producers complained, because the operation of their tubewells depended on (and was limited by) the irregular supply of electricity. Output was consequently low, the yearly average per acre yield for both wheat and paddy amounting to only twelve quintals.

The agricultural workforce was drawn from the 25–30 *Musahar* households located on the village outskirts, and peasant proprietors reported that they experienced no difficulty in obtaining either casual or attached labour. Permanent workers were employed by a master for only six months each year, during which they carried out not only ploughing but also irrigation and harvesting. Payment-in-kind received by such workers included usufruct rights to 0.2 of an acre of land (sharecropped with its owner), one-and-a-quarter kilos of rice for every day worked, and one-tenth of the wheat and paddy crop they collected at harvest-time.[71] During the agricultural off-peak season, attached labourers either worked as casual labour on local urban construction sites or else borrowed subsistence loans of Rs 100–400 from their creditor-employers.[72]

So long as these loans remained unpaid, no attached worker was allowed either to quit employment or to seek work elsewhere (particularly during the peak agricultural season) without first obtaining the permission of his creditor-employer; as one such labouring subject observed, when his master needed him for work, he worked for his master.[73] As in Haryana, inter – and intra-kin group conflict concerning the enforcement of debt-servicing labour obligations that involved sums of less than Rs 200 were settled by the village *panchayat*, which had the power both to impose fines of Rs 50 and to imprison a person for a period of one month.[74]

One consequence of the acute conflict in this village between landholders and agricultural workers over the issue of tenure has been the decline of sharecropping relations. Landholders pointed out that throughout the past decade (1975–85) the incidence of crop sharing had diminished, although previously it was the most common form of tenure. Two reasons were cited for this change: first, tenancy legislation threatened the ownership rights of proprietors who sharecropped; and second, sharecroppers themselves had become more militant during this period, demanding the whole product of leased land rather than the stipulated 50 per cent.

The outcome, landholders explained, was a shift from crop sharing arrangements to labour attachment, an economic transformation which entailed a reduction of usufruct rights: attached labourers received only half the land previously leased to sharecroppers. Under the current system of tenure (*jagir*), landholders both cultivated more of their property and simultaneously retained a higher proportion of its output; the attached labour relation, they concluded, was for them more profitable than sharecropping.

During the peak agricultural season, local males and females were employed as casual labour by village landholders, particularly for the paddy transplanting operation. Both piece-work and time-work was remunerated in kind: the per acre rate for uprooting and transplanting paddy was respectively 15 and 21 kilos of rice, while one kilo of rice was paid to a casual labourer who completed five hours of weeding. There was no evidence that landless casual workers in this particular village either obtained or were bonded on a seasonal basis as a result of loans advanced by employers.

III

Part of the Gangetic alluvial plain, Purnia District lies in the northeastern corner of Bihar and is bounded on the east by West Bengal and on the north by Nepal.[75] Historically, this has been an economically backward area even within the context of Bihar, characterized by a combination of latifundism, sharecropping and immigrant tribal labour.[76] Research conducted in this district over the period December 1989 and January 1990 pointed to the existence of a link between outmigration and the reproduction of female unfreedom, and also to the important role of gender ideology in immobilizing women's labour-power, the object of which was to meet intra-kin group debt servicing work obligations incurred by male borrowing.

Of related significance was the accompanying process of agrarian change: agricultural production in Purnia district was at this conjuncture experiencing the beginnings of a capitalist transformation.[77] This entailed not only the increasing cultivation of commercial crops – particularly tobacco, potatoes, and bananas – and an increased incidence of tractorization, but also a decline in sharecropping relations.[78] Given the received wisdom about tenure and labour relations in Purnia generally, of particular interest was the low incidence of sharecopping in the villages covered during the course of this fieldwork.[79] Although registered as such in the period 1952–58, occupancy tenants (*sikmidars*) were now being evicted from their holdings, and being transformed either into non-occupancy tenants or landless labourers.[80] In the case of Purnia, the eviction of sharecroppers and the consolidation of means of production was licensed as much by what a landholder might legally retain under existing statutes as by the non-implementation of existing tenancy legislation.[81]

4.8 Bonded Labour in Purnia District, Bihar

In most of the fieldwork villages in Purnia, both casual and permanent attached labourers took loans from their creditor-employers to meet off-peak season consumption requirements, and also to finance expenditure necessitated by life-cycle ritual (marriage, death).[82] As long as such debts remained unpaid, the subject concerned was not free to work for other landholders if the creditor-employer himself had work that required completion (the beck-and-call relation referred to by Thorner). Furthermore, in the event of disability, old age, or death, any unpaid debt was passed on to the children of the labourer.[83] In cases where either an indebted worker, or the children and/or female kinsfolk of a worker who was himself no longer able personally to cancel his debts, attempted to enter alternative employment, he/they were physically assaulted and forced back to work on land owned by the creditor-employer to whom the cash/kind debt was owed.[84]

There were only two methods of escape: to find another creditor-employer willing to reimburse the present one (= 'changing masters'), or quite literally to run away (or 'abscond') by migrating elsewhere. Interestingly, although it reported considerable outmigration from Purnia sample villages, the ANSISS/ILO Bihar survey did not investigate either the incidence or the effects of migration.[85] Significantly, there was considerable outmigration from a number of the fieldwork villages studied, amounting in one instance to 23 per cent of the population and a much higher proportion of the workforce. Migrants from these villages found various forms of employment: as agricultural labourers in Punjab and the main Green Revolution area of Uttar Pradesh, as carpet-makers in Allahabad and Banares, as hotel porters in Calcutta, and as unskilled manual labourers in Assam, Gauhati, and Siliguri, engaged on tasks such as road construction (where they earned Rs 300 monthly) or digging ponds and canals.

Unsurprisingly, landholders in these villages reacted in a hostile manner to this increasing incidence of outmigration, and attempted to stem the outflow in two ways. First, by putting pressure on the family members of an indebted labourer who 'absconded' either to secure his return to work or – failing this – to take his place during harvesting and transplantation. And second, by withholding wages from labour generally, a system whereby the landholder retains a portion of wages due so that the worker does not leave his employ. Of particular significance, therefore, is the fact that in Purnia this method of induced debt by withholding wages was applied to casual workers.[86] When harvesting was complete, the employer retained half of the wage due, thereby compelling the worker concerned to remain with him throughout the succeeding operations in the agricultural cycle. Throughout this period the worker received small payments of Rs 10–20 at a time. This continued until *basant pachami*, when payment was finally made. In this way, informants pointed out, employers retained casual workers for a series of operations, and paid them off when labour was no longer needed.

That workers both strongly resent and fight against this method of immobilizing their labour-power was demonstrated in a rather dramatic manner during the course of a fieldwork interview, when a weeping woman appeared, and informed everyone that she had been beaten by the daughter and wife of her employer (a landholder owning 12–15 acres) because she had dared to ask him for the back wages due her. Not having been paid for two to three months, she asked him at least to provide her with breakfast, to which he replied that she must not demand things of him. She then observed that why should she continue working, at which point her employer instructed his wife and daughter to beat her. Significantly, in the conversation that ensued it was pointed out that employer control over their casual workers frequently entailed this kind of physical force.[87]

4.9 Unfreedom, Gender and Migration in Purnia District

This episode also illustrates the important role of gender ideology in reproducing unfree production relations in Purnia district. As in the case of La Convención, Peru, therefore, where unfree labour is reproduced by means of authority embedded in family/kinship/patriarchy, the reproduction of unfree relations in India is also effected by means of the economic and ideological control exercised by males over the labour-power of females within the same kin group, and the requirement for women to meet debt-servicing labour obligations owed to employers by males in the same household who 'abscond' leaving debts unpaid. Accordingly, the withholding of wages and its element of unfreedom as a form of labour control raises crucial questions about the interrelationship between class and gender as forms of empowerment/disempowerment.

Ironically, the act of worker empowerment by men may in some instances be realized at the expense not just of women but of woman-as-worker. Accordingly, the act of migration, which may be empowering for a male worker, is for a female worker disempowering. Whereas an 'absconding' male worker who migrates in this way (literally) escapes bondage and is accordingly transformed from an unfree into a free labourer, this process of emancipation is nevertheless achieved at the cost of a female worker who, as a result of having to meet his debt-servicing labour obligation, is herself transformed from a free into an unfree labourer.

As the above episode from Purnia District confirms, in demanding the payment of wages owed her, and at the same time threatening to withdraw her labour-power if this was not done, therefore, the labouring subject confronted her employer not as a woman but as a *worker*. The landholder, however, refused to recognize this class identity, and instead responded to her as a *woman* – by setting his female kinsfolk on her (= this is a woman's affair, to be settled by women as women). In other words, not only is it the employer who reconstitutes the identity of the labouring subject by shifting the identity of the latter from a threatening discourse (about class) to a less dangerous one (about gender) but this shift is for the subject concerned a disempowering one.

The example of Purnia (and, indeed, other contexts in India and Latin America) suggests two things. First, that the system of withholding wages amounts to nothing less than a period-specific form of unfreedom the object of which is to prevent the worker in general, and female labour in particular, from offering his/her labour-power for sale elsewhere at the point of the agricultural cycle when it is most advantageous to do so. The element of violence it generates also challenges the observation contained in the ANSISS/ILO Bihar survey to the effect that the lack of tension between large landholders and agricultural labourers was due to the lack of consciousness on the part of the latter.[88]

And second, that the discourse about gender as a form of worker disempowerment is also connected with the distinct kinds of sanction each invites from the wider context. Whereas a worker who is female might expect to receive the support of her kin/caste group in a direct confrontation with an employer over issues of pay and conditions, the same worker could expect by contrast to be a target of hostility from this same kin/caste group in the event of an indirect confrontation with the same employer where this involved challenging/defying the right of a husband/brother/father/uncle to insist that a wife/sister/mother/daughter meet the debt-servicing labour obligations incurred by males in her household/family/kin group.

4.10 Conclusion

A comparison of the conditions affecting the reproduction of bonded labour in Nalanda and Purnia Districts of Bihar indicates the existence of both similarities with and differences from those in Punjab and Haryana. The differences challenge the conventional view about the necessity of a link between emancipatory trends and capitalist development, since the borrowing/repayment patterns of attached workers in Nalanda District suggest their relative economic autonomy when compared with counterparts in northwest India. The similarities are equally significant: both northwestern and northeastern India are characterized by acute forms of class struggle, in which 'from below' attempts at emancipation from attachment are countered by 'from above' attempts to impose or reimpose bonded labour relations. As in Punjab and Haryana, unfreedom in Bihar not only encompasses permanent, casual and migrant workers, but its reproduction is linked centrally to patriachal authority/power exercised from within the kinship domain.

An important difference between northeast and northwest India concerns the multi-sourced nature of indebtedness among permanent workers in Bihar. Unlike Haryana, where attachment involved entering an exclusive debt/working relationship with a single creditor-employer, in Nalanda District by contrast it was possible for annual servants to borrow from different landholding and non-landholding subjects simultaneously, even though not bonded to the latter as a result. This situation derived from a combination of circumstances which ensured debt repayment: first, access by an attached labourer to income-generating sharecropped land; and second, his disposition over a low paid or unpaid workforce composed of kinsfolk. Adopting the criterion invoked by Rudra (see Chapter 7), this multi-sourced indebtedness would seem to point to the existence in Nalanda District of an economically less onerous form of bondage when compared with the single-sourced form of indebtedness linked to attached labour relationships in the Haryana village case studies. It is necessary to qualify this, however, by reference to the reduction in Bihar of usufruct rights to land on which such borrowing/debt-repayment depends.

Such an interpretation regarding the relatively greater degree of socio-economic autonomy enjoyed by attached workers in Nalanda District is further supported both by their residential independence and by their ability to finance marriage expenditure from livestock sales. Unlike Haryana, therefore, where permanant attached labour worked full-time in the household of his creditor-employer and where the resulting continuous supervision together with a related inability to tend/own livestock fuelled conflict, bonded labourers in Nalanda District were not only full-time residents of the labourers' colony but also (and therefore) disposed of time in which to raise and tend income-generating livestock (thereby enabling them to finance a large portion of marriage costs from their own earnings).

Turning to the similarities between Haryana and Bihar, it is clear that the control/disposition over household labour-power is central to any understanding of the manner in which attached worker relations are reproduced in both these contexts. In the case of Bihar, the number of household members is usually regarded as a drain on the overall resources available to the domestic unit. However, while it is true that the number of young adults in a family constitutes an important contributory factor in household indebtedness, particularly with reference to marriage expenditure, it is nevertheless true that as *earning* adults such subjects also constitute the means whereby such debt is cancelled.

This points to the possible operation within these units of a *politico-ideological* concept of equal exchange: that is, a system where the father becomes or remains bonded in order to meet the cost of his son's marriage; in turn, the son contributes his earnings to cancelling debt incurred by his parents for medical treatment or marriage of their daughter. This form of reciprocity, it should be emphasized, does not occur between creditor-employer and bonded labourer (where it is placed by revisionist texts considered in Chapter 7) but between the latter subject and members of his family. Neither is it the case that such intra-kin group exchanges constitute *materially* equivalent exchanges, nor are they perceived as such within the domestic unit of the bonded labourer. In whatever form the ideology of intra-kin group reciprocity prevails, therefore, it licenses the reproduction of unfreedom.

This is confirmed by evidence from Purnia District, which underlines the fact that, where unfree labour is concerned, any attempt to theorize intra-kin group exchanges in terms either of material equivalence or as ideologically egalitarian remains problematic. Not only was it the role of women's labour in this particular context to meet debt-servicing labour obligations incurred by male borrowing, but an effect of male outmigration was the transformation of female kinsfolk who remained behind from free into unfree workers. Gender ideology was in this context a disempowering discourse also used by employers, with the dual object of denying the class identity of a female worker in order to reaffirm/reproduce her unfreedom. Rather than an egalitarian discourse licensing materially equivalent exchanges, therefore, the role of gender/kinship ideology was one of power/patriarchy/authority deployed by employers and senior kinsmen for the same purpose: the legitimization and/or enforcement of surplus-extracting (= exploitative) bonded labour relations.

The most fundamental similarity between the fieldwork villages of Haryana and those of Bihar was the increase in landlessness, in so far as this applied to usufruct rights extended to permanent members of the agricultural workforce, and the corresponding decline in the incidence of sharecropping. Just as farmers in Haryana discontinued the *siri* relation and instead them-selves began to cultivate holdings earlier leased to permanent workers, so peasant proprietors in Bihar have themselves begun farming land previously rented out on a sharecropping basis. Even where agricultural labour has been permitted to retain access to such holdings, moreover, there has been a marked decline in both the fertility and area of sharecropped land. Historically, the outcome of this process has been the replacement of crop sharing relations with attached labour that is now either wholly landless (as in Haryana) or possesses usufruct rights only to a reduced micro-holding (as in Bihar).

From the viewpoint of a creditor-employer, the advantage of converting sharecropping tenants into attached labourers in this manner is simply stated: it is a transformation which retains/reinforces the element of unfreedom inherent in the production relation (and hence the availability/subordination of its subject) while simultaneously diminishing the cost of labour-power (embodied in usufruct rights to land). The significance of this development has been that in Bihar – as in Haryana – it also deprives attached labour of an important source of funds with which to finance the marriage of children or repay old debts, which makes such workers *together with the labour-power of their family* more dependent on loans from the creditor-employer. This in turn ensures higher levels of indebtedness, thereby undermining or eliminating incipient attempts on the part of the permanent workforce to establish a modicum of politico-ideological and/or economic independence.

Conflict between peasant proprietors and agricultural workers throughout the state of Bihar during the period in question emphasizes the importance of the need on the part of landholders to impose (or retain) control over the agrarian labour process. This point is further reinforced by the politico-ideological content of the struggles taking place in two of the three fieldwork contexts in Nalanda District, both before and during 1985; in one village attached labour undertook strike action in pursuit of higher wage payments, while in another sharecroppers laid claim to the whole product of leased-in land. Much the same was true of Purnia District at the end of the decade, where workers were migrating in search of better-paid jobs elsewhere or challenging – albeit unsuccessfully – the authority of employers over issues such as withholding wages.

It is equally clear that although casual agricultural workers in Purnia District were engaged an an attempt to commodify their own labour-power, that is to think and act like proletarians, employers were simultanously engaged in trying to prevent this transformation from being realized. This happened in a number of different ways: either at the starting point of the migratory process, where old employers (landholders) tried to prevent indebted workers from 'absconding' by withholding wages; during the migratory process itself, where labour contractors gained control over the labour-power of migrant workers; or at the end-point of this migration, where the new employers (carpet manufacturers in Banares, Allahabad) also attempted to exercise control over the labour-power of their newly acquired workers.

Coupled with its subject's dislike of attachment, together with a corresponding refusal to work in conditions and for payment levels imposed by landholders, the latter rightly perceive such political activity/demands on the part of annual servants as ultimately posing a threat to the existing property structure. In the course of these struggles, therefore, the debt bondage mechanism enables creditor-employers in Bihar – as in Haryana – to re-establish labour discipline (and thus prevent the cost of labour-power from rising) by either restricting or defining the limits to the socio-economic independence of their permanent and/or casual workforce.

NOTES

1. Government of Punjab [1982: 188–9, Table 8.5].
2. Government of Punjab [1982: 128–9, Table 6.6].
3. See Kumar and Desai [1983]; also Pouchepadass [1990].
4. Tiwary [1985].
5. Mundle [1979].
6. See Chopra [1985: 180–81] and Tiwary [1985: 212]. Pointing out that the existence of *kamia* bondsmen was reported in Palamau as early as 1826 [cf. *Banaji*, 1933: 70–71], Chopra rightly criticizes Mundle for stating [1979: 96] that the *kamiauti* system emerged in this district only at the end of the nineteenth century as a result of capitalist penetration. However, this does not of itself invalidate Mundle's general thesis regarding the connection between unfree labour and the appropriation of absolute surplus-value; accordingly, it is possible that accumulation may have either sustained or expanded both the incidence and the importance of debt bondage relations already present in the agrarian labour process. The existence of unfree labour in the latter context does not automatically characterize it as non-capitalist, any more than the presence of hired labour in Ancient Rome constitutes evidence of capitalism.
7. See Vijayendra *et al.* [1984: 130–31]. The same point is made by Winson [1982: 391ff.] with regard to the continuation of unfree production relations in the capitalist agriculture carried out on the East Elbian estates of Prussia during the nineteenth century.
8. See Government of India [1952: 68]. By contrast, Patel [1952: 92–3] observes that bonded labour in Bihar at this same time was almost extinct, due to the existence of a strong *Kisan Sabha*, legal provisions against bondage, and outmigration.
9. See Government of India [1952: 68–9]. Other texts on rural Bihar which support the view that, in terms of unfreedom, attached and bonded labour are essentially the same kind of relationship include Mitra and Vijayendra [1982: 111] and Das [1979: Ch.1; 1983: 56].
10. See Srivastava [1987a: 17]. Although this instruction was withdrawn in April 1981 at the order of Sri K.B. Saxena, he was himself subsequently transferred and his countermanding direction ignored. Official views concerning the presence or absence of bondage are in a large measure reinforced or undermined by prevailing opinion in the academic debates on the subject, and in this respect the work of revisionists (see Chapter 7) has been particularly influential in encouraging government attempts to deny the unfree nature of attached labour (personal communication from Sri K.B. Saxena).
11. See Das [1979: 8–9, 26–9]. For the application of this view to attached labour throughout India during the 1950s, see Ramamurti [1954: 22].

12. As will be seen below, however, there are exceptions to these socio-economic conditions: for example, the occurrence of regionally-specific labour shortages within Bihar itself (a consequence of labour outmigration), and – as in the case of Haryana – the existence of alternative income-generating (forest) resources that enable rural workers to survive the off-peak season when no agricultural employment is available without having to take loans.

13. It should be noted that, in economic terms, this situation is to some degree self-perpetuating. Since labour-power is both plentiful and cheap, there is no need for agrarian producers to invest in more efficient (and costly) labour-displacing technique, which in turn precludes the necessity of further developing the level of the productive forces, and thus reinforces the condition of economic stagnation. For analogous view, see Bhaduri [1973]. This complements the argument that it is largely the scarcity and/or high cost of labour-power which determines technical innovation, a case outlined by Habakkuk [1962] for the pattern of economic development followed by England and the USA in the nineteenth century.

14. For the background to the supply of unfree Indian labour to the British colonies, see Sandhu [1969], Saha [1970], Tinker [1974], Saunders [1984], Marks and Richardson [1984], and Thomas [1985]. The different forms of unfree labour within India during the colonial period are covered in Sarkar [1985].

15. See Omvedt [1980: 192ff.], who observes rightly that:

> There has been little study of these labour-contractors as a significant social stratum, a kind of 'labour aristocracy' that often arose from the ranks of the workers themselves. There is little knowledge, also, about the exact links they had in rural areas with the landlords and headmen who 'released' the labourers to them for recruitment ... the variation in the degree of control by the labour-contractor has been little studied.

Tinker [1974: 50–51] calculates that of the 750,000 labourers recruited for the Assam tea plantations over the years 1882–1904, one-third came from the Chotanagpur region of Bihar. For the way in which labour contractors continued to maintain control over migrant workers through the debt bondage mechanism in both the iron ore and coal mining industries of the Chotanagpur plateau during the first half of this century, see Corbridge [1982: 60–61] and Simeon [1984: 191]. Evidence provided by Sengupta *et al.* [1986] suggests the contemporary resurgence of 'archaic' labour contracting methods in the steel industry of Orissa, a process whereby militant (and therefore more costly) permanent workers are increasingly being replaced with less costly tribal migrants from neighbouring districts in Bihar.

16. See, for example, Connell *et al.* [1976], Oberai and Singh [1983], and Mukherji [1985]. Texts in which migration appears as unproblematically free [e.g, *Patel*, 1952: 93] actually go on to suggest this as a solution to the question of bondage in rural areas, thereby failing to distinguish between physical and economic mobility (about which see Chapters 6 and 7).

17. A survey of employment conditions at the Jharia coalfield on the Chotanagpur plateau of Bihar carried out during 1962 showed that 64 per cent of colliery workers were indebted, mostly to private moneylenders charging interest rates of up to 300 per cent annually [*Srivastava*, 1970: 400, 407 Table 5–30]; there was no evidence, however, that this situation constituted an obstacle to the colliery workers' ability to sell their labour-power. This would not have been the case,

however, had these same coal workers owed debts to labour contractors rather than to moneylenders. Similarly, Vijayendra *et al.* [1984: 146–7] indicate how in Medak District, Andhra Pradesh, a released bonded labourer not in receipt of the rehabilitation assets the government is supposed to provide migrates from his home village to Hyderabad city in order to obtain employment as a casual worker. The income generated by this endeavour is then used to repay the loan owed to his erstwhile creditor-employer, the ex-bonded labourer citing as reasons for this the necessity of fulfilling obligations required by village custom and the continued residence in the village of his wife and child. The 1976 Bonded Labour System (Abolition) Act notwithstanding, these reasons point to the post-abolition persistence in the village context of sanctions to enforce debt obligations in the form of extra-economic coercion against both debtor and his kinsfolk. A similar example is cited by Maharaj [1975: 27] from a survey he carried out in the District of Dhanbad, Bihar, during 1972.

18. Singh and Iyer [1985]. On this estimate, five per cent of migrants coming to Punjab every year can be classified as unfree labourers; however, Sharma [1982: 106] cites a much higher figure in his 1980 survey, and indicates that one in every ten of the migrants to Punjab is bonded at the point of origin. Although making a similar claim that labour contracting is on the decline, Gill [1984: 962] nevertheless indicates that this form of organizing workers still plays an important role in the annual seasonal migratory flow from East Champaran in Bihar to Jullundur District in Punjab.

19. Singh and Iyer [1985: 241] state that in the case of tribals from south Bihar indebtedness – and hence unfreedom – arises from the need to borrow from moneylenders or labour contractors in order to travel to Punjab; however, the same text also points out that non-tribals also have to borrow from moneylenders so as to make the journey to Punjab [1985: 230]. One method of repaying such debts is for migrants to take new loans from Punjabi employers: in these circumstances, bondage does not cease but is merely transferred from one location to another.

20. See Mitra and Vijayendra [1982: 108] and R.A.P.Singh [1985: 77–78].

21. See Marla [1981: 51]. According to this 1978 survey, Palamau District had the largest number of bonded labourers (20,000+) in Bihar; Santal Parganas, Monghyr, Saran and Champaran Districts all contained 10,000–20,000 bonded labourers, and between five and ten thousand were to be found in Gaya and Muzaffarpur Districts. Both Patna and Bhagalpur contained 500–5,000 bonded labourers, and less than five hundred were to be found in Darbhanga and Saharsa Districts. No bonded labour was recorded for the south Bihar districts of Ranchi, Hazaribagh, Dhanbad and Singhbhum, while no data was collected for Shahabad and Purnia Districts.

22. These figures are cited in Das [1979: 4].

23. See Mitra and Vijayendra [1982: 110].

24. In view of the flawed theory used by the First Agricultural Labour Enquiry when differentiating attached and casual workers [*Thorner*, 1962: 173ff.; *Rao*, 1962], it is impossible to quantify the changing incidence of attached labour as a proportion of the total agricultural workforce in Bihar during the post-Independence period. Thus Thorner [1962: 187] observes 'if it is not clear what constitutes an attached worker it does not matter whether the *Agricultural Labour Enquiry* says that in a given state there are 1.3 per cent or 78 per cent of them', and concludes that the true extent of labour attachment at this period, in so far as it referred to farm

servants not free to seek alternative employment, was as a consequence grossly underestimated.

25. At the beginning of the nineteenth century Francis Buchanan noted that share-cropping families (*adhiyar*) in Eastern India outnumbered labouring families (*krishan*) by two to one [*Kumar and Desai*, 1983: 165]. The highest incidence of contemporary share tenancy occurs in northern Bihar, particularly in Saharsa and Purnia districts, while the lowest is to be found in the southern plateau districts of Singhbhum, Ranchi and Hazaribagh.

26. See Bose and Ghosh [1976: 11]. More recent, regionally-specific studies, suggest a higher incidence of sharecropping. Both Ladejinsky [*Walinsky*, 1977: 455] and Mitra and Vijayendra [1982: 98] indicate that over forty per cent of rural house-holds in Purnia District are engaged in sharecropping relationships, while R.A.P. Singh [1985: 53] states that in Begusari District 95 per cent of landowners lease out land to sharecroppers.

27. See Government of India [1983].

28. See Bose and Ghosh [1976: 9].

29. See Jannuzi [1974]. Ladejinsky reports that towards the end of the 1960s land-owners in Purnia District also rotated their tenants in order to defeat the provisions of the 1885 Bihar Tenancy Act, under which a tenant who managed to hold a piece of land continuously for twelve years became entitled to occupancy rights [*Walinsky*, 1977]. As noted in Chapter 3, this kind of 'tenant switching' also occurs in Haryana.

30. Rather than depicting the relationship between sharecropping and unfree labour as a unilinear progression (sharecropping ⇒ debt ⇒ debt bondage), as suggested by some texts [e.g., *GPF/NLI*, 1978: 27], it would perhaps be more accurate to emphasize the element of circularity (sharecropping ⇒ debt ⇒ debt bondage ⇒ rehabilitation ⇒ sharecropping). As has been pointed out by Tiwary [1985: 210], even landless ex-bonded labourers in Santal Parganas District who benefit from government rehabilitation schemes usually become sharecroppers once again, thereby reproducing the very socio-economic conditions which give rise to debt bondage in the first place. This trajectory is confirmed by evidence from Palamau District, where released bonded labourers obtain food for only five-to-six months annually from the small plots of unproductive land received as part of the rehabili-tation process [*Vijayendra et al.*, 1984: 140].

31. See Marla [1981:59].

32. A similar point is made by Bardhan [1984: 120–21], who claims that in Bihar only 21 per cent of sharecropping tenants are required to undertake labour-service for the landowner.

33. See Mitra and Vijayendra [1982: 100]. Other texts support this view:

Right from colonial times there have been attempts by the state to protect *bataidars* through legislation. But the system survived many changes in central Bihar and continues to be in vogue ... the relationship of the *bataidar* with his landlord had all the features of a bonded labour relationship where the *bataidar* willingly does service for the *malik* like [taking] milk or curds to the city, accompanying the *malik* on visits to his relatives, performing services on festive occasions, etc. His economic, social and political life is completely con-trolled by the *malik* (see 'Bihar: Peasants, Landlords and Dacoits', *Economic and Political Weekly*, Vol. XXI, No. 35, 30 Aug. 1986, p.1532).

Dhar [1984: 111] makes the same point.

34. See Beteille [1972].
35. For example, Mandle [1983] argues that the failure to distribute land to ex-slaves in the post-bellum American South weakened their bargaining position in the labour market, and consequently enabled cotton planters to maintain access to a cheap workforce on sharecropping contracts largely of their own choosing. This view is put forward in the case of Bihar by Lal [1977: 25], Mitra and Vijayendra [1982: 97–100], and Tiwary [1985: 187ff.].
36. In Palamau District the incidence of sharecropping plough bullocks (*pasari*) has increased following the abolition of bonded labour [Vijayendra *et al.* 1984:140]. The trend away from sharecropping and towards the engagement of annual farm servants in Haryana is noted in Chapter 3; the same process is reported by Sharma [1982:94,108] with regard to peasant cultivators in Punjab who require a permanent workforce. These examples suggest that in Green Revolution areas where property values are high, producers rapidly discard leasing as a method of obtaining labour.
37. See Martínez-Alier [1971].
38. See Bardhan [1984: 116, 150–51].
39. Fieldwork assistance in Bihar was provided by Professor K. Gopal Iyer, at the time on secondment (as Project Advisor, Land Reforms Unit) to the Lal Bahadur Shastri National Academy of Administration at Mussoorie, and by Dr M.C. Sarkar and Dr A.K. Jha of the A.N. Sinha Institute of Social Studies at Patna.
40. Another difficulty in comparing fieldwork villages in the Nalanda area with those for Bihar as a whole derives from the variable nature of the information presented in the 1971 census. The only data covering all three fieldwork villages referred to population and household: thus village *A* was in demographic terms the largest (282 households with 1,618 inhabitants), followed in this respect by village *B* (132/802) and village *C* (18/129) [*Government of Bihar*, 1973].
41. See Kumar [1986: 53].
42. Government of Bihar [1973], Kumar [1986: 56].
43. See Kumar [1986: 154ff.].
44. See Kumar [1986: 69,71].
45. See Kumar [1986: 128, Table 4.24]. Given the relatively advanced position of Nalanda District within the context of Bihar as a whole, the observations by participants at a Rural Camp organized by the National Labour Institute in Rajgir during the mid-1970s concerning the accompanying socio-economic development are of particular significance. Accordingly, it was reported by Maharaj and Iyer [1975b: 10–11, emphasis added] that:

> In areas where agriculture is no longer a stagnant sector, rents have gone up considerably, and there has been an appreciable increase in the eviction of sharecroppers. Tractorization has made heavy inroads into the demand for labour. There has not, however, been any significant increase in the wage levels as a consequence of increased productivity. *What surprised us more was that agricultural progress was often accompanied by an increase in the incidence of attached labour. It ... did not have any liberating influence on bonded labourers. They continued to be as they were.*

46. The more conservative wing of the CPI has also undertaken wage struggles in Nalanda District [cf. *Maharaj and Iyer*, 1975a: 15]. In the fieldwork villages, its adherents were to be found among landholders and not rural workers. One *Bhumihar* peasant proprietor observed that throughout the block in which the field-

work villages were located, the CPI negotiated 'amicably' with landholders over wage rates, and had thereby precluded the entry of Naxalites into the area.

47. See Bhattacharya [1986: 148–9]. Conflict in the fieldwork villages centred on wage rates, and confirmed the earlier view of Maharaj and Iyer [1975a: 13] that: 'While revising the agricultural wages the Advisory Committee constituted by the Bihar Government also takes into account employers' capacity to pay. Our experience, however ... [suggests that] wage levels in the agricultural sector are regulated more by the ability of the worker to press his claims than by the employers' capacity to pay'.

48. The village was located eight kilometres from Giriak town, and in 1971 it was populated by 1,618 inhabitants and consisted of 282 households. Rather than following the usual fieldwork procedure of interviewing landholders first, and only then going on to interview their workers, in this particular village the pattern was reversed, with problematic effects. Accordingly, information concerning the socioeconomic structure of the village was initially elicited not from its landholders but from the inhabitants of the adjoining *harijan toli*. In the course of one interview, a landholder who with ill-concealed suspicion had been observing from outside the colony the process of questions being put to and answered by his own bonded labourer, suddenly intervened and angrily ordered the latter subject away. As a result of this incident, subsequent attempts to collect information from the landholders themselves proved difficult. Forwarned about the presence of outside researchers interviewing their attached labourers on the politically-sensitive issues of working conditions, debt relations, and wage levels, the landholders misleadingly claimed that no annual servants or permanent workers were employed in this village, and that the casual labour which they did employ was paid a daily cash wage of Rs 8–9 for tasks such as ploughing.

49. For example, one cultivator who owned 1.9 acres found it necessary to lease in a further three acres from another *Bhumihar* landholder, while a cultivator who owned 6.3 acres of land also rented an additional 1.3 acres on a crop-sharing basis from eight to ten other landholders in the same village.

50. The serious implications of this situation for agricultural production may be gauged from the fact that tubewells accounted for 60 per cent of the non-rainfed irrigation in the village, the rest being supplied by tanks (19 per cent), canals (11 per cent) and wells (ten per cent) [*Government of Bihar*, 1972]. Similar information concerning the relative importance of non-rainfed irrigation sources is not available for village *B* or *C*.

51. The total annual payment-in-kind received by a working family of six adults amounted to some nine quintals of paddy and wheat combined.

52. In Nalanda District, only bonded or attached labour has usufruct rights to land [*Maharaj and Iyer*, 1975a]. In this village, even peasant proprietors with very small quantities of land employed attached labour, to whom they sublet a portion of their holdings. Thus the employer of one annual servant himself owned only 1.9 acres; he leased in a further 3.1 acres, of which 0.31 of an acre (six per cent of the land operated and 16 per cent of the land owned) was leased out to his bonded labourer. Another proprietor, who owned ten acres, rented out 1.06 acres (11 per cent of land owned) to his three bonded labourers, a kin group of a father and his two sons. Crop sharing arrangements in this village varied according to the economic contribution of the respective parties: in instances where fertilizer costs were borne equally by both labourer and landholder, the latter subject appropriated

only half the product; where the landholder provided the total cost of seed and fertilizer inputs (because his attached labourer was too poor), however, he also took two-thirds of the crop.

53. For details of both these kinds of multi-sourced indebtedness, see the case studies presented below.

54. Subsistence loans involved small amounts of cash and/or kind, and in this village carried an annual interest rate of 36–50 per cent. One bonded labourer indicated that although he was in debt to his current creditor-employer as a result of periodically borrowing Rs 10 for subsistence purchases, he was nevertheless unsure as to the exact sum owed (his estimate being Rs 100–150). Like all the other labourers in the colony, this subject explained, he accepted his employer's assurances that money was owed. Accounts maintained by landholders were usually settled each June, but in his case this had not been done for the past three years. Another bonded labourer observed that as periods of employment were followed by periods of unemployment, people in his position had to depend on loans and could not leave their master until all such debts had been cleared. An additional cause of indebtedness was the obligatory nature of religious observance and its associated ritual. Hence 'God-service' (*dewa-seva*) entailed animal sacrifice (two pigs, one goat, one pigeon, and one cock) which necessitated expenditure of not less than Rs 1,200. 'If we do not do the service of God', one informant reported, 'evil will befall us'; he added that in order to comply with this religious observance, all *musahars* had to borrow from their creditor-employers. The high cost of the death ceremony (*schraddt*), which amounted to some Rs 1,800 in this village, was a consequence of expenditure both on gifts of utensils and clothes made to officiating Brahmin priests and on the feeding of all the inhabitants in the *musahar* colony. The latter involved purchasing two quintals of rice, 60 kilos of pulse, one-and-a-half quintals of vegetables, and miscellaneous items (such as fuel, salt, spice).

55. The major portion of marriage expenditure was a consequence of having to feed all the inhabitants of the labourers' colony plus outside guests. Loans taken by this bonded labourer were as follows:

Debt (Rs)	Cause	Creditor(s)
2000	Medical treatment	Two landholders, one of whom was the employer.
1000	Marriage	Employer
700	Medical treatment	Three local landholders

56. This informant emphasized that, although he himself was a bonded labourer, his son would not have to replace him as one in the succeeding generation.

57. Finance for the double-marriage ceremony in 1974 originated from the following sources:

Amount(Rs)	%	Source
1300	50	Sale of a cow
800	31	Sharecropping revenue
500	19	Loan from employer
2600	100	

58. The year spent working in the local brick-kiln corresponded to the period between employments as an attached labourer in this village. The informant himself stressed the importance of this outside work undertaken by the whole family as a major source of saving, with which it was possible to pay for the marriage of the younger offspring. Finance for the second double-marriage ceremony came from the following sources:

Amount (Rs)	%	Source
1500	30	Sale of two cows
1500	30	Family income from work in brick kiln
1000	20	Loan from brick-kiln owner
1000	20	Loan from brother-in-law
5000	100	

59. The informant claimed that it would be necessary to repay only half the sum owed to the government.
60. The village is located eight kilometres from Rajgir town. In 1985 the principal crops were paddy and wheat.
61. None of the agricultural labourers owned their house-sites, which belonged to landholders in the village.
62. According to Grierson [1975: 178, 314], the term *harwaha* as used in Bihar around the 1880s was not only interchangeable with the word *kamiyauti*, the term specifying bonded labour, but also referred to (and thus identified) the precise nature of the bonding transaction itself: 'an advance of grain or money or a piece of land given to a ploughman when he is engaged'. The same term, moreover, was used to differentiate a ploughman who received just such an advance from one who did not (*uttha*).
63. One such mixed cash/kind loan consisted of 0.4 of a quintal of rice plus 0.2 of a quintal of wheat, together with Rs 50 in cash. The worker concerned reported that half his total annual harvest wage, amounting to four quintals in all, was allocated to the repayment of cumulative subsistence debts. Attached labourers in this village also borrowed mixed cash/kind loans in order to finance the marriage expenditures of their children.
64. An attached labourer was required to mobilize the labour-power of his whole family for work on behalf of his employer during harvest-time.
65. Other employers claimed that intergenerational bondage had never existed in this village. Interestingly, the politico-ideological linkage in landlord discourse of bondage solely with the indebtedness incurred by an attached labourer for marriage expenditure coincides with the definition of bondage adopted by Breman [1985a: 268]. One attached labourer indicated that he had borrowed Rs 1,800 from an earlier creditor-employer in order to finance the marriage of his son; since the latter had worked for the same employer without usufruct rights to a plot of land, his father now regarded the debt as cleared. It is significant, however, that, calculated in terms of an annual income over the five year period, this sum represented

still only half the market value of produce which an attached labourer would obtain from usufruct rights to even the declining area of a leased holding.

66. For reports of similar landholder responses to worker militancy elsewhere in Bihar at an earlier date, see Maharaj and Iyer [1975a].

67. On this point, Maharaj and Iyer [1975a: 16] note:
The rural poor ... are wholly without reserves and any strike is not merely a test of their moral stamina ... but more so a test of how long they can go without food. We know of it from the experience of striking workers in one of the Patna villages [during the mid-1970s, where] agricultural workers were on strike for a week to press the demand for minimum wages. After three or four days they ran short of food. The landlords saw to it that no grocer sold them anything on credit.

68. As in the case of village *A* in Karnal District, Haryana (see Chapter 3), attached workers in this village were engaged in a continuing defensive struggle to resist the introduction by landholders of external labour during the period of harvesting and threshing wheat. One landholder, owning 12 acres and employing four annual servants, concluded that wherever *Bhumihars* and *Rajputs* existed, there also would be found *Musahars* as attached labourers, thereby indicating the manner in which the latter relationships are reproduced in landholder discourse as a 'state of nature', that is, historically and politically immutable.

69. The village is situated half-way along the Rajgir-Biharsharif road. The main crops in 1985 were paddy and wheat.

70. These tractors were leased out at the cost of Rs 200 per acre. One landholder owning over ten acres ploughed only 16 per cent of this area with a hired tractor, and the remaining 84 per cent with two pairs of plough bullocks. Due to the lack of a secure irrigation supply, he was able to cultivate a second crop on just 64 per cent of his property.

71. The spouse of an attached labourer also worked for the same creditor-employer, both in the domestic context (cleaning out the cowshed) and on agricultural tasks (paddy transplantation, harvesting wheat and paddy).

72. It is important to note that that subsistence debt was necessitated not only by this seasonal unemployment but additionally by the low output of plots leased to attached labourers. One of the latter explained that he also borrowed from his creditor-employer in order to supplement the subsistence shortfall occasioned by the limited productivity of leased-in land, the annual output from his 0.2 of an acre amounting to only two quintals of paddy. During the 1972 survey of bonded labour in Dhanbad District, Maharaj [1975: 27–8] observed a similar decline in yields (from 3.2 to 1.2 quintals) from the increasingly unfertile plots leased to *kamias*.

73. Creditor-employers were most emphatic that labour attachment was initiated not by the taking of loans but rather by the acceptance of usufruct rights to land. This was confirmed by the subjects of these relations, who indicated that access to land continued only for as long as they worked on a beck-and-call basis for its owner.

74. In his investigation of bonded labour in Dhanbad District, Maharaj [1975: 29] also draws attention to the important role played by the village *panchayat* in policing/ enforcing debt obligations. Insubordinate workers were brought before the *panchayat*, sometimes bound with rope, and beaten. Fines imposed on labourers for absence from work were particularly heavy, the penalty for a single day's non-attendance being Rs 30 (a sum equivalent to ten day's wages).

75. Early in 1990 the administrative area corresponding to the District of Purnia was

subdivided into four, and became as a result the Districts of Araria, Kishanganj, Katihar and (a much reduced) Purnia.

76. Over the late nineteenth and early twentieth centuries, one of the largest land-holders in North Bihar, the Maharaja of Darbhanga, owned property in Purnia District [*Henningham*, 1990]. The way in which large landholders in this District utilized the *benami* system of evading ceilings on rural property ownership operated in this district from the mid-1970s onwards is outlined in Nair [1979: 8–23] and Mishra [1993: 216–43]. Although the largest landholders in the field-work villages themselves owned between 100 and 300 acres, political activists in the District reported that some landlords in Purnia continued to own between 500 and 3,000 acres.

77. Purnia District has always featured in discussions about development theory as the epitome of socio-economic backwardness, not just within India but also within Bihar (see, for example, Walinsky [1977: 442–62], Prasad [1989: 27–36], and Nair [1979: 19ff.]). When in 1990 an eminent scholar at the A.N. Sinha Institute was told by me of the emerging capitalist agriculture in Purnia, his response was incredulity, along the lines of 'this kind of process does not occur in that kind of place'.

78. During the late 1980s, of the five main crops grown in the District paddy accounted for 55 per cent of the sown area, wheat and jute 17 per cent each, pulses six per cent and oil seeds four per cent. Only 23 per cent of the net sown area was irrigated and 39 per cent of the area double cropped [*Central Bank of India*, 1988: 34]. However, the number of tractors in the District increased from only 91 in the mid–1970s to 1,548 in the late 1980s [*Nair*, 1979: 17; Central Bank of India, 1988: 34]. According to the District Agricultural Office, the per hectare output of HYV paddy grown in Purnia during 1990 was 25 quintals, compared with only 16 quin-tals for the non-HYV crop; of the 250,000 hectares under paddy, some 43 per cent was high yield variety. HYV wheat output was 22 quintals per hectare, bananas yielded 100 quintals and sugarcane 350 quintals per hectare.

79. In one of the fieldwork villages there was evidence of workforce restructuring by employers. When casuals decided 'not to work according to the employers' will', or organized and presented employers with a demand for higher wages, the response of the landholders in each instance was to recruit substitute labour in the form of other workers from the surrounding area.

80. Thus out of 172 families, only some 10–12 or six per cent in the fieldwork villages were sharecroppers [*Brass*, 1993a]. The inhabitants of one *adivasi tola* pointed out that they were willing to enter sharecropping relations, but proprietors were unwilling to lease out land due to a fear that tribals would occupy it on a permanent basis.

81. Under the land ceilings legislation, big landlords in Purnia District are permitted by law personally to retain a maximum of 15 acres of best irrigated land, or up to 45 acres of worst quality land. Their sons, if over the age of 18, are also permitted to retain the same amount (or one land ceiling unit). Thus a large landholder with five sons over the age of majority can keep *legally* 75 acres of the best land. If his sons are legal minors, they are entitled to one tenth of a ceiling unit, or one-and-a-half acres. Also excluded from the land ceiling assessment are holdings put aside for a daughter's dowry, since this is regarded as an asset which will be transferred out of the landholder's family. Similarly exempted from land ceiling assement over the 1959–70 period is property sold to the government for the Kosi canal, sold

legally, actually gifted to daughters as dowry, or given as *bhoodan*. On the whole, therefore, landholders do extremely well, even out of their legal entitlements to land under the existing legislation, never mind the land held illegally under *benami* or not declared for assessment purposes. Unlike other states, moreover, a landholder in Bihar exercises considerable resumption rights over land held under the ceiling laws. For example, a proprietor who keeps 15 acres under the ceiling and leases this out to others on a sharecropping basis, retains the legal right to take back this land, a right which overrides that of sharecroppers to land which they work. In other words, tenancy laws favouring sharecroppers are abrogated in such instances by the rights of landholders. The sole exception to this rule is the occupancy rights sharecropper, who may still claim ownership to land worked continuously over twelve years.

82. One informant described the attached labour relation as a 'twenty-four hours job', the agricultural working day extending from 4 a.m. to 9 p.m. In addition to ploughing, an attached labourer was required to clean the cattle shed, to tend livestock and supervise the latter grazing. Permanent attachment resulted from debt, generally incurred for marriage, illness or death ceremonies (Rs 500–1,200) and was witnessed by persons from the *harijan tola*. Attached labourers who attempted to work elsewhere without repaying debts owed to an employer were invariably pursued by *goondas* hired by the latter, pysically assaulted and compelled to return. Casuals who borrow for expenditure occasioned by marriage, death or illness, become transformed thereby into permanent attached labourers. Unsurprisingly, therefore, casual workers in Purnia – like their counterparts in Haryana – indicated a strong dislike of attached labour relations and a corresponding preference for casual employment, mainly because the latter permitted them to 'say no to an employer'. And like casual labourers in Haryana, those in Purnia explained that – even though bondage constituted a secure source of employment – they would always refuse to enter attached labour relations voluntarily. Their objection was not to permanent work *per se*, which they all desired, but rather to its accompanying element of unfreedom.

83. When a permanent attached labourer dies, any unpaid debt is passed on to his children who, if they refuse to meet this obligation, are subjected to coercion and/or social pressure. The employer summons the loan witnesses who are required either to confront directly those wishing to renege, to apply physical force, to threaten legal action for the recovery of the loan, or to appropriate any household goods and livestock belonging to kinsfolk of the defaulter.

84. In the fieldwork villages both permanent and non-permanent workers who owed debts to their employers reported that scolding/abuse by the latter was routine. A gang of contract labourers composed mainly of female Oraon tribals, who described themselves as day labourers, stated that they were free to work for others only when their own employer (= master/*malik*) – who owned 300 acres and from whom they all took cash/kind loans – had no need of them. It was pointed out that as he had first call on their labour, they had to work for him when required to do so. Anyone in the gang attempting to seek alternative employment (as some of them had already tried to do) would be forced back to work by the male overseer/contractor supervising their labour on behalf of their employer.

85. See ANSISS/ILO [1988: 118].

86. An important consequence of withholding wages in this manner was that casual workers affected were compelled to borrow in order to survive, a procedure that

carried with it the risk of becoming transformed into a permanent attached labourer. Moreover, in cases where casuals borrowed from and incurred cash/kind debts to the same employer who had withheld their wages in the first place, the effect was to convert the wage form into a debt.

87. Because of the harsh treatment women received from an employer when working as unfree casual labour, they were noticeably more vociferous than men in their criticisms about and opposition to bonded labour relations. Such negative perceptions of unfreedom emanating 'from below' contrast absolutely with the opinion expressed by an Additional Collector (Land Ceilings) in the District, who observed to this writer that, as agricultural labourers now had landholders at their mercy, bondage was non-existent in Purnia; in his view workers who remained with a single employer did so out of choice. The latter corresponds to a discourse about powerful-workers/weak-employers, the politics of which are examined in the second half of this book.

88. For this claim, see ANSISS/ILO [1988: 112].

PART II
Debates

5

Neoclassical and Marxist Approaches to Capitalism and Unfree Labour

Both historically and actually, there is a complex interrelation between the existence of unfree labour and class struggle generated in the course of agrarian transformation. This has in turn given rise to longstanding debates, between neoclassic economics and Marxism and within Marxism itself, about whether debt bondage is a characteristic only of an economically backward (= 'semi-feudal') agriculture or compatible also with agrarian capitalism. The focus of this chapter will therefore be on the respective approaches of neoclassical economics and varieties of Marxism to unfree labour, to the connection between it and capitalism, and to the positive/negative meaning of such relations ('security', 'subsistence guarantee', class struggle and work-force restructuring).

That unfree labour remains a live issue at the end of the millenium is both surprising and yet unsurprising. It is surprising to the degree that varieties of modernization theory have maintained that the global spread of capitalism will be accompanied everywhere by the decline of unfreedom and a corresponding expansion in a free workforce, a view which regards emancipation as a necessary effect of capitalism. In much of the recent debate about economic development, therefore, the transition from pre-or non-capitalist modes to capitalist production is judged to have been accomplished largely on the basis of whether or not free wage labour has replaced pre-existing unfree relations in the agrarian sector. It is unsurprising in so far as not only has this not happened (unfree labour being demonstrably compatible with capitalism) but also because of attempts on the part of neoclassical economic historiography (= 'cliometricians') to revise history by claiming that past forms of unfreedom have not been as coercive and disempowering as depicted.

Broadly speaking, it could be argued that current theoretical disputes about the meaning and thus the presence/absence of unfree labour have their origin in two politically distinct frameworks: Marxism and neoclassical economics. Disagreements about the epistemology structuring the free/unfree opposition, however, also occur within Marxism itself. Because neoclassical economics equates capitalism with worker 'choice', this in effect denies the possibility of a connection between unfree labour and accumulation. Since it regards bonded labour as a pre-capitalist survival, the same is true of one particular variant of Marxism, the 'semi-feudal' thesis. Where capitalist development occurs, therefore, labour must be free. Deprivileging free wage labour as the defining characteristic of accumulation, another variant of Marxism – the deproletarianization thesis – makes the opposite case: that capitalism is not only compatible with unfree labour but in certain situations actually prefers this to a free workforce.

I

In contrast to Marxist interpretations of unfreedom as exploitative relationships which permit the extraction of surplus labour, many texts emanating from the revisionist project which structures much recent writing on unfreedom eliminate the element of coercion from most or all agrarian relationships, and subsequently reclassify them as free wage labour. Hence revisionist contributions to debates about rural labour theorize what Marxists term unfreedom as a form of equal exchange, or a benign (and thus tension-free) arrangement to the benefit of all parties to the relation.[1]

Eschewing objective definitions, these texts adopt subjective criteria when conceptualizing freedom/unfreedom, and consequently maintain that what outside observers wrongly interpret as unfree relations derives from the voluntary entry by rural labour into 'reciprocal' and essentially desirable working arrangements which provide the labouring subject with economic security in the form of a 'subsistence guarantee' or 'employment insurance'. Accordingly, revisionists theorize the debt component of relations such as indenture, peonage, contract or bonded labour as evidence not of the coercive power exercised by employers but much rather of the enhanced bargaining power exercised by workers.

5.1 Neoclassical Economic Historiography and Unfree Labour

Significantly, this revisionist view concerning unfree social relations of production is epistemologically no different from (and in some instances is explicitly determined by) neoclassical economic theory.[2] Within a neo-classical economic framework, silence on the part of the choice-making subject is interpreted as assent: accordingly, a result of a methodological inability and/or theoretical unwillingness to address non-economic aspects of unfreedom, and the consequent failure to problematize coercion (see Chapter 1), is the epistemological impermissibility of unfreedom within a neoclassical economic framework. Having banished coercion, neoclassical economics is left with a form of market essentialism, a reductionist approach whereby anything and everything involving the employer/worker relationship is *ipso facto* proof of the harmonious operation of a free (or 'perfect') market in which choice-making individual labourers express subjective preferences.[3]

The fact that within this framework value is subjective and not objective, and consequently all parties to market exchanges receive the value of their own individual economic contribution and nothing more, necessarily precludes analytical categories such as exploitation, class formation/reproduction, and class struggle. Since neoclassical economic theory cannot accept that in some circumstances employers prefer to recruit unfree labour, and thus may actually strive to bring about an imperfect market, it correspondingly fails to recognize the attempt by either party to change the relationship from what it is to what in the opinion of the respective protagonists it ought to be. This crucial dimension – class struggle – in effect negates the neoclassical view of the market as an arena of harmony, and undermines not only the notion of an equilibrium structuring the exchange between employer and labourer, but also the assumption that rural employers are everywhere and always interested in the operation of a free market, and strive towards its realization.

Since by definition a neoclassical economic framework is premised on the voluntary supply of labour (= 'choice'/'consent') as one of the factors of production in what is – and for adherents of this particular theoretical approach only ever can be – a free exchange between individuals in the context of the market, difficulties emerge when labour is not freely provided by the owner of this commodity. The kinds of problems to which this antinomy gives rise are evident in the neoclassical approach of Shlomowitz to plantation labour during the late nineteenth and early twentieth centuries in a variety of contexts, and especially the way he interprets market exchanges involving the labour-power of unfree workers as evidence for the existence of 'free competition' and thus free labour.[4]

Following a debate with this writer about the presence and meaning of unfreedom, Shlomowitz appears to have qualified his views about plantation labour.[5] He now accepts the validity of two criticisms in particular. First, that on the basis of his original criteria – an essentialist view that the mere existence of employer/worker transactions vindicated claims about a 'well-working market' – it could be argued that chattel slavery itself was free, since exchanges between planters purchasing slaves and labour contractors selling them were also 'the outcome of a free interplay of competitive forces'.[6] And second, that he had failed to differentiate what were in fact two relationally distinct transactions: a direct exchange between worker and employer (a market in free labour-power) on the one hand, and on the other an indirect transaction involving only employers, one of whom transfers a debt-bonded worker to the other (a market in unfree labour-power).[7]

Although Shlomowitz has changed his mind, and now accepts that the existence of a free market in labour does not necessarily require the presence of free labour-power, his neoclassical economic framework is if anything rendered even more problematic. In essence, therefore, his current position amounts to the following proposition: despite the fact that it circulated involuntarily in what were actually exchanges between employers, labour was free. The difficulty with this is that Shlomowitz' acceptance that market competition between employers does not necessarily depend on workers themselves being free has consequences for his teleology: the inability of individuals to express 'subjective preferences' in the market negates the concept of the 'choice-making' subject that is itself central to a neoclassical economic framework.

Much the same kind of difficulty informs what is perhaps the most influential neoclassical economic analysis of unfree labour in recent times: the revisionist account by Fogel and Engerman of antebellum plantation slavery published during the mid-1970s.[8] In the latter text are encountered all the familiar claims of what might be termed a pro-slavery discourse: not only about the 'benevolence' of slaveowners and the 'subsistence guarantee' justification for slavery in the antebellum American south, but also about the 'mild' nature of the slave relation, its essentially benign 'paternalistic' (= 'patronage') character, and how accounts of coercion/cruelty/flogging were exaggerations.[9] According to Fogel and Engerman, therefore, a consequence of the above-average diet, housing, clothing, and medical facilities provided for slaves on the plantation was that they enjoyed a higher standard of living than free workers in the industrial north.[10]

The analysis of Fogel and Engerman also demonstrates the extent to which the epistemological overlap between revisionism and a neoclassical framework stems from a common cause: the emphasis by both on a 'from below' type of agency which, because it is antithetical to the conceptualization of coercion, licenses a discursive slide into the celebration of the plantation system as a context of worker empowerment.[11] Because coercion is either downgraded or missing from Fogel and Engerman's framework, it is impossible theoretically to accommodate both unfreedom and its effects. For adherents of this kind of approach, therefore, an economically successful productive regime can only ever be the outcome of 'choice' exercised by worker and employer alike, and not force.[12] The absence or ineffectiveness of coercion permits in turn the defence not just of slavery and the antebellum plantation but also of capitalism itself: unsurprisingly, therefore, the non-existence of coercion is central both to the seminal work of Fogel and Engerman and also to the many texts on unfree labour informed by a neoclassical paradigm.

In the case of Fogel and Engerman, the ontological structure of this discourse is not difficult to discern. Since in the absence of coercion an economically efficient antebellum plantation could only operate by means of 'incentives' offered to its workers, the latter must as a result have been able to exercise 'choice' and the productive system itself was accordingly based on their consent.[13] If the dynamic of such a system was neither luxury nor conspicuous consumption but rather profit, then the antebellum plantation was a modern capitalist enterprise, and as such could only be based on what for neoclassical economists is an organizationally rational system of market 'choice' involving incentives and rewards.[14] According to Fogel and Engerman, it was precisely the availability on the plantation of better food, clothing and shelter which – given the lack of coercion/force/oppression/exploitation – attracted and retained its workforce.[15]

5.2 Neoclassical Economic Historiography, Capitalism and 'Consent'

Rather than negative sanctions (= coercion/oppression), therefore, the organizing principle of plantation slavery as interpreted by Fogel and Engerman was – and, indeed, could only be – positive inducements (= 'choice'/'consent'): from this a number of things follow. First, what existed on the antebellum plantation was not an oppressive labour regime premissed on coercion exercised by owners against slaves, but rather a 'balance of power' between master and slave.[16] Second, the presence of this equilibrium meant that planters 'were compelled to to recognize the humanity of slaves' and willing to meet the material 'desires of individual slaves'.[17] Third, implicit in such an arrangement are concessions on the part of the masters, who 'compromised ... more than they realized', thereby reproducing the weak-master/powerful-slave stereotype which informs most variants of revisionism.[18] And fourth, a non-coercive regime based on an equilibrium between workforce 'choice' and employer concessions is supportive of the claim that slaves tacitly accepted not just their servitude but also the plantation regime and capitalism itself.[19]

Just how crucial it is for a neoclassical framework in general and for Fogel and Engerman in particular to decouple accumulation and coercion emerges from the way in which they attempt to resolve the difficulties posed for their views by by the economic role in wartime Germany of the concentration camp and its labour regime.[20] Endorsing the argument advanced initially by Genovese, Fogel maintains that 'plantations were organized for a fundamentally different purpose than concentration camps': the former were designed to produce marketable commodities, whereas the non-economic object of the latter was simply to exterminate people.[21] Despite the fact that concentration camps were productive units operating on the basis of unfree labour, therefore, the coherence of Fogel and Engerman's argument (capitalism = harmonious =

'choice'/'consent') depends on the premiss that the plantation ≠ the concentration camp.

The resulting relay-in-statement is revealing: the plantation = a productive unit = economically efficient = operates by consent = non-coercive labour regime; by contrast, the concentration camp = a non-productive unit = non-efficient = non-economic = a coercive labour regime. From this mistaken interpretation – death camps were filled with slave labourers, whose primary function was to produce commodities cheaply, just like their counterparts on the antebellum plantation – Fogel draws a wrong conclusion: namely, that the existence of economic objectives imposed a limit on the oppression exercised by masters. Hence the necessity for the latter to secure the cooperation ('consent'/'choice') of the plantation workforce. By asserting that the concentration camp was not an economic unit, however, a number of comforting conclusions supportive of a neoclassical framework are possible.

First, unlike concentration camps, which are 'irrational' in economic terms, plantations are economically 'rational' institutions: not only are the latter capitalist, whereas by this reckoning the former are not, but ideologically the plantation can also be positioned nearer a more benign image of capitalism, unconnected with horror/starvation/death. Such a view serves to rescue capital from the taint of fascism: in short, it permits Fogel to decouple what is obviously a coercive regime (the concentration camp) from what for him is equally obviously an economically efficient one (the plantation), thereby underlining the core element of his thesis, that capitalist production does not require coercion (capitalism/plantation ≠ force/compulsion).[22]

And second, it also permits Fogel to underline the necessity for planters of gaining the consent of slaves for the work regime, and thus to support his claims about two additional points: 'choice' exercised by slaves is indicative of their willingness to remain on the plantation; hence the essentially non-coercive nature of the plantation work regime, and therefore of capitalism itself. All of this is to be contrasted with the concentration camp, which *was* coercive and based on phsical oppression, but *not* capitalist. In this way, it is possible to maintain that both slavery and the plantation were basically no different from other capitalist relations and institutions.[23]

II

Turning to Marxist interpretations of unfree labour, here it is necessary to distinguish between two different approaches: the 'semi-feudal' thesis, which maintains that capitalism and bonded labour are incompatible, and the contrasting position based conceptually on the existence of deproletarianization.

5.3 Marxism, Free Labour and Capitalism

For Marxists, the necessary starting point for a consideration of the connection between unfreedom and capitalism is Marx's emphasis on the freedom of wage labour in the relationship between labour and capital, the social relation of production that constitutes the distinctive character of capitalism. As is well known, the designation of the freedom of wage labour has a double aspect: labouring subjects ('direct producers') are 'freed' from access to the means of production that secure their reproduction, and consequently they are (and must be) free to exchange their labour-power with capital for wages with which to purchase subsistence.[24]

Both aspects of wage labour capture the difference between capitalism and pre-capitalist modes of production. The first aspect signals the moment of dispossession of pre-capitalist producers, part of the process of primitive accumulation. Dispossession is the condition of the formation of a class of free wage labour which is the second aspect, or moment of proletarianization.[25] The contrast here is that, whereas in pre-capitalist modes of production labour is exploited by means of extra-economic compulsion, under capitalism proletarians are owners of the commodity labour-power which they exchange with capital under the 'dull compulsion of economic forces'. It is necessary to recognize, however, that not all social subjects in all pre-capitalist formations necessarily had property or usufruct rights in land and/or other means of production, let alone that all pre-capitalist formations guaranteed the means of subsistence. Historically, strongly differentiated pre-capitalist formations in Asia and Latin America have contained landless labourers 'available' for recruitment by capitalism.[26] In short, dispossession of pre-capitalist producers was not always necessary to the (initial) formation of a class of capitalist wage labour.

What is the connection between on the one hand the theoretical rationale of the freedom of wage labour and on the other the pervasive incidence of *unfree* wage labour throughout the history of capitalism? Accordingly, two suggestions are made here. First, given this interconnectedness between accumulation and unfree labour, that in particular instances it might be more appropriate to invert the usual way in which the question is posed: that is, to problematize the achievement of free wage labour rather than the existence of unfreedom. And second, that assaults by capital (actual or potential, pre-emptive or reactive) on the freedom of wage labour – the ability of workers to enter *and withdraw* from particular labour markets and labour processes – are a *general* feature of capitalism.[27] That is, the capitalist class as a whole (or its representatives) in some cases, or particular groups/types of capitalists and/or individual capitalists in other cases, seek to define and redefine the labouring subject so as to limit the exercise of his/her freedom as the owner of the commodity labour-power.

Such actions and struggles on the part of capital (with their economic, political and ideological expressions) aim to bring about *deproletarianization*, in the sense of diminishing or eliminating altogether the freedom of wage labour as defined above: the ability of owners of the commodity labour-power to exchange it as they choose. In other words, it is precisely by means of deproletarianization that capital is able to effect a double dispossession of its workforce: both from the means of labour, and also from the means of commodifying labour-power itself. Moreover, the ability of capital to engineer unfreedom in labour markets – to impose restrictions in the process of recruiting workers – has implications for the freedom of capital in using workers in labour processes from which they are unable to withdraw.

On the side of workers, this suggests that their class struggle against capital is commonly a struggle to assert, reassert or extend their freedom to dispose of their own labour-power: either separately from or combined with class struggle to destroy capitalism, therefore, such actions always constitute a potential/actual threat to existing property relations. Accordingly, when workers seek to defend and exercise their freedom as owners of labour-power, they are also required to contest on an individual or collective basis the attempts by capital to impose/reimpose and reproduce unfreedom both in the labour market and the labour process.

5.4 Marxism and Unfree Labour

Unlike neoclassical economics, which seeks either to dissolve the difference between free and unfree labour or else to dismiss its significance, Marxism not only recognizes the importance of this distinction but interprets the existence of the debt bondage relation in one of four ways.[28] The first – and perhaps the most common – regards bonded labour as a non-capitalist relation, and thus as evidence of the 'semi-feudal' (or even 'feudal') nature of agriculture. In contexts where debt bondage is present, therefore, capitalist development must by definition be absent.

By contrast, the remaining three variants of Marxism accept that unfree labour is compatible with capitalism. The second views unfree labour as a specifically colonial experience of capitalist expansion, and argues that accumulation in metropolitan countries is itself dependent on and effected through the maintenance of unfree agrarian relations in peripheral contexts.[29] The third accepts the existence of a connection between capitalism and unfree labour in metropolitan countries, but nevertheless still characterizes the relation itself as a pre-capitalist socio-economic form. Thus unfree labour is central to the reproduction – but not actually part – of the capitalist mode of production.[30]

The fourth position, and the one adopted in this text, locates such relations in the overall framework of struggle between employers and workers. Against the view that characterizes it solely as a pre-capitalist relationship, and in contrast to the preceding ways of situating it on a unilinear historical continuum, where debt bondage relations are ultimately superceded by free wage labour, unfree labour is regarded here as a crucial aspect of class conflict in particular agrarian situations. As such, it may be introduced or reintroduced by employers at any historical conjuncture, in order either to impose capitalist authority over the work place (where a proletariat already exists), or else to preempt the emergence and political consequences of proletarianization.

Because debt bondage is for neoclassical economic historiography and the 'semi-feudal' thesis an archaic remnant to be eliminated by capital at the first opportunity, therefore, both regard capitalism and unfreedom as antithetical. Unlike the latter approaches, which locate bonded labour within a unilinear process of economic development, the deproletarianization thesis accepts that legal emancipation does not necessarily signal an automatic and irreversible relational transformation: in the course of class struggle involving workforce de-/recomposition, therefore, labour can experience a two-way transition, both from freedom to unfreedom and *vice versa*.

5.5 Unfree Labour and the Mode of Production Debate

Significantly, much of the theoretical dispute within Marxism about the presence/absence in the Third World countryside of capitalism and semi-feudalism has turned on the presence or absence in such contexts of unfree labour: this was true not only of the initial exchanges about Latin America but also of those which subsequently characterized the mode of production debate in India.[31] The protagonists belonged to one of two camps: those who interpreted unfreedom as a pre-capitalist (= 'semi-feudal') relation, and those who by contrast maintained that unfree labour was either compatible with capitalism or indeed its preferred relational form.

Exponents of the 'semi-feudal' thesis maintained that moneylending and debt bondage were – and are – archaic relations; because bonded labour was regarded by them as an obstacle to capitalist development, unfree labour in the Indian countryside was categorized as a pre-capitalist remnant to be eliminated by capital at the first opportunity. In the unfreedom-as-a-pre-capitalist-relation framework, therefore, which denies that accumulation is possible in the context of non-mechanized production based on unfree labour, debt bondage is regarded as either unconnected with or indeed an obstacle to capitalist development.[32]

Thus economic stagnation is attributed to an unwillingness on the part of semi-feudal landlords to install labour displacing and productivity enhancing technological improvements because this would undermine their political hold over the indebted tenants from whom they obtain an income based on property rights and usury. Rather than follow the 'rational' economic behaviour of capitalists who employ free labour in order to maximize output and profits, therefore, the landlord class is categorized as uniformly 'feudal' in so far as it prefers instead to combine low growth with the continued employment of bonded labour, a situation which blocks the development of the productive forces (and hence the expansion of capitalism) in agriculture.

However, another variant of Marxism took – and takes – the opposite view, arguing that unfree labour in India and Latin America (and elsewhere) is not merely compatible with capitalism but is in fact reproduced by it.[33] Locating the debt bondage mechanism within the process of class struggle between capital and labour, exponents of this view maintain that unfreedom is method whereby employers impose or reimpose their authority over the labour process. In contrast to the unfreedom-as-a-pre-capitalist-relation view, those who regard debt bondage as compatible with accumulation theorize this in terms of absolute surplus-value extracted from unfree workers in a technically backward labour process formally subsumed under capital. For this reason, adherents of this view question the main assumption of the 'semi-feudal' thesis: namely that contemporary variants of unfree labour are necessarily always and everywhere 'survivals', and thus evidence for the continuation of archaic relational forms.

5.6 Unfree Labour and the 'Semi-Feudal' Thesis

The difficulties faced by the 'semi-feudal' thesis as a result of conceptualizing unfree labour as an intrinsically pre-capitalist relation may be illustrated with reference to the work of Patnaik, one of its most influential exponents.[34] According to her, the forced commercialization of Indian agriculture by landlord, trader and usurer during the colonial era failed to eliminate unfree agrarian relations and consequently to develop capitalism in colonial countries. What occurred in the latter contexts, therefore, was not the separation of the direct producer from the means of production but the pauperization of a still-viable peasantry. Because she perceives the labouring subject as essentially a peasant rather than a worker, Patnaik's idealist teleology downplays the importance or even the the possibility of smallholders being a *de facto* industrial reserve army of labour. For this reason, the process of capitalist restructuring by means of unfree labour formally sumbsumed under capital in the context of a technologically backward agriculture does not arise.

Where poor peasants are involved in the process of workforce decomposition/recomposition, Patnaik conflates what is ideological self-perception as a 'peasant' with the economic reality of these subjects as rural workers. Despite accepting both that these 'peasants' own little or no means of production, and that in their case the proportion of subsistence derived from the sale of labour-power outweighs what is obtained by them from the sale of the product of labour, she nevertheless downplays/underestimates their role as surplus-value yielding workers and persists in reifying them as rent-paying peasants.[35]

Not only does the latter interpretation disregard the fact that such instances do not correspond to 'peasant economy', where a cultivator owns/controls his own means of labour and thus important aspects of his own economic reproduction, but it also ignores those cases where, from the viewpoint of the owner of the means of production, profitability from cultivation exceeds rental yield.[36] Apart from labour-power, such 'peasants' own no property what-soever; to continue to regard them as rent-paying cultivators, therefore, is to wilfully misrecognize the reality of which they are a part.

Patnaik's unwillingness to perceive rural workers behind the surface appearance of (poor) 'peasant economy' derives from a tendency on her part to categorize unproblematically all landed relations together with their institu-tional forms simply as evidence for the existence of 'semi-feudalism'.[37] Indeed, in the face of the evidence she herself and others present, Patnaik appears to do no more than assert that the agrarian structure is pre-capitalist, or that certain forms of economic activity (land purchase, trade, money-lending) are of a 'traditional' character.[38]

Most importantly, essentializing the peasantry in this manner avoids con-fronting the distinction between the formal and real subsumption of labour under capital, and the fact that both permit the extraction of surplus-labour in the form of surplus-*value*.[39] In contrast to Patnaik, for whom the debt bondage mechanism is an archaic survival by means of which unproductive landlords extract pre-capitalist forms of rent from indebted smallholders (tenants, share-croppers), therefore, the unfreedom-as-a-capitalist-relation view is that in the case of a technically backward agrarian labour process formally subsumed under capital the creditor-employer extracts absolute surplus-value from unfree workers who own no property apart from their labour-power. The latter process, it is argued here, amounts to deproletarianization.

5.7 Unfree Labour and Agrarian Transformation

Generally speaking, the process of agrarian change involving the debt mechanism adheres to one of three patterns, in each of which the existing rural population combines a greater or less requirement to sell its labour-power under conditions of unfreedom with equally specific property relations. The first involves a linkage between indebtedness and the attachment of an individual to land, the object on the part of the landowner being to appropriate either surplus labour or surplus product. The most common forms of tenure are sharecropping, serfdom, or labour-service tenancy, and in terms of agrarian change it corresponds either to *peasantization*, or more usually where proletarianization has already occurred, to *repeasantization*.[40]

The second form also entails a linkage between land and debt. Unlike the first variant, however, where indebtedness is used to attach a subject to land, its object here is much rather the opposite: debt constitutes a method of either fully or (more usually) partially separating peasant proprietors from their means of production. The accompanying process of agrarian change is usually presented in terms of *depeasantization* leading to *proletarianization* or *semi-proletarianization*, a transformation associated historically with imperialism, and in particular with the manner whereby large-scale export-oriented colonial plantations acquire control over the labour-power of indigenous smallholders by depriving them of the ability to obtain all their subsistence requirements from their own land.

The main difficulty with this view concerns the way in which the concepts 'proletarianization' and 'semi-proletarianization' are theorized. Because proletarianization is frequently equated only with landlessness and semi-proletarianization with insufficient land for subsistence cultivation, all workers fully or partially separated from the means of production tend to be regarded as free wage labourers, notwithstanding the fact that the labour-power of such individuals may be under the control of a landlord, creditor-employer, labour contractor or a moneylender.[41] Accordingly, this process of agrarian change involves depeasantization combined not with proletarianization or semi-proletarianization but much rather with *deproletarianization*.

The third form is unconnected with land, yet also entails deproletarianization. Unlike the preceding variants, both of which involve employer responses to a workforce composed of subjects either owning means of production or not yet completely separated from the latter, in this instance unfree relations are imposed or reimposed on fully proletarianized workers whose sole property is their labour-power. Such cases, in which the process of agrarian change corresponds to *proletarianization* combined with *deproletarianization*, raise the issue of the connection between unfree relations and worker availability.

5.8 Unfreedom and Labour Availability

Unlike most of the theoretical approaches to the link between debt and agrarian change, the deproletarianization thesis is able to provide an explanation of why unfreedom occurs in both labour-scarce and labour-surplus areas: in the latter because rural workers have insufficient bargaining power and in the former because they have too much. In contrast to the position adopted here, which links the existence of unfree relations to issues of profitability and class struggle, therefore, the presence/absence of unfreedom is generally attributed either to a shortage or to a surplus of labour.[42]

Historically, the existence or introduction into particular agrarian contexts of unfree relations has been associated with the presence in such locations of labour shortages. One of most influential exponents of this view is Nieboer, who argued that as inhabitants of non-capitalist societies usually prefer to work for themselves rather than for others, actual or potential employers of labour-power must rely on unfree workers so long as unappropriated land ('open resources') is still available.[43] Once land becomes private property (or a 'closed resource'), unfree labour ceases to be necessary since the sale of labour-power is now the only method of obtaining subsistence.[44]

The opposing view links the occurrence of unfree relations to a surfeit of agricultural labour that has few or no alternative sources of subsistence. Many texts on rural labour in India are structured by this argument, unfree relations being seen as connected with the existence at different historical periods of labour surpluses in agriculture.[45] Both past and present forms of bondage are theorized as the result of economic immizeration that afflicted large sections of the rural workforce; accordingly, unfreedom is regarded as possessing its origin not in proletarianization – let alone deproletarianization – but in peasant impoverishment which derives from high levels of unemployment. This situation is attributed in turn to demographic growth combined with a lack of industrialization and thus non-agricultural job opportunities.

However, the use of indenture or debt bondage against free workers *already* separated from means of production suggests that reasons for the existence of unfree relations are unconnected with the need of agrarian capitalists to compel unwilling and/or wholly self-sufficient peasant proprietors to sell their labour-power, and raises the issue of the connection between unfreedom and worker availability.[46] In such circumstances, the concept 'labour shortage' possesses a specific politico-ideological meaning. The term is applied by employers not to an absolute unavailability of labour-power (additional workers are needed, yet none exist) but to situations where market forces or political consciousness permit free workers to act as (and reap the benefits from being) proletarians.

It is important to note, therefore, that workforce restructuring can occur in contexts where no actual labour shortage exists, or even where surplus labour is present, as well as in those where labour is scarce. In the latter case, employers will be faced with increasing labour costs because, though not organized on a collective basis, workers are nevertheless aware of the fact that labour-power is much sought after, and attempt to sell this to the highest bidder. However, even in areas where the demand for labour is either met or exceeded by the existing supply, and consequently there is no competition for workers, employers may still be faced with rising labour costs: due to the levels of political consciousness and organization exhibited by workers on the one hand, and on the other because overproduction and the tendency of the rate of profit to fall in the course of capitalist competition generally requires individual producers to cut the price of labour-power. Despite the differences in terms of labour availability, therefore, employer response is in both cases the same: the restructuring of the labour process.

IV

Instances abound across space and time of cost cutting achieved through work-force restructuring involving unfree labour, albeit frequently not theorized as such. Claims by neoclassical economic historiography and exponents of the 'semi-feudal' thesis to the contrary notwithstanding, evidence from the American South and the Sunbelt states, together with sugar plantations in Queensland and the Caribbean, confirms not just a compatibility between unfree labour and agrarian capitalism but also the existence from the mid-nine-teenth century onwards of a process of workforce restructuring involving deproletarianization.

5.9 The Recent History of Deproletarianization

Perhaps the historically most sustained instance of deproletarianization in the Caribbean is the employment of Haitian cane cutters (*kongos*) as contract labour for seasonal work harvesting sugar on both state and privately owned plantations in the Dominican Republic. This annual migration, which began in the 1880s and became more important from the 1920s onwards, was formal-ized with the 1952 inter-governmental agreement licensing payment for and recruitment of Haitian labour. The latter increased in number from around 14,000 annually during the 1960s to 23,000 in 1985, with the result that Haitians constitute over 90 per cent of all cane cutters in the Dominican Republic.[47] Noting that such workers risked arrest as illegal immigrants if found leaving the sugar plantations to which they had been allocated before the six-month harvest season came to an end, the 1983 ILO Commission of

Inquiry concluded that the bilateral contract between the two governments did indeed amount to forced labour.[48]

Part of the ubiquitous and notorious penal labour system which included the chain gang and convict lease, debt peonage in the postbellum South and Sunbelt states arose in cases where white farmers seeking agricultural labour paid the fines of blacks arrested for 'vagrancy', a debt which the latter were then required to repay by means of work on the land of the former.[49] As with other forms of unfreedom, therefore, peonage involved the inability of resident or migrant workers to commodify their own labour-power because of debts owed by them either to a producer or a labour contractor. Not only was its inception in many instances involuntary, in that recruitment was the only alternative to gaol, but the reproduction of peonage invariably exhibited all the characteristics associated with the presence of debt bondage.[50] These included the use of kin labour, the prohibition on working for others as long as debts remain outstanding, the transfer of debts between creditor-employers ('changing masters'), the withholding or non-payment of wages, and the enforcement of debt-servicing labour obligations by means of coercion.

For obvious political and methodological reasons, reliable estimates of the extent of debt peonage are lacking: however, one study conducted in 1907 concluded that at least one third of all planters in the southern states operated this system of bonded labour.[51] It was only during the 1927 Mississipi River flood, when large numbers of unfree black workers among those displaced became temporarily free, that the true extent of peonage was momentarily revealed.[52] In the 40-year period from the 1920s to the 1960s there were continuous and largely unheeded complaints about debt peonage in the southern states generally, and in particular concerning its persistence in California, Florida, Georgia, Alabama, Louisiana, Mississipi, Texas and Arkansas.[53] Based on evidence from the different migration patterns within the United states generally, another estimate calculates that during the mid-1960s a quarter of all commercial growers made cash advances to their migrant workforce, and that in 91 per cent of cases all such loans were repaid.[54]

The extent to which migrant labour employed by farmers in the Sunbelt states is not merely unfree, but also how the latter is itself reproduced by indebtedness to the crew leader, confirms that labour-power circulates in a decommodified form, and also that casuals as well as permanent workers remain trapped by debt peonage.[55] It is similarly clear, moreover, that this coercive link which structures worker/contractor and worker/farmer relations also corresponds to a relation of *production*.[56] Not merely was debt the principal method whereby a crew leader exercised control over members of their work gangs, therefore, but such debt-related control both arises and is possible at many points in this relationship.[57] Thus migrants become indebted as a result of the high prices charged by the contractor for subsistence consumed (the historical basis of the truck system).[58] Similarly, debts are incurred when a contractor (or farmer) either provides labourers with cash advances repayable from future wages or withholds wages that are due.[59]

5.10 Deproletarianization and Capitalist Profitability

These contexts also provide many examples of labour cost reduction by means of displacing free workers with unfree equivalents or converting the former into the latter.[60] One example from the antebellum American South is the Tredegar Iron Works of Virginia, which attempted to offset a competitive disadvantage with Northern and British manufactures by replacing free labour with slaves, thereby lowering the overall cost of labour-power by 12 per cent between 1844 and 1850.[61] The employment of unfree labour in this particular instance was due not to the lack of labour as such but much rather to struggles by members of the existing workforce composed of free labour against attempts by employers to cut costs by wage reduction.[62]

Similarly, had they not been able to use unfree indentured workers as strike-breakers against a local plantation workforce of ex-slaves which had withdrawn its (free) labour in pursuit of higher wages in Jamaica during the mid-1850s, planters would have been compelled to raise pay levels for locals by some 25 per cent.[63] In this respect the situation in Jamaica was no different at the turn of the century, when local workers, who wanted to remain free and were thus unwilling to accept the terms and conditions imposed on indentured labour (to whom they referred as 'slave coolies'), complained that the presence of the latter undermined their own bargaining power and prevented them from earning decent wages on the plantation.[64]

Another example of labour cost reduction through the employment of unfree labour is Queensland, where legislation prevented Pacific island labour from obtaining more lucrative employment outside the sugar plantation, thereby providing the latter with a captive workforce that not only cost less than half other forms of labour-power but also worked longer on a daily/annual basis.[65] It is clear, therefore, that the use of the Pacific Island Labour Acts of the 1880s and early 1890s to restrict Melanesian workers to unskilled manual labouring jobs on the plantation, thereby preventing them from seeking/ holding alternative and better-paid employment outside this sector, and the analogous use of the Masters and Servants Act against time-expired workers similarly attempting to improve pay and conditions, all correspond to a process of deproletarianization.

In the case of the postbellum South, it was capitalist producers in agricultural and non-agricultural economic sectors which benefited from the profitability of the convict lease system.[66] The use of unfree workers to displace free labour in order to restructure the labour process in other parts of the United States was similarly profitable: those who gained most economic advantage from the employment of debt bonded migrants provided/controlled by crew leaders, for example, have been the large commercial growers.[67]

5.11 Deproletarianization and Class Struggle

It is also clear that in all these contexts the imposition/reimposition of unfree relations by employers occurred when the existing workforce began to act consciously as a proletariat. In British Guiana following the end of the apprentice system in 1838, ex-slaves organized themselves into task-gangs and went from plantation to plantation bargaining with owners over wages and conditions, a process which culminated in the strikes of 1842 and 1848.[68] This, and not a labour shortage, was the reason for the dramatic increase in the immigration of Indian indentured workers from 1851 onwards.[69] Much the same happened in Trinidad, where over the 1891–1909 period sugar planters managed to hold down labour costs by importing unfree indentured immigrants in order to undermine the bargaining power of free workers.[70]

Another example of this employer reaction is Puerto Rico where, because newly emancipated ex-slaves began to act as a proletariat and bargain with their erstwhile masters for higher wages and better working conditions, the colonial state reimposed unfreedom during 1874 in the form of contracts preventing freedmen resident on sugar plantations from selling their labour-power without the consent of their employers. When in the 1890s sugar plantation workers on the island struck for higher wages and improved working conditions, employers imported contract labour from the British West Indies.[71]

Significantly, the introduction of Haitian workers into the Dominican Republic during the 1880s followed the first strike by Dominican labour employed on the sugar plantations against the imposition of wage cuts.[72] Both the intensity and determinants of class struggle remained unchanged a century later, when a survey carried out by the National Planning Office in the Dominican Republic pointed out the apparent paradox of largescale public expenditure on the import of Haitian contract labour at a time when some twenty per cent of Dominican workers were themselves unemployed.[73] What emerges clearly from this example is that the historical roots of this seeming contradiction lie on the one hand in the continuing resistance by Dominican labourers to pay and work conditions on sugar plantations (which they regard as the 'work of a slave') combined with a preference for alternative and better-paid employment, and on the other in a corresponding desire by the planters for a cheap, politically docile and immobile workforce.[74]

In this connection, it is significant that in Queensland – as elsewhere – the Masters and Servants Act was used to control labour unrest on the plantation, to stifle complaints and to punish 'troublemakers' for 'insubordination' and 'disobedience'; of equal significance is the fact that the main target of this legislation was the time-expired worker, a category which was increasing as a proportion of the Queensland labour force during the 1880s.[75] It was also used to prevent workers from withdrawing their labour-power and going on strike. In short, the workers against whom the Act was used were the ones with most experience not just of selling their own labour-power and negotiating over its price but also those who were prepared to undertake action to improve pay and conditions.[76]

Much the same is true of California, where the continuous process of agrarian workforce restructuring which occurred from the 1870s to the 1990s was not only a response by employers to workforce unionization and/or militancy but also involved deproletarianization. The profitability of agribusiness throughout this period remained dependent on the existence of a racially segmented rural working class, a situation which permitted capital to draw upon and super-exploit the unfree labour-power of a succession of immigrant and indigenous groups. Central to the accumulation project in this state, therefore, was the unfree and thus low cost labour of Chinese workers during the 1870s, Japanese workers in the 1890s, Indian and Mexican workers at the beginning of this century, Filipinos during the 1920s, that of 'Okies' or 'poor whites' during the 1930s, and again Mexican workers under the *bracero* programme from the 1940s until the mid-1960s.[77]

Not only were all such migrants to California used to curtail/undermine the bargaining power – and thus the cost – of local workers, but they were also used against each other: as soon as one particular wave of migrants showed any signs of organizing and/or militancy, it was rapidly replaced by another.[78] Evidence suggests that workers themselves struggled against the imposition of unfreedom, and frequently expressed the desire either for alternative employment or the same jobs with better pay and conditions.[79] It is equally clear, moreover, that labour contractors collaborated with employers not just in order to keep wages low but also to prevent trade union organization from gaining hold among migrant labour.[80] This process of workforce segmentation along ethic lines continues into the present, in the form of low-cost/unfree undocumented workers currently supplied to California agribusiness by farm labour contractors.

Unfree labour discharged an analogous historical role in the postbellum South, where its function was similarly to curtail/prevent the bargaining power of labour. Not only have convict leasing and debt peonage both been profitable and based on force/compulsion, therefore, but these unfree relational forms were themselves backed up in turn by the presence in the same context of a mutually supportive political/ideological/institutional structure similarly based on coercion.[81] Informed by an all-pervasive racism, this structure extended from the formal institutional apparatus of the state, the legal system, and the police, to violent practices such as vigilantism and – most importantly – lynching.[82] In the case of the latter, for example, it is clear that in the fifty years after 1880 this kind of extra-judicial murder had a powerful negative impact on labour militancy and organization in the American south, where it functioned as a seasonally-specific means of controlling black workers during those periods in the agricultural cycle when the demand for labour-power (and consequently its potential bargaining capacity) was at a peak. As in the other cases outlined here, this example suggests that opposition to the operation of a free labour market came not from workers but from capital.

5.12 Conclusion

The importance of the distinction between free and unfree labour lies in the longstanding debate about the conditions hindering/favouring economic development, at the centre of which is the desirability of market formation on which capitalist development depends. A consequence of landholders utilizing debt bondage to prevent potential/actual workers from personally commodifying their own labour-power is that it prevents or impedes the exchange between buyers and sellers of labour-power. Because unfree labour is regarded by neoclassical economic historians and exponents of the 'semi-feudal' thesis as a non-market ('pre-capitalist') relation which prevents labour-power from becoming and remaining a commodity, it must be incompatible with the formation of a labour market and thus with the development of capitalism itself.

The presence of debt bondage is accordingly interpreted by them both as evidence for the economically irrational behaviour (motivated by 'prestige', 'patronage') on the part of peasants, landlords or planters. For these reasons, both neoclassical economic historians and Marxists who adhere to the 'semi-feudal' thesis tend to regard unfree labour as anachronistic, a pre-/non-capitalist relation that constitutes an obstacle to accumulation. Peasants remain subsistence cultivators and landlords consume rather than invest: the result is economic backwardness. Hence the two difficulties with the way in which bonded labour is interpreted by the 'semi-feudal' thesis. First, such a theorization cannot account for the continued existence or indeed the expansion of unfreedom in what are undeniably areas of capitalist agriculture. And second, this lacunae (capitalism and unfreedom are incompatible) in turn opens up a theoretical space for the neoclassical economic argument that, in a capitalist context, such agrarian relations are not unfree (or bonded) but much rather free wage labour.

Other Marxists take a different view, and argue that in particular situations/contexts unfree labour is the preferred relational form of capitalist producers, since it enables them to segment the labour market, and also to cheapen and/or discipline their workers. Not only is bonded labour compatible with accumulation, but agrarian capitalists utilize the labour-tying mechanism to roll back the negotiating power acquired by workers in the course of labour market formation. Where proletarianization empowers workers, therefore, employers restructure the agrarian labour process (cutting wage costs to raise profitability) by deproletarianizing labour-power (or decommodifying the latter in an economic and politico-ideological sense). According to this view it is employers and not workers or poor peasants who oppose/resist proletarianization. Rather than an archaic relational form constituting an obstacle to (and therefore destined to be eliminated by) capitalism, unfree labour is in certain circumstances an integral aspect of both the initial and continuing accumulation process.

Evidence suggests that in the historical/geographical contexts used by neo-classical economists to illustrate the presence of 'choice-making' workers exercising subjective preferences, what was happening by contrast was a process of workforce restructuring involving deproletarianization. Accordingly, from the mid-nineteenth century onwards in the American South and the Sunbelt states, together with sugar plantations in Queensland and the Caribbean, the twofold objective of deproletarianization associated with unfree relational forms such as chattel slavery, indentured labour, the chain gang, convict lease, and debt peonage, has been to hinder/undermine the development of working class consciousness and struggle. This in turn weakened or prevented unionization, collective bargaining and strike activity, which then guaranteed the continuing presence of a poorly paid and highly exploited workforce. An effect of the latter was to lower the cost of labour-power generally and thereby increase the profitability in all these contexts of agrarian capitalist production.

As will be seen in the following chapters, the idealized image of debt bondage and the inability to recognize it as a form of unfreedom has its epistemological roots in a corresponding failure on the part of revisionist texts to differentiate the peasantry in terms of class. This in turn prevents an under-standing of both the origin and cause of the *enganche* system in Latin America and the attached labour system in India. Hence the objective for the imposi-tion or reimposition of these kinds of unfree relation has not been so much forcing peasants off the land or preventing their access to it (because they would otherwise not sell their labour-power) as an attempt at controlling a growing *proletarian* consciousness. In contrast to the revisionist claim that such relations were necessary because of the absence or the as yet imperfect nature of the labour market, therefore, it is argued here that employers introduce/reintroduce unfreedom in situations where existing labour was withheld/withdrawn as a result of low wages and/or unacceptable working conditions.

NOTES

1. In addition to texts specifically about India and Latin America, which are analysed in Chapters 6 and 7, those subscribing to this view include Miers and Kopytoff [1977], Reid [1983] and Hart [1986a; 1986b].
2. It is not without significance that neoclassical economic theory, which emerged in the 1870s, was an explicitly anti-Marxist response to the development of the labour movement. In politico-ideological terms, it constituted a project of innateness, or the dehistoricizing and reconstituting as immutable of what had been regarded by classical economic theory as terrain changed by conflict. In neoclassical analysis, such terrain became an unchanging and thus a 'natural' socio-economic order.
3. The incompatibility between class struggle and the harmony implicit in the concept of an equilibrium is highlighted in a definition of the latter by one neoclassical economist [*Pearce*, 1981: 32] which points out that '[w]hen applied to markets, equilibrium refers to a situation in which buyers and sellers *agree* prices and quantities' (emphasis added). For the application of a neoclassical economic framework to the analysis of unfree labour in a variety of different contexts and conjunctures, see, *inter alia,* Evans [1970], Brown and Reynolds [1973], Higgs [1977], Cotlear [1979], Galenson [1981], Shlomowitz [1981; 1997], Bardhan [1984], Jagannathan [1987], Srinivasan [1989], D. Lal [1989], Fogel [1989], Pastore [1997] and Steinfeld and Engerman [1997]. For critiques from different theoretical viewpoints of the methods utilized in this process, see Gutman [1975], Sutch [1975], David *et al.* [1976], Greenberg [1977], Mandle [1978: 22–7], Stampp [1980: 72ff.], Fox-Genovese and Genovese [1983: 91ff.], Graves [1984], Brass [1991], Kolchin [1992], Leiman [1993: 78ff.] and Angelo [1997].
4. For the application of a neoclassical economic framework to plantation slavery in the antebellum American South, convict labour in Australia and the postbellum American South, contract labour in the latter context, and indentured Pacific Island labour in Australia, Fiji, and the British West Indies, see Shlomowitz [1981; 1991a; 1992]. A not dissimilar view is the neoclassical argument made by Higgs [1977], who offers a symptomatically harmonious view of agrarian transformation in the American South. However, unlike Fogel and Engerman – for whom it is slavery itself which benefited its subject – Higgs projects the same analytical framework onto the post-abolition period, and depicts a similarly non-coercive process which might be described as proletarianization without class struggle. According to this view, ex-slaves unproblematically abandoned the plantation economy following emancipation, a move which employers in general and planters in particular were powerless to resist: hence the dismissal by Higgs of the efficacy of peonage.
5. For this exchange, see Shlomowitz [1991b] and Brass [1991]. Many of the

criticisms contained in the latter text have also been made subsequently by Williams [1994/95], which Shlomowitz [1994/95] has similarly been unable to refute.

6. That Shlomowitz has qualified his views is evident from a comparison of what for him are the characteristics of two opposed approaches to the analysis of labour/employer transactions, the 'class'/'market' duality (for the details of which see Brass [1997c]). Shlomowitz [1986: 108] initially designated the 'class' position as one based on conflict between capital and labour over wage levels and working conditions, whereas the 'market' position by contrast maintained that the capital/labour relation was 'the outcome of a *free* interplay of competitive forces' (emphasis added). In his most recent text, however, Shlomowitz [1997] has redefined the content of the 'class'/'market' dichotomy. Now the 'class' position consists of the view that employers collude to enserf workers, while the 'market' position is that a *relatively* free market for labour exists. Not only does this 'distinction' have no application outside Shlomowitz' own use of the terms, but the concept of a 'relatively free market' is now so inclusive as to be meaningless, encompassing as it does every known historical form of production relation.

7. As social relations of production have no place in a neoclassical economic analysis, Shlomowitz is in a very real sense unable to conceptualize a process of market-mediated appropriation by capital from labour or by a master from his slave. In this kind of essentialist framework exploitation is necessarily impossible, since by definition markets represent contexts where each factor of production (land, labour, capital) is justly rewarded for its contribution to output. Given that his analysis is informed by the absence of appropriation, therefore, it is unsurprising that Shlomowitz encounters no evidence of exploitation. Hence the view [*Shlomowitz*, 1981: 91] that Melanesian workers employed in the Queensland sugar industry 'were not generally exploited, in the sense of receiving a wage rate less than the value of the marginal product of their labour'.

8. Many of the texts which subsequently challenged negative interpretations of agrestic unfreedom in contexts other than the United States were to some degree influenced by the seminal text on American slavery of Fogel and Engerman [1974]. The latter had an impact on debates from the late 1970s onwards, not only about unfreedom in Southeast Asia, slavery-as-kinship in Africa, and peonage in Latin America and the Caribbean, but also about indentured labour in Australasia. Just as Fogel and Engerman attempted to reverse the earlier negative depiction by Stampp [1964] of plantation slavery in the antebellum American south, therefore, so previous negative depictions – most of which were written/published in the four decades after the 1930s – of unfreedom in Southeast Asia (Lasker [1950]), in Africa (Nevinson [1906], Nzula *et al.* [1979/1933]), in Latin America (Borah [1951], Chevalier [1966], Klarén [1970], Harris [1975]), in the Caribbean (Williams [1964; 1970]), and in the Pacific region (Parnaby [1964]) were themselves questioned: in the case of Southeast Asia by Reid [1983]; in the case of Africa by Hill [1977] and Miers and Kopytoff [1977]; in the case of Latin America by Bauer [1979a; 1979b], Cotlear [1979], Knight [1986a; 1986b; 1988] and Shlomowitz [1991b]; in the case of the Caribbean by Bergad [1983a; 1983b; 1984]; and with regard to the Pacific region by Shlomowitz [1981; 1994/95], Moore [1985] and Munro [1993a; 1995]. Throughout the 1980s and 1990s, however, the attempts at revising the meaning (= sanitizing) of unfree rural labour in all these contexts have themselves become the object of critiques: by Watson

[1980] with regard to Africa; by Loveman [1979] and Brass [1983; 1990b] in the case of Latin America; by Scarano [1984] and Brass [1984; 1986c] in the case of the Caribbean; and by Graves [1984; 1993], Brass [1991; 1994; 1996], Panoff [1994/5] and Williams [1994/95] with regard to the Pacific region. In this connection it is necessary to note that the most important text published during the last two decades reversing the trend towards the sanitization of unfree labour has been in the field of ancient history: namely, the seminal work by Ste Croix [1981], which shows that in the Greek and Roman world 'debt bondage existed ... on a far larger scale than the vast majority of ancient historians have recognized' [*Ste Croix*, 1984: 108].

9. Punishment is dismissed by Fogel and Engerman [1974: 41, 144ff.] as one of the negative myths/misconceptions about unfreedom in the antebellum American south, not least because it then makes possible the claim that – in the absence of coercion – slaves voluntarily remained on the plantation because of the material benefits involved (= 'choice-making individuals exercising subjective preference'). The components of what is termed a pro-slavery discourse are examined more fully in Chapter 8.

10. For the claims about the superior nature of slave diet, medical care, clothing and housing, see Fogel and Engerman [1974: 5, 9, 109ff., 202, 226, 260–63].

11. The centrality of neoclassical economic theory to the revisionist arguments of Fogel and Engerman has been noted by Stampp [1980: 101], who observes that 'their view of slavery may have stemmed in part from a desire to make everything fit comfortably in a neoclassical behavioural model'.

12. For an example of the theorization of indentured migration from India to Surinam in terms of 'choice', see Emmer [1986: 187, 189]. The problematic nature of this view is underlined by the frequent and ambiguous references by Engerman [1986: 263, 268, 276, 282] to indenture as a contract which its subject 'presumably entered into'. Because it lacks a concept of class and hence class struggle, neoclassical economic theory assumes that contracts are agreements between equals, and consequently accepts such arrangements at face value; as a result, the impact of class power on labour relations which derives from this partial application of contractual stipulations remains epistemologically invisible.

13. On this point, see Fogel [1989: 391], who comments:

The discovery that slave plantations were more efficient than free farms challenged my beliefs about the moral problem of slavery ... The notion of efficient plantations created a dilemma because it was difficult to see how individuals so deeply oppressed, without incentive, many demoralized, others determined rebels, could nevertheless produce more output per worker than free farmers. It was not only inconsistent with my vision of slaves as semi-starved, listless workers who barely had the energy to pull themselves through the day, but it seemed to imply a far greater level of labour discipline and a far greater degree of ... acquiescence to the objectives of the planters than I was prepared to entertain.

14. For the view that slavery was determined not by luxury or conspicuous consumption on the part of the planter class but by profit, see Fogel [1989: 188]. Having originally subscribed to the view that plantation slavery was a symptom of traditional agriculture the economic backwardness of which was attributable to masters interested only in conspicuous consumption, Fogel [1989: 389] was subsequently persuaded by the argument of Conrad and Meyer [1965: 43ff.] that mid-nineteenth

century plantation agriculture in the antebellum American South was efficient, and that slavery was in fact compatible with economic growth. That the antebellum plantation was consequently and self-evidently a capitalist enterprise is clear from, for example, Fogel and Engerman [1974: 67–78] and Fogel [1989: 64ff.].

15. As is evident from, for example, the statement by Emmer [1997:14] that 'the system of slavery ... was on the whole an *economically* advantageous institution for slaves and slave owners' (original emphasis), others also claim that slaves as much as masters benefit materially from servitude.

16. For claims about the existence on the antebellum plantation of a master/slave 'balance of power', and the need on the part of employers to meet 'the desires of individual slaves', see Fogel [1989: 189].

17. On the necessity for masters to recognize the humanity of slaves, see Fogel [1989: 189].

18. For the claim that slaveowners were required to compromise, see Fogel [1989: 189].

19. The political significance of this relay-in-statement is examined in Chapter 8.

20. On the economic role of unfree labour generally in wartime Germany, and in particular that of the concentration camps as a source of cheap slave labour, see Ferencz [1979], Hayes [1987], Bellon [1990] and Roth [1997].

21. For claims about the non-equivalence between plantation and concentration camp, see Genovese [1971: 63–6] and Fogel [1989: 188–9]. The rejection by both the latter of an equivalence between plantation and concentration camp derives in part from a desire to rescue black slaves from the negative image associated with the passive, docile 'sambo' stereotype projected by Elkins [1959]. The latter argued that, as in the case of concentration camp inmates, the personality of plantation slaves was reduced to infantilism [*Elkins*, 1959: 104ff.]. It is important to note in this connection that to acknowledge the economic effectiveness of the labour regime either in the concentration camp or on the plantation does not amount to an endorsement of psychologistic explanations which focus on the alleged innate inferiority of their respective workforces. Much rather it is to understand the effectiveness of particular forms of coercive power.

22. It is instructive to compare the view propounded by Fogel and other neoclassical economists, that advanced capitalism does not require coercion, with the contrasting interpretation by Marxists of the link between capitalism, fascism and unfree labour. '[E]ven under conditions where the working class is completely atomized', observes Mandel [1980: 105, original emphasis]:

the laws of the market which determine short-term fluctuations in the price of the commodity labour-power do not disappear. As soon as the industrial reserve army contracted in the Third Reich, workers were able to try, by means of rapid job mobility – for instance into the spheres of heavy industry and armaments which paid higher wage-rates and overtime – to achieve at least a modest improvement in their wages, even without trade union action. Only a violent intervention by the Nazi state to sustain the rate of surplus-value and the rate of profit, in the form of the legal *prohibition* of job changes, and the *compulsory tying* of workers to their job, was able to prevent the working class from utilizing more propitious conditions on the labour market. This abolition of freedom of movement of the German proletariat was one of the most striking demonstrations of the capitalist class nature of the Nationalist Socialist State.

23. This is one of the reasons why Steinfeld and Engerman [1997] maintain that the theoretical opposition between freedom and unfreedom is artificial. Hence their insistence that, as during the nineteenth century 'neither wage labour nor contract labour had a fixed content', wage labour was essentially no different from contract labour, and consequently no real difference existed between wage (= free) labour and contract (= unfree) labour. Their argument that the free/unfree polarity is actually a false (= non-existent) dichotomy licenses a further claim: if no distinction exists between free and slave labour in terms of a requirement to work, then both free and slave labour possess the same ability to choose to work, a difference-dissolving argument that is redolent of the 'choice-making' individual expressing 'subjective preferences' at the centre of neoclassical economic theory.

24. On this point, Marx [1976: 271–2] observes:

> ... labour-power can appear on the market as a commodity only if, and in so far as, its possessor, the individual whose labour-power it is, offers it for sale or sells it as a commodity. In order that its possessor may sell it as a commodity, he must have it at his disposal, he must be the free proprietor of his own labour-capacity, hence of his person. He and the owner of money meet in the market, and enter into relations with each other on a footing of equality as owners of commodities, with the sole difference that one is a buyer, the other a seller; ... The second essential condition which allows the owner of money to find labour-power in the market as a commodity is ... that the possessor of labour-power, instead of being able to sell commodities in which his labour has been objectified, must rather be compelled to offer for sale as a commodity that very labour-power which exists only in his living body.

25. As will become evident in the chapters which follow, because proletarianisation is invariably equated only with landlessness, all workers fully separated from the means of production tend to be regarded as free wage labourers, notwithstanding the fact that their labour-power may be under the control of an employer or labour contractor. For examples of this kind of argument applied to Latin America, the Caribbean, and Asia, see Blanchard [1982: 120–21], Mallon [1983a], Bergad [1983a; 1983b] and Breman [1996]. Similarly, Legassick and de Clercq [1984: 143–4] maintain that contract/indentured migrant labour in South Africa constituted a proletariat because it had been separated from the means of production.

26. On the pre-colonial/pre-capitalist presence and extent of landless labour in Asia, see Kumar [1965], Breman [1990], and Breman and Daniel [1992]. For the presence of landless migrant workforce in mid-nineteenth century Chile, see Bauer [1975a; 1975b].

27. On this point, see texts by, *inter alia*, Kloosterboer [1960], Aufhauser [1973], van Onselen [1976], Corrigan [1977], Legassick [1977], Mundle [1979], Meillassoux [1981: 91ff.], Patnaik [1985], Brass [1986a; 1988], Miles [1987], Cohen [1987], Zegeye and Ishemo [1989].

28. The first and third are specific, while the second and third are in fact variants of the same position. It should be noted that the incompatibility between Marxist and neoclassical approaches to the issue of unfree labour gives rise to a large variety of contradictions, not all of which are capable of solution. Thus the attempt by Olsen [1997] to synthesize Marxism with a neoclassical economic framework is confronted by a common difficulty: namely, the kind of Marxism that is to be combined with neoclassical economics. Some of the points made by Olsen have also been made previously by Bardhan [1986; 1989a] in a similar attempt to synthesize

Marxist and neoclassical development economics; in his case, however, the result amounts not so much to a merger between Marxism and neoclassical economics as a takeover by the latter of the former. The problem Bardhan faces is that his attempted synthesis only seems to work because what he synthesizes with neo-classical economics is in fact 'analytical Marxism', which many would argue is not actually Marxism at all but rather a variant of neoclassical theory itself. Olsen faces a similar kind of problem, in that against neoclassical economics is pitted only the Marxism of those like Prasad [1989] and Bhaduri [1973], who theorize bonded labour as a 'semi-feudal' relation that is accordingly incompatible with capitalist accumulation. Not only is it easy to 'falsify' this kind of straw person Marxism, for example by pointing to the continued existence of bonded labour in capitalist agriculture, but it also opens up a theoretical space for the consequent argument put by neoclassical economics that such agrarian relations in a capitalist context are not unfree (or bonded) but much rather free wage labour.

29. See, for example, Banaji [1978] and Alavi *et al.* [1982].
30. See, for example, Miles [1987: 179–80, 196ff.].
31. The debate about feudalism/capitalism in Latin America is encapsulated in the now classic exchange between Frank [1969a] and Laclau [1977], while its Indian counterpart is presented in the collections by Rudra *et al.* [1978] and Thorner [1982]. For examples of the theorization of unfree labour in Latin America as a pre-capitalist/feudal/semi-feudal relation – by Marxists and non-Marxists alike – see Feder [1971: 149–51], Bauer [1979a: 53, 61], Cotlear [1979: 52], Taylor [1987: 120], and Albert [1984: 109–10].
32. Such a view structured texts not just by Bhaduri [1973: 120–37; 1983] and Prasad [1979: 33–49; 1989: 37–43] but also by Patnaik [1978a; 1978b; 1978c; 1978d; 1978e; 1990; and Patnaik and Dingwaney 1985], Bardhan [1984: 81–83], Breman [1985a: 131, 306–13], Chopra [1985: 212] and Tiwary [1985: 180–81]. It is important to distinguish between the elements of the 'semi-feudal' thesis which are compatible with the unfreedom-as-a-capitalist-relation view and those which are not. The perception by exponents [e.g., *Prasad*, 1989: 36ff., 47–9, 53–4, 95ff.] of the 'semi-feudal' thesis of unfree labour as an obstacle to economic growth, there-fore, is an argument which is incompatible with the view of unfreedom-as-a-capitalist-relation However, the argument that landlords perceive the emergence of free wage labour as a potential threat to existing property rights and political power derived from this is one on which exponents of both the 'semi-feudal' thesis and the unfreedom-as-a-capitalist-relation view can agree. Accordingly, there is no dis-agreement with the 'semi-feudal' thesis as advanced by Bhaduri and Prasad regarding both the existence and the effect of the control exercised by landlords over their workers by means of the debt mechanism; the main objection is that, for them, such control is confined to and indeed indicative of 'semi-feudalism'. As is argued below, capitalist producers also resort to this method of workforce control/discipline in the form of deproletarianisation; that is, imposing or reimposing unfreedom on workers whose sole property is their labour-power.
33. Among this group are to be found McBride [1934: 70], Pearse [1975: 28], Stavenhagen [1975: 100–101], Rutledge [1975: 107ff.], Corrigan [1977], Banaji [1978], Mundle [1979], Thorner [1980: 224–37], Alavi *et al.* [1982], Mallon [1983a], Brass [1986a; 1986b; 1988; 1990b; 1993b], and Lichtenstein [1996]. The eminent Indian Trotskyist, A.R. Desai, adopts a clear position on the mode of production debate, criticizing the view which attributes the presence/absence of

capitalism simply to the corresponding presence/absence of free wage labour, and rightly chides [1984: x] those who 'do not view agrarian production and production relations in the context of the overall transformation of Indian society that is being undertaken actively by the State that has emerged after Independence'. It is equally clear that Desai [1984: 183, 185] not only contextualized the reproduction of unfree relations in terms of class struggle in the countryside but also regarded debt bondage as compatible with agrarian capitalist development. For early references by him (in an essay written and published in 1939) to the role in Indian agriculture of bonded labour, and its connection with indebtedness, see Desai [1961: 87–8].

34. For a more detailed critique of Patnaik's conceptualization of unfree labour, see Brass [1995]. An early and still important critique from within Marxism of a tendency by some Marxists to locate unfree labour in an evolutionary framework is that by Corrigan [1977].

35. Ironically, Patnaik herself appears to accept that poor peasants are in reality no more than 'peasants' when she observes [1978b: 95–6]:

> The terms of tenancy in many cases made it difficult to distinguish between tenant and labourers; for a tenant might provide livestock and labour while landlord provided seed and water; while sometimes the tenant's provision of livestock and labour was itself dependent upon obtaining a loan from the landlord or other sources. In these circumstances the small share of output remaining to the tenant could be regarded as similar to wages, rather than his income from cultivation after payment of rent ... the small peasant ... is often forced to hire himself out as a labourer.

36. On the latter point, see Ghosh [1985: 79]. Furthermore, such a position runs the danger of conveying the impression that, were rents to be reduced or abolished, these subjects would as a result become the efficient peasant family farmers that neo-populists such as Michael Lipton and Paul Richards claim they could be.

37. Hence the odd assertion by Patnaik [1978a: 74; 1978b: 99–100] that, because a 'dominant landlord' takes advantage of worker destitution, he consequently neither seeks to make a profit nor is he a capitalist! This curious piece of 'theory' demonstrates nothing other than her ignorance of the role of the industrial reserve army of labour in depressing wages and/or conditions by diminishing or eliminating the bargaining power of workers *vis-à-vis* capitalists. While Patnaik accepts that 'a tractable labour supply' is the object of moneylending and debt bondage, therefore, she nevertheless persists in regarding the latter as pre-capitalist, despite the fact that agrarian capitalists are themselves also interested both in 'a tractable labour supply' and in the relational forms which give rise to this.

38. See, for example, Patnaik [1978b: 98, 99–100]. A crucial consideration in this regard is the economic role of moneylending and the resulting characterization of the debt bondage relation as either unproductive merchant capital or productive industrial capital. Viewed as a loan, in an inflationary context the interest-free sum advanced to a poor peasant or landless labourer by a capitalist farmer or rich peasant declines in value by the time it becomes due for repayment. Regarded thus, debt bondage operates against the interests of the creditor-employer and to the advantage of the debtor. Viewed in terms of purchasing labour-power, however, debt bondage is in the same inflationary situation a method of obtaining and retaining this resource at an ever-diminishing real 'wage', and in this respect it operates in favour of the creditor-employer and against the debtor. In so far as it constitutes

a way of recruiting and keeping labour-power cheaply, the debt bondage mechanism corresponds not to merchant capital, which exists solely in the sphere of circulation, but rather to a form of productive capital, the object of which is to set and keep in motion the labour process.

39. The theory about distinction between the formal and real subsumption of labour under capital is set out in Marx [1976: 1019–38]. Patnaik [1990: 2–3] is aware that the formal/real subsumption position, whereby the 'analytical distinction between profit and rent was considered unimportant', is the antithesis of her own. Among those who have applied the concept real/formal subsumption of labour under capital to the analysis of agrarian relations in India are Banaji [1978], Mundle [1979: 82ff.] and Gupta [1986]. Unlike the extraction of relative surplus-value, a precondition of which is a reduction in the amount of socially necessary labour time (an objective achieved by raising the organic composition of capital and making labour-power more productive during time spent working), the extraction of absolute surplus-value entails lengthening the working day, which – as is clear from La Convención, Haryana and Bihar (see Chapters 2, 3 and 4) – is what happens in the case of bonded labour. And whereas relative surplus-value extraction involves the real subsumption of labour under capital, and thus requires increasing substantially the level of the development of the productive forces in agriculture, the appropriation of absolute surplus-value may be effected in the context of a relatively underdeveloped 'available, established labour process' [Marx, 1976: 1021] which necessitates only the formal subsumption of labour under capital.

40. This view maintains that debt bondage constitutes an integral component of the landlord/tenant relation, involving the payment of labour-rent for land usufruct rights (see, for example, McBride [1934], Greenidge [1958: 74ff.]). In cases where the concept of unfreedom is limited to the legal attachment of a tenant to land, and such a legal restriction is clearly absent, it is easy to assume that bonded labour is correspondingly absent. Hence the claim made by McBride [1936: 148–9, 156] that during the late 1920s the Chilean *inquilino* was 'free to leave the farm at will', despite the fact that a tenant was 'not allowed to utilize even his free time working on neighbouring farms or at any employment outside of his own hacienda, nor [was] his family free to seek employment elsewhere'.

41. See, for example, Blanchard [1982: 120-21], Bergad [1983a, 1983b], and de Janvry and Vandeman [1987].

42. For a discussion of unfreedom in areas of labour surplus/shortage, and the contrasting significance of control over land and labour in Asia (where a shortage of land was coupled with plentiful labour) and Africa (where land was abundant and labour scarce), see Watson [1980]. Even to regard South Asia generally as a context where labour is always and everywhere in plentiful supply is problematic: as the example of Bihar during the colonial era demonstrates, a landlord discourse about a shortage of workers can operate in a situation of labour surplus [*Pouchepadass*, 1990].

43. See Nieboer [1910]. This view also structures the argument in two recent texts linking the presence of unfree labour in Russia, America, the Caribbean, South Africa and Australia to the existence in all these contexts of a labour shortage [*Miles*, 1987: 205, 214; *Kolchin*, 1987: 18, 359ff.]. The recourse by Andean mineowners or landowners and Caribbean planters to a workforce subordinated by indenture, vagrancy legislation, or the *enganche* system is also attributed to labour scarcities arising from the continued access by peasants to land [*Kloosterboer*,

1960: 197, 199–200; *Bauer*, 1979a: 56–7; *LeGrand*, 1984: 33ff.; *Mallon*, 1986].
The presence of unfree labour in Asia generally during the nineteenth century has
been similarly ascribed to a situation where 'financial inducements alone did not
suffice to disconnect the peasant from his native heath' [*Lasker*, 1950: 210].

44. For a reaffirmation of this view, see Domar [1970] and Dovring [1965]. As Domar
[1970: 31] points out, this argument does not in fact originate with Nieboer, and
can be traced back through Loria's *Les Bases Economiques de la Constitution
Sociale* (1893), Edward Gibbon Wakefield's *A View of the Art of Colonization*
(1834), to Adam Smith's *Wealth of Nations* (1776). Not the least of the difficulties
associated with Nieboer's argument is its compatibility with the idealized
Chayanovian concept of peasant economy and the theory of the articulation of
modes of production. The linkage between the non-existence of private property in
land and a corresponding difficulty in procuring free wage labour for accumulation
in the colonies is also considered by Marx [1976: 934–5].

45. See, for example, Kumar [1965], Patnaik [1985: 9, 11ff.; 1986: 781–93] and
Ramachandran [1990: 258–9]. For a critique of the argument which unproblem-
atically links unfreedom to population density in the case of the Caribbean, see
Bolland [1981: 591–619].

46. Even those who recognize that a proletariat is not a necessary outcome of
depeasantization nevertheless misunderstand the reason why the result is unfree
rather than free relations of production. Thus Miles [1987] attributes unfreedom
not so much to the need by plantations to cut costs by undermining workforce
bargaining power as to resistance by smallholders to proletarianization. Evidence
suggests that struggle conducted by those separated from means of production is
to low wage levels and poor working conditions rather than to proletarianization
per se. For example, even tribals in India who sold their labour-power on a
seasonal basis would withdraw this in circumstances where pay and conditions
were not to their liking: thus in the 1950s Bhil tribals from western India who
migrated to work the cotton, tobacco, and ground-nut cash crops produced in
Gujarat discontinued providing seasonal labour because employers worked them
too hard [*Nath*, 1960: 43–4]. The occurrence of unfree relations in such circumstances would clearly be unconnected with the need on the part of employers to
habituate their workforce to the rhythms of wage labour.

47. For the details of this process, see Díaz Santana [1976], ILO [1983], Lemoine
[1985], and Plant [1987]. The estimated annual demand for Haitian labour by the
Dominican sugar plantation sector alone exceeds 100,000 workers: seasonal
contract labour recruited through the bilateral agreement is therefore only one
category of low-paid Haitian worker employed in the Dominican Republic, others
being resident squatters (*viejos*) and illegal immigrants (*ambafiles*). Many of these
are forcibly rounded up by the military and compelled to work on the sugar plantations during the peak season. Such workers are also employed by Dominican
smallholders engaged in the cultivation of coffee and rice crops.

48. See Plant [1987: 106ff.]. Subsequent investigations by Plant [1987: 84ff.] in the
Dominican Republic during the 1985–86 harvest season revealed that nothing
had changed. Allegations of forcible recruitment and regulation continued; his
conclusion [*Plant*, 1987: 85] is that the intervention by the ILO 'had borne no fruit,
... the situation was as bad as ever'.

49. Evidence of unfree labour in the postbellum American South, and also its interrelationship with the penal system, is contained in Woodson [1918; 1930: Ch.IV],

McWilliams [1945: 142], Kennedy [1946: 48–62], Kloosterboer [1960: 57ff.], Daniel [1972], Ransom and Sutch [1977: 149ff.], Dittmer [1980: 72ff.], Lichtenstein [1996], and Angelo [1997]. Declared unconstitutional/illegal since 1867, peonage has been defined [*Woodson*, 1930: 73] by a judge in a manner which indicates not only its affinity with chattel slavery ('dominion over my person') but also the centrality to its reproduction of debt:

> It is where a man in consideration of an advance or debt or contract says, 'Here, take me, I will give you dominion over my person and liberty, and you can work me against my will hereafter, and force me by imprisonment, or threats of duress, to work for you until that debt or obligation is paid.' Experience has shown, too, that the judge might have added, 'Until I, the planter, shall say that the debt has been paid.'

To the seemingly obvious question 'why don't you leave and get out of it?', one unfree black worker in 1940s Georgia made an equally obvious reply [*Kennedy*, 1946: 61]: 'Because ... the onliest way out is to die out. If anybody tries to leave any other way, the boss man sends the sheriff after him and has him put on the chain gang.' That peonage not only continued into the late 1960s but also retained its mutually supportive connection with the penal system is clear from evidence presented to the Hearings before the US Senate Subcommittee on Migratory Labor [1970b: 433–4]. According to one witness, the young son of a migrant worker,

> the next thing I'd know I'd be there, in jail, and they might never let me out, except if one of the growers comes, and he would say it was OK if they let me out, and he'd pay the fine, but then I'd have to work for him ... They never do anything a lot of people, but work for the same man, because they always are owing him money, the grower, and he is always getting them out of jail, and then they owe him more money.

50. For the link between debt and the recruitment of migrant workers in the late 1960s, see the US Senate Subcommittee on Migratory Labour [1970a: 176–7].
51. For details of this study, see Daniel [1972: 108–9]. Symptomatic of the non-problematization of debt peonage by investigations into migration and tenancy is its absence from three 'classic' fieldwork studies conducted during the 1920s and 1930s: of Mexican immigrants by Gamio [1971] and of rural Alabama by Johnson [1966], neither of which make any reference to debt bondage, and also that of seven southeastern cotton States for the Federal Emergency Relief Administration, in which debt peonage receives only a passing mention [*Woofter*, 1936: 185].
52. For the impact of the 1927 Mississipi flood in confirming reports about the wide-spread incidence of debt peonage, see Daniel [1972: 149ff.]. White national guardsmen surrounded the flood relief camps to prevent unfree black labourers from escaping, and many of the latter who had found refuge in them were subsequently returned to their employers.
53. On the durability of debt peonage in these states, see Daniel [1972: 189]. Writing about the era of Reconstruction, Woodson [1918:154] comments: 'This period has been marked ... by an effort to establish in the South a system of peonage not unlike that of Mexico, a sort of involuntary servitude in that one is considered legally bound to serve his master until a debt contracted is paid.' For instances of the transfer of debt between employers in the Southern States during the twentieth century, see Daniel [1972: 16, 144].
54. The figures contained in the US Senate Subcommittee on Migratory Labor [1970a: 39, 126; 1970c: 1428] provide glimpses of largescale annual migration, extending

from some 2,000 migrants from Florida and Arkansas employed on farms located on the eastern seaboard, to between 28–40,000 in Washington and 83,000 in South Florida. For the estimate of cash advanced by commercial growers, see the US Senate Subcommittee on Migratory Labour [1970a: 251].

55. It is clear from testimony presented to the US Senate Subcommittee on Migratory Labour [1970a; 1970b] that even in the late 1960s debt peonage countinued to flourish. Equating migrant labour relations with debt peonage, one witness made the following observation [*US Senate Subcommittee on Migratory Labor*, 1970b: 353]:

> I must emphasize this word and I use it soberly – peonage. That many of these families are owned for all practical purposes by crew leaders and others who transport them around the country, sometimes with guns at their sides, and tell them that in exchange for this work they owe a certain amount of money to them for the transportation costs, for the food that they have given them, and then when the time comes for paying them, they tell them that they don't have a salary, you haven't worked off so much money you owe me. Then move on to the next place.

56. For the central role of coercion in the reproduction of the migrant/crew leader relation, see the US Senate Subcommittee on Migratory Labour [1970a: 39–40, 43, 100, 192, 195–6, 197, 251; 1970b: 354, 450–51]. According to witness testimony made in Hearings to the US Senate Subcommittee on Migratory Labor [1970b: 354] during the late 1960s,

> There are camps in some of our states where these people [migrant labourers], and many of them have filled out affadavits to this effect, where these people are afraid to leave. They are brought into these camps from other states at so many dollars a head, like cattle, and they don't know they have any rights at all. And, before the presence of guns, who is to ask them to feel any other way?

This testimony about the central role of coercion is corroborated by the labour contractors themselves [*US Senate Subcommittee on Migratory Labour*, 1970a: 195–7, 231].

57. On this point it is necessary to disagree with Cohen [1987: 190ff.], who identifies monopoly over transport and housing as the principal forms of control exercised by crew leaders over the members of their work gangs, and relegates the debt mechanism between these subjects to a subsidiary role. For the importance of debt in the control exercised by crew leaders over migrant labour generally, see the evidence presented to the US Senate Subcommittee on Migratory Labour [1970a: 5–15, 109, 251; 1970b: 158, 161, 247–8]. Much the same is true of migrant agricultural labour employed in South Florida [*US Senate Subcommittee on Migratory Labour*, 1970c: 1442ff.], and also in the northeastern United States, where of all the methods available to the crew leader [*Friedland and Nelkin*, 1971: 52],

> [The m]ost important is the credit system. Most migrants, by the time they begin working, are heavily in debt to the crew leader. Once they start earning, debts are deducted regularly from their pay. Continued dependence on the crew leader's provision of food, whiskey and loans often compounds the debt. ... The arbitrary aspects of the credit system permit the possibility of extraordinary leverage if the crew leader wishes to exercise it.

58. For evidence that migrant farm workers were charged in excess of the prevailing price for subsistence goods purchased from labour contractors, see Shotwell [1961: 225] and the US Senate Subcommittee on Migratory Labour [1970a: 176–7].

59. Many different sources confirm the importance in the United States of withholding wages as a bonding mechanism designed to retain control over agricultural workers by preventing them from commodifying their own labour-power (see, for example, The President's Commission on Migratory Labor [1951: 77–8], Shotwell [1961: 225], the US Senate Subcommittee on Migratory Labour [1970a: 161, 247–8], Samora [1971: 99–100]). In some cases employers withhold wages with the specific object of ensuring the return of migrant workers, while in others it is to avoid having to pay workers at all. Referred to by growers as the 'deposit' or the 'bonus' system, withholding wages from workers ensures that the latter remain with one particular employer throughout the season, otherwise they lose a portion of their overall wage. Significantly, the same practice is interpreted very differently by the workers themselves, who refer to the withholding of wages as the 'bogus' system amounting to the illegal/illegitimate retention by an employer of what is rightfully due them, simply in order to keep them on against their will until the end of the season.

60. Assertions by neoclassical economists to the contrary notwithstanding (see above), not only was the concentration camp under German Fascism part of a productive economic system but its form of unfree labour was also an extremely profitable. During the Second World War some ten million unfree labourers from Russia, Poland, France, Holland, Belgium and other occupied territories were employed in German agriculture and industry, and during the years 1942–44 some 200 German companies (including IG Farben, Krupp, AEG, Telefunken, Siemens, VW, BMW and Daimler-Benz) took 2.5 million unfree labourers from 12 different concentration camps [*Ferencz*, 1979: 112, 186–7]. Given the demand for labour, Ferencz [1979: 24] notes,

no German company had to be coerced into taking labour. On the contrary, the firms had to use all their influence and persuasion to get all the help they needed. The private companies were to pour millions of marks into the coffers of the SS for the privilege of using the camp inmates. An elaborate accounting system was set up to ensure that the companies paid the SS for every hour of skilled or unskilled labour ... The inmates of course received nothing. They remained under the general control of the SS, but under the immediate supervision of the companies that used them.

Daimler-Benz, for example [*Bellon*, 1990: 252],

spent approximately 710 marks a year per person in employing foreign workers during World War II ... During the same years, the firm probably paid one of its workers 2,500–3,000 marks annually in wages, with hundreds of additional marks in social benefits. Whatever the productivity of the foreign workers (and there is reason to believe that it was good), the men and women deported from occupied Europe were a good bargain for Daimler-Benz's operations.

The same was true of IG Farben [*Hayes*, 1987: 344]:

Despite the influx of putatively inferior foreign workers, Farben's sales income per worker in the core corporation was 580 marks higher in 1942 and 806 marks higher in 1943 than in 1939; expenditures for wages, insurance, and social services had fallen by 407 and 194 marks per head, respectively. Thus, at the hight of the war, the enterprise was making roughly 1,000 marks more per worker annually before deductions for general overhead than when the fighting began.

61. On this point see Dew [1966: 30].
62. 'Until the 1840s', observes Stampp [1964: 71],
    the famed Tredegar Iron Company in Richmond used free labour almost exclu-
    sively. But in 1842, Joseph R. Anderson, the commercial agent of the compa-
    ny, proposed to employ slaves as a means of cutting labour costs. The board of
    directors approved his plan, and within two years Anderson was satisfied with
    'the practicability of the scheme'. In 1847, the increasing use of slaves caused
    the remaining free labourers to go on strike, until they were threatened with
    prosecution for forming an illegal combination. After this protest failed,
    Anderson vowed that he would show his workers that they could not dictate his
    labour policies: he refused to re-employ any of the strikers. Thereafter, as
    Anderson noted, Tredegar used 'almost exclusively slave labour except as
    Boss men. This enables me, of course, to compete with other manufacturers.'
63. See Tinker [1974: 217–18].
64. For the details of this, see West India Royal Commission [1897, Appendix C – Part
    XIII: 306, 330, 331, 418].
65. For the details of this process, see Saunders [1982] and Graves [1993].
66. On this point Ayers [1984: 196] observes:
    By 1886 the mining states of Alabama and Tennessee enjoyed the most
    profitable systems: convicts there brought in around $100,000 to each state
    annually – about one-tenth of the states' total revenue. Georgia, Mississipi,
    Arkansas, North Carolina, and Kentucky made the lesser but still respectable
    sums of between $25,000 and $50,000 each per year. Nationally, all prisons
    which did not use the lease system earned only 32 per cent of their total
    expenses, while those who did take advantage of the demand for convict labor
    outside the prison walls earned 267 per cent. In comparison with manufac-
    turing enterprises within the penitentiaries of the North, the profitability of the
    lease system was real and sustained. Substantially lower overhead, more
    profitable products, longer hours, and the more brutal exploitation made pos-
    sible by a disregard for the prisoners health and welfare generated considerable
    short-term profits for the state as well as for the businessman lucky enough and
    callous enough to lease convicts.
    That the employment of prison labour in the United States during the early part of
    the nineteenth century was similarly profitable is clear from Melossi and Pavarini
    [1981: 140].
67. For the argument that it is the large commercial growers which benefit most from
    the employment of debt bonded migrants, see the US Senate Subcommittee on
    Migratory Labor [1970a: 48].
68. About this development Rodney [1981: 33, 43] has commented:
    Less than three years after being emancipated from slavery, the new wage-
    earning class was acting in certain respects like a modern proletariat ... Creole
    Africans in British Guiana constituted themselves into task-gangs and negoti-
    ated with management to have some control over wages, conditions and
    duration of work. They moved from estate to estate in the search for better
    rates; they haggled over the definition of given tasks ... village labor won
    innumerable small skirmishes in its confrontation with estate capital'.
69. An analogous development occurred in post-emancipation Belize, where fol-
    lowing the increased price of mahogony as a result of European railway expansion,
    logging enterprises resorted to the debt bondage mechanism in an attempt to

curtail the enhanced bargaining power of free labour employed in felling trees. As noted by Bolland [1977: 120–21, 124]:

> The intention behind encouraging the immigration of more Africans, whose status was to be virtually that of slaves, was ... to make the apprentices more tractable after Emancipation ... When slavery was abolished, new methods were developed to maintain the submission of the labour force to the masters; primary among these methods was the combination of 'advance' [payment] and 'truck' ... which trapped freedmen in the form of debt servitude ... .

70. On this point, see Ramesar [1984: 60, 65]. The same applied in the case of Surinam [*Emmer*, 1984: 98]. Attributing indentured migration generally to a 'distaste by free labourers to bear the non-pecuniary costs of production upon the plantations', Engerman [1986: 277] implies that everywhere and at all times free labour was unwilling to undertake plantation work under *any* circumstances. Such a view overlooks the fact that planters employed unfree contract/indentured labour because locals were exercising not an absolute but rather a relative unwillingness to work, and withholding their labour-power in order to secure improvements in pay and conditions for the application of this commodity on the plantation itself. In other words, the object of employing unfree labour in such circumstances was to compel free locals to accept plantation work conditions and pay levels that they would otherwise have rejected.

71. See Ramos Mattei [1985: 158–78; 1988: 38]. In the case of West Indian sugar plantations at the turn of the century, the potential dangers posed to employers by an emerging proletarian consciousness among the workforce is highlighted in a revealing memorandum submitted to the Royal Commission by the Rev S.F. Branch, who warned [*West India Royal Commission, 1897, Appendix C – Part VII:* 114]:

> As an alternative to parcelling out estates among labourers for cultivation, the scale of wages should vary with the price of produce. Although it has more or less brought home to the labourer that arrowroot now does not pay, and in some way sugar too (the high local retail prices of sugar makes him suspicious), yet the labourer argues that when these productions sold at remunerative prices there was little advance on the present barely living wage; hence there is a feeling of unfairness that as he did not share in the prosperity of his employer formerly, he should not be called on now to suffer with him when prices are low. The [plantation] labourers in St Vincent have not yet been educated enough to combine for higher wages, but it would be wise if the employers in time, by a liberal policy, gave no occasion for combination. There are not wanting signs that if our industries revive there are some self-seeking persons who will teach the labourer to put pressure on his employer. We have an excitable, suspicious, and still ignorant labouring population, drifting away from the old clerical control, as shown in the numerous new friendly societies, all self-managed, and not as heretofore directed by ministers of religion ... The labourer, by his lay, friendly and religious societies, and his revolt from the healthy control of the Church and ministers of Wesleyan body, shows he is tasting the pleasure of thinking and determining for himself. The employer in the near future must be prepared to reckon with men who are trying to think out the problems of life, but who are still uneducated, and may be dangerous in asserting what they consider to be their rights.

72. See Plant [1987: 17].

73. The official survey explained this paradox in part by reference to the fact that employment of cheap migrant workers from Haiti lowered the price of labour-power and therefore the costs of sugar production in the Dominican Republic [*Plant*, 1987: 69, 98ff.]. Given the hidden labour subsidy in the form of payments made by the State for the recruitment and import of Haitian contract workers, however, not only would the real cost of labour employed in sugar harvesting be much higher but – through taxation – Dominican workers were themselves being invited to make a contribution towards the purchase of their competitors in the labour market. Those who benefit from this transaction are of course the foreign and domestic sugar planters, and not the people of Dominican Republic.

74. When permitted to do so, both Haitian and Dominican labourers sold their labour-power to the highest bidder, the latter subjects 'only moving to the cane fields when the [wage] rates were competitive. In the 1892–93 [sugar] harvest ... there was a marked labour shortage ... because the Dominicans preferred other work. They could earn 4 pesos for a day's work clearing scrub in the mountains, while for a tonne of harvested cane the rate [was] 2–3 pesos' [*Plant*, 1987: 17]. Similarly, during the 1979–81 harvest season, 'Haitians [in the Dominican Republic] preferred to work on rice farms rather than on sugar plantations, but they were rounded up by the army when they were needed to cut cane' [*Plant*, 1987: 83].

75. On these points see Graves [1993: 32, 141–2], who notes that:

> The [Masters and Servants] Act was ... brought to bear when working-class interests were not kept in check by the prevailing market forces ... demands for higher wages or improved working conditions were controlled through the intervention of the Act ... the contract of indenture functioned systematically to minimise the bargaining power of workers.

76. Only in 1911, when the the judiciary dismissed cases brought by employers against their striking workers, did threats of prosecution under the Masters and Servants Act cease to carry force [*Armstrong*, 1983].

77. On this history of labour market segmentation by California agribusiness, together with its role in preventing/pre-empting unionization, see in particular McWilliams [1939] and Krissman [1997]. For accounts of Mexican *braceros* employed in US agribusiness enterprises, see Galarza [1964], Samora [1971], Baird and McCaughan [1979].

78. Restructuring which involved labour of a different nationality/ethnicity/gender occurred as soon as the existing workforce began to organize/unionize: hence reports [*McWilliams*, 1939: 99–100, 118] concerning the frequency of employer discourse about the desirability both of a 'general law prescribing a closed season for strikes during the gathering and movement of staple crops', and solutions along the lines of '[l]ast year our Hindu workers struck, [s]o this year we mix half Mexicans in with them, and we aren't having any labor trouble'. Significantly, the employment in this context of female labour-power was subject to the same consideration: once women began to organize and bargain over working conditions and payment, employers dispensed with their labour-power [*McWilliams*, 1939: 177–9]. Much the same kind of restructuring procedure was operated by agribusiness enterprises in the United States during the 1960s, when unfree contract labour from the Caribbean was (and continues to be) imported specifically with the object of forcing local workers to accept lower wages and less favourable conditions. About this situation the normally conservative US Senate Subcommittee on Migratory Labour [1970a: 178, 185] has commented:

Growers ... have convinced the US Department of Labour that a shortage of domestic farmworkers exists and thus offshore workers are needed. We see very little evidence of such a shortage but rather that the introduction of [unfree migrant] offshore workers has greatly hampered the domestic workers and in some cases has resulted in foreign workers displacing US workers in ... this country. With the foreign workers' arrival, harvesting prices for US labor dropped. As a stable supply of labor was introduced, employers refused to negotiate prices to be paid to US laborers.

Unlike local workers, who can negotiate for higher wages, foreign contract workers have to accept pay levels and conditions imposed by employers, who accordingly 'find it much less expensive with a controlled labor force'. As the case of the struggle conducted by the National Farm Workers Organization against the Californian grape growers during the 1970s confirms, employers frequently used Mexican workers as strikebreakers (see the US House of Representatives Special Subcommittee on Labor [1969]).

79. On this point, see evidence presented to the US Senate Subcommittee on Migratory Labour [1970a: 100]. Asked by the legal counsel to the Senate Subcommittee what kind of legislative protection he would like to have enacted, one migrant replied [*US Senate Subcommittee on Migratory Labour*, 1970a: 216] with great dignity:

The law I would like to see most passed is to be able to bargain like our industrial brothers around the country. If we think we are not being treated fair we would like to be able to sit down and negotiate for better treatment, for a better price, a living wage is all we are after. We are not trying to be multiple millionaires, we want to sit down and eat a half decent meal where we will be satisfied and we know our kids will be. We would like to see that come.

80. Regarding the absence of trade union organization among Mexican migrants employed in the American southwest, and the role in this of the revival of 'patron/client' relations on the part of the labour contractor, the following exchange [*US Senate Subcommittee on Migratory Labor*, 1970b: 473–4] between Senator Mondale and Ernesto Galarza is instructive:

Dr Galarza: In the Southwest, Mexicans rediscover the patrón, but in a different incarnation. He is the labor contractor and the crew leader, and in time becomes what I call ... the patroncito, the little patrón, who accumulates a little capital ... makes loans to his workers, he bails them out of jail, he feeds them on credit, he lets them live in the camp through the winter months until the next season and then collects the back rent. This is the traditional patrón system which has become in the Southwest the core of the [migrant] social system and which in a sense explains the powerlessness of the workers.
Senator Mondale: The patrón is the crew leader?
Dr Galarza: The crew leader.
Senator Mondale: He doesn't want a union, does he?
Dr Galarza: Never.
Senator Mondale: Because that is the end of the role?
Dr Galarza: That's right.
Senator Mondale: So when you want to organize a union in an environment where the patrón system is widespread, the man that the worker depends upon for his job, depends upon for his credit to get out of jail, depends upon as his special pleader with the power system, this man will oppose it and try to deny

him these services ... Once he becomes a troublemaker, he is a marked man in the system, is he not?

Dr Galarza: And if you fall into disgrace or disfavor with your local patrón ... you are in real trouble because you are not only in disgrace with him, but you are in disgrace with those powers above him for whom he is broker, and this is a major disaster in your life and the life of your family and one you try to avoid at all costs.

Senator Mondale: The patrón in turn has to develop a constituency that will use the services that he will provide, and he will want to promise [an employer] a hardworking labor group, and hopefully a labor group that will work for less than someone else's group, is that right?

Dr Galarza: Yes. One of the results, if not one of the stated objectives of the contractor system in the Southwest that I have seen, is to keep the wage scale down and in that its effort has been eminently effective.

It hardly requires pointing out that such an interpretation of 'patron/client' relations contrasts markedly with the highly idealized way in which the same kind of linkages are depicted by revisionist texts on Latin America and India (see Chapters 6 and 7).

81. Noting the important role of all-white Southern juries in the enforcement and perpetuation of the debt peonage relation, Kennedy [1946: 61–2] reports that one juryman admitted to him that, despite substantial evidence confirming its existence: 'we couldn't convict [an employer] for peonage just because he had to whip a few vagabond niggers to keep 'em from runnin' out on their debts!'

82. The link between peak demand for agricultural labour and the incidence of lynching is demonstrated by Beck and Tolnay [1995].

6

The Latin American *Enganche* System

This chapter examines the epistemologically coherent yet theoretically flawed claims made by a number of revisionist texts regarding the meaning and causes of the Latin American *enganche* system. Their problematic definitions of unfreedom include the view that coercion involves overt and continuous maltreatment, and that debt bondage necessarily entails deception. Equally problematic are their reasons for reclassifying the *enganche* as free labour: the apparently free nature of similar kinds of contractual arrangement, the physical mobility of the workforce, the phenomenon of reverse bondage, and voluntary entry into the *enganche* relation. Having redefined debt bondage as free, revisionists then identify economic security (= unfreedom-as-economic-empowerment) as the reason why rural labour enters into and stays within such relations.

The idealized image of debt bondage, and the inability to recognize it as a form of unfreedom, has its roots in a corresponding failure on the part of revisionist texts to differentiate the peasantry in terms of class. This in turn prevents an understanding of both the origin and cause of the *enganche* system in at least some of the Latin American contexts considered. In those instances where class struggle results in an emerging proletarian consciousness, therefore, the object of the debt bondage mechanism is not so much to open up a free labour market (which already exists) but rather to close it down.

As is immediately apparent from much recent writing on agrarian relations in Latin America, the extent to which the *enganche* system corresponds to unfree labour is strongly contested theoretical terrain. In this respect, current debate over the existence/non-existence debt bondage, and whether or not it is a form of unfreedom, replicates many of the issues raised during the mid-1970s by *Time on the Cross*, in which Fogel and Engerman argued that to regard New World plantation slavery as wholly negative was incorrect, since the slaves themselves not only accepted but also secured material benefits from its existence.[1] Rightly seeking to rebut the notorious 'sambo' myth of black responses to plantation slavery, *Time on the Cross* advanced not only the uncontroversial proposition that blacks were not inferior, incompetent, or lazy, but also (and more controversially) that they did well out of slavery. From the latter position it is but a short step to a claim that blacks actually *liked* their servitude.

For much the same reason, many of the texts examined below which project debt bondage in Latin America in a similarly benign or positive manner can also be characterized as revisionist.[2] Like Fogel and Engerman, such texts purge unfreedom of its coercive element; instead, the *enganche* system in Latin America is presented as the outcome of economically rational choice, an harmonious arrangement in a non-antagonistic context which entails materially equal exchange and is therefore of mutual benefit to all parties involved in the relationship. The element of epistemological convergence is quite striking: common to both approaches is the view that because in material terms chattel slaves and bonded labourers were better-off than free workers, they were motivated not by force (or fear thereof) but by pecuniary incentives (= unfreedom-as-economic-empowerment).

Consequently, earlier (= 'traditional') interpretations which projected such relationships in a negative manner are accused of misrecognizing the dynamics of slavery and bondage due to an over-emphasis they placed on the importance of coercion.[3] This enables revisionists to effect a contrast between their own 'modern' framework, whereby the worker is constituted as an active/empowered subject in a capitalist context, with 'traditional' views which not only depict the subject as passive but conceptualize debt bondage as a pre-/non-capitalist relation aimed principally at keeping a peasantry on the land.[4] The chronology is also significant: a number of these texts (Bauer, Cotlear, Cross, and Blanchard) were published towards the end of the 1970s, when the claims about chattel slavery made by *Time on the Cross* would have percolated through to influence those writing about unfree relationships in other contexts.[5]

The object of this chapter is, in short, to examine the assumptions structuring the revisionist perception of unfreedom. What is at issue is not the conjunctural and contextual specificity of the *enganche* relation in Latin America, which is not open to question, but rather the way in which its free/unfree component is theorized.[6] The revisionist position has been criticized elsewhere, notably in the rejoinder by Loveman to Bauer's 1979 text; the gist of the former's response was that the latter had ignored a large body of writing whose findings on the issue of debt bondage undermined the revisionist thesis, a point Bauer himself subsequently acknowledged.[7] Although it highlighted a number of important weaknesses in Bauer's presentation, Loveman's reply was nevertheless unsatisfactory; at no point was the revisionist conceptualization of unfree relations challenged, with the result that the core elements of the thesis escaped scrutiny, and consequently the theoretical framework itself remained intact.

In order to evaluate the way in which these revisionist texts interpret the *enganche* relation, it is necessary to consider the following three points. First, what they regard as bonded labour (its definition). Second, why such relations are not regarded as unfree (alternative theorizations of debt bondage). And third, the reasons given for the existence of these relations (why the *enganche* system occurs).

I

Before considering problematic definitions of unfreedom, it is necessary to emphasize that confusions about the free/unfree labour distinction are by no means confined to revisionist texts. For example, although the Peruvian *enganche* system is described by Collins as a form of debt peonage, she merely asserts that it amounted to 'virtual slavery' without making any reference to the extensive debate as to whether or not this relation corresponds to a form of unfreedom.[8] In support of the view that migration from the Andean highlands to the Tambopata valley was composed of unfree workers, she invokes the studies by McCreery of *mandamiento* labour in Guatemala during the latter half of the nineteenth century, and by Bergad on nineteenth-century Puerto Rico.[9] The difficulty here is that, whereas McCreery does indeed maintain that bonded labour was unfree, Bergad denies this. Indeed, Collins attributes to the latter the opposite view to that which he actually holds: in the text she cites, Bergad argues that the coffee workforce in Puerto Rico during the period in question was not unfree but much rather a proletariat, a claim disputed by this writer in the course of a subsequent exchange on this very issue.[10]

6.1 Unfree Labour and Legislative Abolition

A related problem concerns the tendency to conflate the legislative abolition of unfreedom with the realization of a transition to free wage labour. For example, McCreery regards the abolition in 1945 by the Guatemalan state of pass laws (*libretas*) as evidence for the ending of unfreedom and a corresponding transition to free labour, despite agreeing that the use by employers of coercion and indebtedness as a means of cheapening labour-power continued beyond this date.[11] Whilst important, what the law permits or forbids may not be a very helpful guide to grassroots practice. Thus coercion may exist in law but not in fact, or in fact but not in law.

The difficulties raised by fetishizing legality, and consequently mistaking it for relational emancipation, may be illustrated by the following instances. In the case of nineteenth century Cuba, therefore, legal injunctions preventing the exercise of coercion by masters against apprentices were routinely flouted.[12] Similarly, in Buenos Aires towards the end of the eighteenth century, manumitted slaves were required to continue paying a proportion of their earnings to ex-slaveowners, an arrangement which suggests that emancipation existed in name only.[13] Accordingly, to say that the law permits or disallows unfreedom is to say nothing about why unfreedom is legal or illegal, whether legislation is enforced or disregarded, why this happens and changes, and what social forces benefit from or are disadvantaged by this whole process.

6.2 Debt Peonage and Coercion

In general terms, the different concepts of debt bondage utilized by revisionist texts tend to encompass non-economic definitions of unfreedom; these include maltreatment as an ever-present dimension, and the element of deception. While most of the more important revisionist texts dealing with bonded labour in Latin America rightly identify the existence of debt linked to extra-economic coercion as a crucial aspect of unfreedom, they nevertheless fail to problematise the methodological accessibility of coercion, let alone the different forms this might take.[14] Accordingly, bonded labour is associated largely with the continuous and unremitting existence of physical oppression, the absence of which correspondingly brings into question its element of unfreedom. This definition adheres closely to the popular image of slavery as the maltreatment of individuals physically encumbered and restrained by chains, and subject to continuous brutality by ever-present overseers. Bauer, for example, expresses doubt that sugar plantations on the north coast of Peru 'imposed a harsh and cruel system of debt bondage', and is sceptical of the 'older reports [of the Peruvian *enganche* which] insist that it was harsh and tyrannical'.[15] Similarly, the presence of 'classic debt servitude' in late nineteenth century Mexico is equated by Knight largely with the application of 'harsh corporal punishment'.[16]

Three difficulties confront the revisionist view that unfree labour is characterized by maltreatment. First, continuous physical oppression is counter-productive and therefore uneconomic. Second, no attempt is made to question the methodological accessibility of coercion. And third, instead of recognizing that unfreedom can include oblique forms of socio-economic pressure such as that exercised through kin and quasi-kin networks, and thus does not necessarily entail the actualization of physical oppression, extra-economic coercion is unproblematically conflated with maltreatment. In contrast to the revisionist argument, the view adopted here is that (where and when it occurs) maltreatment is an effect of economic unfreedom, and hence not of itself constitutive of the debt bondage relation. Physical oppression is thus a consequence of the enforced immobility (in the economic sense of the term) of a bonded labourer who cannot re-enter the market (and therefore bargain with his employer over this issue) until his debt has been cancelled.

One reason for not maltreating an unfree worker on a continuous basis is a corresponding diminution in the economic efficiency of the subject affected. This is a particularly important consideration in labour scarce areas such as the tropical lowland areas of Latin America where, as one observer noted with regard to the existence of peonage, an unfree worker 'is a valuable piece of property and if a slave raider travel five hundred miles through forest and jungle-swamp to capture an Indian you may depend upon it that he will not beat him to death merely for the fun of it'.[17] Not all unfree workers are subject to ill-treatment as a matter of course, therefore, since this would clearly be counter-productive (in a literal sense). Instead, the occasional beating-up, physical assault, and even killing of a worker who attempts to abscond or refuses to meet his labour obligations is usually sufficient to demonstrate to the others the consequences of such action.[18]

The fact that some forms of coercion are exercised in an indirect manner similarly reinforces the problem of methodological accessibility. Some revisionists question the the very linkage between debt and coercion. If a landowner controls a worker by means of extra-economic coercion, they ask, why is the 'legal fiction' of debt also necessary for bondage to exist? Their conclusion is that since the landowner anyway has absolute power over the subject concerned, the debt relation is irrelevant to its exercise.[19] Hence unfreedom does not of itself require the presence of a debt relation. The following points can be made in answer to this question.

It is undoubtedly true than in some Latin American contexts the absolute nature of the repressiveness exercised by an employer over his workforce precludes the necessity of debt. However, in so far as this kind of power posesses no politico-ideological legitimacy among the workforce as a whole, it also risks conferring legitimacy on opposition to its exercise. Thus the 'legal fiction' of debt is in the majority of instances necessary precisely because its *material* presence bestows a specific (and potent) form of politico-ideological acceptability (the concept of 'equal exchange') on an exploitative relationship which would otherwise lack this fundamental dimension. It therefore contributes in an important manner to the reproduction of the employer's power and in turn the economic relationship dependent upon this.

Accordingly, the presence of a debt relation between employer and worker (and thus the corresponding existence of a politico-ideological concept of 'reciprocity') facilitates the enforcement of labour-service obligations. Furthermore, in these circumstances the efficacy of the enforcement process does not require that the debtor him/herself perceive the relation as one based on 'equal exchange': if those to whom the debtor is in turn linked by political, ideological, or economic ties themselves perceive the relation as a just transaction, then the most effective structure for enforcement is already in place, since it is through the mobilization of these socio-economic networks that the debtor can be prevailed upon to fulfil his labour-service obligations regardless of whether or not he agrees with the conceptualization of the transaction itself as 'reciprocal' and fair. For precisely this reason, therefore, one of the most important (and ideologically most potent) methods of enforcing debt bondage obligations remains the formal and informal control exerted in the context of actual/fictive kin networks.[20]

6.3 Debt Peonage as Deception

Deception constitutes another defining characteristic of unfree labour in Latin America.[21] Hence the view that the operation of the *enganche* system necessarily entails that its labouring subject be unknowingly or unwittingly recruited into and maintained in debt through trickery. Paradoxically, this theorization is shared by revisionists and non-revisionists alike; in so far as bonded labour is associated largely (or solely) with duplicity, both these opposed viewpoints reproduce the stereotype of those subordinated by this mechanism as passive objects rather than active subjects engaged in class struggle.

On the one hand, therefore, those who regard bonded labour as unfree accept that recruitment based on the *enganche* mechanism involves peasants being 'fooled' by contractors.[22] On the other hand, revisionists also associate the *enganche* with guile on the part of the labour contractor, if only in order to deny both the feasibility of such an arrangement and (hence) the unfree character of the relation itself.[23] Like Cotlear, who questions the extent to which mere trickery could have sustained the *enganche* system over such a long time, Bauer disputes the view that 'families of smallholders and villagers were incapable of learning and each year seemed to stumble drunkenly into the recruiter's grasp'; Miller similarly dismisses the idea that peasants were 'duped into deepening cyles of debt peonage' as an historically inaccurate stereotype derived solely from the literary imaginings contained in Ciro Alegría's *indigenista* novel, *Broad and Alien is the World* (1942).[24] In all these cases the absence of either an initial or a sustainable duplicity on the part of the contractor (or the estate store) is interpreted by revisionists as evidence of the voluntary nature of recruitment and indebtedness effected by means of the *enganche*, and thus as an indication of its non-coercive and free character.

Against these viewpoints it is argued here that the operation of the *enganche* system depends not so much on deception as on compulsion: that is, on the *power* of the dominant class in general, and in particular of creditors or creditor-employers to enforce debt-servicing labour obligations on workers who owe them money. The emphasis on duplicity as an integral aspect of debt bondage derives at least in part from the way in which this relation comes into being.[25] Historically, the inception of the *enganche* relation in Latin America has been linked to the consumption of alcoholic beverages, in the sense that the act of drinking is either itself a cause of indebtedness (to the estate store or the labour contractor) or merely functions as a context in which this form of recruitment is effected.[26] Given this association, therefore, it is unsurprising that deception is perceived as a defining characteristic, since it is inferred that the bonding process operates only on occasions and in circumstances when contractors are able to hoodwink inebriated peasants into accepting cash advances, the implication being that a sober peasant would not incur debt in this manner.

II

Among the reasons advanced by revisionists for rejecting the negative categorization of debt bondage as a form of unfreedom, and reclassifying it as a free relation, are its supposed non-coercive and/or positive aspects: the free nature of similar kinds of contractual arrangement, the phenomenon of reverse bondage, the ability of its subjects to migrate, the voluntary entry into such relations, and their role as a form of economic security or 'subsistence guarantee'. As will be seen in the chapter which follows, these are the same assumptions which structure the perception of unfreedom-as-economic-empowerment informing the revisionist interpretations of attached labour in India. For revisionists generally, therefore, the presence of any or all of these elements constitute evidence of grassroots empowerment, and thus the presence not of unfree but of free production relations.

6.4 Debt Peonage as Economic Security

Significantly, this substantive transformation in meaning (unfree ⇒ free) is generally structured by an epistemologically coherent framework. Given an initial premiss that subjects of the *enganche* system are attracted by, enter into, remain within or change this form of employment voluntarily, it follows that such relations cannot be unfree. This in turn licenses an equally specific form of causation: if subjects enter into and remain in such relationships not because they have to but rather because they want to, this too must be for a particular reason. The latter, it is then argued, is because such arrangements (presented as 'patron-clientage') are a form of subsistence guarantee which provides their subject with economic security.

A supposedly potent argument used by revisionist theory against the characterization of debt bondage in Latin America as unfree is that there is no difference between bonded labour in Third World agriculture and the kind of relationships in metropolitan capitalist countries which link academics, company employees, film stars or sportspersons to their respective institutions through contracts, pension plans or indebtedness to finance companies. All these arrangements are basically the same, and constitute nothing other than non-coercive cash/credit incentives to remain in a particular job.[27]

This comparison ignores a number of crucial distinctions. For example, academics and company employees generally do not owe debts to their employer, nor can they be prevented from resigning in order to take up other employment. More importantly, there is no requirement on their part to repay debts such as bank overdrafts in the form of hard manual labour on rural properties or construction sites owned by the bank at a low wage fixed by the latter. Furthermore, since tenured academics and company employees enjoy the benefits of both high earnings and a full range of the social wage, they are not dependent on cash advances for subsistence.

The usual and generally correct response to this kind of comparison is to dismiss it as irrelevant nonsense.[28] Closer inspection, however, reveals that a parallel does indeed exist, albeit not that proposed by revisionist theory. Comparing the power structure in Hollywood during the mid-1940s to that of the plantation system in the old South, one observer suggests that in a context where studio bosses competed for stars, the contractually unfree position of film actors in this period was in many ways the same as that of plantation slaves or medieval serfs.[29] In a similar vein, a recent social history of professional cricket in England suggests that the benefit system, whereby a player was awarded all the financial proceeds from a particular match, was a method of withholding wages and making cricketers remain with a particular county side in spite of their own best economic interests.[30] These examples confirm yet simultaneously invert the claim made by revisionist theory: hence bonded labour is in some circumstances no different from contractual relations linking film stars and sportspersons to their respective employers not because both are free relations but much rather because both are unfree.

6.5 Debt Peonage as Reverse Bondage

Another influential argument deployed by revisionist texts against the existence of debt bondage is that in many cases it was not the worker who owed money to the landowner but much rather the landowner who owed money to the worker. Bauer makes this point with regard to the *hacienda* system in Latin America generally, while Gibson, Bazant, Brading and Cross make it specifically with reference to *haciendas* in eighteenth and nineteenth century Mexico, and Palacios with respect to Colombian *haciendas* at the turn of the century.[31] The dual inference here is that: firstly, the existence of what is known as 'reverse bondage' demonstrates the advantageous bargaining position of the *hacienda* workforce; and secondly, as the subjects of the latter are not debtors but much rather creditors, they cannot be regarded as unfree.[32]

This is to miss the point, since the object of debt, either in its form of labourer-indebted-to-employer or of employer-indebted-to-labourer is in both cases the same.[33] In so far as the worker is compelled to return in order to pay off or else collect outstanding payments, the employer is assured of a future supply of labour-power.[34] Accordingly, it corresponds to a situation in which payment due a worker at the end of his contract is withheld by the employer precisely in order to retain control over his labour-power, thereby making it unavailable to other employers and rendering its subject economically unfree.[35] In India, for example, where this kind of non-payment is recognized as bonded labour, its object is to force the worker either to take a subsistence loan or to continue working in the hope of eventual payment.[36]

Not only is there no difference between the unfreedom inherent in the structure of debt bondage and 'reverse bondage', therefore, but they are the same in terms of effect. Just as lowering real wage levels through debt bondage permits employers and/or landlords to extract unpaid work from the labourer concerned, so the withholding of a portion of the wage similarly results in unpaid work; in short, both permit the extraction of surplus labour.

6.6 Debt Peonage and Physical Mobility

Yet another characteristic of the revisionist approach to debt bondage in Latin America is the equation of economic freedom with physical mobility by the workforce. Labour migration is accordingly regarded as evidence for the breakdown of extra-economic coercion, and thus incompatible with the continued existence of unfree relations, notwithstanding the fact that in the contexts referred to such movement takes place within the framework of the *enganche* relationship. The epistemological linkage between an initial emphasis on geographical mobility and the subsequent characterization of debt bondage as a non-coercive relation is most marked in the work of Bauer. Thus his view about worker mobility structuring the reinterpretation of bonded labour is first encountered in an earlier text dealing at length with the structure of rural labour in mid-nineteenth-century Chile.[37] A strong sense of physical movement pervades the latter, as evidenced by frequent references throughout to the 'floating', 'nomadic' or 'ambulatory' nature of the agrarian workforce in the Central Valley.[38]

Much the same kind of linkage is made with regard to Peru by both Cotlear and Taylor. Arguing against Burga, who maintains that as a result of incurring debts to the estate store peasants succumbed to the *enganche* and thereby lost the freedom of movement, Cotlear questions the applicability of this latter claim to those who were anyway seasonal migrants, and who were able to return to their own villages at the end of each contract period.[39] Later in the same text, the operation of the *enganche* in Peru at the beginning of the century is linked explicitly to the lack of geographical mobility on the part of the peasantry.[40] By contrast, but in a similar vein, Taylor makes a connection between the ineffectiveness of the *enganche* and the free movement of peasants in the northern Peruvian department of Cajamarca during the period 1870–1900.[41]

For Bauer, Cotlear, and Taylor, therefore, the fact that the *enganche* involves labour mobility, which in turn appears to negate restrictions imposed on workers, is taken as evidence that it constitutes free wage labour. Such a view, however, fails to differentiate between physical mobility (the act of local and/or regional migration) and economic mobility (the relationship governing – and therefore placing limits on – this act). Thus the physical mobility of the labouring subject does not of itself establish the presence of free wage labour; were this so, it would also be necessary to classify both chattel slavery and indenture as forms of free labour-power. Nor does this view take into account the presence of the arrangement known as 'changing masters': in cases where indebted labourers are permitted to find other work only on condition that the new (creditor-) employer pays off what the labourer owes his existing creditor-employer, bondage is merely transferred, not eliminated.[42]

6.7 Debt Peonage as a Voluntary Relation

A teleological effect of banishing coercion from the debt bondage mechanism is that the latter can now be recast as a voluntary relationship, a form of free wage labour and thus evidence for the development of proletarianization. In the case of Latin America, this coercive (unfree) ⇒ voluntary (free) metamorphosis is most evident in the work of Knight. For him peonage ceases to be a unitary relationship characterized by debt-induced unfreedom, and is instead divided into three distinct relations: 'a surrogate proletariat' composed of temporary migrant wage labourers, a 'traditional' peonage that applies to peasant tenants who composed the resident permanent workforce on rural estates, and what he calls the classic debt peonage of Chinese coolies on the coastal plantations of Peru and the indigenous workers employed as rubber tappers on the Amazon during the 1890s.[43] Unlike the last of these three variants, which Knight agrees was 'unmistakably servile and coercive', both the former in his view 'cannot be termed servile relations'.[44] In the case of the first variant, for example, the object of debt is not to impede the ability of the subject to commodify his labour-power, or to control it, but much rather to 'attract workers to commercial plantations'.[45]

The voluntary entry in this manner of workers and/or poor peasants into the *enganche* system is frequently cited as evidence for the free, non-bonded or non-coercive character of this arrangement.[46] Since in these circumstances loans are requested from a creditor-employer, and the recipient willingly agrees to work only for the latter until the debt thus incurred is cleared, the element of coercion is deemed to be absent. Accordingly, such relationships are not regarded as unfree. The problem with this view is that it focuses solely on the *act of recruitment*, and ignores the nature of the subsequent *production relation*; the latter is defined in terms of the former. While recruitment may itself be voluntary, in the sense that the labourer willingly offers himself for work, it does not follow that the production relation which results will be correspondingly free in terms of the worker's capacity to re-enter the labour market.[47] As in the case of chattel slavery, therefore, it is necessary to distinguish the bonded labour relation itself from its different modes of inception and multivariate causes.

Once the *enganche* system has been purged of its negative or coercive element, and consequently reclassified in positive terms as a voluntary (and therefore free) relationship, it then becomes necessary for revisionists to ask why, if not compelled to do so, do peasants nevertheless choose to enter into and remain within such working arrangements. Bonded labour, revisionists then go on to claim, is an attractive type of employment because its subject is provided with economic security in the form of guaranteed subsistence. Accordingly, unfreedom is denied on the grounds that debt bondage amounts to a materially reciprocal exchange between landholder or labour contractor and employee, and thus constitutes for the latter an economically empowering transaction which corresponds to 'patron-clientage'.

For Latin America generally, the *enganche* system is referred to by Bauer as a form of 'paternalism'; he describes the landlord/tenant relation as one of 'patron-clientage', and asserts that the 'pre-1870s hacienda had undoubtedly sheltered, fed, and underemployed far more people than required for production'.[48] Taylor also describes the relationship between the landlord class and the estate workforce in the northern Peruvian sierra towards the end of last century in terms of 'patron-clientage'.[49] Cross attributes a similarly positive role to the debt bondage relation in Mexico, where 'the credit arrangements constituted a kind of insurance, or a nineteenth century social security'.[50] Gibson similarly concludes that in Mexico debt peonage on the colonial *hacienda* 'was an institution of credit, allowing Indians freely to fall behind in their financial obligations without losing their jobs or incurring punishment'.[51]

Much the same kind of claim is made in the case of peonage on the coffee plantations of Guatemala, where according to McCreery there was little incentive on the part of the worker to escape debt since labour contractors and landholders were regarded as sources of ready cash and protection.[52] This claim about the 'benign' nature of planters, landholders and labour contractors shades into and licenses a further claim: that all the latter were actually powerless in dealings with their workforce, the inference being that peonage was unenforceable.[53] It is then possible to argue that, because the unfree component of these relations was a mirage (unfreedom = 'unfreedom' = freedom) consequently they were reproduced not 'from above' by planters, landholders and contractors but much rather 'from below' – by the workers themselves, because such relations were to their advantage. Indeed, McCreery himself argues that it was necessary for landholders to negotiate with workers, because the former had had little actual power over the latter.

6.8 Unfreedom, Subsistence and the Company Store

A variant of the argument that classifies unfree labour as a form of 'security' or 'subsistence guarantee' is the debate about the role of the company store (*tienda, pulperia, el despacho de peones*). The latter constituted the source of subsistence items purchased and consumed by the estate or plantation workforce, and has traditionally been regarded as one of the principal determinants of unfreedom linked to indebtedness.[54]

Unsurprisingly, revisionist texts challenge this negative interpretation of the hacienda store.[55] Cotlear in particular questions this explanation, and laments that the absence of detailed information on the kinds of items sold by these stores precludes an accurate assessment of their role: for example, did migrants purchase items just to consume during the work period itself, or to take back with them to the highlands?[56] His view is that in Peru at the beginning of the twentieth century the estate store fulfilled a positive role, and was the most important source of consumption goods outside the peasant economy, a method whereby seasonal migrants supplemented subsistence shortfalls on their plots in the highlands. What Cotlear argues here is, in short, a variant of the unfreedom-as-economic-empowerment thesis.[57]

In order to sustain this argument, it is necessary for Cotlear to dismiss the main hypothesis linking the store to unfreedom resulting from debt: the view that highland peasants became indebted as a consequence either of items purchased without knowing their cost or of levels of consumption in excess of income are in his opinion both variants of the 'trickery'/'duping' argument, and therefore unsustainable. Similarly unacceptable in his view is the notion that workers were obliged to buy items for which the store charged a monopoly price. He concludes by affirming that the ways in which the store impeded worker mobility remain unclear or unproven.

While Cotlear is correct to reject 'trickery' as the foundation of control exercised over the workforce through the estate store, the issues of expenditure in excess of income, indebtedness generated by overpricing, and impediments to the economic mobility of the workforce consequent on them, cannot be dismissed so easily.[58] Hence expenditure in excess of income is a consequence not of 'duplicity' but rather of low wages combined with either inflation and/or the monopoly position of the store (through the exclusion or non-existence of rival merchants). In such circumstances, where workers had no choice but to purchase from the store, since this was the only source of either subsistence or production requirements consumed in the course of the work contract, credit terms were accepted not unknowingly (as Cotlear implies) but because they were necessary. Caught in the scissors between declining purchasing power and the rising cost of subsistence, workers knowingly incurred mounting debts which in turn affected their ability personally to commodify their labour-power.

Because he questions the existence of unfreedom linked to debt at the estate store, Cotlear does not consider in detail the methods whereby such control was effected. The connection between the purchase of high priced consumption goods, worker indebtedness, and low wages has a long history.[59] For example, it was the foundation of the truck system which endured in Britain from the fifteenth to the nineteenth century. [60] Debt linked to credit advanced at the company store was also a widespread and traditional method whereby Latin American plantations and rural estates producing cash crops for the world market controlled and simultaneously lowered the cost of their workforce.[61] Where remuneration took the form of non-negotiable tokens redeemable only at the store of the estate or plantation in question, the latter retained control over the subsistence (and through this the labour-power) of its workforce.[62] In such a context, payment did not and could not discharge the crucial function of money as a socially acceptable general equivalent of exchange, and workers were consequently prevented from spending their wages elsewhere.

It was possible, moreover, for employers to exercise control through the estate store even when payment took the form of cash. Thus indebted workers in recipt of a money wage would receive only what cash remained after the amount owed had been deducted at source, the balance being insufficient to survive until the next payday without credit at the store. In such circumstances, subsistence was still tied to the store in that workers who still had outstanding advances or loans with the estate were not permitted to seek alternative employment until these had been cancelled, the actual methods of enforcement being the same as for other forms of debt.[63]

Similarly problematic is the view that peasants who migrated from the

Peruvian highlands to the coast or eastern lowlands may have wanted access to goods in order to supplement subsistence shortfalls in their home community. If this refers to a capacity to return to the highlands with items purchased from the estate store, then it implies that either wages were sufficiently high enabling savings to be made, or that downward pressure on wages exercised by inflation and the store monopoly was non-existent.[64]

What is at issue here, therefore, is not the desirability, availability, or necessity of access to subsistence goods obtained from the estate store but the conditions governing and the relationships consequent on this. As with arguments concerning the voluntary entry into unfree relations (famine slavery), the question is not one of resource provision *per se* but rather in exchange for what, and with what implications for the continued ability of the subject to sell his/her labour-power.

Due to the teleological structure of the argument, in its depoliticized form the question of subsistence licenses a false inference. Accordingly, a rejection of the view that rural workers in Latin America remain in unfree labour relationships because of coercion exercised directly or indirectly by their employer necessarily leads to the espousal of the opposing view, that workers stay with a particular creditor-employer voluntarily because they benefit from the arrangement.[65] Extending the logic of this position to other historical contexts, it would be necessary to argue that the reason why chattel slavery on plantations in the American South lasted from the seventeenth to the nineteenth century was because the slaves themselves found it to their liking – which is precisely what is argued in *Time on the Cross* (see Chapter 5).

Since even chattel slavery furnishes its subject with a minimal level of subsistence (and thus could be justified using this particular criterion), any evaluation of benefits has to consider the returns to labour not just from existing relational forms but from the full range of possible alternatives. In short, the argument is a political one, a point that will be considered further in Chapter 8. It is therefore centrally about the class nature and (the opposed) interests of the parties to the relation, and as such concerns not subsistence *per se* but rather how much and in exchange for what. Posed in this manner, the question must take into account not only the necessity of obtaining subsistence (which is obvious and about which there can be no disagreement) but also the political and economic object of the debt mechanism itself.

III

A major theoretical shortcoming in the revisionist thesis is the absence of a concept of agrarian class structure, and therefore class struggle.[66] Thus a common feature of much revisionist writing on the issue of unfree labour in

Latin America is the failure to internally differentiate the peasantry on the *hacienda*, a lacuna which has important consequences for the theorization of debt. Rather than incorporating disparate class elements composed of heterogeneous strata possessing opposed economic and political interests, therefore, the peasantry is regarded as an homogenous social category. The result is a failure to distinguish between actual and formal control exercised by smallholders over their means of production, and hence a corresponding non-recognition of its implications for the presence/absence of together with the class-specific meanings of debt.

6.9 Debt Peonage and the Class Structure

Gibson, Bauer, Cross, Brading and Knight each use specific instances of Latin American estates where peasants were either not in debt to the landlord, or where money was owed but debtors were not subordinated by the *enganche* system, to deny the presence, the unfreedom, or the efficacy of the latter.[67] However, it is clear that the case studies from Peru and Chile cited by Bauer in support of this claim involve 'tenants who were successful and relatively prosperous petty entrepreneurs' and 'well-off tenants', the same being true both of the *arrendatarios* in the Mexican Bajío referred to by Brading, who were 'probably substantial farmers', of the administrative staff on the nineteenth century livestock *hacienda* in the Mexican state of Zacatecas cited by Cross, and of at least some of the 'privileged stratum' of estate tenants in late-nineteenth-century Mexico who are identified by Knight as coming under the rubric of 'traditional'/'voluntary' peonage.[68] In central Mexico during the revolution, it was precisely this 'privileged minority' composed of better-off tenants, administrators, and work supervisors, who refused to join the ranks of the Zapatistas and instead made common cause with the landlord class.[69]

That such better-off elements are not bonded by debt is hardly surprising, because in these circumstances borrowing (when it occurs) has a different cause, outcome, and (therefore) meaning.[70] For rich peasants debt is a means to accumulate, and not a question of survival; they engage in *productive* borrowing that yields a profit out of which repayment can be made.[71] Moreover, unlike poor peasants they sell not their own labour-power but the product of labour; that is, a commodity unconnected with the *enganche* . Their position in the social division of labour on the estate system is more generally as employers of substitute workers (*reemplazantes*); if anything, such producers – like the *arrendires* on the pre-reform estates of La Convención – are not merely not themselves subordinated by but much rather subordinate others through the *enganche* .[72]

Debt incurred by poor peasants, by contrast, possesses a different cause, outcome, and meaning. At this end of the class structure borrowing is in an economic sense unproductive, and occurs not for the purposes of accumulation but rather for survival (a distinction signalled in texts on bonded labour in India by the term 'consumption loan'). Furthermore, unlike rich peasants, poor peasants sell not the product of their labour but labour-power itself; that is, the very commodity the acquisition and control of which is the object of the *enganche* system.[73] Since their principal source of income derives from the sale of labour-power, poor 'peasants' are more accurately characterized as *de facto* workers and not economically autonomous cultivators. By conflating these two distinct types of class subject, yet simultaneously recognizing that rich tenants not only utilize debt to their advantage but are also unaffected by the *enganche* in so far as this involves the immobilization of their labour-power, revisionists wrongly conclude that this is true of *all* peasants on the estate system in Latin America.

Unsurprisingly, the absence of a concept of class results in turn in a fundamental misrecognition concerning the reason for the presence of debt bondage. Thus Cotlear, Bauer, and Knight all regard the *enganche* as a necessary element in the formation of a labour market. Because rural inhabitants were unresponsive to wage incentives or suspicious of market entry, it is implied or asserted, such a relationship was the only way in which peasants could be persuaded to sell their labour-power and so be drawn voluntarily into the process of capitalist production. Since on the one hand the element of coercion has been eliminated, and on the other primitive accumulation made possible, it now becomes feasible within the revisionist framework to argue that bonded labour represents not only an economically progressive tendency (signalling a feudal $\Rightarrow$ capitalist transformation) but also constitutes a development toward or actual evidence of proletarianization.[74]

6.10 Debt Peonage and Class Formation

In the opinion of Cotlear, therefore, the *enganche* plays a crucial role in the formation of a fully operational capitalist labour market, and characterizes the transition period between the absence and presence of the latter.[75] Unlike India, where labour attachment is regarded as a relationship which affects only permanent workers, a central emplacement of the revisionist argument is that in Latin America labour-tying arrangements are applied principally to seasonal workers. Thus Cotlear maintains that the presence or absence of the *enganche* system on Peruvian estates and mines at the beginning of this century was determined ultimately by the corresponding importance (or lack of it) of seasonal migrants in the workforce.[76] Advance cash payment is regarded as a method of making seasonal labour migration possible, and the *enganche* system is accordingly theorized as an important factor in encouraging the formation of a fully mobile rural proletariat. After migration becomes voluntary, this argument goes, the *enganche* ceases to be necessary, a transition marked by the disappearance of the labour contractor.

Bauer similarly observes that in Latin America over the period 1870 to 1930 the *enganche* was necessary in order 'to bring people with precapitalist mentality into the labor market ... at a time when rural people were not yet fully responsive to the wage incentive; when, in other words, a free labor market did not yet exist'.[77] Knight holds much the same view, and argues that the existence of the coercive (as distinct from the voluntary) variant of debt peonage in areas like the Putumayo region of Peru and the Yucatán region of Mexico was a necessary part of habituating pre-capitalist peasants to capitalist work patterns in the context of an imperfect or non-existent labour market.[78] Although Knight accepts that 'the natives were lazy for entirely comprehensible reasons' to do with the working conditions in these contexts, his argument indicates the extent to which the revisionist case reproduces both the 'lazy native' myth that structures employer ideology and the exculpation of chattel slavery by Fogel and Engerman in terms of 'non-pecuniary disadvantage'. Against such a view it is possible to make the following observations.

The difficulty with Cotlear's interpretation is that debt bondage relations affect not just seasonal migrants but also permanent workers. Because the *enganche* system is associated only with the process of migration and its role in the formation of a labour market, this view – akin to saying that slavery ceased with the ending of the slave trade – cannot account for the subsequent persistence of unfree relations among permanent workers who settle and reside locally. If advance cash payment is necessary only to encourage and/or facilitate migration, then why are similar cash advances, with similar conditions, also made to poor peasants and landless labourers already available for hire in the work location itself?

The applicability of debt bondage to seasonal migrants and permanent locals alike indicates that the relation is a means not of encouraging but rather of preventing either the emergence or the operation of a free labour market, and as such can only be understood within a context of class struggle. Thus, the elimination of the labour contractor signals not the end of the *enganche* system but a change in its form. The labourer becomes indebted to the creditor-employer at the point of production, and the portion of surplus labour which previously accrued to the contracting agent henceforth accrues directly to the producer.[79]

In the case of Peru, evidence suggests that the continued resort by employers to the *enganche* in contexts where a free labour market already existed challenges Cotlear's argument that such a mechanism was and is necessary for the inauguration of a wage relation.[80] Similarly, labour contractors were unable to recruit free wage labour in the Mantaro valley during the 1940s, precisely because 'in many villages, the mines [for which the *enganche* was used] remained an unpopular choice for those seeking work ... villagers preferred to work on the irrigation canal [project] ... and on road construction projects'.[81] The same is true of Brazilian Amazonia where, despite the presence in this region of local/migrant free wage labour, there was from the 1960s and 1970s onwards a widely-reported resurgence in the incidence of unfree workers recruited/controlled by labour contractors.[82]

Paradoxically, Bauer's contention regarding the connection between the *enganche* and the absence of a rural labour market is refuted by evidence he himself provides in an earlier text.[83] Notwithstanding his observation that landowners in nineteenth century Chile 'were up against an attitude very different from that held by the modern industrial worker and one that would have to be fundamentally changed', a situation in which 'an expanding market came into contact with archaic [worker] behaviour', it is clear that rural inhabitants were highly responsive to wage differentials, as demonstrated by mass out-migration from the agricultural zone in search of higher wages paid for work on railway construction, both in Chile itself over the period 1852–63 and in Peru during 1868–72.[84] Even within agriculture itself, it seems, labourers 'moved from one work gang to another several miles away for an additional six centavos or an "extra bean in the pot"'.[85] A workforce that not only went from estate to estate to find higher remuneration but also sought better paid employment outside agriculture when this was available cannot be regarded as 'archaic' or exhibiting a 'precapitalist mentality'. Much rather the opposite: in selling its labour-power to the highest bidder on an intra- or inter-sectoral basis, it was in fact acting just like a proletariat.[86]

6.11 Debt Peonage and Class Struggle

With regard to the element of class struggle, here too revisionist texts provide evidence that contradicts claims regarding the crisis-free nature of debt bondage and the corresponding acceptability of this relationship to its constituent subjects. In the case of the northern Peruvian sierra, for example, the period around the First World War was marked by struggles on the sugar plantations as the workforce experienced the effects of rising prices combined with declining real wage levels. According to Blanchard this was a context in which employers regarded the *enganche* as a method of undermining attempts on the part of their workforce both to think and act as a proletariat.[87] In other words, to *deproletarianize* it.

As it appears in many of the revisionist texts on Latin America, the *enganche* system lacks any concept of socio-economic tension, of contradiction. In one sense this is unsurprising, since the presentation of debt bondage as a form of economic security, an harmonious system based on reciprocal exchange, or a transaction whereby loans advanced to poor peasants and labourers are worked off 'at a mutually agreed rate of pay', is in fact the mirror image of and hence necessarily denies the element of class conflict.[88] Despite this, the presence of antagonism cannot wholly be disguised; yet even though the *enganchados* themselves went on strike for higher wages and better working conditions, Blanchard is unable to connect this with the presence of the *enganche*. Struggles over wages and conditions generated in its context are therefore relegated to the peripheral status of 'abuse'. Significantly, this way of marginalizing conflict implies that, although 'excesses' may occur from time to time, the relationship itself is not open to question, a view imputed by the observer to the subjects of the relation. This is the way, for example, in which the conflicts associated with the *enganche* in northern Peru at the turn of the century are referred to by Blanchard, Albert and Taylor.[89]

However, the claim made by Blanchard that the *enganche* survived for as long as it did because of its acceptability to peasant migrants from the highlands notwithstanding, evidence contained both in his own and in other texts suggests to the contrary that the abolition of the *enganche* system – together with the stores owned/operated by contractors – was indeed an important target of strike action on the coastal plantations of northern Peru in which the *enganchados* themselves participated.[90] In keeping with his marginalization of conflict as 'abuses', Blanchard nevertheless persists in attributing the hardships endured by and high levels of suplus appropriated from migrants to factors other than the *enganche* system itself, a position akin to problematizing the experiences associated with chattel slavery solely in terms of poor working conditions, mortality, etc., each of which is perceived as being unconnected with the slave relation *per se*.[91]

6.12 Conclusion

This chapter has examined the epistemologically coherent yet theoretically flawed claims made in revisionist texts by (among others) Bauer, Cotlear, Cross and Knight regarding the meaning and causes of the Latin American *enganche* system over the period 1870–1930. Their problematic definitions of unfreedom include the view that coercion involves overt and continuous maltreatment, and that debt bondage necessarily entails deception. Equally problematic are their reasons for reclassifying the *enganche* as free labour: the absence of a need for the 'legal fiction' of debt, the apparently free nature of similar kinds of contractual arrangement ('binding' film stars, sportspersons or academics to their respective employing institutions), the physical mobility of the workforce (migration, inter-employer debt transfers), the phenomenon of reverse bondage (employer-indebted-to-labourer rather than labourer-indebted-to-employer), and voluntary entry into the *enganche* relation. Having redefined debt bondage as free, these revisionist texts then identify economic security as the reason why rural labour enters into and stays within such relations.

Accordingly, such texts conceptualize the *enganche* not as surplus extraction licensed by extra-economic coercion but rather as harmonious and materially equal exchanges based on 'reciprocity'. Instead of an exploitative institution premissed on compulsion, therefore, the *enganche* is interpreted as 'patron-clientage', a benign and non-anagonistic arrangement to the benefit of all parties to the relation. Reproducing the argument encountered in much neo-classical economic theory about rural development, where micro-level debt appears in the positive disguise of low-interest credit provision by the state or private capital to peasant producers, such texts maintain that indebtedness was an economic incentive by which the Latin American estate provided its workers with consumption goods through its company store.

Against this view it is argued here that the idealized image of debt bondage, and the inability to recognize it as a form of unfreedom, has its roots in a corresponding failure on the part of revisionist texts to differentiate the peasantry in terms of class. This results in an inability to recognize the class-specific meanings/outcomes of debt. Better-off elements on the *hacienda,* composed of administrators, supervisors, and tenants who were rich peasants, engaged in productive borrowing, the object of which was accumulation. For poor peasants, by contrast, debt was for consumption, and thus constituted unproductive borrowing. Unlike the latter, the former did not lead to – and was thus unconnected with – debt peonage. The absence of class also results in the mistaken belief that the *enganche* discharged a crucial economic role in the formation of a rural proletariat: since peasants were otherwise unwilling to commodify their labour-power, it is claimed, debt peonage enabled agrarian capitalists to create a labour market.

This in turn prevents an understanding of both the origin and cause of the *enganche* system in at least some of the contexts considered. In those instances where class struggle results in an emerging proletarian consciousness, therefore, the object of the debt bondage mechanism was not so much to open up a free labour market (which already existed) but rather to close it down. This was because rural workers in many Latin American contexts at this conjuncture were already engaged in commodifying their own labour-power.

NOTES

1. See the preceding chapter for the claims made by Fogel and Engerman [1974] about slavery on the antebellum plantation. As in the case of the latter text, the revisionist case with regard to the Latin American *enganche* system derives in part from a laudable desire to combat negative images of the workers concerned: invoking the 'from-below' historiographical approach of E.P. Thompson, there-fore, Bauer [1979b: 488] stresses the importance of 'not [presenting debt peons] as passive and victimized subjects ... [o]ur understanding is enriched through this work which takes people on *their* terms' (original emphasis). Such a view is basi-cally no different from that encountered in the neoclassical economic framework of Shlomowitz [1991b: 217, 218, 222], for whom the 'more satisfactory' revision-ist interpretation of the *enganche* not only transcends the 'traditional' explanation of this relation by denying that it was 'imposed on powerless workers', but also that it more appropriately views 'most prospective recruits as active and know-ledgeable participants ... rather than as passive and ignorant victims of the system'.

2. In the case of Latin America, the revisionist project is accurately summmed up by one of its exponents [*Gibson, 1964: 255*] as a discourse in which 'the emphasis is reversed from the conventional interpretation of debt labour, for it assumes relative freedom among the workers whose objective was not to escape but to enlarge the indebtedness'. Among the revisionist texts considered below, the main ones are by Gibson [1964], Bauer [1979a; 1986], Blanchard [1979; 1982], Cotlear [1979], Cross [1979], Knight [1986a; 1986b; 1988], Albert [1984], Taylor [1987], Miller [1987], and McCreery [1990; 1997]. Unlike many monographs, which com-ment in passing on the presence/absence of the *enganche* in a given locality at a given period, these texts either make extensive reference to or focus specifically on the relation itself. A number of them – in particular Gibson [1964] and Bauer [1979a] – have in turn influenced others writing about agrarian relations in Latin America (e.g., Langer [1986], Van Young [1981], Edelman [1992]). It must be emphasized, however, that there are important differences within the revisionist approach. Some revisionist texts, such as the neoclassical economic analysis of Cotlear [1979], operate with a sophisticated and internally coherent theoretical framework, while others are merely empiricist (e.g., Miller [1987]). Some who are categorized as revisionists by other revisionists (Favre [1977] by Bauer and Albert, Brading [1977; 1978] by Bauer) actually say little about the *enganche* itself. Others are highly contradictory: for example, both Gibson and Blanchard present the *enganche* system in a positive light, yet each provides much information which indicates that the relationship was based on coercion (see especially Blanchard [1979: 71–3]). Some appear to have changed their views about the *enganche*, and now accept much of the revisionist case: compare, for example, the revisionist assumptions which permeate the more recent texts by Albert [1984], Taylor [1987; 1984] and McCreery [1990; 1997] with their earlier non-revisionist texts (Albert [1976], Rainbird and Taylor [1977], and McCreery [1983; 1986]). Nor is there unanimity regarding the extent to which the revisionist position is acceptable: despite incorporating much of its analytical framework into their own argument, Blanchard [1979: 71–2], Albert [1984: 111], and Miller [1987: 14] nevertheless express reservations about Bauer's seminal 1979 article; by contrast, it is whole-heartedly endorsed by both Taylor [1984: 368] and Knight [1986a: 508].

3. Among the targets of revisionist texts on debt bondage in Latin America are

accounts of this relation contained in Borah [1951], Chevalier [1966], Klarén [1970], Harris [1975], and Rutledge [1975] (see Bauer [1975a: 35ff.,40,46], Cotlear [1979: 4–8]).

4. Because Borah [1951: 39] and Tannenbaum [1968: 11–15, 29–30, 102, 120–21] maintained that the object of the debt bondage mechanism in Mexico was to tie the *hacienda* workforce to the soil, and also that it was a pre-capitalist relationship which prevented agricultural modernization, both are identified by Bauer [1979a: 35 note 2] as exponents of the 'traditional' view on the *enganche*. Ironically, Borah's views [1951: 42] on certain aspects of debt peonage (= worker advantage, patronage) are not so different from those of Bauer himself. Yet another difficulty confronting the 'modern'/'traditional' dichotomy is that Tannenbaum's thesis equating debt bondage with pre-capitalism is in fact shared by revisionists (Favre [1977: 266]) and non-revisionists (Miles [1987], Prasad [1989]) alike. In other words, the theoretical position is altogether more complex than allowed for in an untenable and simplistic opposition between revisionist/modern and anti-revisionist/traditional.

5. As is clear from the comment by Mörner [1973: 201] that 'the traditional view of a necessary connection between *hacienda* and debt peonage must be rejected', revisionist views about bonded labour in Latin America predated the *Time on the Cross* debate of the mid-1970s. The latter, however, served to legitimize and thus gave an added impetus to a revisionist trend already present in the case of Latin America; it is for this reason that the impact of the debate about *Time on the Cross* on interpretations of the *enganche* system is regarded as significant.

6. With the exception of Gibson, whose analysis focuses on the colonial labour regime in Mexico from the sixteenth century onwards, most of the revisionist texts focus on the *enganche* relation in the half century from around the 1870s to the 1920s. Bauer deals with Latin America generally, while the regional emphasis of the others is on Peru (Cotlear, Miller, Blanchard, Albert, Taylor), Mexico (Gibson, Knight, Cross, Brading) and Guatemala (McCreery). Although C. Scott's [1976] theoretically superior analysis of the north Peruvian *enganche* shares the revisionist view that it contributed to the formation of a regional labour market, he nevertheless argues that bonded labour remained an unfree relation until the 1950s.

7. For this exchange, see Loveman [1979] and Bauer [1979a; 1979b]. It has also been pointed out that Bauer ignores the way in which women were specifically affected by unfree relations; for an account of how legislation forced women into bonded labour relationships in Argentina during the latter half of the nineteenth century, see Guy [1981].

8. Collins [1988: 30, 43, 83].

9. Collins [1988: 20]; McCreery [1986]; Bergad [1983a].

10. For the exchange on the presence/absence of unfree labour in Puerto Rico during the latter half of the nineteenth century, see Brass [1984; 1986c] and Bergad [1983a; 1984].

11. A similar difficulty confronts the claim by Tax concerning the end of debt peonage in Guatemala. Having asserted that, following the legal abolition of peonage in 1934, labour was free, Tax [1953: 103, 104–5, 106, 108] then reveals the existence during the early 1940s of what he terms a 'complexity in the wage system'. This turns out to be a situation in which

labourers frequently work for less than the normal wages because ... they receive money in advance for future work. In time of need the Indian asks for, and receives, some money; no interest is involved, but it is understood that he will work off the debt when the other needs him. That time comes, and the employer asks him to work. The Indian, conscious of the favour done him, is not apt to be very demanding.

This 'complexity in the wage system' constitutes nothing other than a beck-and-call arrangement which signals the continued presence in this context of debt bondage, albeit unrecognized by Tax, who interprets the exchange simply in terms of a benign form of 'reciprocity' (= 'the favour done him').

12. See Casanovas [1997].

13. See Johnson [1997].

14. See, for example, Bauer [1979a: 36] and Cotlear [1979]. The latter may be contrasted with C. Scott [1976: 331–2], who is clearly aware of the difficulties involved in attempting to problematize coercion.

15. Bauer [1979a: 37–8]. The same point is made by Langer [1986: 124], and also by Favre [1977: 255] with regard to the role of the *enganche* system in the migration from the central Peruvian highlands to the cotton estates on the coast during the years 1880–1910. Despite Favre's claim that the *enganche* ceased to be necessary after the latter date because highland peasants migrated voluntarily, Figueroa [1984: 72] reports its continued existence in the same region during the 1970s.

16. For this view, see Knight [1986b: 46, 53, 60, 61, 62, 63, 67, 69, 71]. That an apparent non-existence of or decline in physical oppression/punishment leads erroneously to the conclusion that unfree labour is itself non-existent or on the decline is evident from, for example, the view of Gibson [1964: 256] that: '*hacienda* labour might appear ... harsh only in comparison with a twentieth century liberal ideal. To say this is to suggest that in areas such as the Valley of Mexico Indian labour for Spanish employers became progressively less severe, and that it became least severe under the *hacienda*.'

17. Bowman [1920: 25]. The economic contradiction between labour scarcity in the Putumayo region of Peru during the first decade of this century and the maltreatment or killing of workers (= the 'culture of terror') is also noted – but not adequately explained – by Taussig (see Chapter 8).

18. This is the methodological point made by Sutch in connection with the attempt by Fogel and Engerman to equate coercion simply with the incidence of whippings on the cotton plantation in the antebellum American south (see Chapter 1). For an informative case study from early twentieth century Peru of the way in which violence was exercised in order to instil fear into bonded labourers, see Mallon [1983a].

19. This point is made by Cohen [1976: 32–33] in his critique of the study by Daniel [1972] of peonage in the American South. Gibson [1964: 253], Cotlear [1979: 36] and Bauer all make the same point. According to Bauer [1979a: 36], therefore, '[i]n places where landowners wield effective police control themselves or through local political leaders, no excuse, not even the legal fiction of debt is needed to bind workers'. Unlike Cohen, however, Bauer draws a different conclusion: he then goes on to claim that consequently where debt exists, 'it may also be seen as credit'. That is to say, where coercion is present debt is unnecessary; hence the presence of debt necessarily constitutes credit unstructured by coercion.

20. See the first two chapters in this book for details about the way in which actual/ fictive kin pressure is enforced. In his critique of the way in which other texts have interpreted the Peruvian *enganche* system, Cotlear [1979: 35] somewhat

implausibly dismisses the possibility of threats against family or property as an effective method of preventing a worker absconding on the grounds that the texts concerned provide no evidence on this point, an opinion which overlooks the fact that such evidence has generally not been sought. Despite insisting that Mexican peonage was non-coercive, Gibson [1964: 537, 538, notes 186 and 193] admits not only that unmet debts were passed down from father to son but also that workers were unable to leave the *hacienda* without at first clearing such debts (for a similar argument, see Van Young [1981: 261]). In other words, debt-servicing labour obligations were indeed enforced via the kinship domain. The same kind of intra-kin enforcement of bonded labour is suggested by a case-study from 1960s Ecuador [*Feder*, 1971: 31], where debt owed to his landlord by a deceased poor peasant was passed on to his daughter; the latter was consequently faced with a situation in which '[a]t the going wage rate, the yearly earnings would have been insufficient for [her] ever to pay off the debt, even working full time [for his landlord]'. Analogous instances of patriarchal control exercised in the context of the peasant family farm by the male household head over the labour-power of female kinsfolk were also evident in Columbia during the late 1970s and early 1980s [*Reinhardt*, 1988].

21. One reason for not underestimating or dismissing the efficacy/existence of deception in the reproduction of unfree relations is that to do so would eliminate the possibility of false consciousness on the part of the workforce. Another is empirical evidence confirming its presence. In the case of recruitment of workers for tea plantations in northeastern India during the late 1920s, the Report of the Royal Commission on Labour in India [1931: 376] indicates clearly that planters continued to convey the impression to labourers – successfully – that they were subject to the legal sanction of penal contracts long after the latter had in fact been abolished. The intent on the part of the planter class to practice deception regarding the issue of unfreedom is clear from the following observation:

> The planters have shown a lack of confidence in their ability to retain labour, and there has been a constant tendency to rely on restraints of various kinds to keep the labourer on the garden. Even today, where successive amendments of the law have removed all the statutory restraints, there is ample evidence to show that the old faith in restraint in some form persists. The planter, to his own prejudice, has deliberately allowed the old ideas of the penal contract to linger in the minds of his workers. The bonus ... which was given to a labourer when he entered on a 'labour-contract', continues to be paid and is to this day referred to as the 'girmit' or agreement money. It was stated that the discontinuation of the bonus would give rise to discontent as the workers had become accustomed to this lump sum payment; but this does not explain why it is still regarded as an inducement for future service. On many gardens the thumb-impression is taken when the bonus is paid, although this is not done when the worker receives his wages. The explanation given by one witness was that for purposes of audit a receipt was necessary in the case of the bonus, but no such receipts were required in the case of wages. The thumb-impression is usually taken on a register or on a piece of paper, but some planters have devised a form which bears a marked resemblance to the form used in the days of the penal contract, and we came across an instance where the thumb-impression was still being taken on the old form. In theory, the object of the thumb-impression is to bind the labourer by a civil agreement, but as he is

not likely to appreciate the difference between this and the penal contract, the practical result is that he believes himself still bound by a penal contract. In a number of instances the bonus is not in fact claimed, which shows that it continues to be regarded as a gift fatal to the liberty of its recipient. So far as we could ascertain, few steps had been taken to acquaint the labourers with the vital change made in the law; and some officials appeared to be apprehensive of the consequences of any sudden access to knowledge of this kind.

22. See, for example, Feder [1971: 143], Pearse [1975: 32], Núñez del Prado [1973: 20, 47] and Klarén [1977: 243].

23. An exception here is Knight [1988: 110], who although revisionist in terms of his overall approach to the issue of unfree labour, nevertheless links the element of duplicity to the third and coercive variant of his three forms of debt peonage (see below).

24. Cotlear [1979: 8–12, 22–23, 35–36, 38], Bauer [1979a: 38], Miller [1987: 13]. Taylor [1984: 367–8, 371, 376] makes much the same point as Miller about Ciro Alegria's portrayal of the *enganche* in the northern Peruvian Andes over the period 1880 to 1930. It should be noted that disagreement with both Taylor and Miller does not imply a corresponding endorsement of the *indigenista* romanticism of Alegria [1942].

25. Due to a corresponding stress on kidnapping and trickery in the official data, Graves [1984: 112] suggests that there is a similar emphasis on 'the image of the Pacific islands immigrant as a hapless victim of an unscrupulous and coercive recruiting industry' in the case of the recruitment of indentured Melanesian and Micronesian labour for work in Queensland, Fiji, Samoa, Hawaii, New Caledonia, and French Polynesia during the latter half of the nineteenth century.

26. See, for example, Jones [1940: 139–40], Blanchard [1979: 72] and C. Scott [1976: 328].

27. See, for example, Bauer [1979a: 41] and Patterson [1982: 24–7].

28. See, for example, Loveman [1979: 480–81] and Watson [1983].

29. In her study of the power relationships that structured the Hollywood studio system, Powdermaker [1950: 84–5] observes:

> Actors are often loaned by one studio to another without their consent and most of the time without any advance knowledge of the deal. The studio profits by getting more for the deal than it pays as salary ... The feudal characteristic of the power situation lies in the option contract which legally binds directors, actors, and others to the studio for a period of seven years. The employee is not permitted to break his contract for any reason. If he refuses a role the studio suspends him without pay, and formerly the number of weeks of suspension was added to the duration of the contract ... If an actor receives another and better offer while he is under contract, he is not allowed to take it. Court cases in which actors and directors try to break their contracts usually end in victory for the studio. The cases coming to court are the exception but the problem comes up frequently when an actor or director has unusual or unexpected success during the life of the contract. The studio then often gives him a bonus and raises the salary check, but rarely as much as if he were in a bargaining position ... the option contract which binds the employee to the studio for seven years permits the studio to dismiss him at the end of six months or one year, without having to show cause, smacks more of medieval power relations between lord and serf, than of employer and employee in the modern world of industry.

Much the same point is made by Pirie [1981: 10–11, 17–18] and Finler [1988: 50].
30. See Sissons [1988: 129], who describes the benefit as 'a deferred payment against a minimum of ten years consecutive service, and usually against the player's entire first-class career'. In this respect, it fulfils precisely the same economic role as the withholding by an employer of wages owed to an agricultural labourer, a form of unfreedom known as 'reverse bondage' (see below).
31. See Gibson [1964: 252], Bauer [1979a: 43, 45], Bazant [1977: 75], Brading [1978: 24, 26], Cross [1979: 492], and Palacios [1980: 98]. Much the same point is made with regard to Brazil by Holloway [1980: 98–100].
32. In an earlier text, Bauer [1975a: 149] seems to take a view of 'reverse bondage' which recognizes its element of unfreedom. Reporting the deliberations within the Chilean landowners' association in 1881, he observes that landowners 'thought the problem of [labour availability] could be overcome by ... bringing more people on to the estates, and *tying them down by withholding their salary* ... ' (emphasis added). The same is true of Gibson [1964: 252], who observes:

> [Mexican] *haciendas* commonly issued monetary wages on Sunday ... and deferred the maize payments to Tuesday or Wednesday, after the weekly labour had begun. As the manager of the *hacienda* of Molino de Flores, near Texcoco, stated in 1785, this schedule was deliberately established and had 'a thousand advantages', *for it meant that the workers would be induced to stay on the premises* (emphasis added).

33. It is somewhat curious that revisionists like Bauer and Brading fail to note the unfree structure of what they refer to as 'reverse bondage', since this very point is made by Mörner [1973: 200; 1975: 32] and Tovar [1975: 176] in collections to which both the former have contributed. Tovar goes on to suggest that the profitability of Jesuit haciendas in eighteenth century Mexico was linked in part to the reinvestment of capital generated by the withholding of wages.
34. In his study of 'reverse bondage' on *haciendas* in the Cusco region of Peru during the eighteenth century, Macera [1968: cix] emphasizes that its reported object was to maintain control over the economic mobility of the workforce *(la hacienda ... prefería quedar debiendo al indio trabajador para que este volviese 'por su reclamo')*.
35. The 'reverse bondage' relation has been characterized by the ILO as a form of unfreedom. Article 1(f) of the 1957 Forced Labour Convention states that forced or compulsory labour occurs 'as a consequence of the method of payment to the worker whereby his employer defers payment after the agreed date, thereby depriving the worker of a genuine possibility of terminating his employment'. The system of deferred payment, or the retention by the employer of wages until the end of the contract, was part of the legislation incorporated into the 1928 Mozambique Convention between the Portuguese colony and South Africa; its object was specifically to prevent migrants recruited by mines either from 'deserting' to other mines offering higher wages or from working elsewhere in the host nation [*Legassick and de Clercq*, 1984: 148, 151].
36. For instances of further borrowing – and debt – necessitated by the withholding of wages on Mexican estates during the eighteenth century, see Tovar [1975: 178]. For the withholding of wages as a form of bondage in contemporary India, see Chapter 4. In so far as deferred payment deprives workers of a steady cash income, their dependence on employers is either initiated or intensified. Since workers who have no savings and lack access to their earnings are prevented thereby from

entering the market as consumers in order to purchase the cheapest commodities available, an employer is able consequently to regulate not only what items are consumed, and how often, but also the price of subsistence goods themselves. This in turn permits him to charge a higher rate for items his workers consume, which is instrumental in their growing indebtedness. A similar form of employer control over the subsistence costs of the workforce structured both the Truck system and the operation of the company store (see below).

37. See Bauer [1979a: 40, 42; 1975a: Ch.6]. A similar point is made by Weinstein [1986: 60–61, 65, 69, 70], who argues against the effectiveness of debt peonage in Amazonia during the period 1850–1920 on the grounds that rubber tappers could always 'go elsewhere'. Subsequently, however, she contradicts this, and accepts that '[a]ny tapper caught going downriver who could not prove that he had paid his debts would be returned to his [boss] or sent to a worse fate' [*Weinstein*, 1986: 74, note 23].

38. On this point, Bauer [1975a: 57] observes that a 'large number of rural inhabitants who lived outside the system of large estates were called a "floating" or ambulatory mass by the mid-century census takers, and if they stayed put long enough to be counted, entered the statistics as *gañanes* or *peones* – people who had "no residence or fixed destiny." Having indicated that this description of Chilean rural labour had its origins in the census of that period, Bauer then proceeds to unproblematically incorporate this view within his own framework. Thus, the 'lower stratum of rural society' is subsequently characterized [1975a: 145–147] as 'nomadic', 'rootless, often ambulatory masses', 'the great majority [of whom] formed a loose mass of people ... [who] simply moved along the length of Central Chile in search of sustenance ... [m]any documents of the 1840s and 1850s refer to the floating population'.

39. Burga [1976; 1978], Cotlear [1979: 8–12].

40. Cotlear [1979: 45].

41. Hence the view [*Taylor*, 1987: 120] that: '[T]he vast majority of peasants were surprisingly mobile, involved in widely diverse occupations and not tied to ... one *patrón* by extra-economic coercion. If anything, the increased activity of *enganchadores* provided the proletarianized sector of Hualgayoc's population with wider work opportunities ... .'

42. Historical instances of the inter-employer transfer of debt (= 'changing masters') include the northern Mexican state of Coahuila during the eighteenth and nineteenth centuries [*Harris*, 1975: 58–78, 205–30] and the northern Peruvian Department of Huánuco during the late 1880s [*Blanchard*, 1979: 73]. In a similar vein, Knight [1986a: 88] notes that in pre-revolutionary Mexico, '[p]lanters bought each others' peons by transferring their debts from one *libro de hacienda* to another'. This kind of unfreedom also occurred during the early 1950s in Brazilian Amazonia, where as Wolf and Hansen [1972: 127] observe, 'A rubber tapper cannot easily flee from his indebtedness. It is understood in the Amazon that if a worker changes his locale and trader [= storeowner], his new trader must repay the former one and transfer the tapper's debt to his own books.'

43. Knight [1988: 106, 108, 111].

44. Knight [1988: 110, 111].

45. In such instances, Knight [1988: 106, 107] claims, debt 'was an incentive: it operated within a voluntarist, emergent free wage labour system; it did not denote a *de facto* slavery ... this form of debt peonage may be viewed as a variant of free

wage labour ... the conditions of work and remuneration were sufficient to attract workers by means of an advance'.
46. For example, Bauer [1979a: 38], Cotlear [1979: 45] and Albert [1984: 110].
47. As has been noted in Chapter 1, self-enslavement as an alternative to starvation/death is perhaps the best example of 'voluntary' entry into unfreedom.
48. Bauer [1979a: 56, 62]. The following highly idealized description of the landlord/ tenant relation on a coffee *hacienda* in Puerto Rico during the early 1950s is symptomatic. 'The relationship between owner and worker,' observes Steward [1965: 36],

> is typically paternalistic, personal, face to face, and variable ... Between owner and labourer there is a mutual dependency, a system of personal understandings and perquisites. The labourer is paid in wages, but since work is seasonal he is also granted favours in lieu of wages, such as a subsistence plot on which to grow food, or the chance to burn charcoal on shares. The owners takes a personal interest in him, advising him in his affairs and looking to his welfare. In return, the worker renders unpaid services to the landlord and may even supply daughters as servants in the landlord's household.

49. Taylor [1987: 112]. For a similar description of the *enganche* in northern Peru as a 'paternalistic' relation based on 'reciprocity', see Langer [1986: 125–6].
50. Cross [1979: 488, 490].
51. See Gibson [1964: 255], who then observes that 'the amount of debt may be considered in some degree as a measure of the bargaining power of the worker', thereby reproducing the weak-employer/powerful-worker stereotype central to perceptions of unfreedom-as-economic-empowerment. For similar views, see Van Young [1981: 246, 249] and Edelman [1992: 16–17].
52. See McCreery [1997].
53. Claims about unfreedom-as-reciprocity which in turn license images of employers as 'benign' and/or 'powerless' immediately raise the question of precisely who subscribes to this view. It is necessary to ask, therefore, to whom does unfree labour appear as a 'benign' form of 'reciprocity' (= equal exchange) based on 'patronage' and indicative of employer powerlessness? Significantly, a number of revisionist texts rely on – and thus privilege – employer discourse. Gibson [1964: 255], for example, cites with approval 'a survey of the economic condition of New Spain written from the point of view of the Spanish employers in 1788'. In his account of the operation of the Peruvian *enganche* system throughout the twentieth century, Cotlear [1979: 39] similarly relies on the views of labour contractors rather than those of the labourers themselves. And as will be seen below, it is also evident that the views attributed by Bauer to the rural workforce in Chile derive principally from employer opinion on the subject. This overlap between the revisionist views of unfreedom-as-economically-empowering and employer discourse is equally clear from the case of Mexico at the beginning of the twentieth century. When accused by Turner [1911] of employing unfree labour, henequen planters in the state of Yucatán resorted to the 'subsistence guarantee' argument in order to justify the existence of debt peonage [*Chacón*, 1986: 108].
54. See, for example, McBride [1934: 70; 1936: 156–7], Whetten [1948: 103–4], Mintz [1956], Silva Herzog [1959: 134], Feder [1971: 31], and Harris [1975: 216–17]. As the case of bonded labour relations linking rubber tappers to storeowners in Brazilian Amazonia during the early 1950s confirms [*Wolf and Hansen*, 1968: 124ff.], surplus extraction based on unfreedom also operated outside the

Latin American *hacienda*. In this particular instance, the debt mechanism was the method whereby a storeowner maintained control over both the labour-power of the rubber-tapper and also the latex produced by the latter. A similar kind of appropriation was effected in northern Argentina during the 1930s and 1940s by storeowners-cum-contractors who recruited unfree labour for sugar plantations by means of debt; since bonded labour obtained in this manner remained under the control of a storeowner/contractor, to whom payment was made, he also held back between 15 and 30 per cent of the wage received by the former for work on the plantation [*Rutledge*, 1975: 105–6].

55. See Bauer [1979a: 42; 1975b: 408], and also Langer [1986: 123].

56. Cotlear [1979: 37–9].

57. Van Young [1981: 246] makes the same point with regard to eighteenth-century Mexico. Cotlear's argument is contradicted by the evidence. For example, the high price charges by the company store operated by the Cerro de Pasco mine in central Peru at the beginning of the twentieth century enabled this capitalist enterprise to 'take back up to 30 percent of what it paid out [in wages]', and led directly to the impoverishment of unfree workers recruited by means of the *enganche* [*Mallon*, 1986: 203–4, 213].

58. For evidence of deliberate overpricing at the estate store in the case of Peru, see Blanchard [1979: 72–3]. The concept 'duplicity' is itself problematic. Whereas for Cotlear it necessarily entails deception of the workforce, and thus implies ignorance on the part of the latter, the term can also refer to a specific strategem of which the workers may none-the-less be aware. In the case of rubber production in the Brazilian state of Amazónas at the beginning of this century, new labourers were assigned a low-yielding area, the object being precisely to prevent them from being able to cover their subsistence costs and expenses during this period, and thus making debt a necessary outcome [*Ballivián and Pinilla*, 1912: 245–6]. The effectiveness of such a manoeuver depends not on the ignorance of the workforce but rather on the control exercised by the employer over the labour process itself.

59. Acts of violence and arson aimed against the estate store in different Latin American contexts throughout history suggest that workers themselves perceived it as an exploitative institution [cf. *Blanchard*, 1979: 78; *Knight*, 1986a: 286; *Díaz Hernández*, 1981: 39–45]. Knight [1986a: 87] reports that on Mexican estates in the pre-revolutionary era tenants manifested their anger 'when the opportunity arose, against the *cargadilla* (the inflated debt), [and] against the company store and its manipulation of prices and credit'.

60. See Hilton [1960] for a history of the truck system in Britain.

61. See Blanchard [1979: 66, 72] and Katz [1974: 19–20]. That planters themselves perceived the estate store as having an important role of immobilizing the workforce is clear from late nineteenth century Cuba [*R. Scott*, 1985: 42]:

> In the 1880s local shopkeepers initiated a debate on the tax status of such stores, an occurrence interesting primarily for the attitudes it reveals among planters. Freely acknowledging that the main purpose of the stores was control, planters from several sugar areas made it clear that they wished to prevent their workers and [former slaves] from setting foot off the plantation. They were not prepared to accept ... fully free labor.

For an example of how a coffee-producing *hacienda* in nineteenth century Puerto Rico acquired the labour-power of whole families as a result of debt owed by the household head to the estate store, see Díaz Hernandez [1981: 50–51] and Picó [1986: 204].

62. In the case of Puerto Rico during the mid-twentieth century, sugar planters used worker indebtedness to the company store not only to make profits and to prevent workers selling their labour-power elsewhere, but also as a method of strike breaking. 'Coercion', observes Mintz [1956: 369–70],

is also practised through the medium of credit arrangements at the corporation store on [Hacienda Vieja during the late 1940s]. Corporation stores ... were illegalised by law less than ten years ago. But nothing in the law could prevent such stores from legal reorganization as separate corporate entities ... In the event of a strike, all sales became cash transactions after the day of the last paycheck ... Before 1940, the corporation store carried out two important functions in the coordination of work ... First, nearly all earned income was funneled back into the corporation through the store. Second, through the use of token money or tickets, workers could be controlled not only in their purchasing but in their mobility and thereby their search for other work. All older workers today complain bitterly of the almost absolute power corporation stores wielded over them in those times ... .

63. Significantly, employers and landowners themselves perceived the estate store as having a bonding role with regard to their workforce. Thus Bauer [1975a: 149] reports that in 1881 the Chilean landowners' assocation itself suggested 'tying down [workers] ... through the mechanism of the hacienda store' in order to solve what was regarded as a problem of labour availability (see also Bauer [1975b: 408]).

64. Evidence from Latin America and elsewhere suggests that the monopoly position of the estate store was always utilized to generate maximum profits. The trading profit of the *pulpería* on a Brazilian rubber plantation in Amazónas state at the beginning of the twentieth century amounted to some 45 per cent of turnover, and in the Queensland sugar industry during the period 1840–1915 'plantation and urban storekeepers achieved margins of up to 33 per cent over "legitimate profits" through truck' [*Ballivián and Pinilla*, 1912: 246–7; *Graves*, 1983: 114–16]. Items purchased by poor peasants from landlord-owned/operated village stores in China during the mid-1930s were 40–100 per cent costlier than equivalents available in urban areas [*Tawney*, 1938: 45]. Similarly, purchases made on credit at the company store by Bolivian labourers recruited for seasonal work on sugar plantations in northern Argentina during 1970 were between 25 and 30 per cent higher than other local retail outlets; in this particular instance credit was arranged by the labour contractor, through whom purchases were made, and who himself profited from such transactions [*Whiteford*, 1981: 45].

65. Such an argument, for example, structures Blanchard's interpretation of the Peruvian *enganche* system. 'If the *enganche* had been as harmful and exploitative as critics have charged', he asks [1979: 63–4], 'how and why did it manage to survive for as long as it did? ... the survival of the system rested largely on its appeal to [all] the parties concerned ... the majority of workers remained satisfied with the system'. To sustain the claim that workers themselves were satisfied with the *enganche* system, and viewed it in positive terms, necessarily requires extensive access to and knowledge of the ideas held by rural workers themselves. In the case of the Latin American *enganche*, however, the latter point has to be set against the fact that little or no information is available regarding the opinions of rural labour on this subject. The kind of difficulty to which this gives rise may be illus-

trated by Langer's book [1989: 5, 147], where an initial claim that access to *hacienda* records has clarified questions about Bolivian debt peonage is undermined by his subsequent admission that 'practically all ... documents have disappeared, and the few that have survived give only a faint clue to how the labor system actually functioned ... '. Whereas sociologists or anthropologists are sometimes able to elicit the thoughts of contemporary bonded labourers about these relations, and whether or not they are perceived by the subjects concerned as desirable and as a form of 'subsistence guarantee', it is not possible for historians to do this where (as is usually the case) no relevant records exist. Given this methodological lacunae, it is all the more curious that the most ardent proponents of the revisionist thesis concerning the occurrence and meaning of debt bondage in Latin America are themselves historians (Gibson, Bauer, Brading, Favre, Cross, Knight, McCreery), or precisely those who are also the most constrained as regards methodological access to this dimension of agrarian relations. The same kind of methodological difficulty confronts neoclassical economic historiography about Latin America, which maintains that unfreedom is acceptable to its subject yet provides no corroborating grassroots evidence in support of this view, relying instead on motive implied in economic behaviour. Hence the claim by Pastore [1997] that in the case of colonial Paraguay it was material incentives which induced bonded labour voluntarily to increase output, an idealized framework in which the impact of coercion is downgraded or ignored, and in effect replaced by a neoclassical economic concept of the 'choice-making' individual expressing subjective preferences.

66. Bauer, for example, explicitly rejects the usefulness of class as an analytical concept: '[n]or do I believe', he observes [1979a: 487], 'that a line between good and evil can be drawn between ... social classes in the countryside'. A partial exception in this regard is Albert [1984: 111ff.], who notes the importance of class. However, he does not link this to the unfreedom of the *enganche*, nor does he internally differentiate the peasantry.

67. A symptomatic argument is the one expressed by Gibson [1964: 254–5], who maintains that in eighteenth-century Mexico: '[worker] indebtedness ... appears slight in comparison with the reputation of debt peonage as a controlling and universal *hacienda* technique ... in late colonial times debt peonage affected fewer than half the workers on *haciendas*, and ... the large majority of these owed debts equal to three weeks' labour or less'. For a similar view, see Van Young [1981: 253ff.].

68. See Bauer [1979a: 51–2], Brading [1978: 50], and Knight [1988: 109]. Significantly, both the Peruvian case studies cited by Bauer involve estate tenants owning herds of livestock. The *colonos* of Picotani, one of the largest *haciendas* in Puno, were rich peasants who, even as early as 1929, owned substantial numbers of sheep producing wool for the market and earned 'a sizable potential income completely independent of the *hacienda*'; consequently, '[a]lmost none of the colonos there were in debt, both because they had independent access to money and because the *hacienda* had little opportunity to become [their] creditor' [*Maltby*, 1980: 102, 104]. Much the same is true of the large pastoral *haciendas* in the central Andean highlands which belonged to Fernandini, where individual shepherds pastured 300 sheep and were referred to by an estate manager as 'small capitalists' [*Martínez-Alier*, 1977: 44, 76]. The same applies to the Mexican livestock estate studied by Cross [1979: 476], where

the availability of grazing lands to employees, either gratis or with nominal rent, provided important added income potential. Those who benefited most from these arrangements were naturally the administrative staff who possessed sufficient salary and influence to engage in private [economic] activities outside their immediate responsibilities to the *hacienda*. It was not uncommon in nineteenth century Zacatecas for administrative employees on livestock estates to possess herds of goats and sheep numbering in the thousands.

69. According to Katz [1974: 27–28], 'There are some indications that the *acasillados* on the sugar *haciendas* considered their position a privileged one. On the *Hacienda de Santa Ana* the *acasillados* scarcely participated in the Revolution, even though it was located in a Zapatista territory.' In a similar vein, Warman [1980: 61] – a source cited with approval by Bauer [1979a: 48; 1979b: 488] – proclaims that in Morelos '[t]he *hacienda* had no company store nor any other method of tying people down through debts ... [t]he peon was ... a free worker in the liberal sense of the word'. However, it transpires that the category referred to was a small minority of permanently employed staff, consisting mainly of those who discharged bureaucratic, administrative and supervisory roles on the *hacienda* [*Warman*, 1980: 55ff.]. The majority of the *hacienda* workforce, however, was composed of casual/seasonal field labour recruited from the surrounding villages: as another text [*Womack*, 1969: 46–7] shows, in Morelos such workers were dispossessed peasants who – because of low real wages paid by the *hacienda* – were indeed in debt. The result is a double misrecognition: of a small and privileged *hacienda* staff, composed predominantly of petty-bourgois elements, as a proletariat; and of temporary/external manual workers as a peasantry. This in turn leads Warman [1980: 110–12] to a correspondingly problematic conclusion: that in Morelos it was the peasants in the villages who were the authentically revolutionary subjects, while the proletariat on the *hacienda* (= 'children of the *hacienda*') by contrast was a reactionary political force and thus constituted an obstacle to the formation of a revolutionary consciousness.

70. This distinction is more usually acknowledged in the literature on India. For example, Darling [1925] argued that the high incidence of indebtedness among peasants in Punjab at the beginning of this century was an effect not of poverty but of wealth.

71. In the Mexican *hacienda* studied by Cross [1979:488], therefore, the largest debts 'cannot be regarded as liabilities ... [t]hese debts pertain to those credits used for personal investment. Many *hacienda* workers and their wives were in fact small-scale entrepreneurs on the side, and generally obtained their initial capital investment through employee accounts.'

72. Katz [1974: 28] hints as this very possibility in the case of better-off tenants (*acasillados*) in central Mexico during the 1910 Revolution:

At [the *Hacienda* of] Santa Ana, the privileged minority were those tenants who rented land from the *hacienda*, as well as cattle owners who received grazing rights from the *hacienda* and in return rented out their oxen to the tenants. The tenants employed a large group of labourers to work their lands. These *gañanes* or *inditos*, as they were called, constituted the poorest labourers on the *hacienda*.

Much the same is true of Peru at this conjuncture: when the *enganche* became a lucrative business with the establishment of the Cerro de Pasco mining corporation in the central highlands, therefore, it was wealthy peasants with extensive village networks in the area who became the main labour contractors [*Mallon*, 1983a].

73. Revisionists who base their claim that borrowing was non-coercive on what happened in the case of the better-off elements on the estate system usually omit to mention the existence of (and thus the consequences in terms of unfreedom for) indebted poor peasants and agricultural labourers in the same context. This critique can be levelled against Cross [1979: 474ff., 494], who maintains that his case-study of a nineteenth century Mexican livestock estate indicates that only the administrative staff (amounting to no more than five per cent of employees) owed money, and unfree labour was non-existent. However, it emerges that not only was a much larger proportion of the workforce in debt to the *hacienda* throughout the period in question, but also (and more importantly) the levels of indebtedness increased in relation to competition for labour. On average, 23 per cent of estate workers owed money to the landowner over the 1831–83 period, and the annual figure varied between five and 46 per cent; this suggests that debt relations also involved those at the bottom of the estate hierarchy, the semi- and unskilled workers composing the 90 per cent of the workforce [*Cross*, 1979: 483]. Furthermore, the level of worker indebtedness to the *hacienda* store increased dramatically during the years 1831–36, when a state-owned mining company began operating in the vicinity. The latter drew its workforce from the surrounding rural economy, labourers being attracted by the 'much higher wages offered there' [*Cross*, 1979: 485]. Although Cross fails to address the issue, it is unlikely that in such circumstances the landowner would permit the non-administrative components of its workforce to sell their labour-power to the mines so long as money was owed to the estate store, notwithstanding the wage differential.

74. Although Taylor and Albert are right to argue that from the late nineteenth century onwards northern Peru was undergoing capitalist penetration, since they both equate unfreedom solely with 'refeudalization', it is necessary for them to argue that the *enganche* was a free relation and thus constituted evidence of proletarianization [*Albert*, 1984: 109–10; *Taylor*, 1987: 120].

75. Cotlear [1979: 52, 56]. A similar point is made by Figueroa [1984: 72].

76. Cotlear [1979: 40–44]. For a similar argument see Mallon [1986], who maintains that the shift from a seasonal workforce of migrants to a permanent one composed of locals signalled the end of the *enganche* relation in central Peru.

77. Bauer [1979a: 39, 47, 53, 55, 59–62]. See also Pearse [1975: 37].

78. See Knight [1986a:89; 1988:106,112–13]. 'Debt', he states, 'thus figured as an important instrument for the fashioning of a rural proletariat [where] labour was recalcitrant. Indigenous populations, where they existed, were insufficient or (more often) inept, that is they displayed all the feckleness of "lazy natives" who shunned hard work ... .' The use of bonded labour in this manner, Knight [1988: 117] notes, 'should be of particular interest to that growing band of historians who are concerned with the creation of proletariats and the inculcation of the time and work discipline of [agrarian] capitalism'.

79. On the Peruvian north coast sugar plantations at the turn of the century, even labour contractors began switching workers under their control from estate to estate so as to take advantage of higher wages and commissions [*Gonzales*, 1980: 308]. This suggests that on occasion the reason why employers transferred the exercise of the debt mechanism (and the hold over labour this conferred) from the contractor to themselves was precisely to ensure the maximum control over workers employed in their labour process.

80. Thus one text [*Blanchard*, 1979: 82–3] describing how the *enganche* operated in the northern Andes concludes by pointing out that:

> the Indian seemed willing to get involved in the modern sector. An examination of the system certainly shows that the Indian was not inextricably tied to his sierra community and unalterably opposed to work on the coast, as many observers have claimed. He was quite prepared to migrate almost anywhere *if the economic incentives and working conditions were right* (emphasis added).

As has been argued in Chapter 2 with reference to the eastern lowlands of Peru during the mid-1970s, despite the existence within a single agrarian cooperative of different employment opportunities, with correspondingly distinct work conditions, hours of work, levels of remuneration, etc., poor peasants and agricultural labourers who owed debts to rich and middle peasant neighbours were not permitted to choose between them. What did happen, however, was that unfree labour was redeployed by creditor-employers into the free market which already existed on the different sectors of the agrarian co-operative.

81. Long and Roberts [1984: 52]. For evidence of the fact that during the 1970s bonded labour in Peru was not only paid less than free wage labour but also preferred the latter employment to the former, see Chapter 2 and also Figueroa [1984: 72].

82. For evidence about this, see Davis [1977: 121–2], Esterci [1987], America's Watch [1992: 52–73], and Souza Martins [1990; 1997].

83. In the case of Albert, this contradiction occurs within the same text. Having stated that 'Peruvian hacendados were faced with ... a labour force which retained pre-capitalist attitudes toward work', he subsequently indicates that 'it is clear that from a very early period [a wage labour market] did exist in the sierra' [*Albert*, 1984: 109, 110].

84. Bauer [1975a: 148, 149, 152, 165]. Having classified worker attitudes as 'archaic', and based his whole argument on how the need to habituate them to the rhythms of industrial production was effected through the *enganche* system, Bauer [1975a: 57] then admits that:

> the change in condition and attitude of rural people is more difficult to guage ... what people thought or felt about working for others or even for themselves is not recorded ... Workers' attitudes and emotions must still be inferred either from a careful reading of their employers' opinions of them or from their own actions.

Just what constitutes a 'careful reading' of employer opinion about the workforce is never made clear, nor does he suggest how the actions of the labour force are by themselves indicative of worker opinion. In the event, Bauer [1979a: 58–59] ignores the implications for his case of the workers' own actions (see note 86), and instead accepts uncritically the arguments advanced by the landowning class concerning worker 'sloth', 'laziness', etc.

85. Bauer [1975a: 146]. Even in seventeenth-century Chile, tied rural workers possessed 'the right to hire out their labour once they had fulfilled their labour obligations to the landlord' [*Gongora*, 1975: 151]. In other words, an arrangement not unlike the beck-and-call system governing the employment of permanent attached labour in India (see Chapter 7).

86. It is curious that the obvious contradiction between on the one hand the notion of a 'nomadic' or 'ambulatory' rural labour, and on the other the claim that such a workforce is nevertheless 'archaic' and 'pre-capitalist' in its outlook escapes Bauer's notice. Equally curious is the way in which he interprets the response of

the landowning class to this development of a specifically proletarian consciousness. Faced with the prospect of having to pay higher wages or lose their workers, Chilean landowners decided to abandon a free market policy and turn instead to mechanisms designed to restrict the ability of workers to sell their labour-power. 'The solution put forth by a number of hacendados and observers', Bauer [1975a: 165] notes,

> was not to compete on a wage basis because an increased salary often had adverse social effects: workers would squander the entire week's salary in a few hours of revelry or trivial knick-knacks. Rather – and here the ideas of both *progresista* and more traditional landowners coincided – the ill-fated assumptions of *laissez-faire* should be abandoned. If a wage must be paid let only a small part be in [ready cash] and the rest in vouchers redeemable at the *hacienda* store. This would make it more difficult to buy foolish and needless items in the towns from ambulatory merchants and also, hopefully, reduce the amount thrown away on drink and gambling.

What is surprising is that Bauer accepts at its face value this politico-ideological justification, and not only offers no qualifying comments on the concern expressed by landowners for the 'moral' implications of the consumption patterns adopted by their workers but also fails to make the connection between the attempt to tie consumption to the estate store and unfreedom, and similarly the fact that such a response was advocated by both economically backward and advanced landowners.

87. Hence the admission by Blanchard [1979: 70, 71] that:

> [the employment of *enganchados*] had other advantages for employers. It hindered the development of a united labour force with a working-class consciousness, thereby reducing the incidence of labour agitation in the rural sector ... employers continued to view *enganchados* as a non-militant and easily controllable labour force and tried to obtain more of them.

88. Taylor [1987: 111]. It is indeed ironic that Taylor now endorses the concept of class harmony, since in an earlier text [*Rainbird and Taylor*, 1977] he criticizes just such a view informing the revisionist analysis by Martinez-Alier of the *hacienda* system in the Central Highlands of Peru, concluding that 'the whole thrust of his argument gives the impression that socio-economic relations on the Andean haciendas were not strongly exploitative' [*Rainbird and Taylor*, 1977: 66]. For yet another instance of debt peonage theorized in conflict-free terms as a form of 'reciprocity' and worker 'accommodation', see Langer [1989:5].

89. Blanchard [1979: 64, 77, 79, 81; 1982: 123], Albert [1984: 105], Taylor [1987: 111].

90. Blanchard [1979: 78–9], Martínez de la Torre [1949: 300ff.], C. Scott [1976: 326].

91. Hence the following observation [Blanchard 1979: 77]:

> The contention that the system was crushing the Indians was echoed by others who claimed that *enganchados* were returning to their homes 'lifeless' and that ten per cent either died on the coastal estates or on their return to the sierra. If this was true, *it was more a result of the work demanded of the Indians than the system* (emphasis added).

7

Attached Labour in India

This chapter considers the way in which labour attachment in Indian agriculture is theorized, in the seminal 1920s work of Wiser, in the 1950s Agricultural Labour Enquiries, and subsequently in the work of Epstein, Rudra, Bardhan, Breman, Harriss and Platteau. Common to all these texts is a positive conceptualization of attached labour – a view shared with apologists for slavery and serfdom in nineteenth century India – and consequently the downgrading/elimination of its element of unfreedom. Instead, the relation is presented in terms of a materially reciprocal exchange between landholder and worker, a transaction which, it is claimed, from the viewpoint of the latter corresponds to an economically empowering and thus a much sought-after form of job insurance or subsistence guarantee.

By contrast, it is suggested that in India long- or short-term worker attachment is a form of unfreedom corresponding to deproletarianization undertaken by capital in the course of class struggle, and that the agricultural workforce strongly dislikes this kind of tied employment. It is also argued that at a general level the existence of attached labour cannot be understood without regard to the class decomposition/recomposition (or restructuring) that accompanies class struggle in the Indian countryside, the object of which is to discipline (not habituate), control, and cheapen labour-power by preventing or curtailing both its commodification and the growth of a specifically proletarian consciousness.

Warning against a tendency to over-optimism that informs many of the revisionist claims which equate a non-politically-specific process of 'empowerment' with 'patronage', emancipation or proletarianization, the focus here will be on the lineages of the influential argument about bonded labour as the 'empowerment' of rural labour (= unfreedom-as-economic-empowerment). Equally disempowering is the related argument (= 'assertiveness'-as-proletarianization) which, because it conflates worker 'assertiveness' with the negation of bondage, maintains that in India 'from below' agency constitutes evidence for proletarianization.

A parallel exists between the revisionist conceptualization of the *enganche* in Latin America considered in the previous chapter and recent arguments which revise the meaning of bonded labour in India outlined in this one.

Unsurprisingly, therefore, revisionist views concerning unfree labour in both contexts share not just a common epistemology but also tend to emphasize the same kinds of economic themes. If there is a difference, it lies in the greater emphasis placed by revisionist texts about India on debt bondage as an economically desirable form of 'subsistence guarantee', and thus as a benign 'patronage'. This is due perhaps to the pervasiveness of the historical image of rural Asia as an unproblematically labour surplus region.

I

As utilized in the context of debates about the presence/absence/meaning of unfree labour in India, the concept 'empowerment' can be – and has been – deployed in a number of different ways. For those who interpret it as 'patronage' which provides the labouring subject with a 'subsistence guarantee', relations as diverse as agrestic serfdom and chattel slavery in the nineteenth century or permanent attached labour in twentieth century, are all perceived as forms of grass-roots 'empowerment'. Those holding this view, such as Wiser, Epstein, Breman, Harriss and Platteau, have all argued that the decline of 'clientage' (= unfreedom) is for the workers concerned a disempowering process, and that 'patronage'/(bondage) is accordingly a relation which its subjects attempt either to retain or else to reinstate.

7.1 Unfree Labour as Economic Security in the 1800s

In India this kind of argument has a long historical lineage, and is a central element of employer/landlord ideology from the early nineteenth century onwards. Although conceding that sugar in the East Indies was also produced with unfree labour, the apologist for the West Indies sugar lobby George Saintsbury justified this arrangement on the grounds that it provided slaves in both the East and West Indies with economic security.[1] Many of the official reports dealing with rural labour in south India during the early nineteenth century adopted a similar position, and claimed that agrestic bondage was mild, benign and thus a form of 'patronage' which provided workers with a 'subsistence guarantee'.[2]

Much the same is true of south India throughout the latter half of the nineteenth century, when the need for and the provision of a 'subsistence guarantee' following the abolition of slavery in 1843 was a recurring theme in landlord discourse about why ex-slaves continued to work for their erstwhile masters.[3] In a context of enquiries concerning the post-emancipation continuation of agrestic unfreedom, landlords in Kerala not only claimed that ex-slaves chose to remain with them, but also denied the occurrence of complaints by/about slaves/slavery, of collusion between masters to keep wages low, and also of the transfer of ex-slaves as part of landed property transactions.[4] According to landlords, the opposite was the case: coercion was absent, ex-slaves were now free workers and economically better-off than before.[5]

Of particular significance is the relay-in-statement licensed by this argument. In the absence of coercion/compulsion/force, the reason why in Kerala ex-slaves continue in the employment of ex-masters takes on a positive meaning: ex-slaves *choose* to stay because of their need for a 'subsistence guarantee', which erstwhile masters who used to be their patrons are still willing to provide. This in turn is presented by landlords as 'proof' of the fact that masters were not only considerate employers in the past (= prior to abolition), benign dispensers of 'patronage' to their 'clients', but continue to be so even now.[6]

7.2 Attached Labour as Economic Security in the 1920s

An important contribution to this pro-unfreedom discourse about bonded labour in India, and one the influence of which continues into the present, is the study by Wiser of the Hindu *jajmani* system and its operational modalities in the context of Karimpur, a village in the north Indian state of Uttar Pradesh, during a period extending from the mid-1920s to the early 1930s.[7] Involving a process of prestation/counter-prestation between different castes in a particular village, *jajmani* is described by Wiser as an hereditary inter-caste 'service relationship' which generates and sustains customary/reciprocal exchanges and permanent relationships over succeeding generations between a high caste patron (or *jajman*) and his clients, composed of serving-caste workers ('kam-wale' or 'kam karne-wale').[8]

For Wiser, therefore, the *jajmani* relation corresponds not only to an authentically indigenous organizing principle that is reproduced outside and in spite of the wider capitalist system, but also (and thereby) to a form of village level 'subsistence guarantee'.[9] The positive/harmonious characterization of the *jajmani* relation is evident from the way in which Wiser refers to it in terms of 'concessions granted [by the employer] to the different occupational groups', a package which includes 'free residence site', 'rent-free land', 'credit facilities', and 'casual leave', all of which are in his opinion so valuable to a worker that the latter voluntarily rejects the blandishments of urban industrial employment.[10] Describing the *jajmani* system as a source of '[c]ontentment and peace [in] a rural community', Wiser unsurprisingly regards it as evidence for the successful operation of a grassroots and 'natural' economy within the context of Indian village, and concludes approvingly that its 'general contentment and peace should be retained'.[11]

In the case of India, this discourse about unfreedom-as-economic-empowerment, in which unfree labour is depicted as a 'positive good', continued into the post-Independence era, informing official reports and village monographs alike. The characterization of permanent attached labour and debt bondage in terms of a 'subsistence guarantee', and thus from the viewpoint of the worker a desirable and sought-after form of 'patronage', structured not just the All-India findings of the Second Agricultural Labour Enquiry during the mid-1950s, but also many of the individual studies conducted in the same decade.[12]

Rather surprisingly, given that the focus of debate about rural India was increasingly on the necessity of economic development and social change, views about the supposed 'mutuality' of agrestic unfreedom and the benefits it allegedly conferred on permanent attached labour continued to be expressed throughout the 1960s and 1970s.[13] This is particularly true of research undertaken during the 1960s by Breman in south Gujarat and by Rudra in Punjab, and also of research conducted during the 1970s, by Harriss in Tamil Nadu, by Rudra and Bardhan in West Bengal, and by Platteau in Kerala.

Although there is strong competition for this designation, therefore, Wiser's authentic spiritual descendents and contemporary political heirs are Rudra, Bardhan, Breman, Harriss and Platteau, each of whom has at some point endorsed the concept of unfreedom-as-economic-empowerment. On the basis of fieldwork in India, all of them have theorized unfreedom benignly: as a form of 'patronage', to the advantage of what others term bonded labour, and thus freely entered into (not to say actively sought out) by its subject.[14]

7.3 Attached Labour as Economic Security in the 1950s

Since its utilization in the First Agricultural Labour Enquiry (1950–51), the concept 'labour attachment' has undergone a fundamental change in meaning.[15] Initially, therefore, although attached labour was distinguished from casual labour on the basis of characteristics such as a lower rate of remuneration, continuity of employment, and the existence of an oral or written contract, the most important distinction was the restricted freedom of its subject to seek alternative work so long as debts were owed to a creditor-employer.[16]

This linkage between labour attachment and unfreedom remained true of the Second Agricultural Labour Enquiry (1956–57), albeit qualified now in terms of the presence of compensating positive features to counterbalance the negative aspects of the relation.[17] Despite this dilution, the Second Enquiry nevertheless adopted a fourfold classification of labour attachment, in which the element of unfreedom continued to be central: attachment with no debt bondage or tie-in-allotment, with debt bondage only, with tie-in-allotment only, and with both debt bondage and tie-in-allotment.[18]

The extent to which individual monographs based on research conducted during the 1950s misrecognized attached labour and underestimated the existence of bondage due to a positive theorization of 'patronage' can be illustrated by reference to the work of Epstein.[19] In her 1955 study of a village possessing irrigation in the southern Indian state of Karnataka, six categories of farm labour are identified: unpaid household labour, exchange labour, untouchable client labour, contract labour, task-specific group labour, and daily labour. However, attached or bonded labour (*jeeta*) is included only under the rubric of contract labour, despite evidence that debt bondage relations structured at least two other forms of labour, although not identified as such.

Thus Epstein observes that the second of the two kinds of exchange labour (*muyee*) is carried out 'by men for their creditors'.[20] Similarly, untouchable client labour in this context at this conjuncture was 'under the obligation to provide labour for [the] patron whenever the latter requires it'.[21] Elsewhere she notes that untouchables borrow money from their patrons, which suggests a relationship in which cash debts are cancelled with work.[22] In short, both exchange labour and untouchable client labour included bonded labour, the incidence of debt bondage in this particular context being as a result much higher that Epstein herself indicates.

7.4 Attached Labour as a Voluntary Relation

In contemporary analyses of labour attachment in Indian agriculture, the earlier defining characteristic of worker unfreedom is either downgraded theoretically or else discarded altogether. The work of Rudra is symptomatic of this change, and not only illustrates the way in which attachment has become decoupled from the concept of unfreedom but also shows how it has in the process metamorphosed into its opposite, a free labour relation.[23]

The attempt by Rudra (and others: see below) to shift the meaning of labour attachment from a coercive/negative/antagonistic axis to a voluntary/ positive/non-antagonistic one rests on three basic assumptions. The first assumption, that the attached/casual labour dichotomy used by the earlier Agricultural Labour Enquiries is too simplistic, leads Rudra to introduce the intermediate category of 'semi-attachment', which refers to a 'non-casual and timewise somewhat lasting relation of a labourer with one or at most a few employers which falls short of the kind of relation which an annual farm servant has with his employer'.[24]

The two forms of 'semi-attachment' conceptualised by Rudra are each differentiated from 'full' attachment in the following manner: the first 'retains unchanged the condition of the labourer not having the freedom to work for other employers but reduces the duration of the contract to shorter periods, coinciding with the busy periods in agriculture', while the second form 'relaxes the condition regarding freedom of working for other employers ... The labourer has to work for the employer on whatever day the latter would want his services. But on those days on which the employer would not have any work for the labourer the latter would be free to work for any other employer'.[25]

Although Rudra claims to have identified two forms of 'semi-attachment', differentiated from 'full' attachment as regards both duration and mobility, on closer examination this distinctiveness proves illusory. Evaluated in terms of the central criterion outlined by Rudra himself for the purpose of defining production relations – that is, worker freedom and mobility – not only do the supposed differences *within* the category of 'semi-attachment' disappear but the distinctions between the latter and 'full' attachment similarly vanish.[26] Hence the element of unfreedom, which Rudra admits to being present only in the case of the first variant of 'semi-attachment', is actually also present in the second: regardless of whether a worker is required either intermittently over a two month duration or for the whole of this period, therefore, in both these instances labour-power is ultimately controlled not by its subject but by the (creditor-) employer.

The second assumption is that in many cases the long-term duration of either intermittent or continuous labour attachment to one particular employer derives not from the debt mechanism (and thus cannot involve bondage) but rather from the advantages such a relationship bestows on the worker.[27] Rudra is aware that the continued link between 'semi-attachment' and debt poses a serious difficulty for any attempt to decouple labour attachment from unfreedom. As with the concept 'semi-attachment' itself, he endeavours to circumvent this by differentiating the debt category into current consumption loans on the one hand and inherited debt on the other. Of these two forms of indebtedness, he argues, only the latter gives rise to bondage.[28] This, Rudra asserts, is because attached workers obtain consumption loans from different farmers, and thus manage to remain independent of any single creditor-employer; accordingly, 'consumption loans make labourers *as a class* dependent on rich farmers *as a class*, whereas hereditary debts make the dependence relation personalised'.[29]

There are two problems with this view. First, no evidence is produced to support this claim regarding the multi-sourced nature of worker indebtedness; in Haryana, for example, most attached labourers do in fact rely on a single creditor-employer for loans, the repayment of which entails a correspondingly exclusive working arrangement.[30] And second, there is similarly no evidence that hereditary debts personalize a dependency relationship while consumption debts do not; much rather the reverse, in the sense that current indebtedness necessarily entails a personal linkage between borrower and lender that is absent from a debt inherited from the past (where there is no direct connection between the creditor and a person now engaged in repaying the loan).[31]

The third assumption, that both long – and short-term attachment is in essence a free labour relation, begins by rightly challenging the view that a worker's freedom to sell his/her own labour-power is a function of contract duration. Like Thorner, Rudra correctly insists that there is no neccesary connection between longer employment contracts and less freedom on the one hand, and shorter contracts and more freedom on the other. However, rather than using this observation as an opportunity for considering the degree to which casual and/or seasonal labourers are themselves unfree to sell their labour-power (together with the reasons for and effects of this situation), Rudra suggests instead that – like casual/seasonal labour – the long-term attachment of worker to employer is also a free labour relation.[32]

By introducing the category of 'semi-attachment', presenting it in terms of a voluntaristic relation, delinking consumption loans from the concept of debt bondage, and then attributing to attachment the characteristics of daily wage labour, Rudra's symptomatic epistemological trajectory is complete: conceptually, labour attachment has been purged of its unfree content and transformed into a free relation of production. A similar argument informs the way in which debt bondage is theorised in texts by Bardhan and Breman on the subject of rural labour in India.

7.5 Attached Labour as Reciprocity and Patron-Clientage

According to Bardhan, bonded labour is based on hereditary and long-term indebtedness which entails continuous and exclusive work for one employer until a loan taken in the distant past has been repaid.[33] He regards it as a feudal institutional form resting on extra-economic coercion, and concludes that such relationships are of negligible significance in contemporary India.[34] As with Bardhan, the characteristics of unfree labour cited by Breman in connection with *halipratha* servitude in south Gujarat during the first half of this century include the indefinite and inter-generational attachment of an indebted worker and his family to an employer.[35] Extra-economic coercion is central to this relationship, which is similarly regarded by Breman as feudal and more-or-less non-existent in present-day rural India.[36]

With regard to the implications of partial labour mobility and the non-heritability of debt for the free/unfree nature of agrarian relations, neither

Bardhan nor Breman regard labour as bonded unless the relationship is inter-generational, and work is performed exclusively and continuously for a single employer.[37] It remains unclear, however, just why the latter are perceived as defining characteristics – as distinct from historical forms taken by – debt bondage, particularly since the absence of these elements does not of itself prevent labour-power from being unfree (a point conceded in both texts).[38] Bardhan denies the existence of debt bondage in India on the grounds that attached labourers possess the freedom to change jobs, without asking under what conditions and for what reasons this occurs.[39] The fact of job mobility notwithstanding, he fails to note that while there may be a change in the identity of individual creditor-employers disposing of the labour-power belonging to a single attached worker in the latter's lifetime, the relationship between each creditor-employer and the attached labourer is in all cases the same.[40] Having outlined the characteristics of bonded labour, both Bardhan and Breman proceed to indicate why attached labour cannot be regarded as a form of unfreedom. Since it is relevant to an understanding of the manner in which labour attachment is perceived, it is necessary to clarify the epistemo-logical foundations of this view.[41]

Like Fogel and Engerman in the case of antebellum plantation slavery and Cotlear in the case of the Latin American *enganche* system, Bardhan places attached labour firmly within an idealised neoclassical theoretical framework, which banishes the element of coercion and instead emphasizes voluntaristic action by choice-making individuals in an non-antagonistic context where material exchanges between moneylending employer and loan-taking employee are based on reciprocity.[42] Long-term labour-tying arrangements which characterize worker attachment are portrayed by him in terms of 'employment insurance', whereby an employer provides labourers with a house-plot, pre-harvest wage advances, and consumption credit.[43]

In exchange for the latter, a labourer undertakes to work for this particular employer whenever required to do so.[44] Accordingly, the provision of 'job opportunities, regular credit and emergency help' are presented by Bardhan as benign gestures on the part of an employer, rather than as methods of getting rural workers indebted in order to force down wage levels and establish control over the labour process.[45] Employer/employee relationships are as a consequence depicted as harmonious: labourers *choose* to remain in what are conceptualised as non-exploitative contracts based on equal exchange, an arrangement that is of 'convenience to both parties'.[46]

Such a framework permits Bardhan to ignore coercion and class struggle as the determinants of the attached labour system in India, and to argue instead that labour-tying is a mutually-beneficial arrangement which derives solely from the seasonality of agricultural production.[47] Thus, long-term contracts are offered to workers during the lean periods of the agricultural cycle, and in return they provide the employer with a guaranteed supply of labour-power during the peak season.[48]

Implicit in this is the assumption that when the differential earning power in both lean and peak seasons is taken into account, the attached labourer not only receives an equitable overall return on the sale of his labour-power but also achieves security of employment throughout the year. The relatively high level of remuneration obtained in the lean period (when, according to Bardhan, such workers receive a 'wage rate higher than their marginal product') is balanced by the relatively low level of remuneration obtained during the peak season, the inference being that ultimately the lean/peak agricultural wage differential is averaged out.

The difficulty with this argument is that in the majority of instances attached workers receive no payment for the lean period, a point Bardhan himself concedes.[49] What they receive at this time is wages for *future* employment. This arrangement corresponds not to payment for periods of under-or unemployment, therefore, but rather to payment in advance for employment during periods of peak labour demand. In other words, what is actually received during the lean part of the agricultural cycle is a loan for work yet to be done, the object being to commit a labourer thus indebted to work during the forthcoming peak season for less than he might otherwise command at this period.

Denying that permanent attached labour is bonded, or playing down this aspect of the relation, Harriss and Platteau similarly subscribe to the notion of attachment as 'patronage' which provides its subject with a 'subsistence guarantee'.[50] They share with Breman and Bardhan the view that 'patronage' is for the worker a desirable but for the employer an economically irrational form of 'subsistence guarantee', which is generally dissolved 'from above' by 'patrons' against the wishes of 'clients' who wish to retain this arrangement. Because labour-tying is associated with 'patronage', the decline of the latter is wrongly identified as heralding the end of unfreedom.[51]

The confusion to which such a positive interpretation of debt bondage gives rise is evident from the changes of mind it has generated. During the mid-1970s, therefore, Rudra shifted his view about the nature of Indian agriculture: the latter was after all capitalist, and not 'semi-feudal'.[52] Others subsequently did the same. Having initially characterized debt relations between employers and labourers as evidence for 'semi-feudalism' in the agrarian sector, and consequently denied the existence in rural India of a link between the employment of unfree labour, the installation of new technology and/or the process of capitalist development, Breman and Harriss have now also found it necessary to abandon these views.[53] Whereas Harriss has admitted that his original view was wrong, Breman has simply changed his mind without saying that this is what he has done, or why.[54] In a similar vein, Platteau has announced not only that labour-tying by means of debt (= 'patronage') is actually compatible with capitalism, and thus not an archaic pre-capitalist relation, but also that such relational forms are not confined to labour scarce contexts, conclusions which are akin to re-inventing the wheel.[55]

II

Of the many problems which confront historical and current attempts by exponents of unfreedom-as-economic-empowerment to apply the concepts such as 'patronage' and 'moral economy' to bonded labour in rural India and elsewhere, five deserve mention.

7.6 Patronage and 'Patronage'

First, not the least of the difficulties with concepts such as 'patronage' and 'subsistence guarantee' are the historical circumstances in which these kinds of justification have been invoked, the identity of those who have done this and the situation licensed thereby. Accordingly, during the early 1940s (and after) both the German firms that took labour-power from the concentration camps and the Nazi doctors involved in medical experimentation on inmates vindicated such action in terms of a 'subsistence guarantee', claiming that in this way they had saved the unfree workers concerned.[56] (Rather obviously, arguing for the existence of a 'subsistence guarantee' does not of itself constitute proofs of fascist sympathies, nor should such an inference be drawn.)

Second, there is a tendency on the part of exponents of unfreedom-as-economic-empowerment to conflate two distinct phenomena. One is a situation in which there exists a general condition of scarcity (warfare, famine) unconnected with the labour market, and where an employer could arguably be said to provide a starving/destitute subject with a 'subsistence guarantee'. The other is a context where no general condition of scarcity exists, but in which an employer to whom workers owe debts remunerates them at levels he himself fixes, with the result that poverty/starvation is a direct creation of producers themselves, so as to exercise more control over labour-power.[57]

In the latter case, it is impossible to argue that unfreedom and its concommittant low wages and poor working conditions are a redemptive response by a benign employer to an external subsistence crisis faced by his worker, since the necessity for a 'subsistence guarantee' is generated from within the production relation itself, and thus does not pre-exist but is the effect of the transaction between employer and worker.[58] Not only is unfreedom not willingly sought by workers as an alternative to starvation, therefore, but the reverse is frequently true: in India starvation is used by employers as a method of driving recently liberated bonded labourers who wish to remain free back into unfreedom.[59]

Third, and the most difficult politically, is the extent to which terms such as 'patronage' and 'subsistence guarantee' downplay or negate coercion and class struggle. Hence the existence of a contradiction between on the one hand the way in which 'patronage'/'moral economy' interprets these exchanges as being to the benefit of both landholder/patrons and worker/clients, and on the other the Marxist theorization of these same linkages as coercive/exploitative class relationships which license the extraction by 'patrons' of surplus-labour or surplus-value from their 'clients'.[60] In so far as it attempts to combine a 'moral economy' framework with a class analysis, therefore, the concept 'patronage' juggles uneasily with these mutually incompatible (positive/ negative) theorizations of the same relational form.[61]

Fourth, it is clear that for exponents of unfreedom-as-economic-empowerment 'patronage' has a real material component.[62] However, apart from the provision of low paid jobs, no other downwards transfer of resources is identified. That 'patronage' may be simply a materially hollow concept is suggested by the fact that for rural employers the object of tied labour arrangements which are equated with 'patronage' is not merely to keep labour cheap and manageable (by intensifying work schedules without simultaneously increasing payment), but also to obtain access to family/kin labour-power in poor peasant and/or agricultural worker households, a situation hardly compatible with the positive depiction of such relations in terms of above-average material benefits. Accordingly, it is important in such circumstances to distinguish what may be nothing other than ruling class *ideology* of (factually non-existent) resource transfer from any actual redistribution of *material* resources from patrons to clients.[63]

And last, claims about the efficacy of 'patronage' and a 'subsistence guarantee' tend to overlook abundant evidence to the contrary: namely, that historically and contemporaneously there has been little need on the part of workers in many contexts either for 'patronage' or for a 'subsistence guarantee', and where there has, it has not been forthcoming. In the case of southern India during the early nineteenth century, therefore, it is evident that the official claim that agrestic unfreedom constituted a form of 'subsistence guarantee' was without foundation.[64] Not only was no 'subsistence guarantee' actually needed, since even during this era better paid alternative employment was already available in local towns, but when such provision *was* required (illness, old age) landholders in south India refused to supply it.[65]

Much the same remained true of other contexts in India one century later.

Writing in the early 1930s, Mukerjee observed that masters in Bihar did not in fact guarantee their *kamias* employment outside the peak agricultural season, which suggests that during this period no element of 'subsistence guarantee' existed for permanent attached workers.[66] In Kerala during the late 1930s labourers described themselves as 'agricultural serfs, tied down to the landlords ... forced to toil for increasing the wealth of our masters, half-starved and in dirty rags'.[67] Despite frequent claims over the latter part of the nineteenth century by landholders and/or their representatives that they were benign 'patrons' who provided their 'clients' with a 'subsistence guarantee', and that after 1843 agrarian production relations in this state were free, the workers themselves denied the accuracy of these assertions.[68]

Even the Congress Agrarian Reforms Committee, whose report embodied the views of the better-off peasantry and was thus not generally regarded as politically sympathetic to rural labour, notably failed to characterize the instances of agrestic serfdom it encountered during 1948 as forms of 'subsistence guarantee' or 'patronage', much rather the opposite.[69] The same was true of Maharashtra and Gujarat during the mid-1960s, and of Haryana during the mid-1980s, all contexts in which a benign view of bondage as an economically 'empowering' form of 'patronage' or 'subsistence guarantee' was rejected by casual/permanent and free/unfree workers alike.[70]

7.7 'Patronage' and Class Struggle

In order to sustain the unfreedom-as-economic-empowerment view it must be shown that workers attached to a single employer on a seasonal or permanent basis do in fact receive higher wages or larger overall earnings than non-attached labour hired for the equivalent duration to execute similar work.[71] The extensive occurrence of (relative and absolute) *low*-wage labour attachment in rural contexts, however, suggests not only the presence of debt bondage but also that its function as a regulatory mechanism is based on coercion, the purpose being either to prevent workers from seeking available and better-paid alternative employment or – where no better-paid alternative employment exists – to force and keep down real wage levels *tout court*.[72] The combination of attached labour and low wages is incompatible with Bardhan's positive theorization of labour-tying, and thus invites a closer examination of the contexts in which it occurs together with the reasons for this given by Bardhan himself.

For India generally, Bardhan notes a connection between the difficulty of recruitment ('tightness of the labour market'), increasing peak seasonal wage rates, and the importance of attached labour in the rural workforce.[73] Significantly, he also shows that there is a positive correlation between labour-tying, loans provided by a creditor-employer, and areas where agricultural productivity has increased as a result of improved technology.[74] In the context of 'more demand pressure in the labour market relative to supply', such a situation might be interpreted as the successful outcome of bargaining power exercised by those workers who manage to become attached.[75] However, it would be possible to sustain this view only of areas where there was a continuous rise in the level of wages paid to attached labour and where real wages generally outstripped inflation.

This view is contradicted by evidence which Bardhan himself presents. As indicated above, he accepts that during the peak season of the agricultural cycle attached labour obtains a relatively low level of remuneration; he also notes that food prices rise, yet real wages remain low.[76] Furthermore, Bardhan agrees that the principal reason for the existence of labour-tying arrangements linked to credit transactions is that such relationships permit creditor-employers to exercise more effective control over labour-power, a point underlined by findings from the 1979 West Bengal survey which reveal that tied labour did not participate in movements for agricultural wage increases.[77]

All this suggests that, particularly in areas of higher agricultural product-ivity, the attachment of labour through debt is designed basically to check or defuse the development of a specifically proletarian class consciousness, and consequently to instill/reimpose/maintain labour discipline on the one hand and on the other to depress wage levels, either generally (when no better-paid alternative employment is available) or in circumstances where these might otherwise increase (when better-paid work and/or other income generating opportunities are available). As such, it is necessary to characterize the kind of labour attachment referred to by Bardhan as evidence of power exercised not by the worker but rather by the creditor-employer, and hence to the political and economic benefit of the latter and not the former.

Most significantly, the seminal contribution by Wiser to the unfreedom-as-economic-empowerment interpretation of bonded labour has also been challenged, notably on the basis of information which he himself provided. Thus his rose-tinted image of the *jajman*/'kam-karnewala' relationship as a desirable and thus much sought-after form of 'subsistence guarantee' that provided rural labour with cost-free access to village resources (land, credit, employment) has been subjected to extensive criticism, not least because of information to the contrary supplied by Wiser himself.[78] The positive characterization is undermined by evidence that *jajmani* obligations were not only exploitative but that the relation was also structured by economic and/or extra-economic coercion, enforced either by landholders on an individual/collective basis or by caste/community/kin pressure.[79]

It is equally clear from Wiser's description of the relationship as one which '[i]n every instance where the men are giving full-time service they are in debt to their jajmans and paying off the debt through service' that the *jajmani* system is synonymous with bonded labour.[80] Accordingly, a worker does not willingly forgo the possibility of urban employment, as Wiser suggests, but much rather is prevented from doing this. Similarly, the hereditary element, which is interpreted by Wiser as evidence of its acceptability to landholder and worker alike, is due instead to an inability on the part of a worker to break free from the *jajmani* relation due to the existence of inter-generational debt.

III

Some who adhered initially to the unfreedom-as-economic-empowerment interpretation, such as Breman, currently argue that this situation has changed, and that hitherto unfree workers are now free because they are 'assertive'. Like Bauer, Cotlear, Cross and Knight in the case of the Latin American *enganche* system, therefore, the result is unfounded claims about the widespread and unopposed existence in rural India of proletarianization. Equating worker agency or 'assertiveness' with 'empowerment', adherents of this view maintain that 'resistance' against unfree production relations *ipso facto* signals a process of spontaneous 'from below' emancipation. Where such worker agency occurs, therefore, it is claimed that the resulting challenge against unfree relations automatically renders them unviable and leads to their dissolution. This argument, which not only posits the existence of powerful-workers and powerless-employers but also conflates 'assertiveness' with the negation of unfreedom (agency = proletarianization), is for a number of reasons a politically disempowering discourse.

7.8 Assertiveness as Worker Empowerment

To begin with, claims that worker 'assertiveness' is itself 'empowering' are not just wrong but also patronizing, the inference being that 'those below' cannot transcend what has been described accurately in one text as a spontaneous/elemental/(natural) form of 'instinctual political agency'.[81] The sub-text to such claims is the presumption that any/every kind of 'from below' agency has been, is, and must always be 'empowering'.[82] Linked to this is the related assumption, encountered in much of the recent literature about agrarian change in India and elsewhere, that worker 'assertiveness' is 'empowering' simply because it is 'new'. In one sense (and only one) 'assertiveness' and 'resistance' are indeed new, but it is academics and not workers and poor peasants who have discovered these concepts.

Evidence suggests that workers and peasants have always resisted exploitation; in Kerala during the 1890s, for example, landholders and/or their representatives noted with evident anxiety the 'growing independence of the slave classes'.[83] Such 'assertiveness', however, has not always been successful, nor has it necessarily been 'empowering'.[84] Unsurprisingly, therefore, the literature on agrarian change in India (and elsewhere) is replete with texts announcing the imminent demise/decline of unfree relations, and the consolidation of emancipatory trends, predictions which subsequently turned out to be premature or wrong.[85] Since the claims made for the systemically-transforming role of this kind of agency are hugely exaggerated, the political and theoretical usefulness of the concept 'assertiveness' is somewhat limited when applied to rural labour.

Accordingly, there are many examples confirming that, even where/when unfree labour manages to obtain/achieve emancipation from debt bondage, employers generally and agrarian capitalists in particular bide their time and reimpose unfreedom (on the same or different workers) at the earliest opportunity. The absence of this historical dynamic from discussions about bonded labour in India, and in particular from assertions about the declining incidence of unfreedom constitutes an obstacle to the understanding of the relational transformations affecting rural labour. Even when formal emancipation is effected as a result of 'assertiveness', and a bonded labourer manages to obtain employment elsewhere, therefore, landholders reimpose bondage on their workforce as soon as this becomes possible.[86]

As in the case of revisionist texts about the Latin American *enganche* system, part of the difficulty confronting revisionist texts about bonded labour in India stems from the absence or theoretical inadequacy of concepts such as class, class formation and class struggle. Accordingly, processes such as the re-bonding of workers suggest not just that there is no automatic progression from unfreedom to freedom, either historically or currently, but also that as important a consideration as 'from below' agency is the fact and efficacy of class struggle waged 'from above'. The absence of the latter gives rise in turn to two additionally disempowering concepts of worker agency, each of which have implications for positive/negative perceptions of agrestic unfreedom: the powerful-labourer/weak-employer polarity, and 'assertiveness'-as-proletarianization.

7.9 Powerful Labourers, Weak Employers

Claims about worker empowerment as a consequence of 'assertiveness' give rise in turn to the powerful-labourer/weak-employer dichotomy, a view which is not merely fallacious but in class terms also a politically disempowering discourse. Rather obviously, the element of success in any form of 'from below' agency is necessarily constrained by the nature and power of the 'from above' response it elicits.[87] Simply to equate agency with success is rather like saying that Ket's Rebellion or the Peterloo massacre were successful 'from below' mobilisations just because they took place. In many ways, this voluntaristic notion of 'from below' agency (or worker empowerment that takes place in a vacuum) is itself very similar to the concept of an unproblematically choice-making individual at the centre of neoclassical economic theory and post-modernism (on which see Chapters 5 and 8).[88]

In a sub-text which has much in common with landholder ideology, this kind of framework draws a contrast between what it identifies as a polarity between powerful workers and powerless and/or ineffective landholders, an interpretation favourable to the latter in so far as it shifts in the direction of the former the responsibility for any inequalities and oppression which exist.[89] The inference is that since the majority of agricultural labourers possess the capacity to walk away from this if they choose, the fact that they do not do so implies a wish on their part to stay, and thus constitutes an endorsement and simultaneously dissolves criticisms of the economic system in general and of unfree relations in particular.[90] In short, it is a politically *disempowering* discourse which denies or downgrades the importance of 'from above' class rule, and by contrast identifies workers as those who not only undertake but in reality are also the ones who benefit from any struggle which actually takes place.[91]

7.10 Assertiveness as Proletarianization

Those who equate worker 'assertiveness' with 'empowerment' also tend maintain that in India the change from permanent to seasonal or casual employment coincides with a shift from unfree to free production relations, a transformation which in their view similarly constitutes an 'empowering' relational emancipation. Exponents of this view – such as Breman, Jodhka, and Wadley and Derr with regard to shifts in agrarian relations now occurring in Gujarat, Haryana, and Uttar Pradesh – argue likewise (and incorrectly) that, as the process of worker 'assertiveness' is a recent phenomenon, it constitutes additional evidence for proletarianization.[92]

Unfortunately, where unfree relations of production are concerned, many commentators on rural India (and elsewhere) still operate conceptually with a stereotypical continuum on which bonded labour – when it is acknowledged to exist – is regarded as being in the process of replacement by a free work-force. On this point, however, evidence suggests caution. Such a unilinear transition not only assumes the irreversibility of a shift from free to unfree labour but also (and therefore) associates unfreedom with the supposed passivity of pre-capitalist production relations and freedom with workforce agency under capitalism.[93]

What is frequently misunderstood, therefore, is that a shift from permanent attached labour to seasonal and/or casual work signals not the demise of unfreedom but only a change in its form. Thus the extension of unfreedom from permanent to casual labour frequently corresponds to a shift in the immobilising function of debt from a continuous and intergenerational basis to a more period- and context-specific basis. The operationalisation of debt bondage is as a result confined to the months of peak demand in the agricultural cycle, when sellers of labour-power would otherwise command high prices for their commodity. Despite casualization, therefore, what decline in such instances are the pay and conditions but not the workload of the temporary/seasonal/migrant subject who replaces the permanent labourer.

That in India casual employment may have been neither free nor 'empowering' historically is clear from many examples. In the case of late nineteenth and early twentieth century Bihar, therefore, 'the independence enjoyed by the casual worker was necessarily more symbolic than real ... it seems that the agricultural labourer was hardly ever able to hire himself out on a purely economic ... basis'.[94] Writing in the early 1930s, Mukerjee notes that although long-term employment contracts between rural employers and labourers in certain parts of India (Bombay Presidency, Khandesh, Gujarat) were being superceded by more seasonally-specific and/or temporary working arrangements, this did not entail a corresponding decline in the incidence of unfree labour.[95] Equally, in Madhya Pradesh during the early 1940s a ploughman who was a permanent bonded labourer was nevertheless permitted to work for others on a casual basis, but only on condition that he gave wages earned in this manner to his creditor-employer.[96] There are numerous instances from other contexts in India and elsewhere of the retention by employers of wages earned by their erstwhile/actually unfree workers from employment elsewhere, ostensibly as casual labour.[97]

The same is true of what passed for casual labour relations in post-Independence India, and what passes for them even today.[98] During the mid-1960s, landholders in the state of Maharashtra entered into reciprocal arrangements (*vargula*) with one another, exchanging not only bullocks but also the unfree labour-power of their permanent attached workers (*gadis*).[99] One decade later indebted rural workers participating in urban employment guarantee scheme projects on a casual basis during the off-peak agricultural season were not only compelled to withdraw from this and return to the village – despite wanting to stay on and continue getting higher wages – when called upon to so by their village creditor-employers, but were also required to hand over to the latter all earnings generated by such off-farm jobs.[100] Although in such cases rural workers appeared on a hired temporary/casual basis in the labour process of another employer, therefore, they continued to be permanent attached labourers at the beck-and-call of a single creditor-employer.

Hence the presence of casual labour in rural India is not a new phenomenon, neither is it evidence for 'assertiveness', 'empowerment' or proletarianization. While there is indeed a current trend towards casualization, this does not always correspond to a shift from a permanent workforce of bonded labourers to a non-permanent proletariat, and thus to an empowering process of relational emancipation. Much rather the contrary, in that what occurs in such circumstances is that unfreedom is transferred from permanent to non-permanent forms of labour-power. This in turn hints at the presence of a different and disempowering dynamic: not proletarianization but rather *de*proletarianization, or the capitalist restructuring of the agrarian labour process by means of class decomposition/recomposition. In specific contexts, therefore, the trend is not so much towards the formation of a proletariat as away from it.

In the course of this class struggle, the socio-economic structure of rural labour may undergo a multiple and complex transformation: not just in terms of the relational form itself (from free to unfree), but also in terms of the origin (from local to migrant), employment duration (from permanent to casual) and gender (from male to female) of the workers concerned.[101] What is frequently overlooked in analyses of the current shift in employment patterns in rural India is that it is not permanent work in agriculture (and manufacturing) that is declining: the same kinds of jobs are still being done, but now by casuals who may also be females, migrants and unfree. In other words, what is changing is not so much the amount/duration of the work itself (which is what observers usually claim) as the identity, bargaining power and remuneration of those who do it.

7.11 Conclusion

The focus here has been on the way in which attached labour in rural India has been defined (and redefined) over a 200 year period. Initially by apologists for and/or supporters of slavery and serfdom throughout the nineteenth century, then by the Wisers and the Agricultural Labour Enquiries during the first half of the twentieth, and more recently in the work of Epstein, Rudra, Bardhan, Breman, Harriss and Platteau. Common to all these analyses is a positive conceptualization of attached labour, and consequently the downgrading or the elimination of its element of unfreedom.

As in the case of Latin America, the debt servicing labour obligations which structure permanent attachment in India are presented in terms of a materially reciprocal exchange between landholder and agricultural worker, a non-capitalist transaction which it is consequently argued corresponds to a form of employment insurance or 'subsistence guarantee'. Because unfreedom is regarded as incompatible with worker 'resistance'/'assertiveness', the latter is frequently mistaken for evidence of the demise or ineffectiveness of bonded labour, and thus as an indicator of proletarianization

Like the debate about the Latin American *enganche* system, disagreements concerning the presence, meaning and economic role of attached labour in India, both historically and currently, are characterized by two fundamentally opposed interpretations of unfree agrarian relations. One of these is Marxist in origin, and takes a negative view of debt bondage: the relation is based on coercion, is reproduced from above, and its object is to pre-empt/prevent agricultural workers from personally commodifying their own labour-power and the growth of a 'from below' consciousness of class. Labour attachment, either on a long- or short-term basis, is therefore regarded as a form of unfreedom which corresponds to deproletarianization. For this reason, attached labour of whatever employment duration is interpreted as a disempowering agrarian relation.

Exponents of the unfreedom-as-economically-empowering view, by contrast, challenge this negative interpretation. They also adhere to a radically different epistemology: because attached labour in their view corresponds to a desirable and much sought after form of job security or 'subsistence guarantee', it is also perceived by them as the 'from above' provision by benign landholders or creditor-employers of patronage. Consequently, recipients of the latter not only appear as passive but are perceived to be empowered by this working arrangement. For exponents of the unfreedom-as-economically-empowering framework, therefore, attached labour is a 'positive good'.

Such a view has a long history in India. In the colonial era it is encountered in the South from the early nineteenth century onwards, where this discourse was deployed by members of the landlord class or their representatives in order to justify the continued employment of unfree labour. According to these landowners, ex-slaves remained in the service of their ex-masters voluntarily: the relationship was thus benign, non-coercive and free. The same kind of argument was used by the Wisers to explain the persistence and durability of the *jajmani* system in Northern India during the 1920s.

This positive view of labour attachment resurfaced in many of the investigations into the nature of agrarian relations during the post-Independence era. Not only in the 1950s, when it structured both official reports such as the Agricultural Labour Enquiries and also individual monographs, such as that by Epstein about Karnataka, but also in the 1960s and 1970s, when it continued to inform studies of Punjab, Gujarat, West Bengal, Tamil Nadu and Kerala carried out by Rudra, Breman, Bardhan, Harriss and Platteau. Most significantly, these studies revealed little difference between the approach of neoclassical economists (Bardhan, Platteau) and that of self-proclaimed Marxists (Rudra, Breman, Harriss). Of equal significance is the fact that the latter have subsequently changed their minds about the presence, meaning and economic role of unfree labour, a *volte face* that has infused their work with additional contradictions.

These shifts in opinion involve two distinct kinds of voluntarism. Whereas the earlier reinterpretation by Rudra of attached labour as a free relation stemmed largely from economic considerations (the non-heritability of debt, employment duration), those who have changed their minds more recently have reached the same conclusion for different reasons. In the case of Breman, it was mainly because rural workers exhibited agency: given this problematic equation of free labour with 'assertiveness', and the inference that bonded labour is passive, it cannot but follow that all workers who exercise agency must by definition constitute a proletariat. As will be seen in the next chapter, the same kind of epistemology informs the currently fashionable postmodern discourse of Scott, Prakash, and others, about unfreedom-as-cultural-empowerment.

Not the least of the many difficulties facing this positive view of attached labour an an economically empowering form of 'subsistence guarantee' is that it fails to locate the process of determination in the wider context. Historical evidence from India confirms that frequently agricultural workers had no need of patronage; and, conversely, when they had, it was denied them. This indicates that, for the workers concerned, unfree relations not only possessed no economic benefit but may actually have been devoid of any material content. The latter suggests in turn that benign views of unfreedom were and remain part of landholder ideology.

Unlike the provision of subsistence in the case of a pre-existing famine situation, starvation and hunger consequent on low wages paid to unfree labour is not only an effect of debt bondage itself but – from the viewpoint of landholders engaged in struggle with their workers – a desired outcome in terms of negotiating power. Employers in rural India frequently manipulate loans in order to create indebtedness, which in turn enables them to retain and simultaneously lower the cost of labour-power. This dynamic, in which a requirement for subsistence provision is imposed by employers, and thus not an external but an internal aspect of the relation, undermines claims that attachment is a form of 'subsistence guarantee' desired/chosen by workers themselves.

Just as grounds exist for questioning assumptions about the economically empowering aspects of labour attachment, so there are reasons for doubting the claim that worker agency ('from below' assertiveness/resistance) signals the dissolution of attached relations, and is therefore synonymous with emancipation. Since it ignores much evidence to the contrary, the argument that simply because it is new worker agency amounts to relational emancipation is also a politically disempowering one. As in the case of the debate about the Latin American *enganche* system, positive interpretations of attached labour in India have their origins in a corresponding absence or downgrading of a concept of class. In part, this helps to explain the air of Whiggish optimism which pervades claims that unfreedom is either non-existent, unimportant, on the decline, or unenforceable. All the latter, either singly or combined, generate the important 'others' of unfreedom.

Hence the view that, in the absence of coercion, worker 'assertiveness' can only be an indication of grass-roots empowerment, a perception seemingly confirmed by the 'newness' of labour casualization in India. Since attachment is not only deemed to be negated by the physical mobility of the worker but is also associated with permanent employment, the current shift away from the latter and towards the hiring of seasonal, casual and/or migrant labour is seen as further proof of the decline in unfree production relations. However misplaced, the logic of this position is simple: rural workers who migrate, or who are employed on a temporary basis, do not constitute bonded labour.

The conflation of worker 'assertiveness' with employment casualization and relational emancipation, together with the assumption that such processes are 'new' developments, leads in turn to a false conclusion: that wherever/ whenever worker 'assertiveness' is present, bonded labour must by definition be absent. As unfreedom is inefficacious or no longer in evidence, so the argument goes, existing production relations must accordingly be free, and thus confirmation of proletarianization. The link between this epistemology and the conceptual absence of class is manifest in the accompanying deployment of the weak-employers/powerful-workers dichotomy: emancipatory trends are rife because landholders are powerless.

For a number of reasons, this positive view about the non-existence/ decline/dissolution of unfreedom and attached labour is over-optimistic. To begin with, it disregards the fact that, both historically and currently, non-permanent workers have been and are recruited and controlled by means of the debt bondage mechanism. It also overlooks instances where free temporary/ casual labour is transformed into its 'other': a permanent relation that is also unfree. Equally important is the fact that workforce 'assertiveness'/ 'resistance' has always been a dimension of rural conflict, historically no less than now. Indeed, if unfreedom is as incompatible with worker agency as claimed, then it becomes impossible to explain why debt bondage continues to survive in any part of rural India where labour has been 'assertive'.

This tendency to equate 'assertiveness' with empowerment, casualization, migration and proletarianization also overlooks the extent to which any emancipation which results from grassroots agency is merely a transitiory prelude to the rebonding of rural labour. Evidence suggests that, over time, landholders and/or creditor-employers in India do indeed manage to reimpose unfree relations on their workers. Only by ignoring the fact that class struggle is waged as effectively 'from above' as 'from below' is it possible to conclude that history is composed of irreversible victories. Accordingly, in this connection it is important to remember that the assertion by attached labourers of their right to be free is not the same either as achieving this, or as sustaining it once achieved.

NOTES

1. On this point, see Saintsbury [1972]. A current variant of the same argument is that by Baak [1997], who maintains that, after the abolition of slavery in South India during the mid-nineteenth century, ex-slaves chose to remain in their masters' employment as *de facto* unfree labour rather than migrate to European-owned plantations. The reason for this, in his view, was that ex-slaves did well out of this arrangement, in the form of assured employment and food supplies.

2. Examples of optimistic accounts contained in official resports about rural labour, which emphasized the mild/benign nature of unfreedom, are provided by Patel [1952: 84–5] and Hjejle [1967: 93, 96 note 62].

3. The 1872 Report by Dewan Peishkar 'On the Condition of Freed Slaves in Native Cochin', the 'Memo from the Dewan of Cochin to the Resident: On the Slave castes of Cochin' in the same year, and 'Questions on the Condition of the Emancipated Slaves, and Replies, 1890', all contain evidence of the invocation by landlords of the 'subsistence guarantee' argument as a justification for unfree labour [*Kusuman*, 1973: 132, 140, 150].

4. All these claims are encountered in the 1873 memo from the Dewan Peishkar of Padmanabhapuram to the Dewan of Travancore [*Kusuman*, 1973: 145–7], which concludes that '[t]hose [who] continue in the service of their old masters do so from simple choice'.

5. Denying that ex-slaves were maltreated, landlords maintained [*Kusuman*, 1973: 140, 146, 147] that ex-slaves now worked as free labourers, 'acquire property in the shape of land and cattle', and consequently 'all vestiges of slavery have disappeared in South Travancore and that the so-called slave is, in reality, a free man'.

6. See Kusuman [1973: 132–33].

7. The pervasive and enduring influence of Wiser's study on subsequent research into rural labour relations in India is considered by, among others, Beteille [1980: 114], Srinivas [1987: 175], and Wadley and Derr [1989].

8. See Wiser [1936: 3,6].

9. For his interpretation of the *jajmani* system as a form of village level 'subsistence guarantee', see Wiser [1936: 185–6]. Significantly, most of those who utilize an analytical framework structured by the *jajmani* system regard its relational form as a feudal/semi-feudal one (for example, Wiser [1936: 2], Lewis [1955: 151], Beidelman [1959: 6], and – as will be seen below – Breman and Harriss).

10. On these points, see Wiser [1936: 10–11, 95ff.]. The contradictory nature of Wiser's idealized characterization of workers' access to resources owned/

controlled by landholders as being without cost is evident from his description
[1936: 108] of the provision of land as 'free' because '[f]or this no rent is charged
and the employee is expected to render a particular type of service in the village'.
11. Wiser [1936: 177, 187].
12. For examples of the pervasiveness of the 'subsistence guarantee'/'patronage'
     argument as applied to rural India during this era, see among others the texts by
     Patel [1952: 87, 94], Cohn [1955: 56], Srinivas [1955a: 6; 1955b: 26–31], Mayer
     [1960: 79–80], Ishwaran [1966: 36ff.], and Epstein [1967: 233].
13. As the debates about agrarian reform [*Walinsky*, 1977; *Wharton*, 1970] and the
     mode of production in India [*Rudra at al.*, 1978; *Thorner*, 1982; *Patnaik*, 1990]
     and elsewhere [*Frank*, 1969a: 1969b; *Laclau*, 1977] all testify, the presence/
     absence of unfree labour was central to much of the theoretical discussion during
     – and following – the 'development decade' about the presence/absence of
     capitalist production in the Third World countryside. Symptomatic of the con-
     tinued positive characterization during this period of debt bondage as a benign
     form of 'patronage' and 'subsistence guarantee' are the views expressed by
     Frankel [1971: 37–40, 73–4, 108–9, 146–7, 198–9] concerning the negative eco-
     nomic impact of the Green Revolution on the living standards of rural labour in
     Punjab, Andhra Pradesh and Kerala, which is attributed by her to the erosion dur-
     ing the late 1960s of workers' customary arrangements with landowners (=
     'impersonal bargaining arrangements replace customary patron-client relation-
     ships', 'rapid progress of agricultural modernization tends to undermine tradi-
     tional norms of agrarian relationships', etc.).
14. Such views pervade texts by Breman [1974; 1985a; 1989a; 1993; 1996], by
     Harriss [1982a; 1982b; 1992; 1994] and by Platteau [1985; 1992; 1995] and
     Platteau and Abraham [1987]. In each case, there is evident confusion about and
     a misunderstanding of what precisely constitutes unfreedom. In the case of
     Harriss, for example, whether or not he regards particular working arrangements
     as unfree remains unclear. At some points he seems to accept that production
     relations are unfree, but implies that this of no consequence since labourers
     benefit from the arrangement, while at others he disavows the presence of un-
     freedom. It comes as no surprise, therefore, that denying the existence in Tamil
     Nadu of debt bondage [1982a: 239–40, 259–60 note 14], and asserting that
     'attached farm servants called *padials* [are] not bond servants', does not prevent
     Harriss from holding the opposite view: namely, that 'the status of the labourers
     is comparable with that of bond servants' [1977: 237]. All that it is possible to
     say with any certainty is that Harriss [1982a: 239–40] describes in the following
     benign terms ('subsistence guarantee' = 'patronage' = 'reciprocity') what are
     unmistakably bonded labour relations: '[l]abourers are usually attached by debt
     relations ... but in return for his dependence a labourer increases the security of
     his livelihood by assuring himself of employment and by being able to call upon
     the assistance of his patron for small loans ... '. 'The exchange is unequal in the
     sense that patrons benefit more than clients,' Harriss [1982b: 292] notes, 'but the
     relationship provides some guarantee of the clients' right to subsistence and there
     is an element of reciprocity within it'. A decade later, although Harriss is as con-
     fused as ever about the presence/absence/meaning of unfreedom, on the subject
     of 'patronage' his view has not changed: he is still arguing [1992: 208], therefore,
     that in Tamil Nadu 'landholders have not had to resort to the same extent to debt
     bondage as a mechanism for attaching labour but have been able to operate

through the institutions and ideology of patronage'.

15. The attached/casual labour distinction of the 1950s reproduced the earlier dichotomy of long-term farm servant and casual field labourer utilised by the 1921 Census of India, and was itself replaced in the 1963–64 Rural Labour Enquiry by a regular/casual worker classification [*Chatterjee*, 1964: 161]. Significantly, whereas the short-term employment category still remains the same after the first two Agricultural Labour Enquiries, the long-term one by contrast has been changed from 'attached' (denoting unfreedom) to 'regular' (denoting continuity/duration only).

16. The First Agricultural Labour Enquiry described the conditions and characteristics of labour attachment in the following uncompromising manner [*Government of India*, 1952: 32,45]:

> Attached workers are engaged either for a year or at least for a month, but frequent cases of life-long and even hereditary employment were noticed during the enquiry. Driven into debts by their poverty, the agricultural workers have to render life-long service to their creditors whom they cannot repay otherwise ... The average agricultural labourer is not infrequently compelled in times of stress to mortgage his personal liberty. In return for a small sum of money he may happen to need at the moment, he agrees to serve the man from whom he has borrowed. The money is not repaid, nor is it intended to be repaid; but the borrower remains a lifelong bond slave of his creditor ... Involuntary employment is a characteristic feature of agricultural economy. It prevails generally among attached workers whose contracts of employment are determined by the force of tradition and custom. With a view to making the attached workers remain in service for a long time, it is usual for landholders to advance [interest-free] loans ... The inability of workers to repay the advances has led to certain practices of exacting labour either at nominal wages or even without them.

In his critical analysis of the methodological procedures adopted by the Enquiry, Thorner [1962: 177] agrees that: 'In the context of Indian agriculture, the term "attached labourer" has a connotation of unfreedom'.

17. In the Second Agricultural Labour Enquiry, labour attachment is theorised in more ambiguous terms [*Government of India*, 1960: 76, 86]:

> Usually there is a loss of individual freedom for the labourer *though he secures compensatory advantage in the form of security of employment*. In some cases, even family members of the worker are bound to work along with him, *though such instances are few in number*. When there is no work in the field, the attached worker has to do domestic chores. Grant of loans to attached workers with or without interest solely for the purpose of retaining them in service for an indeterminate period is not uncommon, *though it might not contain any pronounced element of agrestic serfdom* ... In spite of contractual obligations which at times deprive attached workers of their freedom, the *redeeming feature is continuity of employment for a longer period even if at times it be at low wages* (emphasis added).

18. For this fourfold classification, see Government of India [1960: 86]. The centrality of unfreedom to the concept of labour attachment used in the Second Agricultural Labour Enquiry is demonstrated not only by a definition which stresses both that

> In many parts of the country advance of loan (not readily repayable) ... is made

by the farm to attached labourers, so that they may be available for work whenever required. Such advancement of loan was termed 'debt bondage' which
binds a debtor and sometimes his family members for life or at least for an
indefinite period till the day of repayment of loan ... The attached labourer or
sharecropper is bound to his master by debt [1960: 86, 286–7],
but also by hints that agricultural workers themselves strongly resented and
resisted this process. Hence [1960: 76, 86]:
    Some attached workers are even not in favour of working on long term
    contracts of employment in view of long hours of work and exacting conditions
    of employment ... The relative decline in the quantum of employment as
    between 1950–51 and 1956–57 ... might also be due to ... reluctance on the part
    of attached labour to being tied down to annual employment contracts ... and
    the general awakening among attached labour in availing leave and holidays
    on festive occasions notwithstanding the stringent provisions contained in
    contracts of employment.
19. Significantly, the restudy by Epstein [1973] during the 1970s of the two South
    Indian villages where she had conducted research during the mid-1950s revealed
    that whereas the incidence of bonded labour in the non-irrigated 'dry' village had
    declined by some 50 per cent, the installation of canal irrigation in the 'wet'
    village had stimulated the development of a capitalist agriculture, and the demand
    for labour doubled accordingly. However, this demand was met not by the
    employment of free wage labour but rather by the utilization of cheaper bonded
    labour, the latter increasing by some 243 per cent over the 1955–70 period
    (calculated from Epstein [1962: 74; 1973: 132ff.]).
20. See Epstein [1962: 73]. 'Such *muyee* labour', she continues, 'is not taken into
    account as payment of interest on debt, but is done simply to "keep in" with one's
    creditors ... The chief moneylenders in the village command the highest amount
    of *muyee* labour.'
21. See Epstein [1962: 73].
22. See Epstein [1962: 105].
23. It should be noted that an important determinant of this transformation in the
    way attached labour relations are theorized is the one alluded to in Chapter 5:
    namely, the difficulty in reconciling the spread of labour attachment with the
    development of a capitalist agriculture. One solution to this problem, adopted not
    only by Rudra but also by Bardhan and Breman (see below), is to redefine attach-
    ment as a form of free labour (a view seemingly shared by Ahlawat [1988: 72]
    with regard to annual contract workers in Haryana). Another solution – the one
    followed here – is to regard the unfreedom that characterizes attachment as the
    outcome of (and therefore compatible with) the class struggle which accompanies
    capitalist penetration of agriculture.
24. Rudra [1987: 757]. The latter's concept of 'semi-attachment' has of course been
    developed in other texts [e.g., *Rudra and Bardhan*, 1983]; the one examined here
    constitutes his most concise intervention on the subject. For another critique of
    Rudra's text, see Srivastava [1987b].
25. Rudra [1987: 758].
26. Rudra [1987: 757]
27. Rudra [1987: 758–9]. The latter's positive theorization is signalled by his use
    of terms such as 'congenial' and 'voluntary' when describing both the existence
    and the renewal of the attached labour relation on the part of the worker. This

idealized theorization is contradicted by the 1987 research findings from Haryana presented in Chapter 3; these indicate that attachment is perceived as neither beneficial nor 'congenial' by its labouring subjects. Significantly, the case of free attached labour mentioned in the First Agricultural Labour Enquiry [*Government of India*, 1952: 275] and cited by Thorner [1962: 177] as evidence that attachment does not necessarily involve unfreedom, is one in which the subjects of these relations take neither loans nor wage advances from their employers; that is, an attached labourer is unconditionally free to seek other employment *only* in circumstances where debt is also absent. As is clear from Rudra's own data [1987: 759–60, Table 2], the latter situation does not apply to his own case study, in which the majority of attached and 'semi-attached' workers owe debts to their employers.

28. The absence of hereditary debt enables Rudra to deny the existence of debt bondage [1987: 758, 759], notwithstanding the widespread borrowing of consumption loans. For a similar mode of theorization, see the comments below on Breman. Here it is anyway necessary to pose a crucial question: what happens to debts owed to a creditor-employer when an attached labourer dies or, because of illness or age, is unable to continue working? The implication of Rudra's argument is that such debts are written off, which, if true, would make nonsense of both moneylending and labour discipline. Accordingly, there would now be nothing to prevent workers borrowing with the full knowledge that the longer these loans remained unpaid, the lesser the likelihood of repayment *per se*; this in turn would destroy the link between the (large) amount of debt owed to a creditor-employer, and the necessity of having to work it off in the form of labour-service. As the data from the Haryana village case studies presented in Chapter 3 indicate, when a labourer dies, gets old, or becomes ill, the debt is automatically passed on to the surviving spouse and/or offspring, an intergenerational form of debt bondage that applies to both attached and casual workers.

29. Rudra [1987: 758, original emphasis]. It is instructive to compare the latter's view, which involves the transformation of dependency on an individual ⇒ group basis, with that of Patel who – although making some of the same assumptions regarding the nature of bonded labour – nevertheless presents a mirror image of the shift in dependency (group ⇒ individual). Thus Patel [1952: 88] comments that the

> liberation [of agricultural workers] from the traditonal bondage itself paved the way for the new type of economic bondage. There were no longer 'serfs' within the framework of the village community, wherein, as a *group* of village menials and servants, they had accepted bondage to a *group* of cultivators. This relationship was replaced by a *new* form of bondage, wherein an *individual* in desperate economic need was forced into bondage to another *individual*. The traditional serfs were 'liberated' to be enserfed (original emphasis).

30. In contrast to the position adopted by Rudra, evidence suggests that labour attachment consequent on capitalist penetration of agriculture entails the replacement of multi-sourced credit linkages by single-source debt bondage. In her analysis of changing agrarian relations in Haryana during the early 1970s, Bhalla [1976: A-29] points out that in the economically backward areas of the state agricultural workers continued to obtain consumption loans from different sources, whereas in the more advanced areas – where new forms of unfree permanent labour had developed following the Green Revolution – multi-sourced consumption loans

had been eliminated: such credit was now obtained solely from an employer. As the 1987 Haryana village case studies presented in Chapter 3 indicate, labourers do indeed take loans from different landholders. But, firstly, these are *casual* workers, and the system of borrowing is sequential not coterminous; and, secondly, the process of attachment itself entails taking a loan from and becoming employed on a long-term basis by a single employer (as Bhalla indicates with regard to the earlier period).

31. Rudra omits to specify the precise nature of personalised dependency, but implies that it entails a benign or positive relational dimension.

32. In contrast to both Thorner and Rudra, it is argued here that, while there is no connection between contract duration *per se* and the freedom or unfreedom of a worker to sell his or her own labour-power, there *is* a link between unfreedom and either long- or short-term labour attachment where debt is also part of the relation. This view is confirmed by Ahlawat [1988: 109], who shows that in Haryana indebted casual workers are unfree. Even government officials recognize that bondage applies not just to long-term but also to short-term agrarian relations. Thus Srivastava [1987a: 14] notes that:

> One of the reasons for the slow progress in identification of bonded labour is a mental reservation, as it were, on the part of some State Governments and officials on the point whether seasonal labourers who have taken advance or loan from their employers, can be called bonded labour. The practice of engaging seasonal labour and paying them some advance which is adjusted against their wages is widespread. The wages are very often below the prescribed minimum wages; and in any case there is some obligation on the part of the worker that he will not leave work till the advance is adjusted or paid off. Thus, technically there is no doubt that such seasonal labour comes within the definition of bonded labour as contained in the Bonded Labour System (Abolition) Act, 1976, and clarified by the Supreme Court in the Asiad case (1982) and the *Bandhua Mukti Morcha* case (1983).

The same text then concludes that strict enforcement of legal provisions on bondage in the case of seasonal workers would not only prove impossible but also disrupt agricultural production.

33. See Bardhan [1984: 81–3]. The latter notes the existence of an alternative definition [1984: 83, footnote 7] that stresses the obligation to carry out non-remunerated work for an employer.

34. Bardhan [1984: 81–4, 124–6, 176, 181 note 18]. Paradoxically, Bardhan undermines his own argument about the non-existence of coercion (and therefore bondage) when he states [1984:79] that one of the purposes of labour attachment through debt is that it makes 'recovery of loans easier ... it [is] easier to *enforce* implicit [tied-labour] contracts' (emphasis added). It is anyway difficult to see how the questionnaire-based method of data collection used by Bardhan would enable him to obtain information on a subject as politically-sensitive as the occurrence and role of coercion in debt enforcement, a doubt confirmed by the examination of his fieldwork schedule for the 1979 village survey in West Bengal [*Rudra and Bardhan*, 1983: Appendix 3]. The series of questions dealing with borrowing and attachment conditions include nothing designed to elicit a response concerning the reaction of a creditor-employer in a situation where his worker or tenant either fails to carry out or else falls behind with debt-servicing labour repayments (see Rudra and Bardhan [1983: 76, 80, 82–5]). Significantly,

Bardhan concedes the existence of precisely such methodological problems with regard to moneylending and the underreporting of tenancy relations [1984: 112–13, 127, 151–2].

35. Breman [1985a: 127–9, 264–5].

36. Breman [1985a: 131, 306–13]. Although Breman's participant-observation method [1985b] is more amenable to obtaining information about coercion, he nevertheless repeatedly asserts that it is no longer an important dimension of agrarian relations. This view lacks conviction, however, given Breman's confusion over the determinant role of fear as distinct from reciprocity when considering the earlier *halipratha* system, the evidence he himself provides concerning the existence of coercion, and finally his admission that labour-contractor/gang-member and seasonal-migrant/employer relationships are in fact structured by coercion [1985a: 268, 312, 411–12].

37. The NLI/GPF survey [*Marla*, 1981: 23] reports that in only three per cent of cases is bondage to one particular creditor-employer actually life-long. Forty-six per cent of cases entail the annual renewal of bondage, and a further 45 per cent of instances are classified as 'indefinite' bondage (that is, not specifying a cut-off point while not being permanent in duration).

38. Referring to the existence of what Thorner [1962: 33] identifies as unfree 'beck-and-call' relationships between indebted workers and their creditor-employers, Bardhan [1984: 3 footnote 9] accepts that an agricultural labourer in receipt of consumption loans and wage advances, yet who does not work for one creditor-employer continuously or exclusively – but whose labour-power is nevertheless at the disposal of the latter whenever and for whatever period he wants so long as debts remain outstanding, 'is not an entirely free participant in the labour market'. Similarly, Breman [1985a: 275] reports that in Gujarat casual labourers who take small loans from farmers are as a result 'not always completely free to sell their services to the highest bidder; at the most favourable times for them – the months of greatest work pressure – some of them have no opportunity of obtaining the maximal price for their labour ... '.

39. See Bardhan [1984: 83, footnote 9].

40. One outcome of this is that although an attached labourer can change the locus of his attachment, he cannot withdraw from the attached labour relationship itself. On this form of 'changing masters' in rural India generally, see Marla [1981: 23]. Evidence from individual case studies about rural labour in different states at particular conjunctures suggests that the transfer of debts between creditor-employers was – and continues to be – a significant phenomenon. In the case of Bihar, therefore, Sinha [1982: 19] reports its occurrence in Hararibagh District during the first two decades of the twentieth century, and Lal [1977: 34–7] indicates that in Gaya District the sale or lease of *kamia* bonded labourers by one creditor-employer to another has always been an integral aspect of debt bondage relationships. Much the same is true of UP, where the 1939 Report of the Royal Commission on Agriculture (cited in Chopra [1985: 166]) noted that rural artisans were 'transferred from capitalist to capitalist in a manner which practically amounts to sale and purchase'. According to Galey [1983: 70], in Uttarkashi District of the same state 'the system makes it impossible to free oneself from debt without borrowing the equivalent sum from a second lender who, with the agreement of the former, will impose the same labour constraints on the borrower'. The transfer of a worker's debt between masters is cited by Breman

[1985a: 127–8] as a characteristic of unfree *hali* labour in Gujarat, while in Thane District, Maharashtra, indebted labourers were 'sold' by one master to another [*Deshpande*, 1982: 118]. Vidyasagar [1985: 146] notes the current practice in Tamil Nadu of changing masters by transferring debt, while Platteau *et al.* [1985: 66, 145] provide detailed information from fishing villages in south Kerala on the way in which unfree crew members transfer debt from one employer to another.

41. The practical and political importance of this task may be illustrated by conflict in Khammam District, Andhra Pradesh, where the CPI(M) resisted attempts by local voluntary agencies to file cases under the 1976 Bonded Labour System (Abolition) Act against rich and middle peasants for keeping 'annual farm labourers in some degree of bondage' [*Balagopal*, 1986: 1402]. Such a conflict, justified by the CPI(M) in terms of maintaining 'peasant unity', poses awkward questions about unity for whom and on what conditions. For an interesting analysis of similar political issues arising from the agrarian struggles in Kerala, see Krishnaji [1986].

42. For analogous theorizations, see D. Lal [1989: 120–26] and Srinivasan [1989].

43. For other examples of the same view, see Dovring [1965: 309] and Jagannathan [1987: 38ff.]. It should be noted that Bardhan presents contradictory views on this point: having denied that the existence of tied-labour contracts in India is determined by the need on the part of poor peasants for 'subsistence insurance', he subsequently states that it is [1984: 80, 175–6]. For a much stronger version of this neoclassical argument, see Platteau *et al.* [1985] and Platteau and Abraham [1987]: despite the fact that there was intense inter-employer competition over – and hence demand for – scarce seasonal labour-power in the three Kerala fishing villages studied, that wage advances were made by an employer specifically with the object of attaching labourers to his own crew, that indebted crew members were as a result not allowed to seek employment with other (more successful) fishing units without first repaying these loans (which they found difficult to do), and that attachment gave rise to conflict between employers and crew members, such relations are nevertheless theorised as 'subsistence insurance', 'subsistence credit', and 'reciprocity'. Indeed, the analytical framework and consequent denial of bonded labour relations notwithstanding [1985: 59–61, 144, 289–90, 374; 1987: 478], both these texts provide an excellent illustration of how exactly the debt bondage system operates.

44. Bardhan [1984: 61, 67, 71–2].

45. Perhaps the best illustration of this idealised presentation of debt bondage is that by Hill [1986: 111–15], in which harvesting is presented as 'an exciting time from which every labourer expects to benefit ... the generosity of employers being enhanced by the sight of grain with which the labourers are rewarded', where bonded labourers 'positively enjoy the security provided and are envied by day labourers', and how in her opinion 'having seen some of these young men at work [as bonded labourers], and lounging about in their employer's house, I certainly got the impression that they were better off than they would have been if living semi-starved at home'. The 'dire poverty of many free labourers in South India', she concludes, 'is a much graver problem than that of bonded labouring', thereby failing to identify the link between these two production relations.

46. Bardhan [1984: 83–4, 86, 124–6, 157, 175]. For a similar view on this point, see Rudra [1987: 758].

47. That seasonality – or rather the period-specific scarcity to which this concept

refers – is in some instances not a 'natural' occurrence but an artificially-induced phenomenon that arises from the manipulation by creditor-employers of cash/kind loans and repayments may be demonstrated by the following examples. In the case of Thanjavur District, Tamil Nadu, during the early 1950s [*Gough*, 1983: 279–80], annual contracts were renewed each year in the month of April, at which point bonded labourers (*panniyals*) received an interest-free cash loan from their employer. This debt was repaid in the form of paddy during the February harvest the following year. What is significant about this seasonal combination of money-loan/kind-repayment is that throughout the April–September period, at the start of which the cash debt is incurred, the price of paddy is high, whereas during the harvest month of February, when the debt is repaid in kind, the price of this commodity is low. Accordingly, workers in Thanjavur who receive a cash loan when the cost of paddy is high are able to purchase insufficient quantities of this staple product, being as a result compelled to borrow more than would otherwise be the case in order to secure an adequate subsistence provision during the period of scarcity. At harvest-time, however, when repayment becomes due, the low price of paddy ensures that a higher proportion of kind wages than might otherwise be the case are devoted to cancelling the debt. Consequently, workers who now have insufficient subsistence provision are once again required to take a loan from their employers, thereby reproducing and simultaneously reinforcing the debt cycle. By taking advantage of seasonal price movements in this way, creditor-employers are able to make their workers dependent on loans, to keep them continuously in debt, and to depress the remuneration they obtain for debt-servicing labour at harvest-time. Such a view is confirmed by Bhaduri [1973: 123 footnote 3] who, writing about a similar period-specific form of borrowing linked to market fluctuations in the price of paddy in West Bengal during 1970, notes:

> It is natural to ask: why does the *kishan* not borrow right after the harvest when prices are low? The answer is simple: he is not given any loan then. The local *jotdar* usually has intimate knowledge of the *kishan's* economic position and will lend him paddy only at the high price season, when typically the kishan's own stock of paddy from the last harvest is exhausted. It is the same answer that I got from several *kishans* when I asked this question.

One comparable variant involves the *kamia* system in Bihar [*Patel*, 1952: 76–77] where, to ensure that debt remained outstanding (and labour obligations continued), creditor-employers stipulated that cash repayment of loans must be made on a particular day during the lean season – when money was scarce – or it would be rejected. Another variant of seasonally-induced debt has also been noted by Bhalla [1976: A-26] in the case of Haryana during the early 1970s, where the

> initial interest-free advance, equivalent to four or five months' emoluments ... is paid [to permanent workers in June, and] constitutes only a part of the amount which will fall due when the next payment is made [in mid-January], which is six and a half months later. Thus a 'gap' is built into most contracts, which tends to produce a period of financial stress for the labourer before the January 'second installment' is received. This becomes one of the factors which make resort to interest-bearing forms of assistance likely during the year.

48. Bardhan [1984: 67–8, 86]. However, as Bardhan himself observes [1984: 77], one consequence of the application of new technology has been the evening out of peaks and troughs in the demand for labour, and thus the seasonality of

agricultural production. The demand for workers has accordingly become more constant.

49. Bardhan [1984: 73].

50. For denials that attached labour is bonded, see Harriss [1982a: 122–3], Breman [1985a; 307–8, 310–11; 1996: 216–7], and Platteau [1995: 767ff.]. Their versions of the argument that unfreedom is a form of 'subsistence guarantee'/'patronage' are noted in Harriss [1982a: 124, 240], Breman [1974: 118, 140, 192; 1985a: 127, 135] and Platteau [1995: 774]; a similar claim has been made by Rogaly [1996] with regard to West Bengal in the early 1990s. Significantly, such views are no different from those of the Indian government, which has long argued that attached labour is a positive good (that is, provides its subject with a 'subsistence guarantee'), and indeed has used this as a justification for not implementing exist-ing legislation abolishing bonded labour. Discussions in which this writer partici-pated in India with lefwing academics and researchers, progressive bureaucrats and comrades engaged in agrarian struggles suggest that none of them regard this idealized view (attached labour = 'subsistence guarantee' = 'patronage' ≠ un-freedom) as having made a useful contribution to the eradication of debt bondage, much rather the contrary. No less significant is the fact that in the mid-1970s the Government of Bihar invoked the 'subsistence guarantee' argument in order to justify its refusal to classify attached workers as bonded labour, to recognize the presence of the latter, and thus to implement existing legislation abolishing debt bondage (on which see Das [1979: 8–9, 26–7]).

51. This is particularly true of Breman [1974: 220ff.] and Platteau [1992; 1995].

52. See Thorner [1982: 1968].

53. For the categorization of debt relations as 'semi-feudal' and the delinking of unfreedom and agrarian capitalism, see Breman [1974: 121–2; 1985a: 131, 306–13] and Harriss [1982a: 98, 103–5].

54. Both the fact of and reasons for his change of mind are set out in Harriss [1992; 1994: 178]. That Breman has also experienced a Pauline conversion on the sub-ject of unfree labour, now regarded by him as central to the process of capitalist accummulation in Gujarat, is outlined in Brass [1997b]. The latter text also shows how as a result of this unacknowledged *volte face* the relational distinctiveness which Breman previously insisted separated the *hali* in south Gujarat from contemporary farm servants, migrants and casual workers seems to have all but vanished.

55. Over the last three decades, these very points have been raised continuously in publications dealing with agrarian transformation, both about India and else-where: for example, during the late 1960s and early 1970s by various contributors to the mode of production debate (Frank [1969a], Thorner [1980: 224–37] and Banaji [1978]), during the late 1970s (Mundle [1979]), and during the early and mid-1980s (Brass [1986a]). That unfreedom/('patronage') is supportive of accumu-lation in agriculture throughout India is therefore most emphatically not some-thing that has surfaced and been recognized as an issue only in the mid-1990s.

56. On this point Bellon [1990: 319 note 112] comments that: 'One still hears today what a defence of Krupp proclaimed almost 40 years ago: that German compa-nies performed a humanitarian service for concentration camp prisoners by employing them at their factories, thus saving them from death in the camps.' As the additional example of Mengele's justification of his medical experiments on concentration camp prisoners demonstrates, this very defence has been advanced

by Nazis themselves. As was made clear in an ITV programme about Mengele broadcast on British television on 17 September 1985, Mengele justified himself to his son Rolf by saying that he *helped* those he selected for medical experiments by saving them from the gas chambers. Those who volunteered for experiments got more food, and Mengele thought that the Jews should build a statue in his honour to commemorate the many lives he had saved in this way. The similarity between the justification of unfreedom as a form of 'subsistence guarantee' as advanced both by Mercedes Benz and by Mengele show that what can be presented by an employer (or others in a position of power) as a virtuous act of saving inmates from the concentration camp can also be – and be seen by the 'beneficiaries' of such virtue as being – a method of getting cheap labour (or 'volunteers' for medical experiments) that in the circumstances has little or no negotiating power. This point is neatly depicted in the film *Schindler's List*, in which a character 'rescued' in this manner asks the main protagonist bluntly (and bravely): 'What's in it for you, Mr Schindler?'.

57. As is clear from Kusuman [1973: 134], this was true of Kerala in the 1870s, where it was the landlord's hold over labour-power which generated the need by workers for a 'subsistence guarantee'. In this particular instance, therefore, the requirement for a 'subsistence guarantee' did not precede and operate independently of landholder power.

58. As has been shown with regard to Bihar in the early 1930s [*Mukerjee*, 1933: 230], Madhya Pradesh in the late 1930s [*Grigson*, 1944: 236], Tamil Nadu in the late 1950s [*Gough*, 1983: 279–80], Haryana in the early 1970s [*Bhalla*, 1976: A-26], and West Bengal during the 1970s [*Bhaduri*, 1973], creditor-employers manipulate cash/kind loans in order to *create* the indebtedness which in turn enables them to retain and simultaneously to lower the cost of their workforce.

59. Joshi [1978] reports that during the mid-1970s landholders in Palamau District, Bihar, denied their erstwhile bonded labourers employment as free workers with the object of starving them back into unfreedom. As one of those affected by this strategy observed [*Joshi*, 1978: 202, 206],

> The zamindars collectively decided that no work should be given to the liberated *dhangar* [labourer]. They wanted to drive us again to the verge of starvation ... The *sahukars* of the village had made up their mind that no local labourer who had been liberated by the government would get work ... The landlords wanted to see us in bondage again.

60. For the conceptualization of 'moral economy', see among others Scott [1977: 23–4]. Breman [1996: 222] and Harriss [1977: 236; 1994: 181–2] also endorse the 'moral economy' framework.

61. As Scott himself has admitted [1977: 21], 'The terms "patron" or "patronage" are morally loaded. To take them at more or less face value is to accept a definition of role behaviour very much in accord with how elites would like to have things seem.'

62. Of the advocates of unfreedom-as-economic-empowerment, Harriss [1994: 185], Breman [1974: 143ff.] and Platteau [1995: 767ff.] all maintain that 'patronage' has a material component that benefits workers.

63. On this point, see Gilsenan [1977] and Li Causi [1975]. That such a view is compatible with the way in which creditor-employers as a class perceive these relationships is supported by the response of factory owners who justify the employment of bonded child labour in their glass-making factories at Firozabad,

Uttar Pradesh, in the following manner: 'What can we do when fathers bring their children to us and beg us to employ them? If we did not help out, these poor people would starve' [*Burra*, 1986: 2033].

64. Pointing out that among the observers of and commentators on agrarian relations in early nineteenth century India only Abbé Dubois drew attention to their coercive aspects, Hjejle [1967: 96] remarks: 'The idea, which I have come across several times, that the slaves at least were entitled to work and to a subsistence, did not hold good in Malabar, Trichinopoly and Tanjore, where their wages were either cut or stopped altogether when there was no employment.'

65. Both the absence of a need for a 'subsistence guarantee' during the working life-time of unfree labourers in south India during the nineteenth century, together with the abandoning by landholders both of old or infirm slaves who were no longer able to work and of tied labour during periods of famine, is outlined by Saintsbury [1972: 12], Saradamoni [1980: 57–60] and Arnold [1984: 79]. Much the same is true of nineteenth century Brazil, where plantation slaves who became too old for work were manumitted by their 'generous' masters [*Degler*, 1976], and also of Bihar during the early 1980s, where creditor-employers encouraged older bonded labourers (whose usefulness as agricultural workers had ended) to free themselves, yet strongly resisted attempts at self-emancipation on the part of young bonded labourers [*Tiwary*, 1985: 203].

66. About this situation Mukerjee [1933: 230] writes: ' ... daily work is not guaranteed by the master, and no food is supplied when there is no work to be done'.

67. For this self-description on the part of the rural workforce, see Kusuman [1973: 154].

68. The details of the workers' complaints are contained in the *Memorandum of the Lower Classes to the Resident, Trivandrum, 1937*, signed by some 200 persons [*Kusuman*, 1973: 153–55].

69. On this point, see All-India Congress Committee [1949: 127–39], much of whose information about the working conditions of rural labour in the late 1940s was based on interviews conducted in Gujarat, Kerala, Tamil Nadu and UP. The negative views expressed in the report on the subject of agrestic unfreedom may have been the result of the perception of this relational form as an effect largely of land-lordism.Writing in the early 1950s, another commentator [*Patel*, 1952: 77] observes: when the bonded labourer agrees to serve under a master, he has promised not to work for any other person. *But the master does not guarantee work for him for the whole year. When there is no work for him, he is given neither food nor grain allowance ... This is also the time when there is hardly any farm work to be found in the neighbourhood* (emphasis added).

70. Hence the observation by Carter [1974: 71] about permanent attached labour in mid-1960s Maharashtra, that:
As the length of their employment increases, their average daily wage decreases. Most are paid entirely in cash. Others are paid partly in cash and partly in food and clothing. People are now increasingly reluctant to work as *gadis*. Since irrigation has made the demand for labour increasingly constant throughout the year, the higher wages of short term employment now tend to outweigh the security of long term employment.
The same point is made by Vyas [1964: 13] and Patel [1964: 108] with regard to Gujarat during the 1960s, and in Chapter 3 with regard to Haryana during the mid-1980s.

71. As the Haryana village case studies presented in Chapter 3 demonstrate, this cal-
culation would also have to take into account the earnings an attached labourer
might expect to obtain from non-wage work, such as livestock ownership.

72. Based on a 1981–82 survey of West Bengal villages, Bardhan and Rudra [1986]
argue that, wage differentials notwithstanding, the absence of inter-village labour
mobility is due not to the existence of regulatory mechanisms impeding this but
rather to the territorial segmentation of the local labour market. The latter derives
in turn from a situation in which labourers 'often look up to their local employers
as providers of sustained job opportunities, regular credit and emergency help
over the years, and may even forgo high short-term wages in nearby villages in
order to maintain their long-term ties' [1986: 91]. Even where bonded labourers
have been released by government intervention, these sentiments – presented here
by Bardhan and Rudra as evidence of benign employers – point to the continued
existence at the village level of coercive mechanisms that permit the enforcement
of debt-servicing labour obligations. The attempt to explain the combination of
labour immobility and wage differentials solely in terms of geographical
determinants turns out to be nothing other than a restatement of the 'subsistence
insurance' position in a new form.

73. See Bardhan [1984: 68–9, 76–7, 80].

74. See Bardhan [1984: 77–81].

75. Alternatively, it might mean that non-attached workers are simply unwilling to
enter attachment at any price, either because of its onerous working conditions
and accompanying maltreatment at the hands of the creditor-employer, or because
of the possibility of higher outside earnings from non-wage economic activity.

76. See Bardhan [1984: 52].

77. See Bardhan [1984: 47, 60, 66, 77–9, 81, 86]; Rudra and Bardhan [1983: 22–4].

78. Critiques of Wiser's interpretation of the *jajmani* system include Lewis [1958:
55ff.], Beidelman [1959], Dumont [1970: 97ff.], and Wadley and Derr [1989].

79. That the power of landholders was based ultimately on coercion exercised against
workers is conceded by the Wisers [1963: 14] when they write of Karimpur
during the late 1920s that:

> [the] leaders of our village are so sure of their power that they make no effort
> to display it ... And yet when one of them appears among the men of serving
> caste, the latter express respect and fear in every guarded word and gesture.
> *The serving ones have learned that as long as their subservience is un-*
> *questioned, the hand which directs them rests lightly. But let there be any move*
> *toward independence or even indifference among them, and the paternal touch*
> *becomes a stranglehold.* (emphasis added).

Additional evidence for the coercive enforcement of *jajmani* work obligations by
means of pressure exercised through the village community is to be found in
Lewis [1958: 58]. On the issue of exploitation, Lewis [1958: 79] comments that
'it seems evident that the relationship between *jajman* and *kamin* lends itself to
the exploitation of the latter'.

80. See Wiser [1936: 64]; at other points, however, he concedes [1936: 164–5, 174]
that it is hard to distinguish the *jajman*/'kam-karnewala' relationship from that of
master and slave. That *jajmani* cannot be differentiated from unfree labour
relations is a point made not just by Beidelman [1959: 9–10] and by Wadley and
Derr [1989: 106] but also by Lewis [1958: 57, 80], who observes that '[a] major
function of the *jajmani* system is to assure a stable labor supply for the dominant

agricultural caste in a particular region by limiting the mobility of the lower castes, especially those who assist in agricultural work ... some of [the *kamins*] are deeply in debt to their *jajmans* [which] gives the Jats an additional hold over their *kamins*'. Even Dumont, who subscribed to an idealized view of the caste system [*Berreman*, 1979: 155–63], accepts that the *jajmani* relation amounts to unfree labour [1970: 100].

81. See Larsen [1993: 282, 285]. This aspect is evident in the admission by two exponents of Scott's 'resistance' theory, that in many instances 'resistance' is no different from accommodation, and thus an acceptance of the *status quo*. Hence the concession by Munro [1993b: 32] that 'even when resistance failed, it was nevertheless admirable that an attempt had been made to beat the odds ... ', while Harriss [1994: 188] similarly concedes that '[s]ome will say, no doubt, that this sort of action [= 'resistance'] ultimately reflects accommodation with the facts of power'.

82. Perhaps nowhere is this kind of epistemology more evident than in the clearly stated view expressed by Lal [1979] in a text celebrating the contribution by Indians to the economy, society and culture of Fiji. 'Over the years many a derogatory myth has been built around the origins and character of Fiji's *girmitiyas*, and these myths have been unfairly and cruelly used on many occasions to remind their descendants of their proper place in society', he observes [1979: 25], ' ... the overwhelming majority [of Indian indentured migrants to Fiji were not undesirable riff-raff but] were young, productive agricultural workers ... who had fallen on hard times and who *chose* to migrate temporarily to alleviate their plight' (emphasis added).

83. On this point, see the responses to 'Questions on the Condition of the Emancipated Slaves, and Replies, 1890' [*Kusuman*, 1973: 149–52].

84. Many examples of worker 'assertiveness' in the past confirm that it is not 'new', nor has it been successful. Hence the numerous instances of unsuccessful 'assertiveness' reported in south India during 1948 by the All-India Congress Committee [1949: 134], when permanent agricultural labourers who had dared to ask for higher wages were physically assaulted by the landholder's hired goondas, who then also burned down the workers' houses and school. That worker 'assertiveness' does not necessarily correspond to empowerment is also evident from an episode in Tanjore during the early 1950s, where an unfree worker who assaulted a landholder responsible for withholding payment due him was beaten severely and ritually humiliated, and where '[m]any other cases similar to [this one] could be quoted' [*Gough*, 1960: 49]. That such employer responses to worker 'assertiveness' continue is evident from the case of Purnia, examined in Chapter 4.

85. Among those who have claimed somewhat prematurely that unfree labour in India as a whole no longer exists are Bardhan [1982: 80, 91 note 18], Rudra [1982: 376–78] and – rather more surprisingly – Thorner [1962: 8]. (To be fair to Thorner, what was being referred to here was *begar* and not the debt bondage relation) The same kind of claims have been made periodically with regard to individual states in the Indian union: for example, Bihar (Mukerjee [1933: 229]), Haryana (Marla [1981: 10], Jodhka [1994]) and West Bengal (Rudra and Bardhan [1983: 17]) have all been identified as contexts where debt bondage is either nonexistent or on the decline, evidence to the contrary notwithstanding (Srivastava [1987b], Ahlawat [1988], and Chapter 3 in this book). Others who initially made claims along these lines now accept that such a prognosis was incorrect: for

example, having maintained initially that 'patronage' associated with permanent attached labour relations was subject to erosion in North Arcot District of Tamil Nadu, Harriss [1992; 1994] now agrees that he was wrong, and that in the period 1974–83 the number of farm servants (*padials*) actually increased. Those from whom the assertion that unfree labour has been eradicated is most frequently heard are, unsurprisingly, government officials and right-wing politicians. Hence the claim made by the Maharashtrian Finance Minister during 1976 that 'the bonded labour system is not prevalent in Maharashtra' was followed by a flood of legal applications for the release of unfree workers, whose existence had been uncovered in surveys condicted by labour organizations in the state. As has already been noted in Chapter 4, much the same happened in Bihar, where the state government announced that attached labour was not unfree. There are numerous historical instances from other contexts of similar denials subsequently being shown to be false. In the case of the Mexican state of Yucatán at the beginning of the century, for example, many of the pro-planter apologists who dismissed as exaggerations the findings by Turner [1911] on the subject of debt peonage subsequently recanted, and conceded that his negative portrayal of unfree labour had after all been accurate [*Chacón*, 1986].

86. There are numerous instances of this process of rebonding workers in India, at many different conjunctures and contexts. It affected migrants within Bihar during the early decades of the twentieth century [*Pouchepadass*, 1990:19], and in the mid-1970s landholders in the same state refused to re-employ free bonded labour with the object of driving them into unfree relations once again [Joshi 1978]. In the case of eastern UP during the late 1960s, Sharma [1978: 165–6] reports that

These positions of labor are not necessarily inheritable from father to son, but indebtedness tends to tie the son to his father's *malik* as well and a bondage much like serfdom is imposed. One Bhumihar revealed to us that when one of his family's agricultural workers attempted to leave their service and support himself by driving a rickshaw, they beat him up and broke the rickshaw one night. After that, he returned to [his master's] service as a laborer.

87. In the case of bonded labour, many examples exist of successful opposition to abolition/emancipation as a result of class struggle conducted 'from above'. Throughout the nineteenth and early twentieth centuries, the legal eradiction in India of praedial slavery and/or debt bondage not only faced effective opposition from employers and/or landholders but grassroots implementation of existing statutes outlawing unfree relations was invariably blocked, circumvented, or simply ignored [*Grigson*, 1944: 217ff.; *Hjejle*, 1967: 96–7, 100; *Naidis*, 1981: 156–7]. Current obstacles to emancipation posed by 'from above' agency are perhaps nowhere better illustrated than in the following observation made during the early 1980s by a grassroots activist in Madhya Pradesh ('The Burden of Freedom', *India Today*, 15 April, 1983). 'The rehabilitation programme will never be permitted to work' he observed, 'it is too dangerous for local political interests. If thousands of bonded labourers start shouting for their rights, it will upset the status quo and the rural power structure. No politician in power would want it to succeed.'

88. See Brass [1993b].

89. There are numerous instances of the deployment by landholders of a discourse projecting weak-landlords/powerful-workers. Denying they were slaveholders, planters in the Mexican state of Yucatán claimed in 1906 that 'planters could not

prevent, even should they desire, freedom and progress from penetrating the plantation environment'. [*Chacón*, 1986: 102].

90. For an example of this view, see Haynes and Prakash [1991: 2, 17]. Echoes of this powerful-labourer/weak-employer discourse were evident in the claim made to an Indian government workshop held in New Delhi during September 1995 to consider the issue of unfree child labour that '[a] child who possesses the skill of carpet weaving or any other craft learned in the family is not a slave but a master'.

91. In ideological terms, the resulting power reversal amounts to a political inversion which licenses landholder discourse along the lines of 'they do not have to be protected from us; much rather, we have to be protected from them'.

92. For claims about the incompatibility between unfreedom and worker 'assertiveness', and consequently that the kind of transformation rural labour was experiencing must be proletarianization, see Breman [1985a: xxi; 1993: 309; 1996: 21, 217, 237, 255] and Jodhka [1994; 1995; 1996]. Because they too equate unfreedom with the *jajmani* relation, and casualization with the emergence of free labour, Wadley and Derr [1989: 106] claim in their restudy of Karimpur that by the mid-1980s bonded labour no longer existed. However, they fail to provide any evidence to this effect, and – like Breman and Jodhka – simply (and wrongly) assume that a non-permanent workforce is composed of free labour-power.

93. It is important to emphasize that the claim made here is not that capitalism everywhere and always attempts to introduce or reintroduce unfree labour, only that in the course of class struggle capital is quite happy to do this where and when necessary. The problem is that many of those who write about transformations in agrarian relations explicitly or more often implicitly adopt what might be termed a 'transition' paradigm. This belief in an unproblematic concept of progress is akin to the Whig interpretation of history, or the presumption that historically everything necessarily and automatically improves. In contrast to the concept 'transformation', therefore, which admits that just as unfree labour becomes free so the latter can in turn revert to the former, the concept 'transition' imparts the idea that the change from unfree to free labour is an once-and-for-all accomplishment. For this reason, it tends to downplay or discount the possibility that the inauguration or restoration of unfree production relations can be the outcome of employer success in the class struggle.

94. See Pouchepadass [1990: 14–15].

95. On this point, see Mukerjee [1933: 236]. It is clear from the formal distinction between slavery-for-life and slavery-for-a-fixed-period that even in ancient India unfreedom applied equally to non-permanent agrarian relations [*Adam*, 1840: 15; *Chanana*, 1960: 109, 115]. In this connection it should be noted that, historically, a limited form of freedom advantageous to the master was itself an aspect of both chattel slavery and bondage in India. Thus in 1829 one observer [*Saintsbury*, 1972: 12] commented:

> In regard to the treatment of masters towards their slaves, it does not appear to be incumbent on them to afford a subsistence to their slaves, except when employed on their business; and then it is on the lowest scale of allowance, being generally no more than two measures of paddy a day; *at other times their slaves are obliged to seek a livelihood at the hands of others, being bound only to return to their masters when the season of cultivation again commences* (emphasis added).

96. See Grigson [1944: 222, 225].

97. In the case of south India during the early nineteenth century, for example, slave-owners in Wynad insisted that an unfree worker who obtained employment on British-owned plantations handed over to them a part of the wage earned [*Hjejle*, 1967: 112]. Similarly, in Madhya Pradesh during the late 1930s 'a bond-servant who takes temporary employment on daily wages pays over the whole of his cash remuneration to his employer' [*Grigson*, 1944: 242]. The same was true of the antebellum American South, where plantation slaves were hired out by their own-ers to other employers [*Robert*, 1938: 198–99; *Starobin*, 1970: 128–37].

98. Noting that the 1950s Agricultural Labour Enquiry concluded that 97.7 per cent of agricultural labour families in Bihar were employed on a casual basis, Pouchepadass [1990: 15] nevertheless stresses that '[t]his percentage ... cannot be taken as the actual figure for free labour'. Even Harriss [1977: 237] accepts that, in the case of Tamil Nadu during the mid-1970s, both casual and permanent labour was attached (= unfree).

99. On this point, see Carter [1974: 72]. As has been noted in Chapter 2, a similar arrangement operated during the mid-1970s in the eastern lowlands of Peru, where rich and middle peasants participating in reciprocal labour groups con-tributed not their own personal labour-power to such exchanges but rather that of debt bonded landless workers or poor peasants in their employ.

100. On this point, see Despande [1982]. For similar examples from Orissa and Andhra Pradesh, see Nagesh [1981: A-111]. About the effects of unfree relations on rural labour employed in government-sponsored urban employment schemes in Maharashtra during the late 1970s Deshpande [1982: 50, 105] makes the fol-lowing observation:

    some workers were getting a better wage rate and were therefore reluctant to leave the work. The *sawkar*, however, appeared at the site and demanded that all those who were [bonded to him] should leave the project work and go back with him to work on his farm. It was interesting to see that none of the workers refused to go with him. The workers always prefer employment on the EGS [employment guarantee scheme] projects as it ensures honourable employment, regular and better wages and fixed hours of work. The working conditions on the *sawkar's* farm were reported to be 'inhuman' as the labourer had to toil for more than 14 hours and moreover the work was very strenuous indeed. With all this, the labourers followed him mutely. ... The creditor can permit the debtor to accept wage work elsewhere; however ... it was found that wages received on such works were appropriated by the creditor.

101. Issues of multiple/complex changes in the relations and conditions of rural employment (from free to unfree, from permanent to casual) and workforce identity (from male to female, from local to migrant) are considered in more detail in Brass [1997c]. For a case study from Andhra Pradesh of how capitalist farmers restructure the agrarian labour process by replacing the labour-power of men who refuse to work as bonded labour with the unfree labour-power of women, see da Corta and Venkateshwarlu [1999]. The latter outline a multiple transformation in the structure of rural labour: from one in which the fulltime jobs in agriculture are filled by a permanent workforce composed of men, to one where work of a similar duration is now done by women who are nevertheless tied labourers employed only on a casual basis.

8

Unfree Labour, Culture and Nationalism

Debates about the meaning of bonded labour have not been immune from the pervasive influence of the dominant ideological agendas of the 1990s. The sub-text of the latter is clear: since fundamental economic and political change is now widely regarded as unfeasible or undesirable, the main – or perhaps the only – form of empowerment available to poor peasants and agricultural labour at the rural grassroots is henceforth to be cultural, as manifested in the equally widespread celebration currently of different/distinct national/ethnic/ indigenous identities. At the centre of this 'new' theory about the kinds of change permitted to the Third World 'other' lies postmodernism, which questions the very existence/possibility of relational emancipation and economic development.

Accordingly, it will be argued that postmodernism propounds something akin to a form of 'cultural individualism', or the politico-ideological equivalent of bourgeois economic individualism, which – when combined with concepts such as 'resistance' and 'popular culture' – dilutes/downgrades/ dismisses unfreedom and creates a space for nationalist ideology. In considering the impact/implications of postmodernism, therefore, this chapter will focus largely on the agenda-setting texts about unfree labour in Asia and the Americas (by Scott, Taussig, Prakash and McCreery), since these demonstrate the epistemological overlap between postmodernism, 'everyday forms of resistance', 'moral economy', 'popular culture', agrarian populism and nationalist ideology on the one hand, and the combined discourses of unfreedom-as-economic-empowerment and unfreedom-as-cultural-empowerment on the other.[1]

What needs emphasizing above all is the politically charged nature of these discourses, in terms of assumptions and effects. Not only is the 'empowerment' of unfreedom frequently linked to an anti-socialist celebration of agrarian populist 'community', therefore, but such arguments tend to emanate from the right of the political spectrum. Unlike earlier exponents of unfreedom-as-economic-empowerment (such as Fitzhugh, Dew, Cardoso, and Phillips), of unfreedom-as-cultural-empowerment (such as the Southern Agrarians), and of a combination of the two (such as Calhoun), all of whom were clearly aware of the conservative politics structuring their own views, current advocates of these two positions (such as Harriss, Breman, Prakash and Scott) are seemingly unaware of the political lineages associated with this discourse.[2] Neoclassical economists (Fogel and Engerman, Bhagwati and Platteau) are exceptions in this regard.[3]

This chapter is divided into three sections, the first of which examines the assumptions structuring the unfreedom-as-cultural-empowerment framework, and in particular the claims made by postmodernism regarding worker 'assertiveness' based on 'hidden transcripts' and 'everday forms of resistance'. The second traces the epistemological continuities between the latter and the 'semi-feudal' thesis, agrarian populism and the discourse of nationalism. The connection between 'assertiveness', casualization and deproletarianization of rural labour, together with reasons why in the context of the global spread of capitalism a discourse equating unfreedom with economic or cultural 'empowerment' is politically disempowering, are all considered in the final section.

I

Unlike exponents of unfreedom-as-economic-empowerment, who stress the material benefits of bonded labour such as 'patronage' and a 'subsistence guarantee', those who adhere to an ostensibly different teleology (such as the Southern Agrarians and – more recently – Scott, Taussig, Prakash and McCreery), declare that the 'empowerment' experienced by these workers is mainly a cultural phenomenon. Like exponents of unfreedom-as-economic-empowerment, therefore, postmodern adherents of an unfreedom-as-cultural-empowerment framework maintain that it is possible for 'empowerment' to be realized within existing relational forms, regardless of whether these are feudal/capitalist, free/unfree or permanent/casual arrangements. And again like those who subscribe to unfreedom-as-economic-empowerment, the assumption is that a desire for 'empowerment' is the same as its realization.

Within a postmodern framework that links 'resistance' to the ideological plurality of the subject, 'popular culture' becomes identified with the 'voice from below', and action based on this accordingly constitutes an authentic expression of the democratic will. Consequently, anything and everything associated with its grassroots manifestation, now increasingly celebrated in that most fashionable form of power-exercised-from-below, the 'primordial' rituals (crowning/decrowning) associated with 'carnival', automatically becomes the embodiment of democratic expression.[4] The difficulty with this is that once the 'popular' is accepted as an *unmediated* construct (or the 'natural' voice of the people), it follows that what is desirable becomes whatever the 'popular' says is so; in short, a procedure that fails to ask precisely how such views are constructed, by whom, and for what political ends.

8.1 Unfreedom as Cultural Empowerment

Many of the original arguments advanced by Fitzhugh and Phillips in the defence of antebellum plantation slavery resurfaced during the 1930s in the discourse of the Southern Agrarians, whose nostalgic and idealized vision of a rural 'world-we-have-lost' was linked to perceptions of southern decline. Unlike the earlier apologists for slavery, however, the focus of the Southern Agrarians was on cultural identity, and they accordingly attempted to recuperate not just the pre-industrial values of a southern landowning class, but also a concept of slavery-as-cultural-empowerment.[5] The latter was invoked through a specifically agrarian folkloric image of 'popular culture' operating on the plantation, which served to emphasize both the benign nature of its regime and simultaneously the 'otherness' of black slave society in the antebellum American south.[6]

Much the same is true of the more recent variants of unfreedom-as-cultural-empowerment, such as the 'from below' agency on the part of unfree labour inscribed in culturally-specific forms of agency manifested in 'everyday forms of resistance' and 'survival strategies'.[7] In so far as it entails an 'adaptive' approach by an individual choice-making subject, the concept 'survival' is compatible with neoclassical economic theory. Within such a framework, moreover, there is an analogous progression in textual interpretation whereby 'survival' shifts rapidly from being an end in itself to being a *positive* counter-vailing aspect of the agrarian context under consideration (plantation, estate, rich peasant holding), a position which then links up with the neoclassical claim that rural workers actively *chose* such (unfree) employment, which consequently could have been neither exploitative nor oppressive.[8]

Significantly, the 'survival strategies' framework is in many ways similar to the notion of 'self-help' which structures much of the currently fashionable theory of grass-roots rural agency. The metamorphosis of 'popular culture' from a passive to an active historical role is thus linked to its being the source of self-empowerment mediating the 'everyday forms of resistance' associated with the work of James Scott.[9] The implication is that opposition to the existing social order derives from a hitherto undiscovered authentic grassroots voice (= 'popular culture', 'carnival'), which can be re-presented by post-modernism as a *de*politicized discourse untainted by discredited overarching metanarratives.[10]

Where resistance (= 'hidden transcripts') occurred on the plantation or estate system, so this argument goes, then the unfree relations of production structuring its labour process were consequently rendered unviable. From this position it is once again a short step to the neoclassical economic argument that, as workers could have made it non-operational had they chosen so to do, the continued existence in such contexts of unfreedom was the choice of the workers concerned, and thus non-coercive/non-exploitative and to their advantage.

8.2 Bonded Labour and 'Everyday-Forms-of-Resistance'

Although Scott claims that 'hidden transcripts' possess 'immanent possibilities', it transpires that these are no more 'empowering' than grumbling under one's breath about someone in authority outside the range of the latter's hearing, a process the disempowering nature of which is accurately characterized as 'letting off steam'.[11] It is, in short, a process of displacement, or nothing more than the recognition by the subject concerned of his/her own powerlessness in a situation that he/she cannot transform through this particular kind of agency ('assertiveness', 'resistance'). Scott recognizes but fails to confront this 'safety-valve' argument: namely, that masters/employers of unfree labour *allow* 'hidden transcripts' and 'sites of autonomy' because these are no more than play-acting and ersatz rebellion, and thus a way of avoiding the occurrence of the real thing.[12]

Insisting that open exchanges (= 'public transcript') between landholders and slaveowners on the one hand and slaves and serfs on the other are characterized by 'prudent' but 'misleading deference', Scott forgets that ruling class power is not only not threatened but actually confirmed and reproduced by such displacement, both in the realm of an inauthentic 'performance' in overt exchanges and a covert but authentic 'hidden transcript'. In support of his view, however, Scott asserts that 'the aggregation of thousands upon thousands of such "petty" acts of resistance have dramatic economic and political effects', an argument which conflates a desire on the part of an unfree worker to change his/her predicament with the actual capacity to do so, and as such is open to at least three objections.[13]

First, that by their very occurrence, such smallscale/everyday acts of 'assertiveness'/'resistance' generate for those who undertake them the delusion of progress that seemingly reinforces the notion of benign 'spaces', and thus consolidate the chimera of economic advance under existing systemic arrangements. Second, in doing so, 'assertiveness'/'resistance' also offers its subjects the excuse for postponing – or cancelling – a more fundamental reckoning with the system itself. And third, the view about the link between smallscale 'assertiveness' and systemic change cannot explain the historical coexistence of oppression and resistance: that is, why in the majority of instances 'assertiveness'/'resistance' neither culminated in attempts (successful or otherwise) at systemic overthrow, nor prevented slavery and other forms of unfreedom from enduring for centuries. Accordingly, to present the arena of the 'hidden transcript' as a potential/actual form of 'empowerment' is quite simply wrong.[14]

Some variants of Marxism also appear to subscribe to a notion of 'hidden transcripts'. Ironically, therefore, attempts by neoclassical economic historiography to combat negative portrayals of black slaves on the cotton plantations of the antebellum American South through arguments about 'positive' aspects of black *economic* participation/autonomy in the plantation system find parallels in attempts by left scholars similarly to challenge negative stereotypes by invoking positive images of a resilient black *culture* (= 'hidden transcripts') produced by plantation slaves themselves.[15] The difficulty faced by both these politically opposed viewpoints is that they license a discursive slide whereby the defence of blacks (implicitly or explicitly) may ultimately – as the case of Fogel and Engerman demonstrates – be transformed into a *celebration* of the plantation, and in particular its mode of unfreedom. This in turn opens up a theoretical space for anti-universalizing/decentered postmodern analysis: the latter objects to (and thus denies the efficacy/existence of) unfreedom on the grounds that, in the overarching metanarratives of colonial and capitalist discourse, free labour is privileged as the totalizing agent of universal progress.

8.3 Bonded Labour in (Postmodern) Theory

Emanating from linguistic/literary theory and rapidly colonizing the social sciences, postmodernism encompasses much of the discourse which permeates (among others) the subaltern studies project, the new social movements framework, resistance theory and the study of popular culture. A form of radical conservatism which denies the fixity of meaning (or the theory of the floating signifier), postmodernism licenses an anti-universalistic, indeterminate, decentering and thus a relativistic interpretation of social existence, in which no particular identity or political view is – or can ever be – privileged.[16] In rejecting totalising/Eurocentric meta-narratives, postmodernism also denies thereby the possibility of a universal process of socio-economic development embodied in the notion of history-as-progress (regardless of whether or not this is actually realised).

Such a view necessarily signals the abolition of the Enlightenment project, or emancipation as the object and attainable end of historical transformation (and along with it socialism and communism). The collective is replaced by the autonomous/fragmented individual subject, action is guided not by class structure/formation/struggle but by subaltern/elite identities and/or those based on ethnicity/gender/religion/region, revolution is replaced by resistance, and in terms of the desirable/(possible) outcome of such action socialism is displaced by bourgeois democracy – or worse. From within a postmodern epistemology, therefore, it is possible not merely to deny the necessity and/or desirability of changing an existing or traditional political order but also to espouse/endorse fascism with a clear conscience.[17] Most of these problematic aspects surface in accounts of bonded labour influenced by postmodernism.

In the postmodern framework of Taussig, for example, the debt peonage relation encountered in the Putumayo region of Peru during the Upper Amazon rubber boom of the early 1900s merges into and becomes nothing more than a specifically cultural manifestation of irreducible 'otherness'/difference.[18] Accordingly, unfreedom possesses only a discursive existence, linked to the construction by Amazonian colonists of a mythological/folkloric image of indigenous horror/terror (based on savagery/rebelliousness/cannibalism), and projected by them on to the tribal workforce they recruited/employed. Rather than connecting the existence of terror/unfreedom in such a context to struggles over the commodification of labour-power, however, and identifying thereby a specifically economic role for terror in the enforcement of unfreedom which in turn licenses the process of capital accumulation, Taussig deprivileges/banishes economics and reifies ideology.[19]

Unsurprisingly, Taussig opts instead for the non-economic/innateness of Foucault's postmodern concept of power, whereby the exercise of terror becomes an irrational end in itself; in short, a Nietzschean view of terror/unfreedom as chaotic, purposeless, and hence unchanging/unchangeable.[20] The resulting analysis oscillates uneasily between two competing discourses about debt peonage in the Upper Amazon region: one by Roger Casement condemning the use of unfree labour for rubber production, the other by employers supporting its use, and (because of 'epistemic murk') neither of which according to Taussig it is possible to categorize as true or false.[21] Like other revisionists writing about the Latin American *enganche* system, Taussig comes close not just to endorsing the 'lazy native' myth, but also to questioning both the actuality of terror – as distinct from the efficacy of discourse about this (= uncorroborated 'stories' which are believed, and thus possess a materiality regardless of whether or not they are accurate) – and ultimately the reasons for together with the existence of debt peonage itself.[22]

8.4 Bonded Labour as Empowering Cultural 'Otherness'

The more recent postmodern (re-)interpretations of unfreedom by Prakash and

McCreery not only attempt to give voice to the mute indigenous subject of Taussig's analysis, but in so doing push the problematic theorization of unfreedom structuring his postmodern framework to its logical conclusion. Since Taussig does not address the issue of how unfreedom was perceived 'from below' by the tribal worker, for him the question of a negative/positive perception of such a relation by the subject of labour does not arise, and consequently remains open. In seeking to answer precisely this question, and attempting to supply this missing voice-from-below, texts by Prakash and McCreery illustrate how a postmodern and revisionist concept of unfreedom in India and Latin America is compatible with the concepts 'popular culture' and 'resistance' theory.[23]

Just as Wiser and Breman (and others) invert the meaning of unfreedom by claiming that it corresponds to an economically 'empowering' form of 'patronage', so Prakash and McCreery invert the meaning of unfreedom by representing it as a culturally 'empowering' form of indigenous 'otherness', also an outcome of worker 'assertiveness'.[24] Accordingly, Prakash maintains that because it lacked a discursive form in the precolonial era, debt bondage in the Indian state of Bihar automatically had no relational existence.[25] For two symptomatic reasons, therefore, the anti-universalizing/decentered postmodern analysis of Prakash objects to (and thus denies the efficacy/existence of) unfreedom.[26] First, because it operated with a universal and enlightenment notion of slavery, the abolition of which was used by the British to equate colonialism with liberation. And second, that in the overarching meta-narratives of colonial and capitalist discourse, free labour is privileged as the totalizing agent of universal progress. Like neoclassical economic theory, which precludes a connection between capitalism and unfreedom by redefining the latter as free wage labour, postmodernism dismisses bondage as a figment of western discourse, thereby banishing it from indigenous accumulation and simultaneously reifying unfreedom as a cultural 'other'.

Equally unsurprisingly is the fact that the *jajmani* relationship is regarded by Prakash as a form of 'patronage', or a specifically 'cultural form of power relations'.[27] For Prakash, therefore, 'the use ... of indigenous categories such as *jajman* and *kamin* allow an empirical access to real life that categories such as landlords and labourers do not provide easily', thereby (re-) privileging 'indigenous' categories over the discourse of political economy ('indigenous' = real, political economy = unreal), a procedure which he himself criticizes with regard to colonial/nationalist/Marxist views on the free/unfree labour distinction.[28] Because for Prakash the postmodernised concept of unfreedom is theorized in Foucaultian terms of a 'corporeal' relationship, whereby power takes the form of physical control by a landholder over the body and not the labour-power of the worker, it is easy for the absence of actual violence to be interpreted as evidence for the benign nature of bondage (= the 'economy of gentleness') and thus the non-existence of unfreedom.[29]

8.5 Politically Non-Specific Empowerment: Arguments Against

Against such a view it is possible to make a number of points. To begin with, not the least of the many difficulties which confront the postmodern framework of Prakash is its refusal to countenance any alternative to a specifically bourgeois/individualist concept of freedom, thereby ignoring completely the socialist approach in which unfreedom is negated by collective freedom based on class. As with Taussig, moreover, this symptomatically postmodern outside-of-discourse/language-there-is-nothing view is a palpably idealist position. And again like Taussig, Prakash fails accordingly to distinguish between an *ideology* of unfreedom (which may indeed have been absent, although precisely what constitutes proof of this remains problematic) and *de facto* unfreedom, which had a material existence that predated colonialism (regardless of whether or not it was identified by its subject as such).

Similarly, the difficulties which beset Prakash as a result of his rejection of a specifically economic concept of free/unfree labour are illustrated by his inability to theorize the connection between unfreedom and the market. Hence the resort to moralizing when confronted by their coexistence, as evidenced by his view that 'the market, it turns out, was nothing but a santitized name given to certain sordid events', and his reference to the market as a 'euphemism' for coercion, whereas in economic terms the concept 'market' is actually an *antithesis* of coercion.[30] His inability to understand why the segmentation of the labour market frequently occurs along ethnic or gender lines derives from a similar cause.[31] Since on the one hand it involves the demobilization of workers' struggles by transforming/deflecting consciousness of class into (false) ethnic/national consciousness and conflict, yet on the other to probe the surface appearance of ethnic/national/gender identity is forbidden to postmodernism, the underlying ('foundational') reasons for segmenting the labour market is not a question that can be posed within such a framework.

This problem keeps coming back to haunt Prakash. Notwithstanding the claim that hierarchical inversion in oral tradition was a form of 'resistance' practiced by unfree labour in the southern part of Bihar in eastern India, therefore, he finally concedes that, after all, it might just be the case that 'the resistance contained in oral traditions was not particularly significant; they may have made the burden of bondage a little easier to shoulder, moderated the impact of hierarchy, but did little to change the "real" condition of the Bhuinyas ... one may say that the oral traditions deluded the Bhuinyas into thinking that they were reconstituting hierarchy and labour relations when, in fact, they did nothing of the sort'.[32] In other words, what is idealized as a form of 'resistance' may amount to no more than a contextually/historically specific form of false consciousness.

Once the postmodern framework of Prakash has conceptually decoupled agararian relations from their material (= 'foundational') base, it becomes possible not merely to deny the existence/efficacy of power-exercised-from-above (= class rule) but actually to invert this: social relations of production thus recast become instead evidence of power-exercised-from-below (= 'assertiveness'). When combined with non-class-specific concepts such as 'everyday forms of resistance' and 'popular culture', therefore, the actions/beliefs imputed to agricultural workers and unfree labour can be (re-) presented by postmodernism as proof not just of the fractured/tenuous or even non-existent character of ruling class power but also of a corresponding process of worker empowerment.[33]

Even the existence of a 'from below' form of cultural autonomy, however, does not preclude the fact that such 'assertiveness' may serve different and opposed class interests, and thus license the very economic oppression and exploitation which postmodernists regard as its 'other'.[34] This is a question that Marxism asks, but one that proponents of unfreedom-as-cultural-empowerment tend to evade or not to pose. In contrast to Marxist analysis, therefore, postmodernists such as Prakash equate cultural autonomy with 'from below' agency, and thus assume that it is automatically a form and process of grass-roots empowerment. The result is that rather than examining how – and why – landholders on occasion also effect control over their workforce through these non-economic aspects of social existence, the latter are nowadays more usually presented simply as part of an unproblematically empowering 'popular culture'.[35]

Another symptomatic text in this regard is that by McCreery, where the culturally-based 'resistance' theory of Scott is combined with a 'survival strategy' framework in order to invert the meaning of unfreedom on coffee plantations in Guatemala during the late nineteenth century. Despite noting that '[f]orce, the coffee planters reasoned, was what the Indian understood, force would do, and force was what the Indians got', that '[l]abor recruiters and state agents in villages jailed workers, beat and defrauded them, kidnapped their wives and children, and burned their houses', that from the 1870s 'the state ... had the ability to deliver effective and immediate violence to the countryside', and that '[l]ife on the run and cut off from ... the community, ... was precarious ... [Labour contractors and village authorities], pressed to deliver labor, ... increasingly took their search for [workers] into every corner of the municipality, making evasion more difficult', McCreery nevertheless claims that the state was powerless to enforce unfreedom on the indigenous population.[36] For this reason, he theorizes the debt bondage relation in a positive fashion, as a mechanism that enabled rural workers 'to force from their employers as much money as possible'; accordingly, bonded labour is subsumed by McCreery under the rubric of 'culture' which – along with folk tales, dances, religious ceremony and ritual – becomes yet another form of unproblematically successful 'resistance' on the part of indigenous communities.[37]

This revisionist position, in which unfreedom is regarded by McCreery as evidence of the enhanced bargaining power of agricultural labour (= worker 'self-empowerment'/'assertiveness'), is virtually indistinguishable from the postmodern views of Taussig, Prakash and Scott. In many ways, these different attempts to revise the meaning of unfreedom constitute a new variety of functionalism. The old functionalism of Durkheim and Parsons maintained that the survival of a particular institutional form (such as religion) was linked to its capacity to satisfy basic societal needs, thereby contributing to what was perceived as social stability; as critiques pointed out, however, this amounted to a framework in which institutions were functional-for-those-who-rule.

By contrast, the new functionalism of the 'survival strategies' theory, 'moral economy' and postmodernism argues that the continued existence of institutional forms such as indenture and debt bondage is similarly linked to their ability to meet basic social needs, but this time not of the subjects but rather of the objects of rule: that is, unfreedom as a relationship that is perceived as being functional-for-those-who-are-ruled. This, it will be recalled, is precisely the claim made by Fogel and Engerman in what amounted to a defence of plantation slavery in the antebellum American South.

II

It is a (much ignored) truism that any attempt to conceptualize worker 'empowerment' must begin by addressing the issue of the socio-economic context in which such 'empowerment' is effected, and hence the limits imposed by systemically distinct political meanings of the concept concerned. For this reason, a general, politically non-specific concept of 'empowerment' is inadequate, and cannot be regarded as sufficient for closing-off the question about what is desirable as a solution to the problem of unfreedom. What, for example, is the benefit which accrues to the agrarian working class (as distinct from individual labourers or categories of labour) from freedom achieved under capitalism? The position taken here is that the attainment of freedom has to be considered on a collective (= workers-as-a-class) basis in relation to socialism, and not simply in individual terms (= workers-as-individuals) under varieties of capitalism.[38] Hence the scepticism about claims of worker 'empowerment' accomplished as a result of a transition from unfree to free labour; as long as the latter is confined to (and defined theoretically in terms of) a capitalist mode of production, the true achievement and extent of worker emancipation must remain problematic.[39]

Whereas liberalism and Marxism both privilege free labour, each draws a different political conclusion from its presence. Liberals regard free labour as an absolute form of 'empowerment', as a vindication of capitalism, and thus its apogee. For Marxism, by contrast, free labour signals only the possibility of transcending capitalism en route to socialism. Marxism therefore privileges free labour only as a means to a particular end: namely, the achievement of socialism, a precondition of which is the ability of workers to combine/act collectively as a proletariat.[40] Developments such as deproletarianization or the recuperation of an idealized village community based on 'moral economy' or 'patronage', which hinder, undermine or reverse proletarianization are accordingly not – and, indeed, cannot be – perceived by Marxism as evidence of worker 'empowerment'. It is necessary to observe, however, that not all variants of Marxism share this view.

8.6 Unfreedom, Semi-Feudalism and Nationalism

In so far as some variants of Marxism continue to insist on the absence from agriculture of capitalism and the unbroken dominance of 'semi-feudal' relations, capitalism must for them remain a politically progressive force. Consequently, their 'Marxism' also remains trapped in the discourse of nationalism. Whilst the latter is perfectly compatible with conservatism, populism and neo-populism (and, indeed, is their political *raison d'être*), the continuing support for nationalism and/or nationalist political discourse in a context of global capitalist development is – or should be – incompatible with Marxism. For an illustration of the difficulties raised by this issue it is necessary to look once again at the symptomatic way in which Patnaik's views about bonded labour are supportive of a nationalist discourse.

Patnaik's argument is that only advanced economic development along the lines of metropolitan capitalism will lead to proletarianisation, and that basically this is the reason both for the continued existence of unfreedom in underdeveloped ex-colonies like India and for the necessity in such contexts of passing through a bourgeois democratic stage. The crux of the problem is, as always, a political issue: whether or not socialism should be postponed until after a 'pure' capitalist stage has been ushered in, by an equally 'pure' democratic bourgeoisie using correspondingly 'pure' (= free) relations of production. The political corollary of the 'semi-feudal' thesis, therefore, is that it is necessary to wait for the arrival of an as-yet-to-be-realised 'pure' form of capitalism before attempting a transition to socialism.

Not the least of the difficulties faced by Patnaik's espousal of the necessity of a bourgeois democratic stage as the only 'pure' form of capitalism that licenses revolution are the contrary examples of Russia in 1917 and China in 1949.[41] Like post-1947 India and many other ex-colonial nations in the Third World, agriculture in Russia and China on the eve of revolution was characterized not only by a low level of productive forces when compared with metropolitan capitalism (Europe, North America), but more importantly the accumulation occurring in these contexts was based on the existence of 'feudal/semi-feudal remnants', or precisely those unfree agrarian relations which Patnaik insists must be eliminated prior to a revolutionary upsurge.

The question, therefore, is how does 'semi-feudalism' (= landlord capitalism) change, and into what is it transformed? The answer given by Patnaik appears to suggest that in the case of India it will be replaced by a bourgeois democratic stage, in which peasant proprietorship reigns supreme. In other words, for Patnaik the abolition of landlord capitalism (= the Prussian path) will lead to peasant capitalism (= the American path), in the process realizing the classic two stages theory of agrarian transformation whereby one form of capitalism (unbenign, landlord, undemocratic) is replaced not by socialism but by another 'pure' form of capitalism (benign, peasant, democratic).[42] In such a two stages pattern of transformation the duty of socialists is to press not for socialism but rather to support elements of the 'progressive' national bourgeoisie and to argue for the redistribution of land on an individual basis to smallholders (= 'repeasantization').[43] About this view the following three observations are in order.

First, and rather obviously, the two stages theory of agrarian transformation ignores the existence and effect of capitalist restructuring. Hence the former identifies while the latter denies the existence of an economic and political distinction between landlord and peasant capitalists. In contrast to the two stages theory, therefore, the Marxist argument made in this book is that, for reasons of cost and discipline, rich peasants no less than landlords engage in restructuring the agrarian labour process and thus also seek to replace free labour with its unfree equivalent. Consequently unfreedom is just as acceptable to those elements of the 'progressive' national bourgeoisie who according to Patnaik would emerge in the democratic stage as representatives of 'pure' capitalism.[44]

Second, where capitalism already exists, arguments in favour of land redistribution in the form of individual peasant smallholdings creates a political and ideological space for agrarian populism (see below). And third, Patnaik's position appears to be no different from the kind of political conservatism traditionally associated with the CPI (Communist Party of India), for whom India continues to be a 'semi-feudal' nation in the agrarian sector of which there are similarly no 'pure' capitalist relations, and the absence of which accordingly precludes a transition to socialism and thus continuing political support for capitalism – in its (fictitious) pursuit of a 'progressive', 'pure' and national identity. Relevant here is the fact that the political object of Frank's attack on the 'myth of feudalism' was the extreme political conservatism of leftist parties in the Third World generally, and those in Latin America in particular.[45]

Like their counterparts in India, these political organizations preferred to enter alliances with the 'progressive' national bourgeoisie against international monopoly capital, in the naïve hope that, once in power, a national bourgeoisie would carry out the tasks of bourgeois democracy, and thus pave the way for a socialist transition that would result in its own dissolution.[46] It is to Frank's great credit that he saw this for the political nonsense that it was, a way by those on the left of avoiding class struggle aimed at the revolutionary capture of power and instead dabbling in a 'safer' but politically disasterous electoral opportunism based on compromise and class collaboration.

The situation faced now by many Third World countries is not one in which a national bourgeoisie that has somehow failed to carry out a transition to 'pure'/'progressive' capitalism must therefore be encouraged to do so by those on the political left, but one in which this class actually strives to prevent exactly this kind of transformation from happening. In such circumstances it is pointless to wait for a democratic stage which capital can anyway do without, and which it not only never intends to establish but to which it is actually opposed.

Accordingly, Patnaik's claim about the necessity of striving for the achievement of a 'pure' capitalist stage which will permit the realisation of the tasks of social democracy – amongst which will be the effective abolition of debt bondage – is quite simply misconceived. It is precisely because capital accumulation based on workforce restructuring that entails the reproduction of unfree labour (= deproletarianization) does not depend on the introduction of this bourgeois democratic stage that the 'tasks of social democracy' will consequently be achieved not by a national bourgeoisie but by the working class, a situation which (as Trotsky pointed out) puts socialism and not an intervening 'pure'/'progressive' capitalist stage on the political agenda.[47]

8.7 Agrarian Populist/(Conservative) Myths of Empowerment

It is not without significance that many of the claims supportive of unfreedom-as-economic-empowerment   and   unfreedom-as-cultural-empowerment   are linked epistemologically to the political discourse of conservatism, agrarian populism and nationalism, all of which are antagonistic to – and indeed in many respects the 'other' of – marxism and socialism.[48] Equally unsurprising is the fact that fear of the effects of emancipation on existing property rights is at the root of the ideological and political concerns expressed historically and currently by those on the right of the political spectrum.

At the close of the eighteenth century, therefore, conservative Junkers such as von der Marwitz defended the presence of agrestic serfdom in Germany by maintaining that unfree workers were no worse off than free counterparts, that 'the serf enjoyed social security from the cradle to the grave' (= 'subsistence guarantee').[49] Not only was serfdom not as coercive as its critics claimed, but what the latter unjustifiably dismissed in negative terms as opression and exploitation was in the view of von der Marwitz much rather a benign form of 'patronage', and thus for its subject an economically advantageous relation. Such arguments invariably concluded with a warning that, since the abolition of serfdom would licence a 'from below' challenge to all other existing forms of property in German society, emancipation should be resisted.

In the case of pro-slavery apologists such as Fitzhugh and Phillips, their arguments about the economic benefit slavery conferred on its subject (= 'subsistence guarantee', 'trickle down' effect) were structured in turn by the view that the plantation not only constituted a non-capitalist institution within the United States which provided its unfree workforce with a refuge from wider capitalist system, in the process representing a 'natural' social order (= 'community') based on a coincidence of economic interests between master and slave, but also – and most importantly – acted as a bulwark against the spread of and need for socialist ideas.[50] In contrast to industrial capitalism, the argument went, the master/slave relation was a non-coercive/benign form of patron/clientage: like conservative Junkers, therefore, apologists for the southern plantation insisted that it provided an albeit unfree workforce with a 'subsistence guarantee'.[51] And again like their German counterparts, southern conservatives defended the agrarian tradition against Northern capitalism on the grounds that the latter would generate a socially disruptive process of class struggle leading to the eventual destruction of the 'natural' social order which its supporters believed the system of plantation slavery to be.[52]

Another defence of antebellum Southern 'community' and 'otherness' that also fuses with nationalism structures the pro-slavery discourse of Calhoun. For the latter, therefore, 'community' is synonymous with class: unlike populism, which maintains that because class is non-existent 'community' embraces everyone, Calhoun accepts that class exists and argues that it must be protected as such.[53] One defends ruling class interests by denying these exist, the other by acknowledging them. Not merely was Calhoun an effective exponent of ruling class 'otherness' by combining a defence of the economic basis (= property rights) of its political power with appeals to an overarching, democratically-constituted national identity which enjoyed divine sanction, therefore, but in his case the threat to property rights was seen to emanate ultimately from unfree labour.[54]

The significance of his pro-slavery discourse lies in its political conclusions. Invoking the existence of a 'concurrent' or 'constitutional' majority, consisting of a numerically minority 'community' with interests distinct from those of the 'absolute' or numerical majority, Calhoun argued that it was the political role of the democratic state to protect the former from the latter.[55] Ostensibly a politically progressive recognition of 'minority rights' within a larger context in which the numerical majority represented an actual/potential political threat, Calhoun's argument was actually a defence of existing property rights of the planter class, by invoking its minority status against reforming and thus hostile majorities.[56]

Most significant, however, is the fact that his argument licenses a discursive fusion been the pro-slavery position and nationalism. Antagonistic to natural rights philosophy, Calhoun maintained not only that economic and political progress was premissed on inequality but further that the only unifying ideology in such circumstances was nationalism.[57] In his view the self-interest of a numerical majority in a nation composed of two kinds of 'community' that were socio-economically unequal could only result in conflict, while the fact that their own interest is protected confers on those slave-owners who enjoy 'minority rights' political status a disinterestedness that enables them successfully to mobilize and lead the nation.[58] As Calhoun himself expressed this, it is only the 'concurrent'/'constitutional' majority (= the numerically minority planter class) which is able to unite 'the most opposite and conflicting interests [blending] the whole in one common attachment to the country'.[59]

Agrarian populist discourse resurfaced during the 1930s in the nostalgic and idealized vision of a rural 'world-we-have-lost' espoused in the United States by the Southern Agrarians. As in the case of Fitzhugh and Phillips, the rejection of progress generally and industrialization in particular was linked to the fear of socialism and communism, each of which was seen by the Southern Agrarians as the inevitable outcome of capitalist development.[60] Again like pro-slavery apologists, the Southern Agrarians regarded smallscale subsistence agriculture – undertaken during this era by black sharecroppers, many of whom were subordinated by peonage – as a politically desirable, historically traditional and culturally 'natural' form appropriate to the southern economy and society, the 'other' of both finance capital and socialism.[61]

8.8 Populist/(Nationalist) Myths of an Empowered Third World 'Other'

Many of these arguments have also been deployed with regard to India. What remains significant about the idealized analysis by Wiser of the Hindu *jajmani* system, therefore, is not the numerous and trenchant criticisms of this, nor even that his positive interpretation reproduces all the stereotypes associated with the pro-slavery argument, but the fact that it is structured by a populist belief in the desirability of reproducing in India a traditional village community. This belief informs Wiser's idealized perception of the *jajmani* relation, which is accordingly presented by him as the vindication of an eternal and ancient principle, as a specifically Hindu and essentially benign form of exchange operating in village India between landholders and the landless, a transaction whereby the latter obtain resources from the former and in turn provide them with labour-power.[62]

Symptomatically, Wiser contrasts the disadvantages of urban existence with what he perceives as the advantages available in the village community in the form of the *jajmani* system. Urban contexts are characterized by the exercise of power and the existence of wealth, both of which in his view are the inevitable outcome of unequal economic transactions in such locations. By contrast, the exchanges that occur within the context of the village community are not just equal but also of non-material for material resources: accordingly, Brahmins seek spiritual and not material power, which they obtain as a result of providing resources for their labourers.[63] For Wiser, therefore, not only do rural employers (unlike their urban counterparts) refuse to take advantage of workers' need for credit but agrestic unfreedom is also equated by him with a form of job security denied to those who are employed in urban contexts.[64]

Other and more recent exponents of the argument that bonded labour constitutes 'patronage' and a 'subsistence guarantee' not merely share the same epistemology as Wiser but – like their eighteenth and nineteenth century European and American counterparts – are in some instances explicitly nationalist and/or anti-socialist in their political outlook.[65] This is particularly true of Srinivas, who essentializes/reifies village India as a repository of an harmonious and 'authentic' indigenous 'otherness', and thus both adopts and advocates a typically populist approach of 'learning from the people'.[66] Not only are traditional Hindu institutions such as caste and religion defended by him against criticisms from what he dismisses as a secular/rationalist Marxism but Srinivas also appears to approve of the politically reactionary RSS, the VHP and the BJP, because they 'protect ... the interests of Hindus, Hinduism and India'.[67]

Suspicions about the an analytical convergence between agrarian populist visions of an harmonious village 'community' and the views about unfreedom-as-economic-empowerment as embodied in texts by Breman and Harriss are not dispelled by the fact that each subscribes to a 'moral economy' framework. Both equate 'depatronization' with the erosion of what they infer is an historically benign 'patronage'/servitude/feudalism by a systemically maleficent calculation/freedom/capitalism, and 'moral economy' refers to the the attempt by those affected to reverse this development. Applied by historians to contexts in which economic growth generates agency by small-holding (= middle) peasants that is premissed on the reassertion by them of pre-capitalist custom/practice regarding consumption, the concept 'moral economy' invariably applies to petty commodity producers harkening back to a mythical golden age. Although Harriss has attempted to circumvent this objection by claiming that 'moral economy' is not a backwards looking invocation of traditional rights to subsistence but rather a form of trade unionism, it is clear that he is mistaken in this belief.[68]

That the 'everyday-forms-of-resistance' framework associated with Scott also possesses affinities with agrarian populism is evident from an earlier text by him, in which much of the theory prefiguring the 'resistance' framework is already present. There Scott argues that peasant societies everywhere are traditional and thus closed economic systems, governed by the politics of scarcity, or what he terms a 'constant-pie' orientation: that is, a zero-sum situation which assumes rigidly fixed or 'natural' shortages.[69] Accordingly, rural society in his view remains largely outside of and impervious to the capitalist system, both the process and effects of socio-economic differen-tiation are contained, and traditional culture survives intact.

The epistemological link to agrarian populism is unmistakeable. Such a framework casts all petty commodity producers in the role of a pan-historical, stereotypical non-accumulating peasant proprietor (the Chayanovian peasant family farm, in other words), the basic 'other' of development theory and socialist planning strategy. For Scott, therefore, peasants are economically backward largely because they want to be (= empowering 'choice'/ 'assertiveness'), because of non-economic reasons (= culturally empowering 'resistance'), and because of reasons to be found within rural society itself. His 'everyday-forms-of-resistance' theory refers simply to the kind of rural grass-roots agency exercised in pursuit of these objectives.

Much the same is true of Prakash's essentialist argument that colonialism made very little impact on India, and that as a result there remained underneath a 'real' India largely undisturbed by its coming/going.[70] This of course permits him not only to reify and celebrate an indigenous discourse as an authentic 'other', resisting economic development successfully, but also to reclassify agrarian relations such as debt bondage as part of these indigenous institutions and discourse. In short, not as unfreedom (= an economic relation) but rather as part of this underlying and eternal 'otherness' (= distinctive cultural practice) that characterized a 'natural' form of 'community' in rural India which antedated and survived colonialism. In so far as it posits the existence historically of a non-economic and culturally innate identity, such an analysis – like that of Scott – cannot be other than supportive of nationalist ideology.

III

Not only is worker 'assertiveness' neither new nor an indicator of the emergence/consolidation of proletarianization, therefore, but there is also an additional reason for questioning the perception by postmodern and 'resistance' theory of politically non-specific forms of worker 'assertiveness' as an unproblematically empowering form of grassroots agency. That unfreedom-as-economic-empowerment, unfreedom-as-cultural-empowerment and 'assertiveness'-as-proletarianization are not simply components of a politically irrelevant ivory tower discourse, unrelated either to current debates about or to the realities of economic development, is evident from their connection with the current agenda of the neo-liberal political right.[71]

The reasons for this are not difficult to discern. Accordingly, the dominance of currently fashionable interpretations both of unfreedom as its 'other' (= freedom) and of workforce agency as grassroots 'empowerment', derive in part from the need of the (nationalist) inheritors of colonial power to have a 'usable past' (a history purged of its 'black legend').[72] More important is the fact that the epistemological complicity of this discourse about worker 'empowerment' – in both its economic and cultural manifestations – with neo-classical economic theory, with agrarian populism with conservative ideology, and with nationalism, has licenced the global deployment by international/national capital of unfree labour in the furtherance of workforce restructuring during the period after the Second World War.

8.9 Unfreedom and Post-War Capitalist Development

From the mid-1970s onwards, a decline in transport and communication costs has resulted in a corresponding decentralization and fragmentation of the industrial labour process, as capital has relocated production both within and between social formations.[73] Accordingly, restructuring has occurred both in metropolitan capitalist countries and also in so-called Third World contexts, where the response of employers to increased levels of unionization has been a similar process of workforce decomposition and recomposition.[74] Under an accumulation project geared largely to export led economic growth, therefore, the historical link between the expansion of a home market and capitalist development has been broken.

Consequently, domestic capital formation is no longer constrained by having to ensure that profit margins are compatible with the continued ability of its own workforce to consume, since accummulation is now focussed on the international market. There is accordingly in theory no specifically economic limit below which wages can be forced, and it therefore becomes possible even for a national bourgeoisie to utilize low-paid workers employed on a casual/temporary basis who are also subordinated by unfree relations of production.[75] In the medium or long term, this trend merely accentuates the overproduction/underconsumptionist crisis of capital at a global level, in that capital everywhere is required to adopt the same cost cutting procedures in order to remain competitive and sell its commodities abroad. The end result is that consumption shrinks as producers everywhere are deprived of their markets. In the short term, however, cutting wage costs by using unfree labour maintains or enhances profitability.

One crucial result of such workforce decomposition/recomposition has been a process of displacement/replacement with regard to existing jobs, rather than – as is frequently claimed by those on the political right – a net increase in employment, albeit with low pay and poor conditions. Hence an important consequence of labour process fragmentation coupled with deskilling is that employers are able not only to locate (or relocate) production in economically backward rural areas but also to recruit a workforce in these contexts. The connection between unfree labour and agrarian restructuring becomes clear when situated within this framework of workforce decomposition/recomposition. It is precisely in such circumstances that it now becomes possible to combine the most advanced forms of technology with 'green' labour subordinated by what are still interpreted as 'pre-' or 'non-capitalist' relations of production.[76]

Another is that when it involves national/regional/ethnic/caste distinctions, this kind of restructuring also enables employers either to block or curb an unfolding proletarian consciousness among existing local workers. The utilization of the reserve army of labour not as an addition to the existing workforce but rather as a substitute for (and thus competitors with) the latter has dire consequences for the development of politico-ideological activity and organization associated with proletarianization. Even in the case of a union-ized and militant workforce, therefore, a defensive response to restructuring which involves the introduction of cheap unfree migrant labour can take the politically reactionary form of racism.[77]

8.10 Divide et Impera: Unfreedom, Culture and Nationalism

In these circumstances, the target of claims about politically non-specific but economically empowering worker 'assertiveness' is frequently workers of an 'other' national/ethnic/cultural/gender identity. When undertaken by employers, the thinly-disguised ideological object of workforce decomposition/recomposition along ethnic lines is to divide and rule, or the reproduction of a 'from below' discourse about 'otherness' designed to dilute international working class opposition to the global spread of capitalism. This in turn creates an ideological space for those on the political right, in metropolitan capitalist and Third World countries alike.

In metropolitan capitalist countries this takes the form of the argument that, as immigration and/or competition from the Third World threatens the living standards of workers, they should unite with employers of the same nationality to demand tariff protection and immigration controls. Much the same is true of so-called Third World countries, except that here workers are encouraged to unite with their own capitalist class in pursuit of these very same jobs by demanding free competition.[78] In short, a reaction that not only undermines what should be international working class solidarity by splitting labour along ethnic/national lines (thereby encouraging racism), but also one that is the stock response of those on the political right to capitalist crisis.

Neither does it come as a surprise that arguments identical to those encountered in postmodern/populist discourse, about the innateness, the desirability, and the empowering nature of cultural 'otherness', together with the kinds of agency ('assertiveness'/'resistance') such a discourse advocates, are now being deployed by those on the political right to defend the employment of unfree labour in the so-called Third World. This, for example, was the kind of reasoning deployed by carpet manufacturers and their supporters in India during the mid-1990s to justify the continued employment by them of unfree child labour.[79]

The latter involved an attempt to construct a relay in statement shifting the debate about unfree child labour from the economic sphere, where there was always the danger of it being categorized as exploitation and oppression, to that of 'culture'/'tradition'/'nation'/'family', where the same relational form could be depicted in an altogether more benign way (unfreedom = not-economic-but-cultural-relation, carpet weaving = tradition = traditional art = culture = sacred, child labour = 'family tradition' = the-domain-of-the-'natural'). Symptomatic of this process was the insistence by some employer representatives that carpet manufacturing in India has always been and is merely a 'cottage industry' based on 'family tradition', that child labour used in this situation could not be categorized as bonded labour, and further that this kind of smallscale economic activity 'is an age-old handicraft of India that finds [its] way in the world market carrying with it the rich heritage and culture of the country'.[80]

Another employers' organization accepted that child labour in the carpet industry was indeed unfree, but nevertheless justified its existence and continuation in much the same terms: namely, that it was a specifically Indian form of cultural 'otherness', both the weaving process and its production relations being described as a 'rich cultural heritage' embodying 'traditional skills' and thus a 'national treasure' which was emblematic of 'Indian tradition' itself. Perhaps the most explicit example of this kind of nationalist discourse was the proclamation that '[t]he need of the hour is to save the child-craftsman [sic] from the clutches of his self-proclaimed saviour who as an alien is intolerant of other people's cultural values and is bent upon destroying age-old Indian traditions ... '.[81]

Similarly, at the European Union and Asian summit in March 1996, heads of government in the former were warned by their counterparts from China, Japan, South Korea and the ASEAN countries not to raise the issues of cheap labour, child labour and poor working conditions in the latter contexts on the grounds that these were 'cultural' issues specific to the nations concerned.[82] To attempt to apply universal standards on child labour, it was argued, was a Eurocentric imposition on Asian countries of inappropriate (= 'other') cultural values.[83]

In much the same vein, Jagadish Bhagwati, a neoclassical development economist, has suggested that legislation which outlaws child labour is a discriminatory practice that is anti-competitive, and thus an obstacle to free trade. Accordingly, he endorses the use of child labour, which in many so-called Third World countries is unfree, since in his view it rightly permits those employers who use it to undercut and outcompete those who do not, a situation of competitive advantage which many less developed countries generally – but not always – have over metropolitan capitalism.[84] What is particularly significant about this is the way in which such exploitation is justified: claiming that 'diversity of labour practices and standards is widespread and reflects ... diversity of cultural values', therefore, Bhagwati – like the heads of government at the Asia/EU summit and the postmodern texts considered above – defends unfree labour in the name of a culturally-specific form of national 'otherness'.[85]

8.11 Conclusion

Not only have arguments in defence of slavery and serfdom tended to coincide historically and contemporaneously with ones about the economically/culturally advantageous and thus 'empowering' nature of unfree relations, but this concept of grassroots 'empowerment' has frequently been reproduced from within an agrarian populist vision about the innateness/desirability of rural 'community' structured by an harmonious/idyllic mututality. In epistemological terms, therefore, over the nineteenth and twentieth century the ideology defending slavery, serfdom and bonded labour in socio-economic contexts as diverse as Europe, the Americas and India has been remarkably consistent, incorporating narratives about unfreedom-as-economic-empowerment and unfreedom-as-cultural-empowerment.

The epistemological linkages are not difficult to discern. An important consequence of the neoclassical economic historiographic perspective of revisionists such as Cotlear, Bardhan, Shlomowitz, Platteau, Pastore, and Fogel and Engerman is that everything which happens in the labour market is defined as 'choice'. It is in this assumption about uncoerced agency on the part of the (willing) subject that the origins of neo-liberal claims by Bhagwati regarding the nationally-specific cultural 'otherness' (= culturally-empowering nature) of contemporary forms of unfree labour in the Third World are to be found.

This is turn licenses workforce decomposition/recomposition, using unfree labour, a process whereby an agrarian bourgeoisie pre-empts proletarianisation through the deproletarianisation of the rural workforce (= decomposition of the working class by means of restructuring), with the object of depoliticizing/cheapening/disciplining it. The latter is in political terms doubly disempowering: not only does it permit the segmentation of the labour market but in ideological terms it enables capital to invoke/reproduce a discourse about the primacy and/or innateness of national/ethnic identity.

For different reasons, the 'semi-feudal' thesis is similarly endorsing of nationalism: it central claim is that the next necessary step in agrarian transformation is to a 'pure' form of capitalism in which capitalists would be 'progressive', as a result of which unfree labour would then be eliminated. To the extent that it encourages support for a 'progressive' national bourgeoisie, therefore, such a view licenses the reproduction not only of what is conceptualized as a benign form of capitalism but also (and thereby) of nationalist ideology.

That the 'everyday forms of resistance' framework is not as radical as it claims is clear for at least two reasons. First, it ignores the fact that much grassroots agency nowadays presented simply as part of an unproblematically empowering 'popular culture' is in many instances no different from accommodation, and thus not merely compatible with but actually supportive of exploitation. And second, like the 'semi-feudal' thesis, it also epistemologically downgrades or banishes revolutionary action, or what for Marxism is the only authentically system-transforming kind of working class agency.

By equating proletarianization with worker 'assertiveness', the impression is conveyed that a process of working-class empowerment has been effected. In this regard, the conceptualization of worker 'assertiveness' is akin not just to the notion of worker 'choice' informing neoclassical economic historio-graphy but also to the 'everyday forms of resistance' framework associated principally with the work of Scott, whereby any/all grassroots action in the so-called Third world is seen as necessarily and fundamentally empowering, as agency capable of politically transforming the existing socio-economic system.

Although this kind of framework does not – indeed cannot – deny the presence of 'from above' coercion and control, much the greater emphasis is placed by it on 'from below' agency', often to the extent of obscuring/negating the efficacy of the 'from above' response. The result is that 'from below' agency – which is necessarily constrained by the nature and power of the 'from above' response it elicits – tends to be depicted as more forceful, effective and system-transforming than it really is. When coupled with the claim that unfreedom is unenforceable, this kind of framework draws an implicit contrast between powerful workers and powerless and/or ineffective landholders. In short, it is a politically disempowering discourse which denies or downgrades the importance of 'from above' class rule, and by contrast identifies workers as those who not only undertake but in reality are also the ones who benefit from any struggle which actually takes place.

Much the same can be said of postmodern theory. It is impossible to under-stand the political impact of postmodernism on analyses of bonded labour and agrarian change generally without reference to the way in which it fuses with and is simultaneously reinforced by the concepts 'everyday-forms-of-resistance', 'moral economy', 'survival strategies' and 'popular culture'. The widespread adoption of the latter is due in part to the way in which such con-cepts challenge the notion of passivity by recognizing the voice and action of those historical categories (women, agricultural labourers, tribals, peasants) usually perceived as mute and/or dominated.

Given a postmodern teleology, whereby freedom is not merely linked to the discourse of colonialism but also and wrongly finds its closure in such a discourse, two things follow. First, a critique of freedom is incorrectly equated with a self-empowering critique of colonialism and capitalism. And second, a defence of freedom is misleadingly conflated with a defence of colonialism and capitalism. Such an framework overlooks the presence of an alternative political trajectory – also springing from the Enlightenment – which regards unfreedom as the the negation not just of bourgeois individualism but also of the collective freedom of the working class in a socialist context. But the latter is of course a transcendence the efficacy of which postmodernism denies, and consequently a form of freedom that it does not – indeed, cannot – recognize.

Part of the difficulty is that the concept 'false' consciousness is epistemologically impermissible within a postmodern framework. Since the latter not merely accepts but celebrates the plurality of the ideological, by definition no form of political consciousness can be categorized as 'false'. Accordingly, postmodernism rejects consciousness of class as an Eurocentric concept which involves an 'outsider' unacceptably imputing a politically appropriate, logically consistent and historically necessary set of universalistic beliefs to particular socio-economic agents. Without a concept of consciousness that discriminates between notions of 'true' and 'false' (which in turn entails the theorization of a *politics* that transcends the randomness of non-specific, amorphous conflictive practices), it becomes possible to identify each and every single components of activity (or existence) as yet another form of 'resistance'.

The politically disempowering nature of claims about grassroots empowerment effected as a result of what is a politically non-specific form of 'assertiveness' is evident from the way in which theoretical frameworks informed conceptually by unfreedom-as-economic-empowerment and unfreedom-as-cultural-empowerment create a space for nationalist ideology. In a sense this complicity is – or ought to be – unsurprising, since not only are Marxism and nationalism antinomic but the epistemological approaches of the texts concerned are also either openly hostile to Marxism (postmodernism, 'resistance' theory), openly supportive of capitalism (neoclassical economic historiography), or both. The significance of the latter emerges clearly when considered in relation to contemporary capitalism.

Post-war capitalist development has been characterized by a continuing relocation of production to less developed countries, where a reserve army of labour has formed as a result of the declining economic viability of peasant smallholdings. This has enabled capital generally to deregulate, divide and cheapen labour. The global response by international/national capital to increased competition, therefore, has been to restructure its labour process by means of workforce decomposition/recomposition, a process which in some contexts has entailed replacing free workers with cheaper 'green' labour composed of unfree/low-paid rural workers employed on a casual/temporary basis.

For national/international capital the economic logic is in both instances the same: since there is no need for local consumers, for competitive purposes wages can be decreased by whatever means possible, especially by deskilling and by the decommodification of labour-power, thereby eliminating or undermining trade union activity. Thus payment made to the workforce can be maintained or lowered without risk to the overall realization of surplus-value.

Combining in symptomatic fashion nationalist ideology with all the components of the discourse proclaiming unfreedom-as-economic-empowerment ('subsistence guarantee', job security) and unfreedom-as-cultural-empowerment (postmodernism, 'popular culture', 'resistance', 'assertive-ness'), neo-liberals such as Bhagwati are then able to argue that attempts at the political empowerment of an unfree workforce in the Third World based on universal notions – such as trade unionization – amount to an inappropriate Eurocentric cultural imposition by developed nations on less developed ones.

Not only is this presented by those on the political right as an infringement of 'natural' national sovereignty, but the object of invoking 'spurious' univer-sal labour standards against different cultural practices such as child labour is also depicted in terms of a populist/nationalist discourse, as an endeavour by 'rich'/'white'/ex-colonizing countries to prevent 'poor'/'non-white'/ex-colonized nations from competing to their best advantage in the global market.

NOTES

1. It must be emphasized that unfreedom-as-cultural-empowerment and unfreedom-as-economic-empowerment are by no means mutually exclusive frameworks, much rather the opposite. The distinction between them is largely one of emphasis. Although his analytical focus is on unfreedom-as-cultural-empowerment, there-fore, Prakash [1990a: 178] – like Wiser, Breman, Harriss and Platteau – also regards the debt bondage relation as a form of 'patronage'. In a similar vein, Harriss [1994] proclaims his affinity with postmodernism, which itself structures the unfreedom-as-cultural-empowerment views of Prakash. Fogel [1989: Ch.6] also endorses the unfreedom-as-cultural-empowerment view

2. When, for example, Harriss [1994: 186] protests that the kinds of view associated with the unfreedom-as-economic-empowerment and the unfreedom-as-cultural-empowerment positions are 'not a romantic notion dreamt up by conservative intellectuals' he merely underlines the extent of his own lack of awareness, not just about those who have advanced them in the past but also about rightwing neo-liberals (such as Bhagwati) who currently espouse them. Alternatively, Harriss may simply be in denial: since he now subscribes to the 'new institutional economics' of the North (Harriss, Hunter and Lewis [1995]) – the mentor of neo-liberals such as Fogel [1989], Shlomowitz [1997] and Pastore [1997], all of whom interpret unfreedom as a benign/'empowering' relation for its subject – it is unrea-sonable to suppose that Harriss any longer experiences real political discomfort with neo-liberal theory.

3. Whatever the criticisms made of neoclassical economists, they cannot be accused of presenting their views as anything other than a defence of the market economy, and hence capitalism itself.

4. For the carnivalesque as a form of power-exercised-from-below, see Bakhtin [1984: 122ff.]. Unsurprisingly, Scott [1990: 175] identifies the carnival as resistence incarnate, 'the ritual location of uninhibited speech ... the only place where undominated discourse prevailed, where there was no servility, false pretences, obsequiousness, or etiquettes of circumlocution'. Needless to say, such a view overlooks the extent to which carnival not merely fails to challenge but actually reinforces and justifies the existing social structure, and is therefore more

accurately categorized as a form of social control (or power-exercised-from-above). For the way in which the carnivalesque in India has on occasion served to reinforce communalism/nationalism, see Cashman [1975] and Freitag [1989].

5. For this point, see Twelve Southerners [1951: 55, 59], where the components of an authentically southern 'popular culture' are clearly delineated in the following manner:

> The South has been rich in the folk-arts, and is still rich in them – in ballards, country songs and dances, in hymns and spirituals, in folk tales, in the folk crafts of weaving, quilting, furniture-making ... If the Southern [artistic] tradition were an industrial tradition, it would deserve to be cast out rather than cherished. It happens, however, to be an agrarian tradition.

6. Perhaps the best-known and most powerful projection in the realm of 'popular culture' of the kind of society and values the loss of which the Southern Agrarians lamented is the film *Gone With the Wind* (1939).

7. See, for example, Lieten, Nieuwenhuys and Schenk-Sandbergen [1989].

8. For just such a positive theorization of 'survival' by female indentured labour on plantations in Fiji, see B.V. Lal [1989: 179].

9. For more recent examples of the ubiquitous 'everyday-forms-of-resistance' theory, see not only Scott [1985; 1986; 1990; 1992] but also Colburn [1989], and Haynes and Prakash [1991]. This 'resistance' framework has now been extended to include not only individual actions undertaken by subordinates with the object of obstructing/denying the process of material appropriation (for example, poaching, footdragging, pilfering, arson, dissimulation, flight) but also those multiple forms/contexts which in Scott's view similarly obstruct/deny the process of cultural/ideological subordination (linguistic disguises, ritual codes/agression, taverns, fairs, rumours, folktales, songs, gestures, jokes).

10. Scott [1990: x] has admitted that his theoretical framework 'shares with postmodernism ... the conviction that there is no social location or analytical position from which the truth value of a text or discourse may be judged'.

11. Regarding the 'immanent possibilities' embedded in what he terms 'hidden transcripts', see Scott [1990: xii]. Accepting that he privileges 'dignity and autonomy' over 'material exploitation', Scott [1990: xi] characterizes 'hidden transcripts' as the way in which: 'slaves and serfs ordinarily dare not contest the terms of their subordination openly. Behind the scenes, though, they are likely to create and defend a social space in which offstage dissent to the official transcript of power relations may be voiced.'

12. The attempt to deal with the 'catharsis through displacement' argument is outlined in Scott [1990: 184–7], his conclusion being that '[i]t would be more accurate ... to think of the hidden transcript as a condition of practical resistance rather than a substitute for it'.

13. See Scott [1990: 192].

14. In his latest text, Scott [1998] extends the concept 'hidden transcripts' to include virually any historical form of anti-state grass-roots activity or agency, thereby rendering 'resistance'/'assertiveness' meaningless in terms of politics.

15. For the economic empowerment of plantation slaves in the antebellum South, see Chapter 5. For examples from the other end of the political spectrum of a 'culturalist' defence of slaves (*not* slavery), see James [1980: 173–90] and Genovese [1975].

16. Unless it is to be regarded as innate, immutable, and therefore part of 'nature', any

concept of 'difference' has – and can only ever have – its origin in a class structure which first assembles and then ideologically consecrates it. By conferring a 'natural' fixity on 'difference', postmodernists who reify/essentialize it simultaneously naturalize the (bourgeois) socio-economic order which constructs this (historically-specific notion of) 'difference' in the first place.

17. On the connection between postmodernism, linguistic deconstruction, decentering/depriviliging and fascism, see Brass [1997a].

18. See Taussig [1984; 1986], whose analysis is aimed at Casement's account of Putumayo (for which see Singleton-Gates and Girodias [1959: 201–315]).

19. At some points Taussig maintains that in the Upper Amazon region a market for labour-power was absent, and is therefore correspondingly dismissive of Casement's attribution of terror/unfreedom to a scarcity of workers; elsewhere, however, he appears to accept not merely the existence of labour shortages but also the economic irrationality of destroying scarce workers and that the object of terror was in fact to increase rubber production [*Taussig*, 1984: 475–7, 488; 1986: 52ff.]. In other words, terror combined with unfreedom possessed a twofold economic object: to intensify output on the one hand, and on the other to warn potential absconders of the consequences of flight/disobedience. As in the case of the tobacco plantations in the Dutch colony of Sumatra, therefore, executions and floggings of tribal workers in the Putumayo region took place in the labour process itself [*Breman*, 1989b; *Taussig*, 1984: 475–7].

20. See Taussig [1984: 491, 495; 1986: 27, 69, 442–3].

21. See Taussig [1984: 470, 494]. This equivocation on the part of Taussig is prefigured in the similarly postmodern ambiguity of de Man [1979: 293], who notes:

> It is always possible to face up to any experience (to excuse any guilt), because the experience always exists simultaneously as fictional discourse and as empirical event and it is never possible to decide which one of the two possibilities is the right one. The indecision makes it possible to excuse the bleakest of crimes because, as a fiction, it escapes from the constraints of guilt and innocence.

The outcome of this framework, in which language is decoupled from material reality, is ethical relativism, which in turn naturalizes horror/terror/(unfreedom). That such a position licenses complicity with fascism is confirmed by the cases not only of de Man himself but also of Heidegger and Blanchot.

22. See Taussig [1984: 490, 494; 1986: 60, 65–6] for his views on the 'lazy native' and his questioning of the actuality of terror/unfreedom.

23. See Prakash [1990a; 1990b; 1992a; 1992b] and McCreery [1990]. The main target of this postmodern critique is Marxism in general, and in particular its privileging of 'the economic' , dismissed by Prakash [1992a: 2, 3, 11, 12, 13, 14, 15–16, 21] as 'foundational'. Unsurprisingly, Prakash [1992a: 3, 11, 21, 34, 35–6] also regards the Eurocentric/Enlightenment/Emancipatory economically-based notion of class differentiation as inapplicable to the Indian countryside, and rejects this in favour of an approach which emphasizes the 'cultural' formation of labour.

24. That 'assertiveness' is frequently no more than 'existence' is conceded by Prakash [1992a: 43] when he notes that: 'reading dissonance in the cultural forms which landholders and labourers lived their social lives is ... difficult because, as anthropological studies of village India amply demonstrate, transactions imbued with

such institutions as caste hierarchy and patriarchy appear to have the status of unquestioned habits, as matters of everyday routine'.

25. See Prakash [1990b: 197–8].
26. See Prakash [1992a: 4,16–17].
27. See Prakash [1992a: 37].
28. See Prakash [1992a: 1, 6, 38].
29. See Prakash [1992a: 6, 16; 1990a: 185].
30. See Prakash [1992a: 29,31].
31. See Prakash [1992a: 31ff.].
32. See Prakash [1991: 170].
33. This is true, for example, of the attempt by Prakash [1992b] to inscribe 'resistance'/'assertiveness' into the spirit cults of south Bihar. A not dissimilar problem confronts those neoclassical economic historians who attempt to address the role of culture in the reproduction of unfree relations, except that in this case the difficulty is perceived as being not so much unfreedom-as-cultural-empowerment as its negation: that is, an inability on the part of slaves to manifest an 'authentic'/ 'empowering' and a specifically slave cultural 'otherness'. Arguing for the existence of a close connection between political power and culture, Fogel wrongly concludes that a denial of the latter amounted to a politically disempowering process of deculturalization. 'Perhaps the most important point that has emerged from the work of cultural historians', observes Fogel [1989: 400], 'is the intimate connection between political power and culture. As long as slaves were subjected to virtually unrestrained personal domination, were denied citizenship, and were highly constrained in economic opportunity, they were unlikely to achieve a large degree of cultural self-identification.' By focusing on whether or not masters dominated slave culture, therefore, Fogel [1989: 399] confuses two distinct phenomena. The question should be whether or not masters dominated via slave culture, not slave culture itself. Accordingly, it was unnecessary for masters to shape slave culture in order to exercise dominance, merely to allow this to exist. The self-identification unfree labourers on the antebellum plantation were allowed/encouraged to develop was as slaves, and the cultural autonomy they exercised underwrote this perception: slaves have their own culture, and it is the culture of slaves. Had they been other than slaves, they would – like urban workers – have developed a culture consonant with this. In other words, Fogel identifies a problem where none exists.
34. Perhaps the most obvious example of this is the apartheid system in South Africa, where the discourse about an ethnically empowering 'otherness' was deployed in order to segment the labour market along racial lines with the disempowering object of legitimizing the institutionalization of an unfree black workforce. One of the few socialists to oppose this on political grounds was S.P. Bunting [*Roux*, 1944: 35], who in 1917 warned against the dangers of white racism among the labour movement in the following uncompromising (and still relevant) terms:

It is a challenge to the socialists who recognize the class struggle; a sneering intimation to the underpaid, undereducated, unskilled toilers that they need not hope for the cooperation of the whites, who, on the contrary, will oppose their efforts at emancipation; a wilful decision of the 'trustees' of the working class movement to sell it for a 'place in the sun', where they clink glasses with magnates, with the d-d [blacks] as their footstool ... The wages system for ever, they chuckle, provided ours are high and yours are low; an injury to one is an injury to all – unless he's black. Down with capitalist exploitation – of 'Europeans' only ... Fools! Do they [= the white working class] not see that they are tools in the hands of the capitalist, who flatters and pampers them not because he doesn't want cheap black labour, but because he does: who retains them as white boss boys, trading on their silly pride, while he educates the Natives eventually to oust them; who uses them not to keep the [black worker] out but only to keep him down ... .

35. Indeed, on occasion and for a variety of reasons, worker cultural autonomy can be extremely supportive of landholder power, which suggests in turn that 'popular culture' based on the ideology of non-class identity (gender, tribe, caste, region, nation) is not always an unproblematically 'from below' phenomenon. The disempowering way in which rural employers in Bihar utilize gender identity to reproduce unfree labour has already been noted in Chapter 4. There is also evidence from many parts of India, and especially from Punjab, Haryana and some parts of UP, that where it occurs the displacement by local workers by out-state migrants – either on a temporary or a permanent basis – is the reinforcement of an 'insider'/'outsider' polarity that splits working class ideological and organizational solidarity. This indeed may be one of the reasons for the rise of non-class identity politics among the ranks of rural labour in some of these contexts. The fact that on occasion parties of the left have been complicit with this merely compounds the difficulty. Even some exponents of a neoclassical economic historiography recognize this fact; for example, Fogel [1989: 399] makes the point that masters in the antebellum plantation south permitted/encouraged only those forms of cultural expression that fitted in with their own 'grand designs': namely, 'the creation of a new worker'. His epistemology, however, prevents him from pursuing the implications of this fact. Although cultural autonomy was indeed compatible with the economic objective of higher slave productivity, therefore, Fogel fails to mention the reason for this: divide-and-rule the workforce by emphasizing non-worker identity.

36. See McCreery [1990: 161, 164, 166, 168].

37. See McCreery [1990: 167, 169, 172]. For a similar claim linking the negation of bondage to grassroots resistance by rubber tappers in the Amazon area, see Weinstein [1983; 1986].

38. That a number of unfree labourers may in a few isolated instances actually like their situation is for Marxism irrelevant, since what matters is not this or that particular individual but the class. If the collective interests of the rural working class are adversely affected by the individual interests of a small number of unfree labourers, then the individual interests of the latter must necessarily be overridden by those of the former.

39. On this point see, among others, Grossman [1997] and Kössler [1997]. This is a corollary of the view that economic growth necessarily emancipates and thus 'empowers' workers. It cannot be without significance, therefore, that even as late as the 1970s arguments downplaying the effects of apartheid by liberals opposed to the imposition of sanctions against South Africa were based on assumptions about the efficacy of 'empowerment' achieveable under capitalism. Hence the assertion by Merle Lipton, among others, that as the economic position and bargaining power of black workers was improving, left to itself the process of capitalist development in South Africa would in time undermine the oppressiveness of

the apartheid system. As Legassick and Innes [1977] pointed out, such claims were not merely false empirically but could only be made by ignoring the fact that the profitability of accumulation in South Africa was premissed on the existence of a workforce that was unfree.

40. It is precisely the inability to countenance the significance of this step as a precondition for the transcendence of capitalism that constitues an obstacle for post-modern analyses of unfree labour. In the case of Prakash, for example, his post-modern teleology inevitably leads to a rejection of proletarianization as a desirable outcome for rural labour in India, since the conceptual origin of freedom and free labour-power stems from what for postmodernism is the doubly-tainted 'foundationalism' of Eurocentric/Enlightenment metanarratives and colonial discourse.

41. Chattopadhyay [1978: 238ff.] makes exactly this point, which Patnaik failed to answer.

42. The characterization by Patnaik [1995: 90] of the Prussian path of agrarian transition as one in which unproductive landlords employ bonded labour – but not for profit – is in marked contrast to an earlier view [*Patnaik*, 1978b: 101–2, 110, 113], when she maintained that such landlords were 'investing in land improvement, and producing for profit with hired labour', and further that during the colonial era India was following neither the Prussian nor the American path of agrarian transformation. Her initial characterization of the Prussian road suggests that landlords not only used free labour but also invested in the labour process – one of Patnaik's own criteria for capitalism – in order to generate profit.

43. Like Patnaik, Breman [1996: 242–3] also suggests that 'repeasantization' is a desirable political solution. The reformist politics to which this kind of argument gives rise were accurately described some 30 years ago by A.R. Desai [1984: 151–2] in the following manner:

All three [left] parties at present assume that the state structure which has been elaborated by the Indian bourgeoisie is in fact and can work as a neutral institution which can be utilized for both good and evil. All of them assume that the basic task confronting socialists is to rectify the errors committed by the ruling class. According to them, to pursue this task they should ... include in their programmes attempts at changing the personnel of the central and state governments, and demand association of non-government groups in framing national policies, and even the formation of a coalition National Government composed of members of different parties or composed of the best men in the country, irrespective of their party affiliations ... These parties are thus engaged only in the task of counteracting ills arising out of the implementation of bourgeois policy, of healing wounds caused by the Indian bourgeois programmes. They are not interested in organizing movements to destroy the perennial source of these evils, the very structure which is being generated by the Indian bourgeoisie.

44. The sample of 66 'relatively big landowners' interviewed by Patnaik [1978b: 109, 125–7; 1978c: 167] in 1969 contained a category of eight 'urban entrants' (or 'gentlemen farmers'), referred to by her as 'pure' capitalists, or those 'urban and monied people' from the bureaucracy, industry, or the professions, who had turned to cultivation because of its profitability. What is of particular interest here is that, in her initial contribution to the mode of production debate [*Patnaik*, 1978a: 75], she also observed with regard to the 508 adult male farm servants in her 1969 sample that on 'all except two holdings they were in some form of debt bondage',

which suggests that unfree labour was indeed employed by at least some of those in her category of 'urban entrants'. In terms of production relations, therefore, 'pure' capitalists appeared to be no different from the 'impure' capitalists in Indian agriculture who used 'semi-feudal' agrarian relations. Having put in a brief appearance in her early contributions to the debate, however, this category of 'urban entrants'/'pure capitalists' together with the implications for her argument of its production relations, vanished rather suddenly and mysteriously.

45. See Frank [1969a].

46. That it is not – nor has it ever been – the intention of any component of the Indian bourgeoisie to usher in a bourgeois democratic stage that would empower workers as workers has long been clear to many of those concerned with problems connected with an agrarian transformation in India, from Kalecki [1976] in the 1950s to A.R. Desai [1984] in the 1960s. On this issue Patnaik's views are predictably confused. Having conceded that 'no third world bourgeoisie ever has or ever is going to carry out ... the practical tasks of the classic radical bourgeois revolutions', and by implication accepted the theory of permanent revolution, she then asserts that the two-paths approach is nevertheless still relevant, as a consequence of which the 'semi-feudal characterization is appropriate' [*Patnaik*, 1995: 91–2]. Astonishingly, and the antithetical nature of their politics notwithstanding, Patnaik manages to subscribe to both views simultaneously within the confines of a single text!

47. This is in essence the theory of permanent revolution [*Trotsky*, 1962: 8, 12]: 'that the democratic tasks of the backward bourgeois nations lead directly ... to the dictatorship of the proletariat and that the dictatorship of the proletariat puts socialist tasks on the order of the day ... an uninterrupted ... revolution passing over directly from the bourgeois stage into the socialist [one]'.

48. As has been argued elsewhere [*Brass*, 1997a], the discourse-for of agrarian populism is supportive of rural-based smallscale uniform/harmonious/'natural' economic activity (artisanry, peasant family farming) and culture (religious/ethnic/national/regional/village/family identities derived from 'nature'). By contrast, its discourse-against expresses opposition to urban-based largescale industrialization (finance capital, the city, manufacturing, collectivization, planning, massification) and its accompanying institutional/relational/systemic effects (class formation/struggle, revolution, socialism, bureaucracy, the state), all of which are perceived by agrarian populism not only as non-indigenous/inauthentic/'alien' internationalisms imposed on an unwilling and mainly rural population by 'foreigners', but also (and therefore) as responsible for the erosion of hitherto authentic local traditions and values.

49. For arguments defending serfdom, which in late eighteenth century Germany was 'virtually indistinguishable from slavery', see Epstein [1966: 201ff.]. The same kinds of claims have been made by conservatives about other kinds of unfree labour elsewhere in Europe at this conjuncture. Hence the deployment by Hutt [1954] of an identical argument in defence of child labour used by British factory owners during the early 1800s, to the effect that masters were 'men of humanity', that such work was well-paid, 'wholesome' and light in nature, and that child labourers were 'free agents' (= 'choice-making' subjects) who were no less healthy than other children

50. The defence of slavery in the nineteenth-century antebellum South by apologists such as Phillips [1918; 1929; 1939] focused on what were perceived to be the

economic benefits conferred by the plantation on its slaves. For the argument that slavery is a 'natural' condition in Nature, see Phillips [1939: 125] and Tise [1987: 119 Table 5.7]. When combined with an anti-socialist discourse, this tradition-invoking and backward-looking anti-capitalism is revealed as nothing other than a reactionary form of agrarian populism. The sub-text is unambiguous: the price of industrialization was the accompanying growth of an urban proletariat, which was both politically disruptive and a bearer of 'alien' beliefs/values. Since capitalism inevitably leads to class war, and thus eventually to socialism, the avoidance of the latter is best served by remaining under a slave system. 'I believe', warned Fitzhugh in 1857 [*Wish*, 1960: 102, 124],

> that under the banners of Socialism and, more dangerous, because more delusive, Semi-Socialism, society is insensibly, and often unconsciously, marching to the utter abandonment of the most essential institutions – religion, family ties, property, and the restraints of justice. [...] As modern civilization advances, slavery becomes daily more necessary, because its tendency is to accumulate all capital in a few hands, cuts off the masses from the soil, ... and increases the necessity for a means of certain subsistence, which slavery alone can furnish ... .

51. For the defence of slavery in the antebellum American south both as an essentially benign kind of 'patronage', and thus as a desirable (and by inference a sought-after) form of 'subsistence guarantee' denied to poor white tenants in the rural south and industrial workers in the urban north, see Fitzhugh [*Wish*, 1960: 59] and Phillips [1939: 116, 154, 194–205, 212–15]. As Tise [1987: Ch. 5] demonstrates, in a variety of guises (for example, 'Labor protected against every contingency of life', 'Free [Blacks] more degraded than slaves') the 'subsistence guarantee' argument is an historically pervasive component of landholder discourse about planta-tions. Although these pro-slavery arguments refer specifically to the antebellum American south, it is clear from Dean [1976] and Tise [1987] that similar themes informed pro-slavery discourse on plantations in Brazil and the British West Indies. Much the same is true of Mexico at the beginning of the twentieth century: when accused by Turner [1911] of employing unfree labour, henequen planters in Yucatán similarly resorted to the 'subsistence guarantee' argument in order to justify the existence of debt peonage [*Chacón*, 1986: 108]. That rural employers in Tamil Nadu during the mid–1970s similarly invoked the 'subsistence guarantee' argument in order to justify low wages paid to their bonded labourers is clear from evidence contained in Harriss [1982a: 124], although the latter does not himself make this point.

52. Debates on slavery which took place during the 1840s were structured by an under-lying fear of a threat to property relations on which this 'natural' social order in the South depended [*Kaufman*, 1982: 121ff.]. Concerned that an emergent rural proletariat would ultimately demand the expropriation of the Southern landowning class, therefore, anti-abolitionists such as Cardozo and Dew advocated ruling class unity between Northern property owners and Southern planters in defence of slavery in order to counter a potential working class challenge to existing property rights throughout the whole of the United States. For the links between pro-slavery discourse and conservatism, see Tise [1987: 238–60].

53. Unlike populists, Calhoun [*Lence*, 1992] not only accepted the existence of class and class struggle but incorporated each into his conservative political framework. Whereas for populism 'community' is composed of those having the same

political interests, for Calhoun by contrast it is composed of those having different interests. In contrast to populism, which denies that class transects 'community', Calhoun insists that precisely because communities are not socio-economically homogeneous it is necessary to recognize both the presence and the political implications of this 'difference'/'otherness' within its context. Instead of extending the concept 'community' to cover different class subjects – inclusive of employer and worker or master and slave alike – he applies it in an exclusive way; a 'community' composed of employers or slaveholders co-existed with that formed by workers or slaves.

54. As Eaton [1965: Ch.IV] and others have shown, following the successful uprising in San Domingo during the 1790s, fear of slave insurrection remained a pervasive element in the concerns of the southern antebellum planter class.

55. For the differences between a numerical/'absolute' majority and a 'concurrent'/ 'constitutional' one, see Calhoun [*Lence*, 1992: 21, 23–4].

56. The protection of the existing property structure was enshrined in a broader and apparently innocent argument; namely, that no change affecting 'minority rights' should proceed without the agreement of the minority concerned. In other words, in the antebellum South no reforms based on forcible expropriation – such as slave emancipation and property redistribution – could be effected, either by the northern state or by the slaves themselves (= the 'absolute'/'numerical' majority) without the consent of the minority southern planter class (= the 'concurrent'/ 'constitutional' majority). In effect, Calhoun's argument amounted to a class veto on any 'from below' policy and action where this came into conflict with 'from above' political interests.

57. See Lence [1992: 43–4]. Not the least of the many difficulties with this argument is the fact that, having dismissed any such thing as 'natural rights', Calhoun in effect restores this very concept; namely, the 'natural' existence of socio-economic unequal ownership/control of resources that structure the prefiguring 'community' interests which for him give rise to 'minority rights', or what he terms a 'concurrent'/'constitutional' majority.

58. See Lence [1992: 26]. Completing the relay-in-statement, Calhoun [*Lence*, 1992: 30–31] is now able to marshall a number of seemingly powerful arguements. First, that the 'concurrent'/'constitutional' majority unites the nation, whereas a 'absolute'/'numerical' majority divides it. Second, that any government reflecting the interests solely of a 'absolute'/'numerical' majority is and can only ever be based on force. And third, that one incorporating/protecting the interests of a 'concurrent'/'constitutional' majority is by contrast based on compromise and also truely representative of the whole people. Since for Calhoun 'the voice of the people' is indistinguishable from that of God, it follows that electoral representation not based upon the views of the 'concurrent'/'constitutional' majority is not merely not self-government but a system without either national or divine support, and thus doubly illegitimate in political terms.

59. On this point see Lence [1992: 37–8]. The same text by Calhoun continues:

> By giving to each interest, or portion, the power of self-protection, all strife and struggle between them for ascendency, is prevented; and, thereby, not only every feeling calculated to weaken the attachment to the whole is supressed, but the individual and the social feelings are made to unite in one common devotion to country ... instead of faction, strife, and struggle for party ascendency, there would be patriotism, nationality, harmony ... .

60. That industrialisation was rejected by the Southern Agrarians largely because capitalism would lead to socialism and communism is clear not only from their own observations on this linkage [e.g., *Twelve Southerners*, 1951: 49–50; *Conkin*, 1988: 74–7, 174], from the perception of Marxism as their 'other' [*Conkin*, 1988: 98–9, 110, 112, 150, 160] but also from the fact that I'll Take my Stand was originally entitled 'Tracts Against Communism' [*Conkin*, 1988: 71].

61. The presence of unfree labour and smallholder peonage in the American south during this era is discussed in Chapter 5. For programmatic statements by the Southern Agrarians regarding the desirability of a back-to-the-land movement based on subsistence agriculture carried out on individual smallholdings, see Conkin [1988: 106, 110–13, 125].

62. Hence the claims made by Wiser [1936: 17, 136] about the *jajmani* relation that 'we have here a system which is very similar to or identical with the religio-socio-economic plan of occupations outlined 2,000 years ago by Hindu philosophers and law-makers', and also that '[t]he Hindu Jajmani System is a disintegrated form of the ancient Village Commune'. His conclusion [1936: 175] is both symptomatic and instructive:

> The Hindu Jajmani System represents an interrelationship built up on clearly defined function. It represents the organization of a community based on the Hindu belief that God 'assigned separate duties and occupations to each individual from birth', these duties being fixed as the functions of a father and mother in a family. Its strength in giving stability and psychical integration to Indian village communities through centuries is undisputed. It is demonstrated in what exists today in Karimpur [and] possesses many features which are the envy of modern rural communities today.

63. For this argument, see Wiser [1936: 162, 165]. Although a number of texts [e.g., *Srinivas*, 1987: 175; *Wadley and Derr*, 1989: 81] note in passing that Wiser was a Christian missionary, none attempt to link this fact to his idealized portrayal of the *jajmani* system. That the latter embodies the same kind of structure and replicates core elements of Christian belief/practice most certainly would not have escaped Wiser himself. It could be argued, therefore, that – like Christianity – the Hindu *jajmani* system is premissed on an unequal but functional/'natural' form authority/hierarchy, and one that (it is claimed) is recognized and accepted by all parties to the relationship. This hierarchy/authority is also underwritten socially and ideologically, both by its great historical antiquity and by religious practices/beliefs. Not only does the power of the *jajman* over his subordinates replicate that of God over humanity, therefore, but this inherent inequality is offset by a discourse which emphasizes egalitarianism: namely, both the benign nature of this power and the reciprocal exchanges it licenses. Unsurprisingly, the *jajmani* system also shares with Christianity the view that the benefits conferred on their respective adherents take the form of spiritual rewards. Hence the emphasis by the discourse of each on the realm of the sacred, as embodied in the renunciation of earthly (= material) existence, and the related processes of 'service' and 'self-sacrifice'. It is noteworthy that a parallel exists between this religious justification of bonded labour in India, and the supportive ideological role played by Roman Catholic discourse – particularly about fictive kinship – in the reproduction of the Latin American *enganche* system (see Chapter 2).

64. The contrast between evil-city and pure-village is evident from the assertion [*Wiser*, 1936: 110] that, where the conditions governing the availability credit are

concerned, '[i]n the city undue advantage may be taken of a man's adversity [but] in the village the jajman knows that it is his "kam karnewala" or his "kam karnewala's" sons who will serve him and his sons ... '. An employer's continuing control over the labour-power of a labourer who is permitted to work in towns on a period-specific or seasonal basis is depicted in similarly idealized terms: '[t]here are very few employees in cities'. Wiser [1936: 115] observes, 'who have so much freedom that they can leave their job, and yet keep it'. For other examples of the same kind of argument, see Wiser [1936: 186].

65. Writing about unfreedom in Asia, Leach [1967: 14–15] observes:

Class, caste slavery ... each of these words is liable to carry overtones which suggest the exploitation of the underprivileged by the overprivileged ... we need to be on our guard against initial prejudices of this sort. Marxism has so infected our thinking that we not only take it for granted that it is in the nature of modern society that there should be class struggle but we are also inclined to believe that unqualified equality, unqualified freedom and the utopia of a classless society are sensible political goals for all right-thinking men ... Freedom and classlessness are political ideas; they have no place in socio-logical analysis, which must necessarily be concerned with social constraints and status differences. The word slavery (as we use it today) suggests that we can readily distinguish between social constraints which are morally justifiable and those which are not. I deny this.

66. The idealized view held by Srinivas [1992: 9] regarding the harmonious nature of pre-colonial village India is evident from his claim that '[i]n recent years, caste has come to be seen as a divisive institution, but in traditional pre-British India, the castes of a village or small region, formed an interdependent economic and social whole, having certain common beliefs, ideas and values'. Hence the admiration he expresses [*Srinivas*, 1992: 146] for the 'powerful village headman' in Rampura because in his view this subject was 'a tremendous factor for stability and peace in the village'. He also attributes his advocacy of 'learning from the people' to an anthropologist's closeness to the village 'community', and accepts that 'the people he is studying, and their culture ... to some extent inhibits his becoming an agent of change' [*Srinivas*, 1992: 106–7]. Much the same kind of approach structures analyses of the peasantry in Latin America. For example, Andean peasant economy and 'verticality' are concepts applied to the organizational modalities of smallholders in the Peruvian highlands [*Fonseca Martell*, 1973; *Alberti and Mayer*, 1974]. 'Verticality' refers to exchanges between peasants, rural com-munities, or land-based kin groups occupying different Andean ecosystems, where survival not surplus is the object of production. Exponents of this view argue that such culturally-determined reciprocity, as embodied in traditional community institutions (*mink'a, ayni, compadrazgo*), constitutes an indigenous levelling mechanism which guarantees the subsistence of the rural population. It also prevents capital accumulation and peasant differentiation, and thus accounts for the continued existence of the Andean peasantry. For a more recent version of this argument, see Marglin [1998].

67. See Srinivas [1992: 5, 10, 11].

68. For this defence of 'moral economy', see Harriss [1994: 181ff., 188]. As the main exponents of the 'moral economy' framework themselves agree [*Wolf*, 1971a: xviii, xiv, 276ff.; 1971b: 60; *Thompson*, 1991: 188–9, 260; *J.C. Scott*, 1976: 189], 'moral economy' is a politically conservative discourse that is indeed tradition-

invoking, backwards-looking, and about peasant subsistence. Like post-modernism, the 'moral economy' position of Thompson [1991: 184ff.] allocates primacy to customs, traditions, culture, and practices as these already exist within the peasantry and the working class, a view which contrasts with that of Marxists who have tended to emphasize the backward-looking, politically reactionary and historically transcendent role of much of what passes for resistance based on an already existing 'popular culture' (racism, nationalism, religion). Lenin [1961: 349ff.], for example, warned against the opportunistic espousal/endorsement of spontaneous conflict 'from below' simply because this happened to be taking place, and emphasized instead the importance of party organization structured by a specifically political input into the formation of what would eventually become a consciousness of class.

69. For his 'constant-pie' approach, see Scott [1968: 94ff., 119ff.]. In many ways, he has not departed substantially from this theoretical analysis. Hence the myth of a stereotypically undifferentiated/non-accumulating, subsistence-oriented, resistance-engaging peasantry which pervades his current work, is prefigured in earlier views; on the one hand regarding a pre-given situation of 'natural' material scarcity (a view he shares with neoclassical economic theory), and on the other concerning the presence/role of levelling mechanisms (wealth traded for prestige) whereby actual/potential rich peasants are made to disgorge their surpluses by the village poor through carnivalesque redistributive rituals (fiesta, potlach), a process which can be perceived as evidence of successful resistance-from-below mediated in the form of 'popular culture'.

70. See Prakash [1992a: 18].

71. Those on the political right have long understood that, to be successful, any defence of capitalism must be based on the acceptability of the argument that it licenses worker empowerment. It comes as no surprise, therefore, to find that in his defence of capitalism against criticisms from economic historians such as Dobb and the Hammonds, Hayek [1954: 15–17] not merely invokes the 'subsistence guarantee' argument but maintains this is one of the benefits extended by owners of capital to the proletariat as a whole. More recently, the political provenance of discourse about unfreedom-as-economic-empowerment may be gauged by the fact that during the 1980s something akin to the 'security'/'subsistence guarantee' argument was deployed by rightwing opinion in the UK (see *The Guardian*, London, 2 Feb. 1989 and 15 July 1988). In the course of a House of Commons debate on proposals to abolish Wages Councils that protect low paid workers, therefore, a Junior Employment Minister in the Conservative government sought to justify the payment of low wages by arguing that 'a job is better than no job, and low pay is better than no pay'. Another Conservative MP observed similarly that: 'People have said they do not want to go back to Victorian sweatshops. Would we not be better off if the country was one sweatshop, hard at work instead of having three million unemployed?'

72. The creation of a 'usable history' has been one of the more significant political results to emerge from the combined impact of the *Time on the Cross* debate about chattel slavery in the antebellum American south on the one hand, and of the ubiquitous 'everyday-forms-of-resistance' framework structured by postmodern-ism on the other, each of which has reinforced attempts to revise the meaning of unfree labour in the United States, Latin America, India, and Australia.

73. See, *inter alia*, Fröbel *et al.* [1980], Cohen [1987] and Harris [1987].

74. This process of workforce restructuring has been most marked in Europe and the United States, where capitalist production has brought into being what Cohen [1987: 25ff.] describes as a 'regional political economy'. In the case of the United States, for example, this has involved at a general level the relocation of manufacturing from the eastern seaboard states (where the workforce is unionized and exhibits a high degree of political consciousness) to the Sunbelt states (where the incidence of workforce unionization and political consciousness is low). Even within the latter context, however, the accumulation process requires a continuous decomposition/recomposition of the workforce. So as to remain competitive in an increasingly global market, US agribusiness capital – both at home and abroad – has to raise profitability not only by installing new technique but also by constantly reducing labour costs. This it achieves through the importation of a deskilled captive immigrant workforce from neighbouring states, in order to undermine (or pre-empt) actual (or potential) organization/unionization on the part of existing labour (see Chapter 7).

75. The political constraint, in the form of struggle by the workforce to maintain or restore wage and consumption levels, remains, of course. But as the history of the last two decades of the twentieth century underlines, this political constraint is subject to constant and piecemeal erosion by an increasingly global capitalism.

76. On this point, Cohen [1987: 174–5] unnecessarily concedes that 'the balance of logic and evidence is behind those who argue for a dual labour market thesis, rather than those who adhere to a displacement argument ... [i]t is the case that workers with job security, good wages, a recognized skill and union protection are hardly likely immediately to go down-market to a job characteristically occupied by an illegal migrant, even if faced with unemployment'. What occurs here, however, is not so much well-paid/skilled/unionized workers refusing to go down-market, as low-paid/unskilled/non-unionized labour moving up-market. It is precisely in circumstances where the application of new technology results in deskilling that it becomes possible for capitalists to offer even up-market jobs either to the present incumbents at lower wages and poorer conditions or (more usually) to unfree migrants. This is exactly the kind of transformation to which Castells (cited in Cohen [1987: 111]) refers when he writes: 'A twentyfirst century capital and a nineteenth century [workforce] – such is the dream of monopoly capital in order to overcome its crisis.'

77. This, for example, was how the seeds of fascism were sown in Austria, when German workers attempted to protect themselves from economic competition in the labour market by Czech migrants [*Whiteside*, 1962]. For other examples, from the West Indies and Australia, of racism generated as a result of workforce restructuring – but not necessarily interpreted as such – see Beachey [1957: 109], Tinker [1974: 217, 218–19] and Hunt [1978]. Similar instances of indigenous working class racism involving Latin American labour include attacks against illegal Mexican immigrants to the USA during the 1950s [*Cohen*, 1987: 52–3, 129–30, 187, 193ff.] and against unfree Haitian immigrants during the 1980s by local free workers being displaced in the commercial agriculture of the Dominican Republic [*Plant*, 1987: 69–70].

78. In defence of the continued employment in the Indian carpet weaving industry of unfree child labour recruited from landless and poor peasant families in rural areas, just such a discourse – stressing the need for national ideological unity in the face

of economic competition from foreign carpet manufacturers – has been mounted from the mid-1990s onwards, not just by the employers themselves but also by their apologists and government officials. The following are typical examples of this discourse: '[the effect of restriction on the employment of child labour] is to kill the industry ... with an aim to deprive the livelihood of two million workers from downtrodden and weaker section of the society ... it will place us in a disadvantageous position against our competitors [for] whom there is no such restriction', 'Emergence of such a picture [child labour = unfree] in the overseas markets will not only tarnish the image of the country but will also damage exports', 'Any ban imposed [on exports] would completely destroy the carpet industry [and] would render at least 1.5 million adult workers of the carpet Industry unemployed [and] devastate 1.5 million familes', etc. For all the latter, see documents submitted by the All-India Carpet Manufacturers Association, the Carpet Export Promotion Council, and the Office of the Development Commissioner for Handicrafts to the Workshop on 'The Elimination of Child Labour in Hazardous Occupations', held in New Delhi on 13–14 September 1995, and organized by the Ministry of Labour for District Collectors and District Heads.

79. The importance for employers of the unfreedom-as-cultural-empowerment discourse is clear from documents submitted to a Workshop on 'The Elimination of Child Labour in Hazardous Occupations', held in New Delhi on 13–14 September 1995.

80. See Carpet Export Promotion Council, 'A Position Paper on the Problem of Child Labour in the Indian Carpet Industry', 30 December 1994; and also S.S. Shukla, 'The Child Labour in Carpet Industry – Its Different Aspects', both documents submitted to the New Delhi Workshop in September 1995.

81. See 'Position Paper on Problem of Child Labour in Carpet Industry', All-India Carpet Manufacturers' Association, and J. Jain, 'A Great Indian Tradition – Prospects and Perspectives: Employment of Child Labour in Carpet Industry', both of which were submitted to the New Delhi Workshop in September 1995. With the exception of CPM representatives, the Lok Sabha supported the call by a rightwing BJP member for the endorsement of similar views (see 'MPs Seek New Definition of Child Labour', *Indian Express*, New Delhi, 1 June 1995).

82. The fact that the economic crisis which affected Thailand, Malaysia, Indonesia, the Philippines, Korea and Japan during 1997, was caused in part by the continuing relocation of capitalist production to China, where the industrial reserve army of labour following deregulation/decollectivization has ensured cheaper and thus more profitable forms of labour-power, not merely upholds the accuracy of Marxist analysis but also puts to rest the oft-heard claim that it is the cultural 'otherness' of Asian capitalism which is the basis of its continuing and crisis-free economic development. Marxists can only smile when they contemplate the prospect of words being eaten by those [e.g., *Hawthorn*, 1991; 1993] who have long insisted on East Asian exceptionalism, and maintained that the stability of the Tiger capitalist economies not only confounded Marxist theory about economic crisis and infrastructural 'foundationalism' but also made them the only development model for the rest of the so-called Third World (and indeed metropolitan capitalist countries) to follow. Such views simply mimic the least tenable aspects of earlier and more sophisticated arguments, advanced by those like Jacobs [1958] and the populist Bellah [1957; 1970], that Japanese economic success was an Eastern variant of the Protestant ethic.

83. On the deployment at the Asia-Europe summit in Bangkok during March 1996 of a discourse about cheap labour as part of 'cultural otherness' – and thus off-limits to universals embodied in international standards – see Pilger [1996]. As is clear from an account of the Japanese and Chinese cotton industry written during the late 1920s by the General Secretary of the International Federation of Master Cotton Spinners' and Manufacturers' Associations, this kind of employer justification of low wages, poor working conditions and unfreedom in terms of 'cultural otherness' has a long lineage. Hence the observation [*Pearse*, 1929: 93] that: 'When investigating [labour] conditions in the Far East one has frequently to regard them with Eastern and not with Western spectacles, and particularly in the case of wages, hours of work, food amusement, housing, *so-called restraint of liberty*, etc.' (emphasis added). This rose-tinted picture of unfreedom as a culturally empowering form of 'otherness' contrasts markedly with the accounts provided by the young women employed in Japanese textile mill workers [*Tsurumi*, 1984; 1990], who not only regarded these same working conditions and unfree production relations as disempowering but also struggled (unsuccessfully) to transform them. During the last decades of the nineteenth century, the response of employers to strike activity by young women workers in the textile mills was to impose further restrictions on the freedom of the workforce. About this process Tsurumi [1984: 17] comments:

> Female workers ... initiated work stoppages and wild cat strikes. They did so especially during the 1880s and 1890s before the dormitory system became widespread and employer control tight ... The response of managers to such strikes was to build more dormitories for workers, to lock their workers more securely in these dormitories, to supervise them more thoroughly both on and off the factory floor, to strive to keep them too exhausted to unite and fight ... Such responses probably made strikes less likely to erupt spontaneously and harder to continue once they had begun ... As dormitories became an integral part of factory architecture, undoubtedly it became almost impossible for outside labour organizers to reach the women in the textile mills. But there is little evidence that the textile hands' "passivity" was anything but forced upon them by their employers.

84. Urged on by India, the non-aligned nations passed the Delhi declaration condemning metropolitan capitalist countries for threatening to boycott imports made by child workers, the 'conscience clause' in the GATT, a position endorsed by European and North American employers of this kind of unfree labour in the so-called Third World. An example of this emerged in a television programme about the employment of child labour in Tirrichipur, South India, called 'T-Shirt City' because of the large numbers of T-shirts made here for Sears in the USA ('Newsnight', BBC 2, 1 March, 1995). Local Indian managers interviewed agreed that the reason for the employment of children in the manufacture of T-shirts was because they were cheaper than adults and did not organize in unions. Unsurprisingly, the 'subsistence guarantee' argument justifying the employment of unfree child labour was also encountered in the same programme: on this occasion it was advanced by a German buyer who, lamenting the fact that children in Tirrichipur missed school, stated that their parents nevertheless needed the money child labour earned, and that by working and generating income children were simply reciprocating parental provision. The same buyer concluded by dismissing child labour legislation as a 'sentimental European luxury' which Third

World countries were unable to afford, thereby reproducing the 'cultural other-ness' argument advanced by Bhagwati.

85. For this view, see Bhagwati [1993; 1995: 28], whose argument against protection-ism and its 'interference' with free trade includes among its targets not just tariffs (= protection of national capitalists) but also labour legislation (= protection of national workforces), each of which is condemned for undermining free trade. The target of his most recent text – published by the Institute of Economic Affairs, a rightwing 'thinktank' – is the argument that, in the name of the desirability of uni-versal standards, international trade should take place on the basis of uniform (= international) working conditions. His view, by contrast, is that world trade ought to be conducted on the basis of the absence of such standards. Significantly, Bhagwati reproduces here the same kind of argument as did British imperialism during an earlier era, when it maintained that those who wished to apply universal standards of labour legislation in its colonies simply did not understand the extent to which these standards were inapplicable in a culturally 'different' context such as India.

Conclusion

On the face of it, unfree labour would appear to be an economic anachronism in a world that is dominated by the expansion of monopoly capitalism based not only on the free wage relation, advanced technology, greater mobility of labour and capital, but also on mass unemployment coupled with a trend towards job casualization in the form of sub-contracting and part-time working. Even acknowledged cases of unfreedom, such as the use of forced labour by each side during both world wars, the continuing existence of peonage and unfree migrants in the southern United States, together with an unfree black workforce under the South African apartheid system, can seem to be systemic aberrations, unconnected with modern capitalist production. This approach is itself compounded by the frequent tendency to categorize unprob-lematically as free wage labour all workers who are not (or are no longer) chattel slaves. Yet, as the cases presented throughout this book attest, much of the evidence points to the opposite conclusion: rather than an archaic relational form constituting an obstacle to (and thus destined to be eliminated by) capitalism, unfree labour is an integral aspect of both the initial and continuing accumulation process. This conceptual decoupling of capitalism and unfree labour is due in part to the influence of postmodernism and the current unfashionability of political economy.

Since political economy conceptualizes labour-power as the private property of the subject, and thus an actual/potential commodity over which its owner has disposition, it is the latter aspect – and only the latter aspect – which determines its free or unfree character. In so far as debt bondage or peonage entail a period-specific loss on the part of an indebted worker and/or his (or her) kinsfolk of this capacity personally to commodify their own labour-power, these production relations do not correspond to free wage labour as defined by political economy. Although important, all other considerations, such as the category of worker (migrant/local, permanent/casual) involved, the monetization or non-monetarization of payment received by the latter, the long- or short-term duration of employment, its continuous or non-continuous nature, the actualization or non-actualization of physical maltreatment, the heritability or non-heritability of debt itself, and whether or not workers are assertive or perceive such arrangements as empowering, do not of themselves characterize a production relation as free or unfree.

To some degree, therefore, the resurgence, academic dominance and theoretically problematic nature of culturalist 'new' (postmodern, resistance) theory about debt bondage is a consequence of abandoning either the definition of unfreedom advocated by political economy, or the methodological approach of the latter to the presence, meaning and systemic role of bonded labour. Many of the changes in agrarian relations and forms of consciousness and agency linked to them identified by culturalist analyses as 'new' developments have a long history, and are thus not in fact 'new'. And where developments are indeed new, they are not necessarily empowering. Unsurprisingly, when it unites with history, political economy confounds most of these claims about the empowering nature of unfreedom, its absence or decline, and the 'newness' of 'assertiveness' as an emancipatory trend.

The misrecognition/misinterpretation of unfree labour by the revisionist accounts criticized in the second part of the book also possesses its origin in problematic methodologies. These extend from the utilization of non-economic definitions of unfreedom not recognized by political economy, from which stems a misunderstanding of its historically/contextually specific connection with the process of class formation/struggle, to questions about the nature/accessibility of coercion, and a consequent failure to investigate the direct/indirect enforcement of debt-servicing labour obligations. It is these methodological deficiencies which are partly responsible for perceptions of contemporary unfreedom as, variously, a non-capitalist relation destined to be replaced with free labour, a method of converting smallholders into workers in order to create a market in free labour, an empowering relation preferable to free labour, or as a form of free labour itself. Such misunderstandings give rise in turn to false notions about the political efficacy of worker agency (empowerment, resistance, assertiveness), and the systemic (political, economic) changes consequent on this.

On the basis of case-study materials from fieldwork conducted in Peru and India over the 1974–90 period, and in contrast to most of the texts considered in the second part of the book, it has been argued that debt bondage is an unfree relation the object of which is to discipline (not habituate), control and cheapen labour-power by preventing or curtailing both its commodification and the growth of a specifically proletarian consciousness. It has also been suggested that unfreedom exists regardless of whether or not recruitment is voluntary, that currently it affects mainly landless workers, and that it applies as much to migrants as locals and to non-permanent as to permanent categories of worker. Bonded labour operates efficiently, even where debts are owed not by but to the worker (= reverse bondage, withholding wages), and where physical mobility (= beck-and-call arrangements, inter-employer debt transfers) or grassroots 'assertiveness'/'resistance' occurs. Moreover, it is enforced as effectively by forms of coercion (= direct and/or indirect pressures) operated from within the peasantry or rural labour – via actual/fictive kinship or caste networks – as by a landlord class or the state.

Again in contrast to many of the views examined in the second part of this book, evidence from Peru, India and elsewhere indicates that unfree labour is not just compatible with accumulation and even technologically advanced levels of production, but in certain situations agrarian capitalists actually prefer this to a free workforce. It is also argued that at a more general level the existence of unfree labour cannot be understood without regard to the process of class decomposition/recomposition (or restructuring) that accompanies class struggle, whereby free labour is transformed into its unfree relational 'other', and that consequently debt bondage can occur in both labour scarce and labour surplus areas (in the latter because rural workers have insufficient bargaining power, in the former because they have too much). Accordingly, many of those who become bonded labourers are workers who previously commodified their own labour-power, and thus ceased to be part of a proletariat. For this reason, unfree labour in Peru and India (and elsewhere) has been conceptualized as a process of *deproletarianization*, or the decommodification of labour-power that its owner had earlier offered for sale in an already-existing market for this particular commodity.

Historically and actually, the *enganche* system in Peru and attached labour in India constitute forms of debt bondage encountered in many different rural contexts throughout Latin America and Asia. Essentially, each consists of a relationship whereby cash or kind loans advanced by a creditor (usually – but not necessarily only – a landlord, a merchant, a moneylender, a labour contractor, or a rich peasant) are repaid in the form of compulsory labour-service by the debtor personally and/or by members of his domestic/affinal/fictive kin group (poor peasants or landless labourers plus spouses, sons and daughters, co-parents and godchildren). Since workers (permanent or seasonal, migrant or local) recruited in this manner lose the right to personally commodify their labour-power (in other words, to sell it on the open market) until the original or subsequently incurred debt has been cleared, it is impossible to characterize this kind of arrangement as free labour.

In the Peruvian province of La Convención, and also in the Indian states of Punjab, Haryana and Bihar, indebtedness not only affected poor peasants and agricultural workers but its structure and outcome was in most cases the same. Borrowing was undertaken by every category of rural worker (permanent/non-permanent, migrant/local), usually from a single creditor-employer or labour contractor, and most commonly in order to meet non-recurrent expenditure (marriage, illness, death). Such borrowing immobilized the labour-power of the debtor by preventing its owner from personally commodifying what in many cases was the only commodity its subject possessed. Although not necessarily interest-bearing, any loan which remained unpaid due to the illness, incapacity, death or flight of the debtor was usually inherited by the kinsfolk of the latter on an intra-or inter-generational basis.

Debt-servicing work obligations incurred in these circumstances, by permanent/casual locals and/or migrants, were all enforced either directly on the subject concerned or – more commonly – indirectly. The latter entailed recourse by a creditor-employer to the authority structure embodied in locally-powerful caste and/or actual/fictive kin networks, a process reinforced ideologically not only by religion and patriarchy but also by a discourse stressing intra-kin/caste 'reciprocity'/'obligation'/'duty'. In the case of Haryana, for example, this was possible because landholders threatened to deprive livestock owning households from access to fodder unless they in turn put pressure on local indebted workers belonging to the same caste to comply with debt-servicing labour obligations. By using bonded labour subordinated in this manner, agrarian capitalists in Peru and India retained continuous or beck-and-call access to and exercised better control over a workforce in a competitive labour market – where this would not otherwise be possible.

Accordingly, the function of debt bondage operated by creditor-employers in the agrarian sectors of La Convención during the 1970s, Punjab and Haryana during the 1980s, and Bihar in 1990 was increased control over and a reduction in the cost of *all* the components of their workforce. Both these objectives were achieved by constricting or eliminating the free movement of labour in the market. Thus, permanent local workers had either to accept wage cuts and more onerous work conditions or face displacement by cheaper migrant labour. Migrants who settled permanently in Punjab, for example, were prevented from either improving work conditions and wage levels through unionization or (perhaps more importantly) from making common cause with displaced local workers. Similarly, both local and migrant labourers who worked on farms for only part of the year were prevented by the debt bondage mechanism from selling their labour-power to the highest bidder at the most advantageous point in the agricultural cycle when they would otherwise possess the bargaining power to do this. As in the case both of Haryana and of La Convención in Peru, this transformation involved a restructuring process undertaken by capitalist producers, whereby the more costly (free) labour components of their workforce were replaced by less costly and more easily regulated (unfree) components.

The second part of the book examines and challenges a number of enduring and more recent stereotypes which inform much of the theory about the presence, meaning, and economic role of unfree labour in general and the debt bondage relation in particular, not just in Latin America and India but also in the United States, the Caribbean and Australia. These include the view that, where it exists, bonded labour is a non-capitalist relation, corresponds to a benign form of 'patronage', is characterized only by intergenerational debt, does not apply to migrants or casual/seasonal employment, operates only in a technologically backward labour process, and cannot exist without the legislative sanctions enforced by the state.

Such theory is structured in turn by three interrelated assumptions regarding the nature of agrarian change in India and Latin America. First, that unfree relations are everywhere destined to be eliminated in the course of capitalist development. Second, that because unfree relations are an economically empowering form of patronage, labour market imperfections are always the fault of peasants or workers resisting the attempts of capital to proletarianize them. And third, that capitalist penetration of agriculture invariably transforms peasants into proletarians, in the full meaning of the latter term. Each of these assumptions, it has been argued, is wrong.

That a connection exists between unfree labour and capitalism is something that has been known about for a very long time by those who recognize the importance of political economy. However, as the example of neoclassical economics and Marxism indicates, the recognition of this fact can lead in very different political directions. Thus the precise nature of the link between capitalism and unfree labour, and whether or not workers and employers benefit from this, is the subject of a longstanding and continuing debate. Neoclassical economic theory denies or dilutes the existence of unfree labour: since it defines all transactions between capital and labour in terms of 'choice', any act of entry into a working arrangement is accordingly deemed by neoclassical economic theory to be evidence of non-coerced agency on the part of the (willing) subject, and thus proof for the existence of a free labour market. Rural workers not only choose to remain bonded labourers, therefore, but they do so because such relations are for them benign/non-antagonistic arrangements which are economically empowering. If debt bondage is reproduced as a consequence of 'choice-making' workers exercising subjective preferences, moreover, then such relations must be free.

Much the same kind of epistemology structures revisionist arguments which interpret the *enganche* system in Latin America and attached labour in India as a form of 'subsistence guarantee', 'job security' or 'patronage' based on economic incentives rather than compulsion. The mutually reinforcing components of this discourse are all in place: the need on the part of labourers for a 'subsistence guarantee' licenses the efficacy of patron-clientage, which in turn seemingly appears to provide a reason for workers choosing to remain with an existing employer. In so far as this supports the view of landlord/ worker relations as non-coercive, both before and after abolition, and thus the claim that landlords are benign employers, such a discourse is also supportive of the unfreedom-as-economic-empowerment argument.

Common to all these approaches, therefore, is the perception of coercion as unfeasible/unenforceable/non-existent, of employers as correspondingly weak (= disempowered), consequently of unfree labourers as 'choice-making' subjects, and thus of unfreedom itself as a form of 'from below' empowerment (either in economic or cultural terms, or both). In the absence of a concept of class and class struggle, the wish of revisionists to show that bonded labourers in India and Latin America are not passive victims (= disempowered) but active subjects (= empowered) leads inevitably to positive interpretations of the *enganche* relation and attached labour. In short, a view that licenses epistemological and political convergence with neoclassical economic historiography.

Faced with the co-existence of unfreedom and capitalist production, yet unable to theorize the connection between them, one particular variant of Marxism (the 'semi-feudal' thesis) is in some senses a mirror image of the neoclassical approach. The latter accepts the presence of capitalism, and accordingly redefines unfree relations of production as a form of free wage labour; the former, by contrast, accepts the presence of unfreedom, but redefines the mode of production itself as pre-capitalist. Within such a framework, therefore, relations like debt bondage retain their 'feudal' connotation: unconnected with accumulation, unfreedom is seen instead as an archaic survival through which unproductive landlords extract pre-capitalist forms of rent from smallholding peasant proprietors, sharecroppers, or estate tenants. Although not revisionist, in the sense that it downgrades or denies the presence of unfreedom, the 'semi-feudal' thesis nevertheless shares the complicitity of the former in creating a space for the political appropriation by nationalism of the discourse about unfree labour. In so far as it continues to insist on the absence from agriculture of capitalism, and the unbroken dominance of 'semi-feudal' relations, therefore capitalism must for this variant of Marxism remain a politically progressive force. Consequently, exponents of the 'semi-feudal' thesis remain trapped in the discourse of nationalism.

The latter, however, derives its main strength from a number of currently fashionable analyses structured by the perception of unfreedom as a form of cultural empowerment. Influenced by a postmodern endorsement of 'popular culture', concepts such as 'hidden transcripts' and 'everyday forms of resistance' seemingly reinforce claims about the efficacy of worker 'assertiveness' in the face of employer oppression/power. When coupled with the objection by postmodernism to the effectiveness/existence of unfreedom, both because it constitutes a specifically indigenous form of cultural 'otherness' and also because free labour is itself a figment of colonial discourse, the resulting epistemology is not merely supportive of nationalist discourse (unfreedom = cultural relation = authentic national identity, whereas freedom = economic relation = inauthentic identity imposed by colonialism) but also fuses with notions of unfreedom-as-economic-empowerment that inform neo-classical economic historiography.

Ostensibly, these two paradigms are not merely different but antithetical: whereas unfreedom-as-economic-empowerment infers that workers passively accept their bondage/'patronage', unfreedom-as-cultural-empowerment by contrast posits the existence of grass-roots agency ('assertiveness') that is seemingly incompatible with 'patronage'. On at least one crucial point, however, both these paradigms agree: like unfreedom-as-economic-empowerment, therefore, unfreedom-as-cultural-empowerment characterizes worker emancipation as a process that occurs only within existing (= unfree) production relations.

For each, not only is unfreedom as empowerment in either its economic or cultural form equally possible in a pre-capitalist or capitalist context, but adherents of both paradigms interpret worker 'assertiveness' as a vindication of their own viewpoint. Whereas exponents of unfreedom-as-economic-empowerment regard such grass-roots agency as evidence for proletarian-ization, and thus for the *de facto* realization of emancipation, exponents of unfreedom-as-cultural-empowerment simply categorize worker 'assertive-ness' as yet more evidence for the affirmation/reaffirmation of cultural identity/values. Within the much wider process of global capitalist expansion, therefore, 'assertiveness' becomes a form of economic 'empowerment' linked to workforce casualization or else an 'empowering' cultural reaction to this process.

Unlike proponents of unfreedom-as-cultural-empowerment, for whom employer agency exercised 'from above' seems to be either non-existent or ineffective, for Marxists the fundamental issue remains whether, why and when such 'from below' agency is or is not successful. What Marxism argues is not that unfree workers exercise no degree of control over their lives, but that on the economically important issue of the commodification of labour-power – precisely because it is so crucial to the the process of capital accumulation – their capacity to do this on an untrammelled basis is severely constrained by a variety of means and measures (legislation, indebtedness, violence, etc.). On specifically cultural matters (religion, language, customs, etc.), however, employers can indeed afford to be 'generous', and concede varying degrees of autonomy without actually threatening their own economic power. What is important in this regard is not to mistake the latter for the former, which is what much of the analysis structured conceptually by unfreedom-as-cultural-empowerment actually does.

The significance of the enduringly positive/endorsing characterization of unfree labour, either by those who regard it as an economically 'empowering' form of 'patronage', or by those who perceive it as an 'empowering' form of cultural 'otherness', lies in the increasing acceptability (and hence importance) of this relational form to an internationally expanding capitalism engaged in a global process of workforce restructuring/recomposition. Since the current pattern of agrarian transformation suggests that the future role in the new international division of labour for the major portion of the so-called Third World peasantry is not subsistence cultivation but rather the part-time/full-time provision of labour-power, questions such as the free/unfree character of this worldwide industrial reserve army of labour, together with its accompanying forms of consciousness/agency, are politically and economically crucial.

Because they disregard/downplay the element of class struggle, exponents of unfreedom-as-economic-empowerment and of unfreedom-as-cultural-empowerment tend to forget that worker passivity is no more a sign of unfreedom than 'assertiveness' is of free labour-power. Even a concept such as 'assertiveness' – which celebrates 'from below' agency – fails to address the central issue of class struggle: namely that it is both a 'from below' and a 'from above' process. Those who see 'assertiveness' simply as a form of cultural 'empowerment', or as economic 'empowerment' (= proletarianization) overlook the limits posed for 'from below' empowerment by class struggle waged 'from above'. The absence or fragility of the latter, however, licences powerful-workers/weak-employers dichotomy, or the inference that agricultural workers could have rendered debt bondage inoperable had they chosen to do so. That they did not is then taken as evidence both for its non-coercive/non-exploitative nature and for the claim that, where it operates, ruling class power is exercised with the consent of the labourer him/herself and not against the wishes of the latter.

Not the least of the many difficulties confronting endorsements of unfreedom-as-economic-empowerment, unfreedom-as-cultural-empowerment and 'assertiveness'-as-proletarianization, are the interrelated assumptions that free labour is always the preferred relational form of capital, that consequently the latter encourages the development of the former, and that the creation of a rural proletariat is irreversible. These kinds of argument maintain not only that the path towards emancipation is clear of obstacles but also that politically non-specific forms of 'empowerment' are ends in themselves, the inference being that once accomplished the objectives have not only been realized but are now unalterable. Unsurprisingly, the result has been that claims about bonded labour in India and Latin America (and elsewhere) have been characterized either by a denial/dilution of its element of unfreedom, or – where the latter has been conceded – by false dawns, in the form of periodic announcements that unfreedom was unimportant, on the decline or a thing of the past.

By contrast, the view taken here is that historically unfreedom has not been empowering, since in the past – no less than now – it has coexisted with worker 'assertiveness'. For the same reason, neither can contemporary forms of unfreedom be regarded as having been undermined by 'assertiveness', a form of agency which bonded labour continues to exhibit in the present. It is also argued that in the course of class struggle proletarianization is indeed reversible, and that consequently the outcome of much agrarian conflict in which worker 'assertiveness' was unsuccessful/ineffective has been – and is – not proletarianization but rather its disempowering 'other', deproletarianization. Just as the formation of a rural proletariat can be the product of class struggle, so the latter process can also lead to its unmaking (= disempowerment).

As fundamental as not mistaking deproletarianization for its 'other' is understanding the political significance – and thus the desirability – of proletarianization. The importance of the latter as an objective of socio-economic transformation stems from the fact that frequently rural proletarianization is sought only by workers and not employers who – because it threatens agrarian property relations and hence their economic power – oppose it. This is the reason why proletarianization is not always realized and sustained, and not (as exponents of unfreedom-as-economic-empowerment and unfreedom-as-cultural-empowerment argue) because Marxism was wrong about the significance/possibility/desirability of proletarianization or because it has been and remains an inappropriate outcome for poor peasants and workers in India and Latin America.

Bibliography

Adam, W., 1840, *Slavery in India*, London: Smith, Elder & Co.

Agar, H., 1944, *A Time for Greatness*, London: Eyre & Spottiswoode.

Ahlawat, S.R., 1988, *Green Revolution and Agricultural Labour*, New Delhi: Deep & Deep.

Alavi, H. and J. Harriss (eds.), 1989, *Sociology of 'Developing Societies': South Asia*, London: Macmillan.

Alavi, H. *et al.*, 1982, *Capitalism and Colonial Production*, London: Croom Helm.

Albert, B., 1976, 'An Essay on the Peruvian Sugar Industry, 1880–1920', University of East Anglia, Norwich.

Albert, B., 1984, 'The Creation of a Proletariat on Peru's Coastal Sugar Plantations: 1880–1920', in Munslow and Finch [1984].

Alberti, G. and E. Mayer (eds.), 1974, *Reciprocidad e Intercambio en los Andes Peruanos*, Lima: Instituto de Estudios Peruanos.

Alegria, C., 1942, *Broad and Alien is the World*, London: Nicholson & Watson.

Alfaro, J. and T.Ore, n.d., *El Desarrollo del Capitalismo en La Convención y Los Nuevos Movimientos Políticos de Campesinos con Tierra, 1963–73*, Memoria de Bachiller, Lima: Universidad Católica del Peru.

All-India Congress Committee, 1949, *Report of the Congress Agrarian Reforms Committee*, Madras: Madras Publishing House.

America's Watch, 1992, *The Struggle for Land in Brazil: Rural Violence Continues*, New York: Human Rights Watch.

Anderson, B., 1993, *Britain's Secret Slaves: An Investigation into the Plight of Overseas Domestic Workers*, London: Anti-Slavery International.

Angelo, L., 1997, 'Old Ways in the New South: The Implications of the Recreation of an Unfree Labor Force', in Brass and van der Linden [1997].

Anon., 1899, 'Slavery in Modern Scotland', *The Edinburgh Review*, Vol.CLXXXIX.

ANSISS/ILO, 1988, 'The Dynamics of Employment and Poverty in Bihar', unpublished report, Patna.

Araya, J. *et al.*, n.d., *Los Trabajadores Eventuales en el Cultivo del Café*, Lima (no publisher listed).

Archer, L. (ed.), 1988, *Slavery and Other Forms of Unfree Labour*, London: Routledge.

Armstrong, J., 1983, 'The Sugar Strike, 1911', in D.J. Murphy (ed.), *The Big Strikes: Queensland 1889–1965*, St.Lucia: University of Queensland Press.

Arnold, D., 1984, 'Famine in Peasant Consciousness and Peasant Action: Madras, 1876–8', in R. Guha (ed.), *Subaltern Studies III*, Delhi: Oxford University Press.

Arnold, D., 1988, *Famine: Social Crisis and Historical Change*, Oxford: Blackwell.

Arora, D.R. and B. Kumar, 1980, 'Agricultural Development and Rural to Rural Migration', Department of Economics and Sociology, Punjab Agricultural University, Ludhiana.

Aufhauser, K.R., 1973, 'Slavery and Scientific Management', *Journal of Economic History*, Vol.33, No.4.

Ayers, E.L., 1984, *Vengeance and Justice: Crime and Punishment in the Nineteenth Century American South*, New York: Oxford University Press.

Baak, P.E., 1997, 'Enslaved Ex-Slaves, Uncaptured Contract Coolies and Unfree Freedmen: "Free" and "Unfree" Labour in the Context of Plantation Development in Southwest India', in Brass and van der Linden (eds.) [1997].

Baird, P. and E. McCaughan, 1979, *Beyond the Border: Mexico and the US Today*, New York: NACLA.

Bakhtin, M., 1984, *Problems of Dostoevsky's Poetics*, Manchester: Manchester University Press.

Balagopal, K., 1986, 'Agrarian Struggles', *Economic and Political Weekly*, Vol.XXI, No.32, 9 Aug.

Ballivián, M.V. and C.F. Pinilla, 1912, 'Monografía de la industria de la goma elástica en Bolivia', Dirección General de Estadística y Estudios Geográficos, Bolivia.

Banaji, D.R., 1933, *Slavery in British India*, Bombay: Taraporevala Sons & Co.

Banaji, J., 1978, 'Capitalist Domination and the Small Peasantry: Deccan Districts in the Late Nineteenth Century', in Rudra *et al.* [1978].

Bandhua Mukti Morcha, 1983, *The Crusade Against Slavery*, New Delhi: Bonded Liberation Front.

Barbira-Scazzocchio, F. (ed.), 1980, 'Land, People and Planning in Contemporary Amazonia', Centre of Latin American Studies Occasional Publication No.3, Cambridge.

Bardhan, P., 1984, *Land, Labour and Rural Poverty*, Delhi: Oxford University Press.

Bardhan, P., 1986, 'Marxist Ideas in Development Economics: An Evaluation', in Roemer [1986].

Bardhan, P., 1982, 'Agrarian Class Formation in India', *The Journal of Peasant Studies*, Vol.10, No.1.

Bardhan, P. and A. Rudra, 1986, 'Labour Mobility and the Boundaries of the Village Moral Economy', *The Journal of Peasant Studies*, Vol.13, No.3.

Bardhan, P. (ed.), 1989a, *The Economic Theory of Agrarian Institutions*, Oxford: Clarendon Press.

Bardhan, P. (ed.), 1989b, *Conversations Between Economists and Anthropologists: Methodological Issues in Measuring Economic Change in Rural India*, Delhi: Oxford University Press.

Bauer, A.J., 1975a, *Chilean Rural Society from the Spanish Conquest to 1930*, Cambridge: Cambridge University Press.

Bauer, A.J., 1975b, 'La Hacienda "El Huique" en la estructura agraria del Chile decimonónico', in Florescano [1975].

Bauer, A.J., 1979a, 'Rural Workers in Spanish America: Problems of Peonage and Oppression', *Hispanic American Historical Review*, Vol.59, No.1.

Bauer, A.J., 1979b, 'Reply', *Hispanic American Historical Review*, Vol.59, No.3.

Bauer, A.J., 1986, 'Rural Spanish America, 1870–1930', in L.Bethell (ed.), *The Cambridge History of Latin America*, Vol.IV, Cambridge: Cambridge University Press.

Bazant, J., 1977, 'Landlord, Labourer, and Tenant in San Luis Potosí, Northern Mexico, 1822–1910', in Duncan *et al.* (eds.) [1977].

Beachey, R.W., 1957, *The British West Indies Sugar Industry in the Late 19th Century*, Oxford: Basil Blackwell.

Beall, J., 1990, 'Women Under Indenture in Natal', in Bhana [1990].

Beck, E.M. and S.E. Tolnay, 1995, 'A Season for Violence: The Lynching of Blacks and Labor Demand in the Agricultural Production Cycle in the American South', in van der Linden and Lucassen [1995].

Beckles, H.M., 1989, *Natural Rebels: A Social History of Enslaved Black Women in Barbados*, London: Zed Press.

Beidelman, T.O., 1959, *A Comparative Analysis of the Jajmani System*, New York: J.J. Augustin Inc.

Béjar, H., 1970, *Peru 1965: Notes on a Guerrilla Experience*, New York: Monthly Review Press.

Bellah, R.N., 1957, *Tokugawa Religion*, Glencoe, IL: Free Press.

Bellah, R.N., 1970, *Beyond Belief: Essays on Religion in a Post-Traditional World*, New York: Harper & Row.

Bellon, B.P., 1990, *Mercedes in Peace and War: German Automobile Workers, 1903–1945*, New York: Columbia University Press.

Bergad, L.W., 1983a, 'Coffee and Rural Proletarianization in Puerto Rico, 1840–1898', *Journal of Latin American Studies*, Vol.15, Part I.

Bergad, L.W., 1983b, *Coffee and the Growth of Agrarian Capitalism in Nineteenth Century Puerto Rico*, Princeton, NJ: Princeton University Press.

Bergad, L.W., 1984, 'On Comparative History: A Reply to Tom Brass', *Journal of Latin American Studies*, Vol.16, Part I.

Berreman, G.D., 1979, *Caste and Other Inequalities*, Meerut: Folklore Institute.

Béteille, A., 1972, *Inequality and Social Change*, Delhi: Oxford University Press.

Béteille, A., 1980, 'The Indian Village: Past and Present', in E.J. Hobsbawm *et al.*, *Peasants in History: Essays in Honour of Daniel Thorner*, Calcutta: Oxford University Press.

Bhaduri, A., 1973, 'A Study in Agricultural Backwardness under Semi-Feudalism', *The Economic Journal*, Vol.83, No.329.

Bhagwati, J., 1993, *India in Transition: Freeing the Economy*, Oxford: Clarendon Press.

Bhagwati, J., 1995, *Free Trade, 'Fairness' and the New Protectionism: Reflections on an Agenda for the World Trade Organization*, London: Institute for Economic Affairs.

Bhalla, S., 1976, 'New Relations of Production in Haryana Agriculture', *Economic and Political Weekly*, Vol.11, No.13.

Bhalla, S., 1977, 'Changes in Acreage and Tenure Structure of Landholdings in Haryana, 1962–72', *Economic and Political Weekly*, Vol.12, No.13.

Bhalla, S., 1983, 'Tenancy Today: New Factors in Determination of Mode and Level of Rent Payments for Agricultural Land', *Economic and Political Weekly*, Vol.28, Nos.19–21.

Bhana, S. (ed.), 1990, *Essays on Indentured Indians in Natal*, Leeds: Peepal Tree Press.

Bhattacharya, N., 1985, 'Agricultural Labour and Production: Central and South-East Punjab, 1870–1940', in K.N. Raj *et al.* (eds.), *Essays on the Commercialization of Indian Agriculture*, Delhi: Oxford University Press.

Bingham, H., 1951, *Lost City of the Incas*, London: Phoenix House.

Blanchard, P., 1979, 'The Recruitment of Workers in the Peruvian Sierra at the Turn of the Century: The Enganche System', *Inter-American Economic Affairs*, Vol.33, No.3.

Blanchard, P., 1982, *The Origins of the Peruvian Labor Movement, 1833–1919*, Pittsburgh, PA: University of Pittsburgh Press.

Blanco, H., 1972, *Land or Death: The Peasant Struggle in Peru*, New York: Pathfinder Press.

Bohannan, P. and J. Middleton (eds.), 1968, *Marriage, Family, and Residence*, New York: American Museum of Natural History.

Bolland, O.N., 1977, *The Formation of a Colonial Society: Belize from Conquest to Crown Colony*, Baltimore, MD: Johns Hopkins University Press.

Bolland, O.N., 1981, 'Systems of Domination after Slavery: The Control of Land and Labor in the British West Indies after 1838', *Comparative Studies in Society and History*, Vol.23, No.1.

Borah, W., 1951, *New Spain's Century of Depression*, Berkeley, CA: University of California Press.

Bose, S.R. and P.P. Ghosh, 1976, *Agro-Economic Survey of Bihar*, Patna: Associated Book Agency.

Bowman, I., 1920, *The Andes of Southern Peru*, New York: American Geographical Society.

Brading, D., 1977, '*Hacienda* Profits and Tenant Farming in the Mexican Bajío, 1700–1860', in Duncan *et al.* [1977].

Brading, D., 1978, *Haciendas and Ranchos in the Mexican Bajío: León 1700–1860*, Cambridge: Cambridge University Press.

Brass, T., 1980, 'Class Formation and Class Struggle in La Convención, Peru', *The Journal of Peasant Studies*, Vol.7, No.4.

Brass, T., 1982, 'Class Formation and Class Struggle in la Convención, Perú: The Case of Pintobamba Grande, 1940–75', unpublished D. Phil. thesis, University of Sussex.

Brass, T., 1983, 'Of Human Bondage: Campesinos, Coffee and Capitalism on the Peruvian Frontier', *The Journal of Peasant Studies*, Vol.11, No.1.

Brass, T., 1984, 'Coffee and Rural Proletarianization: A Comment on Bergad', *Journal of Latin American Studies*, Vol.16, Part I.

Brass, T., 1986a, 'Unfree Labour and Capitalist Restructuring in the Agrarian Sector: Peru and India', *The Journal of Peasant Studies*, Vol.14, No.1.

Brass, T., 1986b, 'Cargos and Conflict: The Fiesta System and Capitalist Development in Eastern Peru', *The Journal of Peasant Studies*, Vol.13, No.3.

Brass, T., 1986c, 'Free and Unfree Rural Labour in Puerto Rico during the Nineteenth Century', *Journal of Latin American Studies*, Vol.18, Part I.

Brass, T., 1986d, 'The Elementary Strictures of Kinship: Unfree Relations and the Production of Commodities', *Social Analysis*, No.20.

Brass, T., 1988, 'Slavery Now: Unfree Labour and Modern Capitalism', *Slavery and Abolition*, Vol.9, No.2

Brass, T., 1989a, 'Trotskyism, Hugo Blanco and the Ideology of a Peruvian Peasant Movement', *The Journal of Peasant Studies*, Vol.16, No.2.

Brass, T., 1989b, 'Beer Drinking Groups in a Peruvian Agrarian Cooperative', *Bulletin of Latin American Research*, Vol.8, No.2.

Brass, T., 1990a, 'Peasant Essentialism and the Agrarian Question in the Colombian Andes', *The Journal of Peasant Studies*, Vol.17, No.3.

Brass, T., 1990b, 'The Latin American *Enganche* System: Some Revisionist Reinterpretations Revisited', *Slavery and Abolition*, Vol.11, No.1.

Brass, T., 1991, 'Market Essentialism and the Impermissibility of Unfree Labour: A Reply to Shlomowitz', *Slavery and Abolition*, Vol.12, No.3.

Brass, T., 1993a, 'Migration, Tenancy and Bondage in Purnea District, Bihar', in B.N.

Yugandhar and K.G. Iyer (eds.), *Land Reforms in India*, New Delhi: Sage Publications.

Brass, T., 1993b, 'Some Observations on Unfree Labour, Capitalist Restructuring, and Deproletarianization', in Brass, van der Linden and Lucassen (eds.) [1993].

Brass, T., 1994, 'Contextualizing Sugar Production in Nineteenth Century Queensland', *Slavery and Abolition*, Vol.15, No.1.

Brass, T., 1995, 'Reply to Utsa Patnaik: If the Cap Fits ... ', *International Review of Social History*, Vol.40, Part 1.

Brass, T., 1996, 'The Return of "Merrie Melanesia": A Comment on a Review of a Review', *The Journal of Pacific History*, Vol.31, No.2.

Brass, T., 1997a, 'The Agrarian Myth, the "New" Populism and the "New" Right', *The Journal of Peasant Studies*, Vol.24, No.4.

Brass, T., 1997b, 'Immobilized Workers, Footloose Theory', *The Journal of Peasant Studies*, Vol.24, No.4.

Brass, T., 1997c, 'Free and Unfree Labour: The Debate Continues', in Brass and van der Linden [1997].

Brass, T. and M. van der Linden (eds.), 1997, *Free and Unfree Labour: The Debate Continues*, Berne: Peter Lang AG.

Brass, T., van der Linden, M. and J. Lucassen (eds.), 1993, *Free and Unfree Labour*, Amsterdam: IISH.

Breen, R., 1983, 'Farm Servanthood in Ireland, 1900–40', *Economic History Review*, Vol.36, No.1.

Breman, J., 1974, *Patronage and Exploitation: Changing Agrarian Relations in South Gujarat, India*, Berkeley, CA: University of California Press.

Breman, J., 1985a, *Of Peasants, Migrants and Paupers: Rural Labour Circulation in Capitalist Production in West India*, Delhi: Oxford University Press.

Breman, J., 1985b, 'Between Accumulation and Immizeration: The Partiality of Fieldwork in Rural India', *The Journal of Peasant Studies*, Vol.13, No.1.

Breman, J., 1989a, 'The Disintegration of the *Hali* System', in Alavi and Harriss [1989].

Breman, J., 1989b, *Taming the Coolie Beast: Plantation Society and the Colonial Order in Southeast Asia*, Delhi: Oxford University Press.

Breman, J., 1990, *Labour Migration and Rural Transformation in Colonial Asia*, Amsterdam: Free University Press.

Breman, J., 1993, *Beyond Patronage and Exploitation: Changing Agrarian Relations in South Gujarat*, Delhi: Oxford University Press.

Breman, J., 1996, *Footloose Labour*, Cambridge: Cambridge University Press.

Breman, J. and V. Daniel, 1992, 'The Making of a Coolie', *The Journal of Peasant Studies*, Vol.19, Nos.3–4.

Brown, W.W. and M.O. Reynolds, 1973, 'Debt Peonage Re-examined', *Journal of Economic History*, Vol.33, No.4.

Burga, M., 1976, *De la Encomienda a la Hacienda Capitalista: El Valle de Jequetepeque del Siglo XVI al XX*, Lima: Instituto de Estudios Peruanos.

Burga, M., 1978, 'La Hacienda en el Peru 1850–1930: Evidencias y Método', *Tierra y Sociedad*, No.1.

Burra, N., 1986, 'Glass Factories of Firozabad: II – Plight of Child Workers', *Economic and Political Weekly*, Vol.21, No.47.

Caballero, M., 1986, *Latin America and the Comintern 1919–1943*, Cambridge: Cambridge University Press.

Cambranes, J.C., 1985, *Coffee and Peasants: The Origins of the Modern Plantation*

Economy in Guatemala, 1853–1897, Stockholm: Institute of Latin American Studies.

Carter, A., 1974, *Elite Politics in Rural India*, London: Cambridge University Press.

Casanovas, J., 1997, 'Slavery, the Labour Movement and Spanish Colonialism in Cuba (1850–1898)', in Brass and van der Linden [1997].

Cashman, R., 1975, *The Myth of the Lokamanya*, Berkeley, CA: University of California Press.

Castro Pozo, H., 1947, *El Yanaconaje en las Haciendas Piuranas*, Lima: Compañia de Impresiones y Publicidad.

Central Bank of India, 1988, *District Credit Plan 1988–90: Purnia*, Patna: Central Bank of India.

Chacón, R.D., 1986, 'John Kenneth Turner, *Barbarous Mexico*, and the Debate about Debt Peonage Slavery in Yucatán during the Porfiriato', *Peasant Studies*, Vol.13, No.2.

Chanana, D.R., 1960, *Slavery in Ancient India*, New Delhi: People's Publishing House.

Chatterjee, K.D., 1964, 'The Agricultural Labour Enquiry', in Government of India (Labour Bureau, Ministry of Labour), *Labour Survey Techniques*, Simla: Government of India Press.

Chattopadhyay, P., 1978, 'Mode of Production in Indian Agriculture – An "Anti-Kritik"', in Rudra *et al*. [1978].

Chaudhuri, K.N. and C.J Dewey (eds.), 1979, *Economy and Society: Essays in Indian Economic and Social History*, Delhi: Oxford University Press.

Chevalier, F., 1966, *Land and Society in Colonial Mexico: The Great Hacienda*, Berkeley, CA: University of California Press.

Chevalier, J., 1982, *Civilization and the Stolen Gift: Capital, Kin and Cult in Eastern Peru*, Toronto: University of Toronto Press.

Chiriftirado, A. *et al*., 1975, *Comunidades Nativas de Selva Central: Diagnostico Socio-económico*, Lima: Dirección General de Organizaciones Rurales, Unidad de Apoyo a las Comunidades Nativas.

Cholia, R.P., 1941, *Dock Labourers in Bombay*, Bombay: Longmans, Green.

Chopra, S., 1985, 'Bondage in a Green Revolution Area: A Study of Brick Kiln Workers in Muzaffnagar District', in Patnaik and Dingwaney [1985].

Choy, E. *et al*., 1970, *Lenin y Mariátegui*, Lima: Biblioteca Amauta.

Chuan-Hua, L., 1934, *Facing Labor Issues in China*, London: George Allen & Unwin.

CIDA, 1966, *Tenencia de la tierra y desarrollo socio-económico del sector agrícola: Peru*, Washington, DC: Panamerican Union.

Clammer, J. (ed.), 1978, *The New Economic Anthropology*, London: Macmillan Press.

Cohen, R., 1987, *The New Helots: Migrants in the International Division of Labour*, Aldershot: Gower Publishing.

Cohen, W., 1976, 'Negro Involuntary Servitude in the South, 1865–1940: A Preliminary Analysis', *Journal of Southern History*, Vol.42, No.1.

Cohn, B.S., 1955, 'The Changing Status of a Depressed Caste', in Marriott [1955].

Colburn, F.D., 1989, *Everyday Forms of Peasant Resistance*, New York: M.E. Sharpe.

Collins, J.L., 1988, *Unseasonal Migrations: The Effects of Rural Labor Scarcity in Peru*, Princeton NJ: Princeton University Press.

Conkin, P.K., 1988, *The Southern Agrarians*, Knoxville, TN: University of Tennessee Press.

Connell, J. *et al*., 1976, *Migration from Rural Areas*, New Delhi: Oxford University Press.

Conrad, A.H. and J.R. Meyer, 1965, *Studies in Econometric History*, London: Chapman & Hall.

Corbin, D.A., 1981, *Life, Work, and Rebellion in the Coal Fields: The Southern West Virginia Miners, 1880–1922*, Urbana, IL: University of Illinois Press.

Corbridge, S., 1982, 'Industrial Development in Tribal India: The Case of the Iron Ore Mining Industry in Singhbhum District, c.1900–1960', in N. Sengupta (ed.), *Fourth World Dynamics: Jharkhand*, New Delhi: Authors Guild Publications.

Corrigan, P., 1977, 'Feudal Relics or Capitalist Monuments? Notes on the Sociology of Unfree Labour', *Sociology*, Vol.11, No.3.

Cotlear, D., 1979, 'El Sistema de Enganche a Principios del Siglo XX: Una Versión Diferente', Bachelor's thesis in Economics, Universidad Católica, Lima.

Craig, W.W., 1967, 'From Hacienda to Community: An Analysis of Solidarity and Social Change in Peru', Latin American Program Dissertation Series No.6, Cornell University.

Craig, W.W., 1969, 'Peru: The Peasant Movement of La Convención', in H.A. Landsberger (ed.), *Latin American Peasant Movements*, Ithaca, NY: Cornell University Press.

Cross, H.E., 1979, 'Debt Peonage Reconsidered: A Case Study in Nineteenth-Century Zacatecas, Mexico', *Business History Review*, Vol.53, No.4.

Cuadros, C.F., 1949, 'El "arriendo" y la reforma agraria en la Provincia de la Convención', *Revista Universitaria del Cusco*, No.96

da Corta, L. and D.Venkateshwarlu, 1999, 'Unfree Relations and the Feminization of Agricultural Labour in Andhra Pradesh', *The Journal of Peasant Studies*, Vol.26, Nos.2–3.

Daniel, C.E., 1981, *Bitter Harvest: A History of California Farmworkers 1870–1941*, Ithaca, NY: Cornell University Press.

Daniel, P., 1972, *The Shadow of Slavery: Peonage in the South 1901–1969*, Urbana, IL: University of Illinois Press.

Darling, M.L., 1925, *The Punjab Peasant in Prosperity and Debt*, London: Oxford University Press.

Das, A.N., 1979, *Does Bihar Show the Way?*, Calcutta: Research India Publications.

Das, A.N., 1983, *Agrarian Unrest and Socio-Economic Change in Bihar, 1900–1980*, New Delhi: Manohar Publications.

Das, A.N. and V. Nilkant (eds.), 1979, *Agrarian Relations in India*, New Delhi: Manohar Publications.

Das, A.N., Nilkant, V. and P.S. Dubey (eds.), 1984, *The Worker and the Working Class*, New Delhi: PECCE.

David, P.A. *et al.*, 1976, *Reckoning with Slavery: A Critical Study in the Quantitative History of American Negro Slavery*, New York: Oxford University Press.

Davis, S.H., 1977, *Victims of the Miracle*, Cambridge: Cambridge University Press.

de Janvry, A. and A.Vandeman, 1987, 'Patterns of Proletarianization in Agriculture: An International Comparison', in M.D. MacLachlan (ed.), *Household Economies and Their Transformations*, New York: University Press of America.

de Man, P., 1979, *Allegories of Reading*, New Haven, CT: Yale University Press.

de Reuck, A. and J. Knight (eds.), 1967, *Caste and Race: Comparative Approaches*, London: J. & A. Churchill.

Dean, W., 1976, *Rio Claro: A Brazilian Plantation System, 1820–1920*, California CA: Stanford University Press.

Deere, C.D., 1978, 'Differentiation of the Peasantry and Family Structure: A Peruvian

Case-Study', *Journal of Family History*, Vol.3, No.4.

Deere, C.D., 1990, *Household and Class Relations: Peasants and Landlords in Northern Peru*, Berkeley CA: University of California Press.

Degler, C.N., 1976, 'The Irony of American Negro Slavery', in H.P. Owens (ed.), *Perspectives and Irony in American Slavery*, Jackson, MI: University of Mississipi Press.

Desai, A.R., 1961, *Rural India in Transformation*, Bombay: Popular Prakashan.

Desai, A.R., 1984, *India's Path of Development: A Marxist Approach*, Bombay: Popular Prakashan.

Deshpande, V., 1982, *Employment Guarantee Scheme: Impact on Poverty and Bondage among Tribal Workers*, Pune: Tilak Maharashtra Vidyapeeth.

Dew, C.B., 1966, *Ironmaker to the Confederacy: Joseph R. Anderson and the Tredegar Iron Works*, New Haven, CT: Yale University Press.

Dhar, H., 1984, 'Bataidars of Bihar – Some Reflections', in Das *et al.* (eds.) [1984].

Díaz Hernández, L., 1981, *Castañer: una hacienda cafetalera en Puerto Rico (1868–1930)*, Ponce: Academia de Artes, Historia y Arquelogía de Puerto Rico.

Díaz Santana, A., 1976, 'The Role of Haitian Braceros in Dominican Sugar Production', *Latin American Perspectives*, III, No.1.

Dingwaney, M., 1985, 'Unredeemed Promises: The Law and Servitude', in Patnaik and Dingwaney [1985].

Dittmer, J., 1980, *Black Georgia in the Progressive Era 1900–1920*, Urbana, IL: The University of Illinois Press.

Domar, E.D., 1970, 'The Causes of Slavery and Serfdom: A Hypothesis', *Journal of Economic History*, Vol.30, No.1.

Douglas, M., 1964, 'Matriliny and Pawnship in Central Africa', *Africa*, Vol.34, No.4.

Dovring, F., 1965, 'Bondage, Tenure, and Progress: Reflections on the Economics of Forced Labour', *Comparative Studies in Society and History*, Vol.VII, No.3.

Dumont, L., 1970, *Homo Hierarchicus*, London: Weidenfeld & Nicolson.

Duncan, K. *et al.* (eds.), 1977, *Land and Labour in Latin America*, Cambridge: Cambridge University Press.

Eaton, Cl., 1965, *The Freedom-of-Thought Struggle in the Old South*, New York: Harper & Row.

Edelman, M., 1992, *The Logic of the Latifundio: The Large Estates of Northwestern Costa Rica Since the Late Nineteeenth Century*, Stanford, CA: Stanford University Press.

Elkins, S., 1959, *Slavery: A Problem in American Institutional and Intellectual Life*, Chicago, IL: University of Chicago Press.

Emmer, P.C., 1984, 'The Importation of British Indians into Surinam (Dutch Guiana), 1873–1916', in Marks and Richardson [1984].

Emmer, P.C., 1997, 'European Expansion and Unfree Labour', *Itinerario*, Vol.21, No.1.

Emmer, P.C. (ed.), 1986, *Colonialism and Migration: Indentured Labour Before and After Slavery*, Dordrecht: Martinus Nijhoff Publishers.

Engerman, S.L., 1986, 'Servants to Slaves to Servants: Contract Labour and European Expansion', in Emmer (ed.) [1986].

Ennew, J., 1981, *Debt Bondage – A Survey*, London: Anti-Slavery Society for Human Rights.

Epstein, K., 1966, *The Genesis of German Conservatism*, Princeton, NJ: Princeton University Press.

Epstein, T.S., 1962, *Economic Development and Social Change in South India*, Manchester: Manchester University Press.

Epstein, T.S., 1967, 'Productive Efficiency and Customary Systems of Rewards in Rural South India', in R. Firth (ed.), *Themes in Economic Anthropology*, London: Tavistock.

Epstein, T.S., 1973, *South India: Yesterday, Today and Tomorrow*, London: Macmillan.

Esterci, N., 1987, *Conflicto no Araguaia: Peões e Posseiros Contra a Grande Empresa*, Petrópolis: Editora Vozes Ltda.

Evans, R., 1970, 'Some Notes on Coerced Labor', *Journal of Economic History*, Vol.30, No.4.

Favre, H., 1977, 'The Dynamics of Peasant Society and Migration to Coastal Plantations in Central Peru', in Duncan *et al.* [1977].

Feder, E., 1971, *The Rape of the Peasantry*, New York: Anchor Books.

Ferencz, B., 1979, *Less Than Slaves: Jewish Forced Labor and the Quest for Compensation*, Cambridge, MA: Harvard University Press.

Figueroa, A., 1984, *Capitalist Development and the Peasant Economy in Peru*, Cambridge: Cambridge University Press.

Finler, J.W., 1988, *The Hollywood Story*, London: Octopus Books.

Fioravani-Molinié, A., 1982, 'Multi-Levelled Andean Society and Market Exchange: The Case of Yucay (Peru)', in Lehmann [1982].

Fioravanti, E., 1974, *Latifundio y sindicalismo agrario en el Perú*, Lima: Instituto de Estudios Peruanos.

Florescano, E. (ed.), 1975, *Haciendas Latifundios y Plantaciones en América Latina*, México: Siglo Veintiuno Editores.

Fogel, R.W., 1989, *Without Consent or Contract: The Rise and Fall of American Slavery*, New York: W.W. Norton.

Fogel, R.W. and S.L. Engerman, 1974, *Time on the Cross: Volume I – The Economics of American Negro Slavery*, London: Wildwood House.

Folbre, N., 1982, 'Exploitation Comes Home: A Critique of the Marxian Theory of Family Labour', *Cambridge Journal of Economics*, Vol.6, No.4.

Fonseca Martell, C., 1973, *Sistemas Económicas Andinos*, Lima: Biblioteca Andina.

Fortes, M., 1970, *Kinship and the Social Order*, London: Routledge & Kegan Paul.

Fox-Genovese, E. and E.D. Genovese, 1983, *Fruits of Merchant Capital: Slavery and Bourgeois Property in the Rise and Expansion of Capitalism*, New York: Oxford University Press.

Frank, A.G., 1969a, *Capitalism and Underdevelopment in Latin America*, New York: Monthly Review Press.

Frank, A.G., 1969b, *Latin America: Underdevelopment or Revolution*, New York: Monthly Review Press.

Frankel, F.R., 1971, *India's Green Revolution: Economic Gains and Political Costs*, Princeton NJ: Princeton University Press.

Freitag, S., 1989, *Collective Action and Community: Public Arenas and the Emergence of Communalism in India*, Berkeley, CA: University of California Press.

Friedland, W.H. and D. Nelkin, 1971, *Migrant Agricultural Workers in America's Northeast*, New York: Holt, Rinehart & Winston.

Fröbel, F., Heinrichs J. and O. Kreye, 1980, *The New International Division of Labour*, Cambridge: Cambridge University Press.

Galarza, E., 1964, *Merchants of Labor: The Mexican Bracero Story*, Santa Barbara, CA: McNally & Loftin, Publishers.

Galenson, D., 1981, *White Servitude in Colonial America*, Cambridge: Cambridge University Press.

Galey, J.-C., 1983, 'Creditors, Kings and Death: Determinations and Implications of Bondage in Tehri-Garhwal (Indian Himalayas)', in Malamoud [1983].

Gamio, M., 1971, *Mexican Immigration to the United States*, New York: Dover Publications.

Gandhi Peace Foundation and National Labour Institute (GPF/NLI), 1978, *National Survey on the Incidence of Bonded Labour: Preliminary Report*, New Delhi: National Labour Institute.

Gellner, E. and J.Waterbury (eds.), 1977, *Patrons and Clients*, London: Duckworth.

Genovese, E.D., 1971, 'Rebelliousness and Docility in the Negro Slave: A Critique of the Elkins Thesis', in Lane [1971].

Genovese, E.D., 1975, *Roll, Jordan, Roll: The World the Slaves Made*, London: André Deutsch Limited.

Ghosh, J., 1985, 'Differential and Absolute Land Rent', *The Journal of Peasant Studies*, Vol.13, No.1.

Gibson, C., 1964, *The Aztecs Under Spanish Rule: A History of the Indians of the Valley of Mexico 1519–1810*, Stanford, CA: Stanford University Press.

Gill, I., 1984, 'Migrant Labour: A Mirror Survey of Jullundur and East Champaran', *Economic and Political Weekly*, Vol.19, Nos.24–5.

Gillion, K.L., 1962, *Fiji's Indian Migrants: A History to the End of Indenture in 1920*, Melbourne: Oxford University Press.

Gilsenan, M., 1977, 'Against Patron–Client Relations', in Gellner and Waterbury [1977].

Góngora, M., 1975, *Studies in the Colonial History of Spanish America*, Cambridge: Cambridge University Press.

Gonzales, M.J., 1980, 'Capitalist Agriculture and Labour Contracting in Northern Peru, 1880–1905', *Journal of Latin American Studies*, Vol.12, Part 2.

Gonzales, M.J., 1985, *Plantation Agriculture and Social Control in Northern Peru, 1875–1933*, Austin, TX: University of Texas Press.

Goody, J., 1959, 'The Mother's Brother and the Sister's Son in West Africa', *Journal of the Royal Anthropological Institute*, Vol.89, No.1.

Gough, K., 1960, 'Caste in a Tanjore Village', in E. Leach (ed.), *Aspects of Caste in South India, Ceylon and North-West Pakistan*, Cambridge: Cambridge University Press.

Gough, K., 1981, *Rural Society in Southeast India*, Cambridge: Cambridge University Press.

Gough, K., 1983, 'Agricultural Labour in Thanjavur', in J.P. Mencher (ed.), *Social Anthropology of Peasantry*, Bombay: Somaiya Publications.

Government of Bihar, 1972, *Census of India 1971*, Series 4 – Bihar (District Census Handbook: Patna, Part X-A), Patna: Secretariat Press.

Government of Bihar, 1973, *Census of India 1971*, Series 4 – Bihar (District Census Handbook: Patna, Part X-B), Patna: Secretariat Press.

Government of India, 1952, *First Agricultural Labour Enquiry [1950–51]*, Vol.I (Agricultural Wages in India), Delhi: Government of India Press.

Government of India, 1960, *Second Agricultural Labour Enquiry [1956–57]*, Vol.I (Report), Simla: Government of India.

Government of India, 1983, *Census of India 1981*, Series 4 – Bihar (Part II), New Delhi: Registrar General and Census Commissioner, Government of India.

Government of Punjab (India), 1982, *Statistical Abstract of Punjab*, Chandigarh: Economic and Statistical Organization.

Graves, A., 1983, 'Truck and Gifts: Melanesian Immigrants and the Trade Box System in Colonial Queensland', *Past and Present*, No.101.

Graves, A., 1984, 'The Nature and Origins of Pacific Islands Migration to Queensland, 1862–1914', in Marks and Richardson (eds.) [1984].

Graves, A., 1993, *Cane and Labour: The Political Economy of the Queensland Sugar Industry 1862–1906*, Edinburgh: Edinburgh University Press.

Greenberg, M, 1977, 'The New Economic History and the Understanding of Slavery: A Methodological Critique', *Dialectical Anthropology*, Vol.2, No.2.

Greenidge, C.W.W, 1958, *Slavery*, London: George Allen & Unwin.

Grewal, S.S. and M.S. Sidhu, 1981, 'A Study of Migrant Agricultural Labour in Punjab', *Indian Journal of Labour Economics*, Vol.24, No.3.

Grierson, G.A., 1975, *Bihar Peasant Life*, Delhi: Cosmo Publications.

Griffiths, D.C., 1987, 'Nonmarket Labor Processes in an Advanced Capitalist Economy', *American Anthropologist*, Vol.89, No.4.

Grigson, W.V., 1944, *The Aboriginal Problem in the Central Provinces and Berar*, Nagpur: Government Printing, C.P. and Berar.

Grossman, J., 1997, 'The Right to Strike and Worker Freedom and Unfreedom: In and Beyond Apartheid', in Brass and van der Linden [1997].

Guillet, D., 1980, 'Reciprocal Labour and Peripheral Capitalism in the Central Andes', *Ethnology*, Vol.19, No.2.

Gupta, D., 1986, 'Formal and Real Subsumption of Labour under Capital – The Instance of Sharecropping', in A.K. Gupta (ed.), *Agrarian Structure and Peasant Revolt in India*, New Delhi: Criterion Publications.

Gupta, J., 1985, 'Himalayan Polyandry: Bondage Among Women in Jaunsar Bawar', in Patnaik and Dingwaney [1985].

Gutman, H.G., 1975, *Slavery and the Numbers Game*, Chicago, IL: University of Chicago Press.

Gutman, H.G., 1976, *The Black Family in Slavery and Freedom, 1750–1925*, Oxford: Basil Blackwell.

Guy, D., 1981, 'Women, Peonage, and Industrialization: Argentina, 1810–1914', *Latin American Research Review*, Vol.16, No.3.

Habakkuk, H.J., 1962, *American and British Technology in the Nineteenth Century*, London: Cambridge University Press.

Halperin, R. and J. Dow (eds.), 1977, *Peasant Livelihood: Studies in Economic Anthropology and Cultural Ecology*, New York: St Martin's Press.

Hanagan, M. and C. Stephenson (eds.), 1986, *Proletarians and Protest: The Roots of Class Formation in an Industrializing World*, New York: Greenwood Press.

Harris, C.H., 1975, *A Mexican Family Empire: The Latifundio of the Sánchez Navarros 1765–1867*, Austin, TX: University of Texas Press.

Harris, N., 1987, *The End of the Third World*, London: Penguin Books.

Harriss, J., 1977, 'Implications of Changes in Agriculture for Social Relationships at the Village Level: The Case of Randam', in B.H. Farmer (ed.), *Green Revolution?*, London: Macmillan.

Harriss, J., 1982a, *Capitalism and Peasant Farming*, New Delhi: Oxford University Press.

Harriss, J. (ed.), 1982b, *Rural Development: Theories of Peasant Economy and Agrarian Change*, London: Hutchinson University Library.

Harriss, J., 1992, 'Does the "Depressor" Still Work? Agrarian Structure and Development in India – A Review of Evidence and Argument', *The Journal of Peasant Studies*, Vol.19, No.2.

Harriss, J., 1994, 'Between Economism and Postmodernism: Reflections on Research on "Agrarian Change" in India', in D. Booth (ed.), *Rethinking Social Development*, Harlow: Longman Scientific & Technical.

Harriss, J., Hunter J. and C.M. Lewis (eds.), 1995, *The New Institutional Economics and Third World Development*, London: Routledge.

Hart, G., 1986a, *Power, Labor, and Livelihood: Processes of Change in Rural Java*, Berkeley, CA: University of California Press.

Hart,G.,1986b, 'Exclusionary Labour Arrangements:Interpreting Evidence on Employment Trends in Rural Java', *The Journal of Development Studies*, Vol.22, No.4.

Hasnain, N., 1982, *Bonded for Ever: A Study of the Kolta – A Cis–Himalayan Tribe*, New Delhi: Harnam Publications.

Hawthorn, G., 1991, "Waiting for a Text?": Comparing Third World Politics', in J. Manor (ed.), *Rethinking Third World Politics*, London: Longman.

Hawthorn, G., 1993, 'Liberalization and "Modern Liberty": Four Southern States', *World Development*, Vol.21, No.8.

Hayek, F.A., 1954, 'History and Politics', in Hayek (ed.)[1954].

Hayek, F.A. (ed.), 1954, *Capitalism and the Historians*, London: Routledge & Kegan Paul.

Hayes, P., 1987, *Industry and Ideology: I.G.Farben in the Nazi Era*, Cambridge: Cambridge University Press.

Haynes, D. and G.Prakash (eds.), 1991, *Contesting Power: Resistance and Everyday Social Relations in South Asia*, Delhi: Oxford University Press.

Heath, D.B. and R.N. Adams (eds.), 1965, *Contemporary Cultures and Societies of Latin America*, New York: Random House.

Hellie, R., 1982, *Slavery in Russia 1450–1725*, Chicago, IL: University of Chicago Press.

Henningham, S., 1990, *A Great Estate and Its Landlords in Colonial India: Darbhanga 1860–1942*, Delhi: Oxford University Press.

Higgs, R., 1977, *Competition and Coercion: Blacks in the American Economy, 1865–1914*, Cambridge: Cambridge University Press.

Hill, P., 1977, *Population, Prosperity and Poverty: Rural Kano 1900 and 1970*, Cambridge: Cambridge University Press.

Hill, P., 1986, *Development Economics on Trial*, Cambridge: Cambridge University Press.

Hilton, G.W., 1960, *The Truck System including a history of the British Truck Acts, 1465–1900*, Cambridge: Heffer.

Hjejle, B., 1967, 'Slavery and Agricultural Bondage in South India in the Nineteenth Century', *The Scandanavian Economic History Review*, Vol.15, Nos.1 and 2.

Hobsbawm, E.J., 1969, 'A Case of Neo-Feudalism: La Convención, Perú', *Journal of Latin American Studies*, Vol.1, No.1.

Hoel, B., 1982, 'Contemporary Clothing "Sweatshops", Asian Female Labour and Collective Organization', in J.West (ed.), *Women, Work and the Labour Market*, London: Routledge & Kegan Paul.

Holloway, T.H., 1980, *Immigrants on the Land: Coffee and Society in São Paulo, 1886–1934*, Chapel Hill, NC: University of North Carolina Press.

Holmstrom, M. (ed.), 1990, *Work for Wages in South Asia*, Delhi: Manohar Publications.

Honig, E., 1986, *Sisters and Strangers: Women in the Shanghai Cotton Mills, 1919–1949*, Stanford, CA: Stanford University Press.

Huertas Vallejos, L., 1974, *Capital Burocrático y Lucha de Clases en el Sector Agrario: Lambayeque, Perú, 1920–50*, Lima: Seminario de Historia Rural Andina.

Huizer, G., 1983, 'Social Polarization as a Disruptive Force in Cooperatives: The Case of the Te Huyro Central Cooperative in La Convención, Peru', *Boletín de Estudios Latinoamericanos y del Caribe*, No.35.

Hutt, W.H., 1954, 'The Factory System of the Early Nineteenth Century', in Hayek (ed.) [1954].

Huxley, M. and C Capa, 1965, *Farewell to Eden*, London: Chatto & Windus.

Indian School of Social Sciences (ed.), 1976, *Bonded Labour in India*, Calcutta: Indian Book Exchange.

International Labour Conference, 1962, *Forced Labour*, Geneva: International Labour Office.

International Labour Organization, 1983, 'Report of the Commission of Inquiry [into] the Employment of Haitian Workers on the Sugar Plantations of the Dominican Republic', *ILO Official Bulletin*, No.66.

Ishwaran, K., 1966, *Tradition and Economy in Village India*, London: Routledge & Kegan Paul.

Jacobs, N., 1958, *The Origin of Modern Capitalism and Eastern Asia*, Hong Kong: Hong Kong University Press.

Jagannathan, N.V., 1987, *Informal Markets in Developing Countries*, New York: Oxford University Press.

James, C.L.R., 1980, 'The Making of the Caribbean People', in *Spheres of Existence*, London: Allison & Busby.

Jannuzi, F.T., 1974, *Agrarian Crisis in India: The Case of Bihar*, Austin, TX: University of Texas Press.

Jaschok, M., 1988, *Concubines and Bondservants: The Social History of a Chinese Custom*, London: Zed Press.

Jodhka, S.S., 1990, 'Development and Debt – A Sociological Study of the Changing Credit Relations in Haryana Agriculture', D.Phil. thesis, Panjab University, Chandigarh.

Jodhka, S.S., 1994, 'Agrarian Changes and Attached Labour: Emerging Pattern in Haryana Agriculture', *Economic and Political Weekly*, Vol.29, No.39.

Jodhka, S.S., 1995, 'Agrarian Changes, Unfreedom and Attached Labour', *Economic and Political Weekly*, Vol.30, Nos.30–31.

Jodhka, S.S., 1996, 'Interpreting Attached Labour in Contemporary Haryana', *Economic and Political Weekly*, Vol.31, No.21.

Johnson, C.S., 1966, *Shadow of the Plantation*, Chicago, IL: University of Chicago Press.

Johnson, L., 1997, 'The Competition of Slave and Free Labour in Artisanal Production: Buenos Aires, 1770–1815', in Brass and van der Linden [1997].

Jones, C.L., 1940, *Guatemala: Past and Present*, Minneapolis, MN: University of Minnesota Press.

Joshi, R.S., 1978, 'Two Liberated Bonded Labourers of Palamau', *National Labour Institute Bulletin*, Vol.4, No.5.

Kaerger, K., 1979, *Condiciones Agrarias de la Sierra Sur Peruana (1899)*, Lima: Instituto de Estudios Peruanos.

Kalecki, M., 1976, *Essays on Developing Economies*, Hassocks: Harvester Press.

Kamble, N.D., 1982, *Bonded Labour in India*, New Delhi: Uppal.

Kapadia, K., 1995a, 'The Profitability of Bonded Labour: The Gem-Cutting Industry in Rural South India', *The Journal of Peasant Studies*, Vol.22, No.3.

Kapadia, K., 1995b, 'Women Workers in Bonded Labour in Rural Industry (South India)', paper presented at the Congress on 'Agrarian Questions' held in Wageningen, the Netherlands, during May.

Katz, F., 1974, 'Labor Conditions on Haciendas in Porfirian Mexico: Some Trends and Tendencies', *Hispanic American Historical Review*, Vol.54, No.1.

Kaufman, A., 1982, *Capitalism, Slavery and Republican Values: Antebellum Political Economists 1819–1848*, Austin TX: University of Texas Press.

Kennedy, S., 1946, *Southern Exposure*, New York: Doubleday.

Kennedy, S., 1959, *Jim Crow Guide to the USA: The Laws, Customs and Etiquette Governing the Conduct of Nonwhites and Other Minorities as Second-Class Citizens*, London: Lawrence & Wishart.

Klarén, P.F., 1970, *La Formación de las Haciendas Azucareras y los Orígenes del Apra*, Lima: Instituto de Estudios Peruanos.

Klarén, P.F., 1977, 'The Social and Economic Consequences of Modernization in the Peruvian Sugar Industry, 1870–1930', in Duncan *et al.* [1977].

Kloosterboer, W., 1960, *Involuntary Labour since the Abolition of Slavery: A Survey of Compulsory Labour Throughout the World*, Leiden: E.J. Brill

Knight, A., 1986a, *The Mexican Revolution – Volume 1: Porfirians, Liberals and Peasants*, Cambridge: Cambridge University Press.

Knight, A., 1986b, 'Mexican Peonage: What Was It and Why Was It?', *Journal of Latin American Studies*, Vol.18, Part I.

Knight, A., 1988, 'Debt Bondage in Latin America', in L. Archer (ed.), *Slavery and Other Forms of Unfree Labour*, London: Routledge.

Kolchin, P., 1987, *Unfree Labor: American Slavery and Russian Serfdom*, Cambridge, MA: Harvard University Press.

Kolchin, P., 1992, 'More *Time on the Cross*? An Evaluation of Robert William Fogel's *Without Consent or Contract'*, *Journal of Southern History*, Vol.58, No.3.

Kössler, R., 1997, 'Wage Labour and Despotism in Modernity', in Brass and van der Linden [1997].

Krishnaji, N., 1986, 'Agrarian Relations and the Left Movement in Kerala: A Note on Recent Trends', in A.R. Desai (ed.), *Agrarian Struggles in India after Independence*, Delhi: Oxford University Press.

Krishnamurty, J. (ed.), 1989, *Women in Colonial India: Essays on Survival, Work and the State*, Delhi: Oxford University Press.

Krissman, F., 1997, 'California's Agricultural Labor Market: Historical Variations in the Use of Unfree Labor, c.1769–1994', in Brass and van der Linden [1997].

Kulkarni, S., 1979, 'Bonded Labour and Illicit Moneylending in Maharashtra', *Economic and Political Weekly*, Vol.14, No.9.

Kulkarni, S., 1982, 'Law and Social Change: The Case of Legislation relating to Bonded Labour in India', in D.B. Gupta *et al.* (eds.), *Development, Planning and Policy*, New Delhi: Wiley Eastern.

Kumar, D., 1965, *Land and Caste in South India: Agricultural Labour in Madras Presidency in the Nineteenth Century*, Cambridge: Cambridge University Press.

Kumar, D. and M. Desai (eds.), 1983, *The Cambridge Economic History of India, Volume 2 [c.1757–c.1970]*, Cambridge: Cambridge University Press.

Kumar, J., 1986, *Land Use Analysis: A Case Study of Nalanda District, Bihar*, New Delhi: Inter-India Publications.

Kusuman, K.K., 1973, *Slavery in Travancore*, Trivandrum: Kerala Historical Society.

Lacey, M., 1981, *Working for Boroko: The Origins of a Coercive Labour System in South Africa*, Johannesburg: Ravan Press.

Laclau, E., 1977, 'Feudalism and Capitalism in Latin America', in *Politics and Ideology in Marxist Theory*, London: Verso.

Laite, J., 1981, *Industrial Development and Migrant Labour*, Manchester: Manchester University Press.

Lal, A.K., 1977, *Politics of Poverty: A Study of Bonded Labour*, New Delhi: Chetana Publications.

Lal, B.V., 1979, 'Fiji *Girmitiyas*: The Background to Banishment', in Vijay Mishra (ed.), *Rama's Banishment: A Centenary Tribute to the Fiji Indians 1879–1979*, Auckland: Heinemann Educational Books.

Lal, B.V. 1989, 'Kunti's Cry: Indentured Women on Fiji Plantations', in Krishnamurty [1989]

Lal, D., 1989, *The Hindu Equilibrium: II – Aspects of Indian Labour*, Oxford: Clarendon Press.

Lane, A.J. (ed.), 1971, *The Debate Over Slavery: Stanley Elkins and His Critics*, Chicago, IL: University of Illinois Press.

Langer, E.D., 1986, 'Debt Peonage and Paternalism in Latin America', *Peasant Studies*, Vol.13, No.2.

Langer, E.D., 1989, *Economic Change and Rural Resistance in Southern Bolivia, 1880–1930*, Stanford, CA: Stanford University Press.

Larsen, N., 1993, 'Postmodernism and Imperialism: Theory and Politics in Latin America', in E. Amiran and J. Unsworth (eds.), *Essays in Postmodern Culture*, New York: Oxford University Press.

Lasker, B., 1950, *Human Bondage in Southeast Asia*, Chapel Hill, NC: University of North Carolina Press.

Leach, E., 1967, 'Caste, Class and Slavery: The Taxonomic Problem', in de Reuck and Knight (eds.).

Leach, E, 1982, *Social Anthropology*, London: Fontana.

Legassick, M., 1977, 'Gold, Agriculture, and Secondary Industry in South Africa, 1885–1970: From Periphery to Sub-Metropole as a Forced Labour System', in Parsons and Palmer (eds.).

Legassick, M. and D. Innes, 1977, 'Capital Restructuring and Apartheid: A Critique of Constructive Engagement', *African Affairs*, Vol.76, No.305.

Legassick, M. and F. de Clercq, 1984, 'Capitalism and Migrant Labour in Southern Africa: The Origins and Nature of the System', in Marks and Richardson [1984].

LeGrand, C., 1984, 'Labor Acquisition and Social Conflict on the Colombian Frontier, 1850–1936', *Journal of Latin American Studies*, Vol.16, Part I.

Lehmann, D. (ed.), 1982, *Ecology and Exchange in the Andes*, Cambridge: Cambridge University Press.

Leiman, M.M., 1993, *The Political Economy of Racism*, London: Pluto Press.

Leiten, G.K., Nieuwenhuys, O. and L. Schenk-Sandbergen (eds.), 1989, *Women, Migrants and Tribals: Survival Strategies in Asia*, New Delhi: Manohar.

Lemoine, M., 1985, *Bitter Sugar* London: Zed Press.

Lence, R.M. (ed.), 1992, *Union and Liberty: The Political Philosophy of John C. Calhoun*, Indianopolis, IN: Liberty Fund.

Lenin, V.I., 1961, 'What Is To Be Done?' *Collected Works*, Vol.5, Moscow: Foreign Languages Publishing House.

Lenin, V.I., 1964, 'Development of Capitalism in Russia', *Collected Works*, Vol.3, Moscow: Foreign Languages Publishing House.

Levidow, L., 1981, 'Grunwick: The Social Contract Meets the 20th Century Sweatshop', in L. Levidow and B.Young (eds.), *Science, Technology and the Labour Process – Volume I*, London: CSE Books.

Lewis, O., 1955, 'Peasant Culture in India and Mexico: A Comparative Analysis', in Marriott [1955].

Lewis, O., 1958, *Village Life in Northern India*, Urbana, IL: University of Illinois Press.

Li Causi, L., 1975, 'Anthropology and Ideology: The Case of "Patronage" in Mediterranean Societies', *Critique of Anthropology*, Nos.4–5.

Lichtenstein, A., 1996, *Twice the Work of Free Labor: The Political Economy of Convict Labor in the New South*, London: Verso.

Long, N., 1984, 'Introduction', in Long (ed.) [1984].

Long, N. (ed.), 1984, *Family and Work in Rural Societies: Perspectives on Non-Wage Labour*, London: Tavistock Publications.

Long, N. and B. Roberts, 1984, *Miners, Peasants and Entrepreneurs: Regional Development in the Central Highlands of Peru*, Cambridge: Cambridge University Press.

Long, N., and Richardson, P., 1978, 'Informal Sector, Petty Commodity Production, and the Social Relations of a Small-scale Enterprise', in Clammer [1978].

Loveman, B., 1979, 'Critique of Arnold J. Bauer's "Rural Workers in Spanish America: Problems of Peonage and Oppression", *Hispanic American Historical Review*, Vol.59, No.3.

Macera, P., 1966, *Instrucciones para el manejo de las haciendas Jesuítas del Peru (ss.XVII–XVIII)*, Lima: Universidad Nacional Mayor de San Marcos.

Macera, P., 1968, *Mapas coloniales de haciendas Cuzqueñas*, Lima: Universidad Nacional Mayor de San Marcos.

Macera, P., 1974, *Las Plantaciones Azucareras en el Peru, 1821–1875*, Lima: Biblioteca Andina.

Maharaj, R.N., 1975, 'The Bonded Labour System in India', *National Labour Institute Bulletin*, Vol.1, No.2.

Maharaj, R.N. and K.G. Iyer, 1975a, 'Field Report from Rajgir (Nalanda, Bihar) – Part I: The Rural Poor and their Problems', *National Labour Institute Bulletin*, Vol.1, No.10.

Maharaj, R.N. and K.G. Iyer, 1975b, 'Rural Camp at Rajgir: Some Observations', *National Labour Institute Bulletin*, Vol.1, No.11.

Malamoud, C. (ed.), 1983, *Debts and Debtors*, New Delhi: Vikas Publishing House.

Mallon, F.E., 1983a, 'Murder in the Andes: Patrons, Clients, and the Impact of Foreign Capital, 1860–1922', *Radical History Review*, No.27.

Mallon, F.E., 1983b, *The Defense of Community in Peru's Central Highlands: Peasant*

Struggle and Capitalist Transition, 1860–1940, Princeton NJ: Princeton University Press.

Mallon, F.E., 1986, 'Labor Migration, Class Formation, and Class Conciousness among Peruvian Miners: The Central Highlands, 1900–1930', in Hanagan and Stephenson [1986].

Maltby, L., 1980, 'Colonos on Hacienda Picotani', in Orlove and Custred [1980].

Mandel, E., 1980, 'Labour and the State in Nazi Germany', in T. Nichols (ed.), *Capital and Labour: Studies in the Capitalist Labour Process*, London: Athlone Press.

Mandle, J.R., 1978, *The Roots of Black Poverty: The Southern Plantation Economy after the Civil War*, Durham, NC: Duke University Press.

Mandle, J.R., 1983, 'Sharecropping and the Plantation Economy in the United States South', *The Journal of Peasant Studies*, Vol.10, Nos.2–3.

Marcoy, P., 1872, *A Journey Across South America*, Vol.II, London: Blackie & Sons.

Marglin, F.A. (ed.), 1998, *The Spirit of Regeneration: Andean Culture Confronting Western Notions of Development*, London: Zed Books.

Mariátegui, J.C., 1968/1928, *Siete Ensayos de Interpretación de la Realidad Peruana*, Lima: Biblioteca Amauta.

Marks, S. and P. Richardson (eds.), 1984, *International Labour Migration: Historical Perspectives*, London: Maurice Temple Smith.

Marla, S., 1977, 'Bonded Labour in Medak District (AP)', *National Labour Institute Bulletin*, Vol.3, No.10.

Marla, S., 1981, *Bonded Labour in India*, New Delhi: Biblia Impex.

Marriott, M., 1955, *Village India: Studies in the Little Community*, Chicago, IL: The University of Chicago Press.

Martínez de la Torre, R., 1949, *Apuntes para una interpretación marxista de Historia Social del Peru* (Vol.IV), Lima: Compañía Impresora Peruana.

Martínez-Alier, J., 1971, *Labourers and Landowners in Southern Spain*, London: George Allen & Unwin.

Martínez-Alier, J., 1977, *Haciendas, Plantations and Collective Farms*, London: Frank Cass.

Marx, K., 1976, *Capital – Volume I*, London: Penguin.

Matos Mar, J. and J.M. Mejía, 1982, 'Casual Work, Seasonal Migration and Agrarian Reform in Peru', in Peek and Standing [1982].

Mattera, P., 1985, *Off the Books: The Rise of the Underground Economy*, London: Pluto Press.

Mayer, A.C., 1960, *Caste and Kinship in Central India*, London: Routledge & Kegan Paul.

McBride, G.M., 1934, 'Peonage', in *Encyclopaedia of the Social Sciences*, Vol.12, New York: Macmillan.

McBride, G.M., 1936, *Chile: Land and Society*, New York: American Geographical Society.

McCreery, D., 1983, 'Debt Servitude in Rural Guatemala', *Hispanic American Historical Review*, Vol.63, No.4.

McCreery, D., 1986, "An Odious Feudalism": *Mandamiento* Labor and Commercial Agriculture in Guatemala, 1858–1920', *Latin American Perspectives*, No.48.

McCreery, D., 1990, 'Hegemony and Repression in Rural Guatemala, 1871–1914', *Peasant Studies*, Vol.17, No.3.

McCreery, D., 1997, 'Wage Labor, Free Labor, and Vagrancy Laws: The Transition to Capitalism in Guatemala, 1920–1945', in Brass and van der Linden [1997].

McWilliams, C., 1939, *Factories in the Field: The Story of Migratory Farm Labor in California*, Boston, MA: Little, Brown.

McWilliams, C., 1945, *Ill Fares the Land: Migrants and Migratory Labour in the United States*, London: Faber & Faber.

Meillassoux, C., 1981, *Maidens, Meal and Money*, Cambridge: Cambridge University Press.

Melis, A., Dessau, A. and M. Kossok (eds.), 1971, *Mariátegui: Tres Estudios*, Lima: Biblioteca Amauta.

Mellor, J., 1983, *The Company Store: James Bryson McLachlan and the Cape Breton Coal Miners 1900–1925*, Toronto: Doubleday Canada.

Melossi, D. and M. Pavarini, 1981, *The Prison and the Factory: Origins of the Penitentiary System*, London: Macmillan.

Miers, S. and I. Kopytoff (eds.), 1977, *Slavery in Africa: Historical and Anthropological Perspectives*, Madison, WI: University of Wisconsin Press.

Miles, R., 1987, *Capitalism and Unfree Labour*, London: Tavistock Publications.

Miller, R., 1987, 'Some Reflections on Foreign Research and Peruvian History', in Miller (ed.) [1987].

Miller, R. (ed.), 1987, *Region and Class in Modern Peruvian History*, Liverpool: Institute of Latin American Studies.

Miller, S., 1967, 'Hacienda to Plantation in Northern Peru: The Processes of Proletarianization of a Tenant Farmer Society', in Steward (ed.) [1967].

Mintz, S., 1956, 'Cañamelar: The Subculture of a Rural Sugar Plantation Proletariat', in J.H. Steward (ed.), *The People of Puerto Rico*, Urbana, IL: University of Illinois Press.

Mintz, S. and E.J. Wolf, 1968, 'An Analysis of Ritual Co-Parenthood (*compadrazgo*)', in Bohannan and Middleton [1968].

Mishra, S.C., 1993, 'Problems in Pursuing Land Ceiling Cases: A Case Study of Purnia District', in B.N. Yugandhar and K. Gopal Iyer (eds.), *Land Reforms in India: Volume 1 – Bihar*, Delhi: Sage.

Mitra, M. and T.Vijayendra, 1982, 'Agricultural Labourers and Peasant Politics: Rural Proletarianisation in Purnea, Bihar', in A.N. Das (ed.), *Agrarian Movements in India: Studies on Twentieth Century Bihar*, London: Frank Cass.

Mitter, S., 1986, *Common Fate, Common Bond: Women in the Global Economy*, London: Pluto Press.

Moore, C., 1985, *Kanaka: A History of Melanesian Mackay*, Port Moresby: University of Papua New Guinea Press.

Moreno Fraginals, M., Moya Pons, F. and S.L. Engerman (eds.), 1985, *Between Slavery and Free Labor: The Spanish-Speaking Caribbean in the Nineteenth Century*, Baltimore, MD: Johns Hopkins University Press.

Mörner, M., 1973, 'The Spanish American Hacienda: A Survey of Recent Research and Debate', *Hispanic American Historical Review*, Vol.53, No.2.

Mörner, M., 1975, 'En Torno a las Haciendas de la Región del Cuzco desde el Siglo XVIII', in Florescano [1975].

Mukerjee, R., 1933, *Land Problems of India*, London: Longmans, Green.

Mukherji, S., 1985, 'The Process of Wage Labour Circulation in Northern India', in G. Standing (ed.), *Labour Circulation and the Labour Process*, London: Croom Helm.

Mukhtyar, G.C., 1930, *Life and Labour in a South Gujarat Village*, London: Longmans, Green.

Mundle, S., 1979, *Backwardness and Bondage*, New Delhi: Indian Institute of Public Administration.

Munro, D., 1993a, 'The Pacific Islands Labour Trade: Approaches, Methodologies, Debates', *Slavery and Abolition*, Vol.14, No.2.

Munro, D., 1993b, 'Patterns of Resistance and Accommodation', in B.V. Lal, D. Munro and E. Beechert (eds.), *Plantation Workers: Resistance and Accommodation*, Honolulu: University of Hawaii Press.

Munro, D., 1995 'Revisionism and Its Enemies: Debating the Queensland Labour Trade', *The Journal of Pacific History*, Vol.30, No.2.

Munslow, B. and H. Finch (eds.), 1984, *Proletarianization in the Third World: Studies in the Creation of a Labour Force under Dependent Capitalism*, London: Croom Helm.

Nagesh, H.V., 1981, 'Forms of Unfree Labour in Indian Agriculture', *Economic and Political Weekly*, Vol.16, No.39.

Naidis, M., 1981, 'The Abolitionists and Indian Slavery', *Journal of Asian History*, Vol.15, No.2.

Nair, K., 1979, *In Defense of the Irrational Peasant: Indian Agriculture after the Green Revolution*, Chicago, IL: University of Chicago Press.

Nath, Y.V.S., 1960, *Bhils of Ratanmal*, Baroda: Maharaja Sayajirao University of Baroda.

Neira, H., 1968, *Los Andes: Tierra o Muerte*, Madrid: Editorial ZYX.

Nevinson, H.W., 1906, *A Modern Slavery*, New York: Harper & Brothers.

Newman, R.K., 1979, 'Social Factors in the Recruitment of the Bombay Millhands', in Chaudhuri and Dewey [1979].

Nieboer, H.J., 1910, *Slavery as an Industrial System*, The Hague: Martinus Nijhoff.

North-Coombes, M.D., 1990, 'Indentured Labour in the Sugar Industries of Natal and Mauritius', in Bhana [1900].

Núñez del Prado, O., 1973, *Kuyo Chico: Applied Anthropology in an Indian Community*, Chicago, IL: University of Chicago Press.

Nzula, A.T. *et al.*, 1979/1933, *Forced Labour in Colonial Africa*, London: Zed Press.

Oberai, A.S. and H.K. Manmohan Singh, 1983, *Causes and Consequences of Internal Migration: A Study in the Indian Punjab*, Delhi: Oxford University Press.

Olmsted, F.L., 1953, *The Cotton Kingdom: A Traveller's Observations on Cotton and Slavery in the American Slave States*, New York: Alfred A.Knopf.

Olsen, W.K., 1997, 'Marxist and neoclassical Approaches to Unfree labour in India', in Brass and van der Linden [1997].

Omvedt, G., 1980, 'Migration in Colonial India: The Articulation of Feudalism and Capitalism by the Colonial State', *The Journal of Peasant Studies*, Vol.7, No.2.

Orlove, B., 1977, 'Inequality among peasants: the forms and uses of reciprocal exchange in Andean Peru', in Halperin and Dow [1977].

Orlove, B., 1980, 'Landlords and Officials: The Sources of Domination in Surimana and Quehue', in Orlove and Custred [1980].

Orlove, B.S. and G. Custred (eds.), 1980, *Land and Power in Latin America: Agrarian Economies and Social Processes in the Andes*, New York: Holmes & Meier.

Page Arnot, R., 1955, *A History of the Scottish Miners*, London: George Allen & Unwin.

Palacio Pimentel, G.H., 1962, 'Relaciones de trabajo entre el patrón y los colonos de los fundos de la Provincia de Paucartambo', *Revista Universitaria del Cusco*, No.120.

Palacios, M., 1980, *Coffee in Colombia 1850–1970*, Cambridge: Cambridge University Press.

Palmer, R. and N. Parsons (eds.), 1977, *The Roots of Rural Poverty in Central and Southern Africa*, London: Heinemann.

Panoff, M., 1994/95, 'Workers, Recruiters and Planters in the Bismarck Archipelago, 1885–1914', *The Journal of Pacific Studies*, Vol.18.

Parnaby, O.W., 1964, *Britain and the Labour Trade in the Southwest Pacific*, Durham NC: University of North Carolina Press.

Pastore, M., 1997, 'Staples, Endowments, Institutions and Development in Agrarian Frontiers: A Neo-Institutionalist Analysis of Sixteenth- and Seventeenth-Century Paraguay', in Brass and van der Linden [1997].

Patel, J.M., 1964, 'Agricultural Labour in a South Gujarat Village', in Vyas (ed.) [1964].

Patel, S.J., 1952, *Agricultural Labourers in Modern India and Pakistan*, Bombay: Current Book House.

Patnaik, U., 1978a, 'Capitalist Development in Agriculture – A Note', in Rudra *et al.* [1978].

Patnaik, U., 1978b, 'Development of Capitalism in Agriculture', in Rudra *et al.* [1978].

Patnaik, U., 1978c, 'Development of Capitalist Production in Agriculture', in Rudra *et al.* [1978].

Patnaik, U., 1978d, 'On the Mode of Production in Indian Agriculture – A Reply', in Rudra *et al.* [1978].

Patnaik, U., 1978e, 'Class Differentiation within the Peasantry', in Rudra *et al.* [1978].

Patnaik, U., 1985, 'Introduction', in Patnaik and Dingwaney [1985].

Patnaik, U., 1986, 'The Agrarian Question and the Development of Capitalism in India', *Economic and Political Weekly*, Vol.21, No.18.

Patnaik, U., 1995, 'On Capitalism and Agrestic Unfreedom', *International Review of Social History*, Vol.40, Part 1.

Patnaik, U. (ed.), 1990, *Agrarian Relations and Accumulation: The 'Mode of Production' Debate in India*, Bombay: Oxford University Press.

Patnaik, U. and M. Dingwaney (eds.), 1985, *Chains of Servitude: Bondage and Slavery in India*, Madras: Sangham Books.

Patterson, O., 1982, *Slavery and Social Death: A Comparative Study*, Cambridge, MA: Harvard University Press.

Pearce, D.W., 1981, *The Dictionary of Modern Economics*, London: Macmillan.

Pearse, A., 1975, *The Latin American Peasant*, London: Frank Cass.

Pearse, A.S., 1929, *The Cotton Industry of Japan and China*, Manchester: International Federation of Master Cotton Spinners' and Manufacturers' Associations.

Peek, P. and G. Standing (eds.), 1982, *State Policies and Migration*, London: Croom Helm.

Phillips, U.B., 1918, *American Negro Slavery*, New York: D. Appleton.

Phillips, U.B., 1929, *Life and Labor in the Old South*, Boston, MA: Little, Brown.

Phillips, U.B., 1939, *The Course of the South to Secession*, New York: D. Appleton-Century.

Phongpaichit, P., 1982, *From Peasant Girls to Bangkok Masseuses*, Geneva: International Labour Organization.

Picó, F., 1979, 'Deshumanización del trabajo, cosificación de la naturaleza: los comienzos del café en el Utuado del Siglo XIX', *Cuadernos de la Facultad de Humanidades*, No.2.

Picó, F., 1986, *Historia general de Puerto Rico*, Río Piedras: Ediciones Huaracán.

Pilger, J., 1996, 'Tales from Tigerland', *New Statesman & Society*, 16 Feb.

Pirie, D., 1981, *Anatomy of the Movies*, New York: Macmillan Publishing.

Plant, R., 1987, *Sugar and Modern Slavery*, London: Zed Press.

Platteau, J.P., 1992, *Aristocratic Patronage as an Ingredient of the Caste System: Formal Analysis and Dynamic Considerations*, London: Suntory-Toyota International Centre for Economics (LSE).

Platteau, J.P., 1995, 'A Framework for the Analysis of Evolving Patron-Client Ties in Agrarian Economies', *World Development*, Vol.23, No.5.

Platteau, J.P., and A. Abraham, 1987, 'An Inquiry into Quasi-Credit Contracts: The Role of Reciprocal Credit and Interlinked Deals in Small-scale Fishing Communities', *The Journal of Development Studies*, Vol.23, No.4.

Platteau, J.P. *et al.*, 1985, *Technology, Credit and Indebtedness in Marine Fishing – A Case Study of Three Fishing Villages in South Kerala*, Delhi: Hindustan Publishing.

Pouchepadass, J., 1990, 'The Market for Agricultural Labour in Colonial North Bihar 1860–1920', in Holmstrom [1990].

Powdermaker, H., 1950, *Hollywood the Dream Factory*, Boston, MA: Little, Brown.

Prakash, G., 1990a, *Bonded Histories: Genealogies of Labour Servitude in Colonial India*, Cambridge: Cambridge University Press.

Prakash, G., 1990b, 'Bonded Labour in South Bihar: A Contestatory History', in S. Bose (ed.), *South Asia and World Capitalism*, Delhi: Oxford University Press.

Prakash, G., 1991, 'Becoming a Bhuinya: Oral Traditions and Contested Domination in Eastern India', in Haynes and Prakash [1991].

Prakash, G., 1992a, 'The History and Historiography of Rural Labourers in Colonial India', in Prakash (ed.) [1992c].

Prakash, G., 1992b, 'Reproducing Inequality: Spirit Cults and Labour Relations in Colonial Eastern India', in Prakash (ed.) [1992c].

Prakash, G. (ed.), 1992c, *The World of the Rural Labourer in Colonial India*, Delhi: Oxford University Press.

Prasad, P., 1979, 'Semi-Feudalism: The Basic Constraints of Indian Agriculture', in Das and Nilkant [1979].

Prasad, P.H., 1989, *Lopsided Growth: Political Economy of Indian Development*, Bombay: Oxford University Press.

Pumaruna, A. [ps. Letts, R.], 1968, *Perú: Revolución; Insurrección; Guerrillas*, Lima: Ediciones Vanguardia Revolucionaria.

Rainbird, H., and L. Taylor, 1977, 'Relations of Production and Relations of Exploitation: A Re-analysis of Andean Haciendas', *Bulletin of the Society for Latin American Studies*, No.27.

Ramachandran, V.K., 1990, *Wage Labour and Unfreedom in Agriculture: An Indian Case Study*, Oxford: Clarendon.

Ramamurti, B., 1954, *Agricultural Labour – Essential Statistics [All-India First Agricultural Labour Enquiry]*, New Delhi: Government of India Press.

Ramesar, M.D., 1984, 'Indentured Labour in Trinidad 1880–1917', in Saunders [1984].

Ramos Mattei, A., 1985, 'Technical Innovations and Social Change in the Sugar Industry of Puerto Rico, 1870–1880', in Moreno Fraginals *et al.* [1985].

Ransom, R.L. and R. Sutch, 1977, *One Kind of Freedom: The Economic Consequences of Emancipation*, Cambridge: Cambridge University Press.

Rao, M., 1999, 'Agrarian Power and Unfree Labour', *The Journal of Peasant Studies*, Vol.26, Nos.2–3.

Rao, V.K.R.V. (ed.), 1962, *Agricultural Labour in India*, London: Asia Publishing House.

Reid, A. (ed.), 1983, *Slavery, Bondage and Dependency in Southeast Asia*, St. Lucia: University of Queensland Press.

Reinhardt, N., 1988, *Our Daily Bread: The Peasant Question and Family Farming in the Colombian Andes*, Berkeley, CA: University of California Press.

Reserve Bank of India, 1954, *Report of the Committee of Direction, All-India Rural Credit Survey: Volume II – The General Report*, Bombay: Reserve Bank of India.

Reyeros, R. 1949, *El Pongueaje: La Servidumbre Personal De Los Indios Bolivianos*, La Paz: Empresa Editora 'Universo'.

Risley, H.H., 1908, *The People of India*, Calcutta: Thacker, Spink.

Robert, J.C., 1938, *The Tobacco Kingdom: Plantation, Market and Factory in Virginia and North Carolina 1800–1860*, Durham, NC: Duke University Press.

Robertson, C.C. and M.A. Klein (eds.), 1983, *Women and Slavery in Africa*, Madison, WI: University of Wisconsin Press.

Rock, D. (ed.), 1975, *Argentina in the Twentieth Century*, London: Duckworth.

Rodney, W., 1981, *A History of the Guyanese Working People, 1881–1905*, London: Heinemann.

Rodríguez Pastor, H., 1969, *Caqui: Estudio de una Hacienda Costeña*, Lima: Instituto de Estudios Peruanos.

Roemer, J. (ed.), 1986, *Analytical Marxism*, Cambridge: Cambridge University Press.

Rogaly, B., 1996, 'Agricultural Growth and the Structure of "Casual" Labour-Hiring in Rural West Bengal', *The Journal of Peasant Studies*, Vol.23, No.4.

Roth, H.-D., 1983, *Indian Moneylenders at Work: Case Studies of the Traditional Rural Credit Market in Dhanbad District, Bihar*, New Delhi: Manohar.

Roth, K.H., 1997, 'Unfree Labour in the Area under German Hegemony, 1930–45: Some Historical and Methodological Questions', in Brass and van der Linden [1997].

Roux, E., 1944, *S.P.Bunting: A Political Biography*, Cape Town: The African Bookman.

Royal Commission on Labour in India, 1931, *Report of the Royal Commission on Labour in India*, London: HMSO.

Rubbo, A. and M. Taussig, 1983, 'Up Off Their Knees: Servanthood in Southwest Colombia', *Latin American Perspectives*, Vol.10, No.4.

Rudra, A., 1982, *Indian Agricultural Economics: Myths and Realities*, New Delhi: Allied Publishers Private.

Rudra, A., 1987, 'Labour Relations in Agriculture: A Study in Contrasts', *Economic and Political Weekly*, Vol.XXI, No.17, 25 April.

Rudra, A. and P. Bardhan, 1983, *Agrarian Relations in West Bengal*, Bombay: Somaiya Publications.

Rudra, A. *et al.*, 1978, *Studies in the Development of Capitalism in India*, Lahore: Vanguard Books.

Rural Wing of the NLI, 1977, 'The Dark World of Jeeta Gadus', *National Labour Institute Bulletin*, Vol.3, No.12.

Rutledge, I., 1975, 'Plantations and Peasants in Northern Argentina: The Sugar Cane Industry of Salta and Jujuy, 1930–43', in Rock [1975].

Rutledge, I., 1977, 'The integration of the highland peasantry into the sugar cane economy of northern Argentina, 1930–43', in Duncan and Rutledge (eds.).

Saha, P., 1970, *Emigration of Indian Labour (1834–1900)*, Delhi: People's Publishing House.

Saintsbury, G., 1972/[1829], *East India Slavery*, Shannon: Irish University Press.

Saksena, R.N., 1962, *Social Economy of a Polyandrous People*, Bombay: Asia Publishing House.

Samora, J., 1971, *Los Mojados: The Wetback Story*, Notre Dame, IN: University of Notre Dame Press.

Sánchez, R., 1977, 'The Model of Verticality in the Andean Economy: A Critical Reconsideration', *Bulletin of the Society for Latin American Studies*, No.27.

Sánchez, R., 1982, 'The Andean Economic System and Capitalism', in Lehmann [1982].

Sandhu, K.S., 1969, *Indians in Malaya: Immigration and Settlement, 1786–1957*, London: Cambridge University Press.

Saradamoni, K., 1980, *Emergence of a Slave Caste: Pulayas of Kerala*, New Delhi: People's Publishing House.

Sarker, T., 1985, 'Bondage in the Colonial Context', in Patnaik and Dingwaney [1985].

Saunders, K., 1982, *Workers in Bondage: The Origins and Bases of Unfree Labour in Queensland, 1824–1916*, St. Lucia: University of Queensland Press.

Saunders, K. (ed.), 1984, *Indentured Labour in the British Empire, 1834-1920*, London: Croom Helm.

Scarano, F.A., 1984, *Sugar and Slavery in Puerto Rico: The Plantation Economy of Ponce, 1800–1850*, Madison WI: University of Wisconsin Press.

Schmeichen, J.A., 1984, *Sweated Industries and Sweated Labor*, London: Croom Helm.

Scott, C., 1976, 'Peasants, Proletarianisation and the Articulation of the Modes of Production: The Case of the Sugar-Cane Cutters in Northern Peru, 1940–69', *The Journal of Peasant Studies*, Vol.3, No.3.

Scott, J.C., 1968, *Political Ideology in Malaysia*, New Haven, CT: Yale University Press.

Scott, J.C., 1976, *The Moral Economy of the Peasant*, New Haven, CT: Yale University Press.

Scott, J.C., 1977, 'Patronage or Exploitation?', in Gellner and Waterbury (eds.) [1977].

Scott, J.C., 1985, *Weapons of the Weak: Everyday Forms of Peasant Resistance*, New Haven, CT: Yale University Press.

Scott, J.C., 1986, 'Everyday Forms of Peasant Resistance', in J.C. Scott and B. Kerkvliet (eds.), *Everyday Forms of Peasant Resistance*, London: Frank Cass.

Scott, J.C., 1990, *Domination and the Arts of Resistance: Hidden Transcripts*, New Haven, CT: Yale University Press.

Scott, J.C., 1992, ''Domination, Acting, Fantasy', in C. Nordstrom and J. Martin (eds.), *The Paths to Domination, Resistance and Terror*, Berkeley, CA: University of California Press.

Scott, J.C., 1998, *Seeing Like a State*, New Haven, CT: Yale University Press.

Scott, R.J., 1985, 'Explaining Abolition: Contradiction, Adaptation, and Challenge in Cuban Slave Society, 1860–1886', in Fraginals, Pons and Engerman (ed.).

Seiler-Baldinger, A., 1980, 'Indians and the Pioneer Front in the North-East Amazon', in Barbira-Scazzocchio [1980].

Seminario de Investigación sobre Movimientos Campesinos, 1974, *Regimen de Hacienda y Luchas Campesinas: Huyro – La Convención*, Lima: Universidad Nacional Mayor de San Marcos.

Sengupta, N. *et al.*, 1986, 'Contract Labour in a Steel Plant', *Economic and Political Weekly*, Vol.21, No.48.

Shankaran, S.R., 1983, 'Methodology for Identification of Bonded Labour Applicable to Telengana Districts of Andhra Pradesh', a paper presented at the 'National Seminar on Identification and Rehabilitation of Bonded Labour', organized by the National Labour Institute and the Ministry of Labour, New Delhi, 7–9 Feb.

Sharma, M., 1978, *The Politics of Inequality: Competition and Control in an Indian Village*, Honolulu, HI: University Press of Hawaii.

Sharma, M., 1982, 'Impact of Migratory Labour on the Rural Economy of Punjab', *Man & Development*, Vol.4, No.3.

Shlomowitz, R., 1981, 'Markets for Indentured and Time-expired Melanesian Labour in Queensland, 1863–1906', *Journal of Pacific History*, Vol.16, No.2.

Shlomowitz, R., 1986, 'The Fiji Labor Trade in Comparative Perspective, 1864–1914', *Pacific Studies*, Vol.9, No.3.

Shlomowitz, R., 1991a, 'On Punishments and Rewards in Coercive Labour Systems: Comparative Perspectives', *Slavery and Abolition*, Vol.12, No.2.

Shlomowitz, R., 1991b, 'The Latin American *Enganche* System: A Comment on Brass', *Slavery and Abolition*, Vol.12, No.3.

Shlomowitz, R., 1992, 'The Genesis of Free Labour in the American Civil War', *Slavery and Abolition*, Vol.13, No.3.

Shlomowitz, R., 1994/95, 'The Queensland Labour Trade: A Comment on Williams', *The Journal of Pacific Studies*, Vol.18.

Shlomowitz, R., 1997, 'The Transition from Slave to Freedman Labor in the Cape Colony, the British West Indies, and the Post-bellum American South: Comparative Perspectives', in Brass and van der Linden [1997].

Shoemaker, R., 1981, *The Peasants of El Dorado: Conflict and Contradiction in a Peruvian Frontier Settlement*, Ithaca, NY: Cornell University Press.

Shotwell, L.R., 1961, *The Harvesters: The Story of a Migrant People*, New York: Doubleday.

Sidhu, D.S. and S.S. Grewal, 1981, *Agricultural Growth and Employment Shifts in Punjab*, New Delhi: Birla Institute of Scientific Research, Economic Research Division.

Sieghart, P., 1983, *The International Law of Human Rights*, Oxford: Clarendon Press.

Silva Herzog, J., 1959, *El agrarismo mexicano y la reforma agraria*, México DF: Fondo de Cultura Económica.

Simeon, D., 1984, 'Industry and Workforce in Chotanagpur: An Outline of the Structural Characteristics (1920s and 1930s)', in Das *et al.* [1984].

Singh, A.J. and D.S. Sidhu, 1976, 'New Farm Technology and Agricultural Labour', in S.M. Pandey (ed.), *Rural Labour in India*, New Delhi: Sri Ram Centre for Industrial Relations and Human Resources.

Singh, M., 1981, 'Migrant Labourers in Rural Punjab', M.Phil. thesis, Department of Sociology, Punjab University, Chandigarh.

Singh, M. and K.G. Iyer, 1981, 'Migrant Labourers in Rural Punjab', *Human Futures*, Winter.

Singh, Master Hari, 1980, *Agricultural Workers' Struggle in Punjab*, New Delhi: People's Publishing House.

Singh, R.A.P., 1985, *Kin, Clan and Land Reforms*, Jaipur: Rawat Publications.

Singleton-Gates P. and M. Girodias, 1959, *The Black Diaries*, London: Sidgwick & Jackson.

Sinha, B.B., 1982, *Society in Tribal India*, Delhi: BR Publishing Corporation.

Sissons, R., 1988, *The Players: A Social History of the Professional Cricketer*, London: The Kingswood Press.

Skar, H.O., 1982, *The Warm Valley People*, Oslo: Universitetsforlaget.

Skar, S., 1984, 'Interhousehold Co-operation in Peru's Southern Andes: A Case of Multiple Sibling-Group Marriage', in Long (ed.) [1984].

Smith, G., 1985, 'Reflections on the Social Relations of Simple Commodity Production', *The Journal of Peasant Studies*, Vol.13, No.1.

Souza Martins, J., 1990, *O Cativeiro da Terra*, São Paulo: Editora Hucitec.

Souza Martins, J., 1997, 'The Reappearance of Slavery and the Reproduction of Capital on the Brazilian Frontier', in Brass and van der Linden [1997].

Srinivas, M.N., 1955a, 'Introduction', in M.N. Srinivas (ed.), *India's Villages*, Calcutta: West Bengal Government Press.

Srinivas, M.N., 1955b, 'The Social System of a Mysore Village', in Marriott [1955].

Srinivas, M.N., 1987, *The Dominant Caste and Other Essays*, Delhi: Oxford University Press.

Srinivas, M.N., 1992, *On Living in a Revolution and Other Essays*, Delhi: Oxford University Press.

Srinivasan, T.N., 1989, 'On Choice among Creditors and Bonded Labour Contracts', in Bardhan (ed.) [1989a].

Srivastava, A.K., 1987a, 'Identifying bonded labour, a knotty problem!', *Yojana*, Vol.31, No.8.

Srivastava, A.K., 1987b, 'Labour Relations in Agriculture', *Economic and Political Weekly*, Vol.XXI, No.46, 14 Nov.

Srivastava, V.L., 1970, *A Socio-economic Survey of the Workers in the Coalmines of India (with particular reference to Bihar)*, Calcutta: Scientific Book Agency.

Stampp, K.M., 1964, *The Peculiar Institution: Negro Slavery in the American South*, London: Eyre & Spottiswoode.

Stampp, K.M., 1980, *The Imperiled Union: Essays on the Background of the Civil War*, New York: Oxford University Press.

Starobin, R.S., 1970, *Industrial Slavery in the Old South*, New York: Oxford University Press.

Stavenhagen, R., 1975, *Social Classes in Agrarian Societies*, New York: Garden City.

Ste Croix, G.E.M. de, 1981, *The Class Struggle in the Ancient Greek World*, London: Duckworth.

Ste Croix, G.E.M. de, 1984, 'Class in Marx's Conception of History, Ancient and Modern', *New Left Review*, No.146.

Steinfeld, R.J. and S.L. Engerman, 1997, 'Labor – Free or Coerced? A Historical Reassessment of Differences and Similarities', in Brass and van der Linden [1997].

Steward, J.H., 1965, 'Analysis of Complex Contemporary Societies: Culture Patterns of Puerto Rico', in Heath and Adams [1965].

Steward, J.H. (ed.), 1967, *Contemporary Change in Traditional Societies: Volume III – Mexican and Peruvian Communities*, Urbana, IL: University of Illinois Press.

Stoler, L.A., 1985, *Capitalism and Confrontation in Sumatra's Plantation Belt, 1870–1979*, New Haven, CT: Yale University Press.

Sturtevant, D.R., 1976, *Popular Uprisings in the Philippines 1840–1940*, Ithaca, NY: Cornell University Press.

Sutch, R., 1975, 'The Treatment Received by American Slaves: A Critical review of the Evidence Presented in *Time on the Cross'*, *Explorations in Economic History*, Vol.12, No.4.

Tadman, M., 1989, *Speculators and Slaves: Masters, Traders, and Slaves in the Old South*, Madison, WI: University of Wisconsin Press.

Tannenbaum, F., 1968, *The Mexican Agrarian Revolution*, Hamden CT: Archon Books.

Taussig, M., 1984, 'Culture of Terror – Space of Death: Roger Casement's Putumayo Report and the Explanation of Torture', *Comparative Studies in Society and History*, Vol.26, No.3.

Taussig, M., 1986, *Shamanism, Colonialism, and the Wild Man*, Chicago, IL: University of Chicago Press.

Tawney, R.H. (ed.), 1938, *Agrarian China*, Shanghai: Kelly & Walsh.

Tax, S., 1953, *Penny Capitalism: A Guatemalan Indian Economy*, Washington, DC: Smithsonian Institute.

Taylor, L., 1984, 'Literature as History: Ciro Alegria's View of Rural society in the Northern Peruvian Andes', *Ibero-Amerikanisches Archiv*, Vol.10, No.3.

Taylor, L., 1987, 'Earning a Living in Hualgayoc, 1870–1900', in Miller (ed.)[1987].

The President's Commission on Migratory Labor, 1951, *Migratory Labor in American Agriculture – Report*, Washington DC: US Government Printing Office.

Thomas, T.N., 1985, *Indians Overseas*, London: The British Library.

Thompson, E.P., 1991, *Customs in Common*, London: Merlin Press.

Thorner, A., 1982, 'Semi-Feudalism or Capitalism? Contemporary Debate on Classes and Modes of Production in India', *Economic and Political Weekly*, Vol.17, Nos.49–51.

Thorner, D. and A. Thorner, 1962, *Land and Labour in India*, Bombay: Asia Publishing House.

Thorner, D., 1980, *The Shaping of Modern India*, New Delhi: Allied Publishers.

Tinker, H., 1974, *A New System of Slavery: The Export of Indian Labour Overseas 1830–1920*, London: Oxford University Press.

Tise, L.E., 1987, *Proslavery: A History of the Defense of Slavery in America, 1701–1840*, Athens, GE: University of Georgia Press.

Tiwary, S.P., 1985, 'Bondage in Santal Parganas', in Patnaik and M. Dingwaney [1985].

Tovar, H., 1975, 'Elementos constitutivos de la empresa agraria jesuita en la segunda mitad del siglo XVIII en México', in Florescano [1975].

Trotsky, L., 1962, *The Permanent Revolution [1928] and Results and Prospects [1906]*, London: New Park Publications.

Tsurumi, E.P., 1984, 'Female Textile Workers and the Failure of Early Trade Unionism in Japan', *History Workshop Journal*, No.18.

Tsurumi, E.P., 1990, *Factory Girls: Women in the Thread Mills of Meiji Japan*, Princeton NJ: Princeton University Press.

Tupayachi, I., 1959, 'Un Ensayo de Econometría en La Convención', *Revista Universitaria*, No.117.

Turner, J.K., 1911, *Barbarous Mexico*, London: Cassell.

Twelve Southerners, 1951/[1930], *I'll Take My Stand: The South and the Agrarian Tradition*, New York: Peter Smith.

United Nations/International Labour Office, 1953, *Report of the Ad Hoc Committee on Forced Labour*, Geneva: Imprimeries Réunies.

US House of Representatives Special Subcommittee on Labor, 1969, *Employment of 'Green Card' Aliens During Labor Disputes*, Washington, DC: US Government Printing Office.

US Senate Subcommittee on Migratory Labor, 1970a, *Migrant and Seasonal Farmworker Powerlessness – Part 1: Who Are the Migrants?*, Washington, DC: US Government Printing Office.

US Senate Subcommittee on Migratory Labor, 1970b, *Migrant and Seasonal Farmworker Powerlessness – Part 2: The Migrant Subculture*, Washington, DC: US Government Printing Office.

US Senate Subcommittee on Migratory Labor, 1970c, *Migrant and Seasonal Farmworker Powerlessness – Part 3: Farmworker Legal Problems*, Washington, DC: US Government Printing Office.

van der Horst, S., 1942, *Native Labour in South Africa*, London: Oxford University Press.

van der Linden, M. and J. Lucassen (eds.), 1995, *Racism in the Labour Market: Historical Studies*, Berne: Peter Lang.

van Onselen, C., 1976, *Chibaro: African Mine Labour in Southern Rhodesia 1900–1933*, London: Pluto Press.

Van Young, E., 1981, *Hacienda and Market in Eighteenth-Century Mexico: The Rural Economy of the Guadalajara Region, 1675–1820*, Berkeley, CA: The University of California Press.

Vasquez, M.C., 1961, *Hacienda, Peonaje y Servidumbre en los Andes Peruanos*, Lima: Editorial Estudios Andinos.

Vidyasagar, R., 1985, 'Bondage in Santal Parganas', in Patnaik and Dingwaney [1985].

Vijayendra, T., Ghatak, M. and V.R. Rao, 1984, 'Rehabilitation of Bonded Labour: Study of Two Cases', in Das, Nilkant and Dubey [1984].

Villanueva, V., 1967, *Hugo Blanco y la Rebelión Campesina*, Lima: Editorial Juan Mejía Baca.

Vyas, V.S., 1964, 'Agricultural Labour in Four Villages: Some Observations', in Vyas (ed.) [1964].

Vyas, V.S. (ed.), 1964, *Agricultural Labour in Four Indian Villages*, Vallabhvidyanager: Sardar Vallabhbhai Vidyapeeth.

Wadley, S.S. and B.W. Derr, 1989, 'Karimpur 1925–1984: Understanding Rural India Through Restudies', in Bardhan (ed.) [1989b].

Walinsky, L.J. (ed.), 1977, *Agrarian Reform as Unfinished Business*, New York: Oxford University Press.

Warman, A., 1980, *'We Come to Object': The Peasants of Morelos and the National State*, Baltimore, MD: Johns Hopkins University Press.

Watson, J.L. (ed.), 1980, *Asian and African Systems of Slavery*, Oxford: Basil Blackwell.

Watson, J.L., 1983, 'A Cook's Tour of Slavery', *The Times Higher Education Supplement*, 8 July.

Watts, M., 1992, 'Peasants and Flexible Accumulation in the Third World – Producing under Contract', *Economic and Political Weekly*, Vol.27, No.30.

Weinstein, B., 1983, 'Capital Penetration and Problems of Labor Control in the Amazon Rubber Trade', *Radical History Review*, No.27.

Weinstein, B., 1986, 'The Persistence of Precapitalist Relations of Production in a Tropical Export Economy: The Amazon Rubber Trade, 1850–1920', in Hanagan and Stephenson [1986].

West India Royal Commission, 1897, *Report of the West India Royal Commission*, (Appendix C, Vol.III, Parts VI–XIII: Proceedings, Evidence and Documents relating to the Windward Islands, the Leeward islands, and Jamaica), London: HMSO.

Wharton, C.R. (ed.), 1970, *Subsistence Agriculture and Economic Development*, London: Frank Cass.

Whetten, N.L, 1948, *Rural Mexico*, Chicago, IL: University of Chicago Press.

Whiteford, S., 1981, *Workers from the North: Plantations, Bolivian Labor, and the City in Northwest Argentina*, Austin, TX: University of Texas Press.

Whiteside, A.G., 1962, *Austrian National Socialism before 1918*, The Hague: Martinus Nijhoff.

Williams, E., 1964, *Capitalism and Slavery*, London: Andre Deutsch.

Williams, E., 1970, *From Columbus to Castro: The History of the Caribbean 1492–1969*, London: Andre Deutsch.

Williams, T.D., 1994/95, 'The Queensland Labour Trade – "A Well Working Labour Market"?', *The Journal of Pacific Studies*, Vol.18

Winson, A., 1982, 'The 'Prussian Road' of Agrarian Development', *Economy and Society*, Vol.11, No.4.

Wiser, W.H., 1936, *The Hindu Jajmani System*, Lucknow: Lucknow Publishing House.

Wiser, W.H. and C.V. Wiser, 1963, *Behind Mud Walls, 1930–60*, Berkeley, CA: University of California Press.

Wish, H. (ed.), 1960, *Antebellum: Writings of George Fitzhugh and Hinton Rowan Helper on Slavery*, New York: Capricorn Books.

Wolf, E.R., 1971a, *Peasant Wars of the Twentieth Century*, London: Faber & Faber.

Wolf, E.R., 1971b, 'Peasant Rebellion and Revolution', in N. Miller and R. Aya (eds.), *National Liberation: Revolution in the Third World*, New York: The Free Press.

Wolf, E.R., and E.C. Hansen, 1972, *The Human Condition in Latin America*, New York: Oxford University Press.

Womack, J., 1969, *Zapata and the Mexican Revolution*, New York: Alfred A. Knopf.

Woodson, C., 1918, *A Century of Negro Migration*, Washington, DC: Association for the Study of Negro Life and History.

Woodson, C.G., 1930, *The Rural Negro*, Washington, DC: Association for the Study of Negro Life and History.

Woofter, T.J., 1936, *Landlord and Tenant on the Cotton Plantation*, Washington, DC: Works Progress Administration, Division of Social Research.

Zavala, S., 1978, *El servicio personal de los indios en el Perú: extractos del siglo xvi*, Vol.1, México: El Colegio de México.

Zavala, S., 1979, *El servicio personal de los indios en el Perú: extractos del siglo xvii*, Vol.2, México: El Colegio de México.

Zavala, S., 1980, *El servicio personal de los indios en el Perú: extractos del siglo xviii*, Vol.3, México: El Colegio de México.

Zegeye, A. and S. Ishemo (eds.), 1989, *Forced Labour and Migration: Patterns of Movement within Africa*, London: Hans Zell Publishers.

Author Index

Subject Index